AT THE INTERSECTION

REVISIONING RHETORIC
A Guilford Series
Karlyn Kohrs Campbell and Celeste Michelle Condit
Series Editors

At the Intersection:
Cultural Studies and Rhetorical Studies
Thomas Rosteck, Editor

Reading Nietzsche Rhetorically
Douglas Thomas

Contemporary Rhetorical Theory:
A Reader
*John Louis Lucaites, Celeste Michelle Condit,
and Sally Caudill, Editors*

Rhetoric in Postmodern America:
Conversations with Michael Calvin McGee
Carol Corbin, Editor

Analyzing Media: Communication Technologies
as Symbolic and Cognitive Systems
James W. Chesebro and Dale W. Bertelsen

AT THE INTERSECTION

CULTURAL STUDIES
AND RHETORICAL STUDIES

Edited by
Thomas Rosteck

THE GUILFORD PRESS
New York   London

© 1999 The Guilford Press
A Division of Guilford Publications, Inc.
72 Spring Street, New York, NY 10012
http://www.guilford.com

Printed in the United States of America

This book is printed on acid-free paper.

Last digit is print number: 9 8 7 6 5 4 3 2 1

Library of Congress Cataloging-in-Publication Data is available
from the Publisher.

ISBN 1-57230-398-0 (hard)
ISBN 1-57230-399-9 (pbk.)

PREFACE

This is a book that began with a conviction. It began with the firm belief that the oldest form of political and cultural critique and the newest have something to say to each other.

This collection has its more direct genesis, as most intellectual work does, in other places and other times. It began with my introduction to what was then called "British Cultural Studies" during my graduate student days in communication arts. It has been sustained by a regular course I teach on communication and cultural studies, and it was brought to its present juncture by the difficult and perplexing questions asked by my graduate students: Is there a connection between rhetorical studies and cultural studies? How are they the same? How different? What, if anything, can we gain by thinking about them together? And it was the reaction to my essay "Cultural Studies and Rhetorical Studies" that served to show me that many of my colleagues were both very interested and very involved in working through the issues and possibilities where rhetorical studies and cultural studies seem to intersect. And so it was that the need for the present collection became clear.

It seemed convincing to me then that, precisely because rhetorical studies and cultural studies come to us with complex and contested histories, because both are multiaccentual and are activated in different ways in different discursive contexts to serve several academic projects, the meaning and potential functions of rhetorical studies and cultural studies may best be determined in relation to one another. This moment of articulation is the ground for the present collection. And so, it is to exploring, to describing, to defining, and to enhancing this nexus and the issues that arise at such points of contact that *At the Intersection* is dedicated.

It is perhaps not so surprising that, as yet, very little literature soberly takes up whether and why we even ought to consider the two most important contemporary critical disciplines together. And there has been no sustained reflection on what it might mean, who might benefit, and how we might go about bringing them into contact. Some clarifications, then, are called for at the outset. Given the title of this collection, there is doubtless a presupposition that cultural and rhetorical studies do indeed somehow intersect. So, I must come clean on one bias that propels this collection and is shared by each contributor to it, namely, the enabling vision that rhetorical studies and cultural studies address specific and parallel questions about culture, critical practice, and interpretation, and that articulating or theorizing about them together might invigorate them both. This collection of essays makes a tentative case for their interrelationship and begins explicating the issues, problems, and questions that arise in the wake of this linkage. So, the essays contained here consider vitally important and exceedingly difficult questions, including the relationship between symbol use and history, the most effective blend of theory and practice, what case studies of communication/cultural behavior should "look" like, and more broadly the whole purpose of academic work in communication/cultural studies.

In initiating discussion of these kinds of questions, the original essays here not only take up matters of critical practice, including how one might study rhetorical culture and the relations or borrowings that could occur between rhetorical studies and cultural studies, but also include the more immediate issues of current academic practice, of assessing the future of rhetorical studies and cultural studies in the (postmodern) university, the challenges of culture studies for the discipline of communication, and the insights of rhetoric for those in cultural studies. In short, these essays seek to illuminate issues of history, society, textuality, and reception in provocative ways, and to develop the practice of a cultural rhetorical studies and that of a rhetorical cultural studies.

Because both rhetorical studies and cultural studies are transdisciplinary and cross the borders of traditional academic divisions, issues such as these are best engaged across established disciplinary lines. So *At the Intersection* takes very seriously the call that the best academic work should question received and traditional disciplinary boundaries and ultimately seek to create a new language of critique. The result is that *At the Intersection* provides a space both to engage the connection between cultural studies and rhetorical studies and simultaneously to address anew central issues of identity, subjectivity, and academic discipline and pedagogy. To accomplish this, it brings together for the first time a very diverse group of scholars and teachers from numerous academic domains. The contributors to this volume are housed in departments of communication, rhetoric, and English language and literature, but also in interpretive studies, humanities, and American studies.

Since one of the clearest parallels between cultural studies and rhetorical studies is the way each exemplifies complex uses of theory in practice, each of these contributors was asked to combine theoretical inquiry and analytical praxis, and thus to demonstrate—to model—the benefits of a cultural rhetorical study. While some essays focus on the discourse of rhetoric or of cultural studies itself, others ground their arguments in the analysis of cultural artifacts or events. These generalizations notwithstanding, each essay embodies the defining characteristic of the best of both rhetoric and cultural studies, that is, a binding together of theoretical sophistication with case analysis. They do not speak with one mind, and I did not try to enforce my own understanding of these critical questions upon them. Rather each essay in its own way is searching for a means to describe the intersection of cultural studies with rhetorical studies.

Each contributor attempts to address the rhetorical-cultural "split/ debate/schism/overlap." Though they sometimes use different terminology, including cultural rhetoric studies (Mailloux), rhetorical-cultural analysis (Aune), cultural rhetorical studies (Rosteck), or pragmatic analysis (Mechling and Mechling), each contributor takes seriously the idea that the structural relationship between these two critical inquiries needs to be made clear so as to deepen the scholarly and the political possibilities of each. Each essay operates with the understanding that the production of a cultural critique—however it is done and whomever does it—takes place within a particular social, historical, cultural, institutional, and textual situation. As cultural/political practice itself, this book gives new demonstration to the broader implications of intellectuals as cultural workers and of rhetorical studies as a form of discursive challenge to a variety of political, academic, and cultural spheres. The aim is thus to call into question accepted and orthodox answers of how we ought to position ourselves and our students in relationship to complex structural and economic changes occurring in higher education and society more broadly.

Also, it should be said here at the start that At the Intersection takes up only one part of the cultural studies movement. Considered broadly, one of the dominant paradigms in cultural studies takes its heritage from literary studies, cultural anthropology, and sociology, and, using approaches more typical of the historical and analytic models of such interpretive disciplines, concentrates upon textual or discursive practice. At the Intersection takes as its horizon this textual or critical domain of cultural studies; each essay emphasizes "textual" approaches rather than either production-based studies or more anthropological perspectives on "lived cultures."

Finally, reflecting my own predilections, At the Intersection is not much given to interest in turf battles, nor to how one might define what "cultural studies" or "rhetorical studies" is or is not. Again, given my prejudices, it concentrates much more on the goal of beginning to think about how we might use whatever is available to get on with the business of understanding the way power is maintained through discursive practice and the use of symbols. But I also clearly recognize that these are days of crisis in the humanities and in academic quarters. These are dangerous days of shrinking educational budgets, declining federal support, and debate over the role of higher education, which have the inevitable result that definitional struggles and questions of disciplinary identity entail dire material consequences. The cumulative insights of this collection and the vision of its purpose suggest that a cultural rhetorical studies can meaningfully engage the conditions that have produced this crisis.

*   *   *

This is the background on the professional, disciplinary, political, and pedagogical aims and purposes of this collection, namely, to begin to think in terms of a "cultural rhetorical studies." *At the Intersection* is not the end of such discussions but a spur to begin them. Certainly there are questions that are not treated as comprehensively as others; and there are what some will see as important issues that are not addressed at all. But I am confident that the overall aim has been richly realized by the outstanding and original essays contributed by this distinguished group of scholars. I am deeply grateful for the time, energy, and seriousness that they invested in this project and for the diligence and consistent goodwill with which they completed it.

An original compilation such as this owes debts to many in addition to its contributors. I am grateful to those whose hospitality and good humor made editorial work more agreeable than it often is—in that regard, I am particularly indebted to Fulbright College, in Fayetteville, for a sabbatical that supported my final work in assembling the essays. I gratefully acknowledge, too, the patient support and advice of my editors, Peter Wissoker at The Guilford Press, without whose conviction this collection would not have been possible, and of the Revisioning Rhetoric series, Karlyn Kohrs Campbell and Celeste Michelle Condit.

CONTENTS

AT THE INTERSECTION

INTRODUCTION

APPROACHING THE INTERSECTION
Issues of Identity, Politics, and Critical Practice

All ideas come with a history. And in these last days of the century, one would be hard-pressed to find two concepts overlaid with more tradition and accumulated meanings than rhetoric and culture. Both have been used in many contexts by diverse traditions to serve distinct intellectual, ideological, and political ends. As a result of this history of reception and usage, both rhetoric and culture come to us as slippery concepts, notoriously difficult to immobilize and pin to one and only one sense or meaning.

Yet, it is also an irony of our present circumstance that the two academic fields with arguably the largest stake in the terms *culture* and *rhetoric*—namely, cultural studies and rhetorical studies—are both in ascendance. Cultural studies, of course, rides a wave of fashionability, what some have called an "unprecedented boom," "flourishing and proliferating across space, institutions, and disciplines" (Grossberg, "Toward," 131). More and more, cultural studies is represented as "charismatic" and "progressive" and as capable of speaking to the significant issues that face our increasingly multicultural society in these times. Partly this may reflect the "intellectual promise" that cultural studies holds out, "an attempt to cut across social and political interests and address many of the struggles within the current scene." It may also reflect the role that culture is now seen to play in the maintenance of society—as the "social production and reproduction of sense, meaning and consciousness, . . . [and] the sphere of meaning, which unifies the spheres of production (economics) and social relations (politics)" (Hartley, "Culture," 68).

The fortunes of rhetorical studies too are on the upswing. In discipline after discipline there is evidence of what has been called the "interpretive turn," the realization that the givens of any field of activ-

1

ity—including the facts it commands, the procedures it trusts in, and the values it expresses and extends—are socially and politically constructed, that these givens are fashioned by human beings through public discourse rather than delivered by nature, and that these givens ultimately and inevitably serve the interests of one group over another. Fields as diverse as literary studies, economics, history, and the physical sciences have each experienced this revolution.[1] Rhetoric's current ascendance may be due in part to its central concern, that of understanding how language and other symbolic systems provide frameworks through which we make sense of experience, construct our collective identity, produce meaning, and prompt action in the world. Also, this "revived interest" in rhetoric is compatible with the contemporary assumption that much of what we know and experience is structured by sign systems or texts that we "inhabit and encounter" (Hartley, "Rhetoric," 266).

At a glance, then, cultural studies and rhetorical studies seem to share in much that is taken to be important these days: both aiming to reveal the relationship between expressive forms and social order; both existing within the field of discursive practices; both sharing an interest in how ideas are caused to materialize in texts; both concerned with how these structures are actually effective at the point of "consumption"; and both interested in grasping such textual practices as forms of power and performance.

Why then the assumption, clung to as conventional wisdom in many quarters, that the courses of the two, rhetorical studies and cultural studies, run independently along parallel and incompatible trajectories?

* * *

History also changes things. In the second edition of *Key Concepts in Communication and Cultural Studies,* inserted almost parenthetically after discussion of the term *rhetoric,* one finds this sentiment: "If rhetoric didn't already exist it would no doubt have to be invented" (Hartley, "Rhetoric," 266). Beside its whimsy (and playfully clever punning), this entry compresses into epigrammatic form the "call" for rhetoric—or for its "rediscovery"—in the discourse of critical cultural studies. In fact, should we follow this thread, there seems a nascent realization that, as one scholar in cultural studies puts it, "rhetoric offer[s] a major route into the study of contemporary culture" (Silverstone, 182). Others, too, have called for a turn to "the insights and the modes of analysis of rhetoric" in studies of culture (Morley, *Television,* 208), and, even more explicitly, still others have pointed out recently that "cultural studies has been deeply, if broadly, textual and rhetorical" (Nelson and Gaonkar, 9).

Fittingly, this "call for rhetoric" in the literature of critical cultural studies is matched by a "call for cultural studies" in communication and rhetoric, a summons that is also hard to overlook. Certain recent books from communication presses have explored the "rhetorical dimensions of culture" (e.g., Brummett, *Rhetoric, Rhetorical Dimensions*). In 1993 the National Communication Association sponsored its first summer conference devoted to the theme "Cultural Studies in Communication." A recent review in the *Quarterly Journal of Speech* proclaimed cultural studies a field "hard to ignore" (Fitch), and the 1997 National Communication Association convention featured nearly a dozen panels on "cultural studies."[2]

* * *

We find ourselves then in the present context of having two intellectual pursuits with increasing contemporary influence, ever more frequent "calls" for rapprochement between the two, and a dawning realization that rhetorical studies and cultural studies address specific and often similar issues about culture, critical practice, and interpretation. However, the matter of whether or not or even why we ought to engage in the postmodern propensity to reinvent, that is, to metamorphose or attempt to ally—these two important contemporary critical disciplines remains highly unsettled. Three broad concerns appear to drive the debate at the point where rhetorical studies and cultural studies intersect. The first has to do with the inevitable matters of disciplinarity, the consequences of the arbitrary jigsaw puzzle of academic domains and departments. Any rethinking of how cultural studies and rhetorical studies might relate to each other necessarily involves the real-world politics of the academy and how each discipline trains and authorizes work in its own behalf. In relation to this are the serious and consequential questions of what it means to define one's work as "rhetorical" or as "cultural." The second concern derives from the relationship of both cultural studies and rhetorical studies to "real" political action and to the ideological purpose of each, respectively. As they have developed historically, cultural studies and rhetorical studies have constructed quite clear yet very different conceptions of their social and political end(s) or purpose(s).

The third issue, which energizes the thinking about the relationship between rhetorical studies and cultural studies, stems directly from the analytic protocols and critical methodology of each discipline. Both cultural studies and rhetorical studies entail certain assumptions about discourse, reading, and history, and they arrive in their present circumstance bundled with methods of analytic practice, sets of values, critical theories, and assumptions about effect. This issue engages the problems of how one might best define history or context, what sorts of "objects" ought be studied, what "objects" or "texts" do or mean and what role readers/auditors play in this, and finally the right relations between object(s) and analyst.

DISCIPLINARITY AND IDENTITY

Both historically and conceptually, the debate over the crossdisciplinary relationship between cultural studies and rhetorical studies has been something more than a passing controversy without consequence. Instead, what is indisputable is that, under the pressure of the book market, the dictates of the academic job marketplace, and academic cultural capital in general, the relationship between these two disciplines weighs heavily in considerations of the identity of each and the possibilities and pitfalls of merging or joining them together—all the more so because any major change might affect the academic lineage and thus the domains of study open to each group of scholars. Related but no less crucial issues include whether or not one or the other term logically subsumes the other. What academic lineage is involved? Did rhetorical studies "beget" cultural studies—or vice versa? Is cultural studies really just rhetorical analysis applied to nontraditional practices?

Most of the time such questions about academic influence articulate themselves in terms of the histories, the essentialized identity, or the influence of cultural studies and rhetorical studies upon each other. One way to respond is to see a commonality—what Cary Nelson (in Chapter 8 of this volume) calls the shared "metaphor of linguisticality"—that is at the heart of both cultural studies and rhetorical studies. As Nelson argues here, the two disciplines have always broadly shared much the same approach and subject matter, and the relationship has been a vital and formative one for cultural studies, which in "its founding moments depended upon careful interrogation of texts" and the "close analysis of traditional sorts of texts." As Nelson's interpretation of the seminal *Policing the Crisis* makes clear, in cultural studies' earliest work at the Birmingham Centre for Contemporary Cultural Studies, obvious links with rhetorical analysis and with close reading traditions were established from the outset.

Others see this historical relationship less as formative than deforming. Lawrence Grossberg, for instance, argues that, largely as a result of being housed in communication departments, American cultural studies has adopted a partial and debilitating practice. Such studies, what he calls "communicational cultural studies," concentrate too much on textuality and interpretation, so much so as to exclude a complete analysis. Instead, Grossberg argues, such "conflation" of communication and cultural studies has reduced the key problems of cultural studies to issues of signification and textuality ("Toward," 139–140). Thus, he laments, it reduces the object of cultural studies to "a concern with texts and/or audiences which can be analyzed in isolation from their place within the material contexts of everyday life" (141).

While Grossberg does not directly address rhetorical studies per se, his criticism is serious. However, there are other possible narratives of the relationship between rhetorical studies and cultural studies. Bruce E. Gronbeck (Chapter 11) provides one alternative history by locating an indigenous critical cultural project in the legacy of the intellectual scene of the 1930s in and around the "small" magazine the *Partisan Review*. In contrast to Grossberg's narrative, which locates the formative episode of cultural studies in departmental siting, Gronbeck sees the crucial break coming under the influence of positivism, with the cultural-rhetorical and critical models of intellectual critique being replaced by a social scientific paradigm increasingly interested in description, categorization, and prediction and less concerned with political critique and theorization.

But should the two disciplines move toward a kind of alliance or even "become" the other? One way to confront this weighty issue is to realize that an inescapable factor in the overall debate has been the influence of popular culture. As several contributors to this volume point out, our current fascination with popular culture and with its role in social formation has the effect of making whatever is popular seem worthy of serious study; one need but pursue the titles of current doctoral research theses to appreciate how much and how broadly the popular has become the center of recent academic work (Nelson and Gaonkar, 1–5). As an academic area historically and conceptually predisposed to the popular, cultural studies thereby attains a higher level of visibility, which certainly contributes to its academic institutionalization and to a kind of disciplinary colonization fostered through proliferating professional associations, conferences, celebrity practitioners, journals, and high-profile books. There is nothing sinister about any increasing convergence between rhetorical and cultural studies. As John M. Sloop and Mark Olson (Chapter 10) suggest, because the "study of culture" is a relatively open-ended phrase, there is a tendency for rhetorical studies and cultural studies partially to "merge into one another rather than having separate projects." Others have explained it slightly differently. Nelson has argued that these days, as the analytical pursuits of literary studies, rhetorical studies, history, women's studies, and cultural studies more and more focus on either *nontraditional* or *the same* artifacts and practices, the walls traditionally thought to separate the two disciplines become ever more porous (Nelson and Gaonkar).

But there is the danger (as Sloop and Olson warn in Chapter 10) that the high visibility that cultural studies currently enjoys inevitably encourages some scholars in rhetorical studies to recast or attempt to recast their own work as "cultural." Faced with the demands of an academic marketplace that places an increasing premium upon "culture studies" as a descriptor, some rhetorical studies scholars naturally tend to assert that they also "do cultural studies." One of the ominous conclusions of this trend is that, should market forces continue to fuel developments in academic practice, one or the other discipline might lose its identity altogether, with conceivably dire consequences for social justice at large.

A closely related and equally knotty problem concerns defining the proper practical relationship between cultural studies and rhetorical studies. Should rhetorical studies take wholecloth the presumptions or perspectives of cultural studies? Should it take any elements? What does rhetorical studies offer to cultural studies that it presently lacks or overlooks? One possible response is to hold firmly to the distinctions between the two disciplines and to avoid any tendency to collapse one into the other. Sloop and Olson, for example, argue against the too easy use of the term *cultural studies* in rhetorical studies and lament the "ease" with which cultural studies and rhetorical studies have been made interchangeable. They caution scholars to consider what is "really at stake in the joint articulation of cultural studies/rhetorical studies." What might well happen, they argue, is that the strengths of both disciplines might be weakened as they are conflated, that is, we might well end up with an "apoliticized" cultural studies and an overgeneralized "analytical" rhetorical studies.

But this outcome need not necessarily result. As I argue in Chapter 9, an alternative reading of the literature of rhetorical studies finds cultural studies dormant but already present within that tradition. Following out this line of rediscovery, I suggest that a "cultural rhetorical studies" is not an aberration or a change in direction for rhetorical studies but more a recovery of tendencies already prefigured in the history of the field. Rather than one discipline collapsing into the other, I see a more hopeful prospect where preservation of the unique nature of the two disciplines can go hand in hand with progress on critical problems specific to each.

Others see it differently still. Patrick Brantlinger (Chapter 12) enters this controversy from a novel direction. Instead of dealing with distinctions and histories, Brantlinger asks that we consider the very real possibility that rhetorical studies and cultural studies have already merged, that they are, with their shared interest in the concrete practice of cultural critique and with the linguisticality that Nelson has identified, both positioned as antithetical to "Theory." Brantlinger advances the controversial idea that it is in and through this antitheoretical dimension that rhetorical studies and cultural studies find themselves most closely identified with each other. Some might take issue with such a counterintuitive position, but Brantlinger's essay resets the issues of the relationship between the two metadiscourses within the contemporary university on a quite different and more common footing than is usually assumed.

Other contributors begin with the insight that cultural studies and rhetorical studies do, after all, share certain areas of theoretical agreement and practice. Thus, an identity forged in praxis might serve as the anchor point to erect considerations of the essential relationships between cultural studies and rhetorical studies. Henry Krips (Chapter 7) maps such an analysis by working backward from the shared interest of cultural studies and rhetorical studies in the relationship among images, representation, and ideology. For him, this is a model for the ultimate unity of the two fields. James Arnt Aune (Chapter 2) pursues this insight by focusing on what he defines as the essential abilities and myopias of each discipline. Indeed, Aune argues that rhetoric seems especially adept at analyzing political strategy but rather weak at mapping trajectories of popular desire; on the other hand, cultural studies is robust in drawing attention to issues of gender, performance, and desire in the popular media but rather unconcerned with analyzing conventional political discourse. Aune's essay is an especially provocative attempt to "use" both disciplines' perspectives where they seem most able to further the fullest disclosure and critique. Thomas S. Frentz and Janice Hocker Rushing (Chapter 13) agree, noting that both cultural studies and rhetorical studies are focused on the process of influence, with this great difference: rhetoric traditionally has been concerned with how a struggle for power happens through legitimate social institutions, whereas cultural studies assumes that political empowerment occurs outside legitimate social institutions and in resistance to those institutions.

One of the insights apparent at the intersection seems to be that practitioners, when they do their analytical and critical work, concern themselves chiefly and finally with the ultimate and complete disclosure of the artifact or practice being studied rather than dogmatically attempting to separate their work into its "cultural" and "rhetorical" components. This approach seems grounded in the assumption that such distinctions themselves are finally arbitrary and that reproducing them in critique results in what amounts to an amputated a priori analysis. For example, Steven Mailloux (Chapter 3) interchangeably uses the approaches of classical and sophistic rhetorical theory and those of contemporary reception theory to deal with current political cultural discourse. Neither he nor Aune rely on a distinction between the disciplines of cultural studies and rhetorical studies, instead implying that what is really at stake is less a question of whether one is being "rhetorical" or "cultural" in approach than it is one of how best to investigate the way stability or change is structured into social discourse. Carole Blair and Neil Michel (Chapter 1) make the same point in a slightly different way. They take the Astronauts Memorial as text and find that the subject matter resists both a more or less orthodox "rhetorical reading" or a "cultural studies" one. Instead, they appropriate certain methods from both rhetorical studies and cultural studies. As they conclude, reading a text through rhetorical theory is "not wrong, but it is only one kind of reading." We might push this conclusion further to suggest that, concomitantly, reading a text through cultural studies perspectives is also "only one kind of reading."

Finally, and related to the other conclusions, the debate over future disciplinary relations between cultural studies and rhetorical studies has real material consequences that are anything but trivial. What will determine the eventual outcome? First among such determining factors is the rather precarious position of both rhetorical studies and cultural studies in what Brantlinger has called the "modern corporate university" (*Crusoe's*, 23–28). Often less able than some other disciplines to offer justification for increased funding and staffing when framed within the reigning market model of higher education, cultural studies and rhetorical studies find themselves pitted unwittingly (though sometimes deliberately) as adversaries. Of course, this is even more complicated by the phenomenon of convergence that I mentioned earlier. As Nelson argues (Chapter 8), whichever course we ultimately choose automatically forecloses job opportunities for our graduates. And, as he has made clear, the way we define whether we are doing "cultural studies" or "rhetorical studies" manifests itself at the crucial point of the hiring process for new doctoral graduates (Nelson and Gaonkar, 3–5). Sloop and Olson (Chapter 10) are also concerned about the effects that our present deliberations over the shape of the field will have on the next generation of scholars.

THE POLITICS OF CRITIQUE

For any intellectual practice, but especially for those such as cultural studies and rhetorical studies that have a stated interest in the social and the material world, the connection between critique and intervention in political life is a complex one. In rhetorical studies, as Gronbeck (Chapter 11) points out:

> The ideological turn has spawned a running battle between those who believe that analytically controlled rhetorical analysis generates human understanding (in the tradition of Black [*Rhetorical Analysis*]) and those who demand that critics must push past the disinterestedness of rational analysis and into the realm of ideological critique and political action.

Indeed, rhetorical studies arrives in its present circumstances bearing the determining weight of this historical incompatibility. On one side are the "traditionalists," who urge the analysis of a text's rhetorical devices free and clear of any subjective personal involvement (Hill, "Turn," 122). Bill Nothstine, Carole Blair, and Gary Copeland have explained this perspective in part by noting the historical coincidence of the formation of modern academic departments of speech and the rise of an "ideology of professionalism" in American higher education. As they see it, in the wake of this "professionalism," rhetorical studies/criticism becomes more "scientistic," with its findings or conclusions more directed to other "critics" as demonstrations of "scholarly virtuosity" (43) and its practitioners more satisfied with amoral theoretical explanations (45). As this occurs over time, the political edge of rhetorical studies is blunted, and it becomes "disengaged" from public life and "unable" to render "judgment" or guidance that might shape public action, deliberation, or critique. The net result is that "the possibility for critics and for their criticism to serve as a genuine source of knowledge, power, or ethics in a public culture is diminished almost to zero" (45).

In a way the issue of political neutrality or engagement has not progressed much beyond the seminal exchange between Forbes Hill and Karlyn Kohrs Campbell (Karlyn Kohrs Campbell, "Conventional Wisdom," "Response"; Hill, "Conventional Wisdom," "Reply") and others over the role and obligations of the social critic. Their debate revisited the basic dispute of the classical tradition, centered upon the dispassionate analysis of argumentation, versus a more engaged critique that ultimately wishes to confront the abuses of power through ideologically weighted discourse. And, however advantageous it might be to think that rhetorical studies has gotten beyond this debate, nonetheless residues of it remain that have significantly shaped contemporary rhetorical studies (Gaonkar, "Very Idea"; Jasinski).

But, as with the other issues treated here, rhetorical studies does not present a single, uniform treatment of the political responsibilities of critique. While the influence of the traditionalists remains forceful, some rhetorical work clearly follows a tendency toward ideological exposure (Wander, "Ideological Turn" and "Third Persona"). There is a clear tradition of such ideological studies in rhetoric, often taking the form of discourses that are not even usually recognized as "political." Such studies range from Dennis Mumby and Carole Spitzack's analysis of the ideology of television news to Farrell Corcoran's reading of news magazine coverage of a Soviet attack on a Korean airliner. Another nontraditional type of work has been the various studies sponsored under the banner of feminism or work influenced by feminism. Indeed, for many such critics working today, rhetorical studies analysis is undertaken with a clear and explicit political purpose, and with the desire to reveal how ideology and power are manifest through rhetorical struggle. As Celeste Michelle Condit (Chapter 6) observes, this work is very different from traditional work: not only does it seek to expose how taken for granted ideology is but also, importantly, it seeks to have clear political effects on the historical world in which we live.

Related to this traditional tendency in rhetorical studies toward political "neutrality" (notwithstanding the foregoing exceptions), there is a second charge leveled against the discipline with increasing frequency these days, namely, the tendency to assume a rather naive stance toward the practices of public discourse as they really occur in our contemporary postindustrial and increasingly multicultural society. Indeed, public communication nowadays has changed in ways that render the traditional model of the intentional persuasive agent and subject-centered producer of discourse rather quaint. It is apparent we live now in a more managerial and more self-consciously ideological age than we have hitherto allowed, thus undercutting previous assumptions that our "democratic society" means or sponsors an "open marketplace of ideas." Rhetorical studies, in general, has not been too concerned with questions of the tactical management of discourse by public relations experts or communication consultants, nor of what it means when a "public" is accessible to rhetors only through a heavily regulated and expensive mass media (Sproul, 474).

When we turn to cultural studies, the situation is more ambivalent. As originally formulated, cultural studies was not politically neutral. On the contrary, critique and analysis, it was agreed, "should" lead to intervention and to community building. Thus cultural studies, early on, maintained commitment to critical and political objectives. As the editors of the popular volume *Cultural Studies* put it, "cultural studies [is] not simply a chronicle of cultural change, but an intervention in it, ... not simply scholars providing an account but ... politically engaged participants" (Nelson, Grossberg, and Treichler, 5).

It is ironic, then, that some have lately observed in the recent practice of cultural studies a significant departure from such political engagement (Ferguson and Golding, xxiv). Indeed, this "retreat from politics" has been seen as the inevitable effect of a contemporary practice preoccupied with popular culture, where the real dynamics of power and inequality become displaced onto textual politics. This development is accompanied by an overriding interest in the theoretical and the textual (Carey, "Reflections"; Gitlin). The outcome is a form of study remote from life, the almost complete abandonment of real politics from the cultural studies purview, and concentration instead on the affirmative, pleasurable, and thus redemptive responses of audiences. As Douglas Kellner has put it, the "postmodern turn in cultural studies" decenters actual politics "in favor of emphasis on local pleasures, consumption, and the construction of hybrid identities from the material of the popular" (104).

This displacement of politics in both disciplines manifests itself concretely in the kinds of discourses that seem to preoccupy them. Cultural studies has shown a reluctance to consider discourses that are overtly political. James Aune criticizes cultural studies for neglecting overt political matters while criticizing rhetorical studies, on the other hand, for overemphasizing "official discourse" at the expense of context and history (*Rhetoric and Marxism*). As he puts it, all too often cultural studies displays a benign neglect of political rhetoric and an accompanying inattention to the strategic dimension of politics (269). Aune has gone on to point out that cultural studies has been especially reluctant to adequately attend to public political discourse, rather preferring, as he puts it, to look to subcultures and lived experience as the proper subject for study. Tony Bennett has reached a similar conclusion and urges more cultural studies attention to the actual institutions and organization of real (as opposed to academic) politics.

But, as Nelson (Chapter 8) so vividly demonstrates, in its founding days British cultural studies *was* fully and completely involved in the study of public discourse and in discourses distinguished as political, ranging from public speeches to judicial decisions to parliamentary debate. While it might seem that such texts were solely within the purview of rhetoric, Nelson argues that the early projects of The Birmingham Centre show the dimensions of what we might call a cultural rhetorical studies.

Several contributions to this volume address the politics of critique with the implicit conclusion that cultural studies and rhetorical studies have much to learn from each other in this regard. As Elizabeth Walker Mechling and Jay Mechling (Chapter 5) argue, criticism is always "interested" and is "never neutral" in part because the critic wants to make a difference in the world and wants criticism to have moral and political consequences. In his essay (Chapter 2) Aune takes up this challenge and professes a quite specific political agenda for the critic, who in his view should practice a "new type of rhetorical-cultural analysis" that transcends differing forms of cultural and political discourse. What a new kind of cultural critique should do, Aune says, is investigate how rhetorical forms interact with audience desire and anxiety in particular historical circumstances. The political is served by looking for "positive opportunities for political organizing and rhetorical mediation of the contradiction between information and body." For Barry Brummett and Detine L. Bowers (Chapter 4) texts are sites of struggle with potential rhetorical effects, and an understanding of how texts create subjects or objects can also create more awareness of how the discursive construction of race is struggled over rather than just dictated by discourse. Mailloux (Chapter 3) examines the "Culture Wars" with the understanding that disputes over curriculum change and cultural diversity ("Western Greats," "identity politics," "Eurocentrism," or "ethnic studies") are but covers for a more serious criticism of the "liberalism" of the academy in the 1990s. He investigates the circulation of topics within this debate, from the academic to the popular and back again, in hopes of sponsoring an intervention. Gronbeck (Chapter 11), calling upon cultural criticism to reconnect with its history, shows how this same tendency toward apparent apoliticism has been manifest in American cultural studies in contemporary times. Gronbeck's conclusions are not particularly encouraging, for he sees the maintenance today of a distinction between a politically engaged cultural critique and a truly detached, perhaps pedagogical, analysis.

On the other hand, Brummett and Bowers (Chapter 4) along with Frentz and Rushing (Chapter 13) both seek to invigorate the orthodox practice of rhetorical criticism to serve specific political purposes. Brummett and Bowers offer demonstration of the insight that the struggle over textual positions has the potential to create awareness and hence intervention in the politics of race and racial stereotype(s). They recognize that how texts reflect and reproduce struggles for meaning are also struggles for power. For Frentz and Rushing, a larger political struggle entails reestablishing the connection between institutional structure and social consciousness to save community, and they envision the alliance of cultural studies and rhetorical studies as the most promising strategy to accomplish this reconnection.

But it is just this sense of the hopeful purpose of a cultural rhetorical practice that provides, for Patrick Brantlinger (Chapter 12), a delicious paradox. He notes that both rhetorical and ideological critique have as their goal enlightenment or emancipation from the illusions generated by rhetoric and ideology. To the good, such "emancipatory" social theory harbors ameliorative "utopian ideals." But, at the same time, Brantlinger warns that we not get carried away with the metaphor, for it begs the very serious question of whether or not rhetoric/ideology critique can actually be subversive or oppositional. Instead, Brantlinger holds that the neopragmatic position promoted by both Mailloux and Mechling and Mechling is antitheoretical, and thus it gives up any possibility of disturbing the status quo. He lodges the serious complaint that such neopragmatism is more consonant with and supportive of a peculiar brand of liberal pluralism than it is of a true political radicalism. This position, if sustained, would undermine the assumption that a "pragmatics" of rhetoric could ever function except as a form of sophisticated ideological apologetics.

METHODOLOGY

One key set of concerns over the intersection between rhetorical studies and cultural studies centers on methodology. In a way, this is perhaps the most pivotal debate of all, for, as Nelson (Chapter 8) notes, disputes about the relationship between rhetorical studies and cultural studies are in reality disputes about discursive practices—that is, about which methods and analytical techniques are validated and privileged. Positions in the debate are, of course, determined by many factors, but we can group them heuristically. On the one hand, some have suggested that cultural studies has always been undeniably shaped by rhetorical studies. Cary Nelson and Dilip Gaonkar, for instance, review some early cultural studies and conclude that interchange between "cultural studies acolytes and traditional rhetoricians" has occurred frequently, even if in many cases it is as yet unacknowledged. They conclude that "cultural studies has been deeply, if broadly, textual and rhetorical in its methodology" (9). Others, however, take a less sanguine perspective and seek to maintain quite distinct walls of separation between the disciplines. Still others take a more moderate position and consider how rhetorical studies may serve as a means for cultural analysis and vice versa.

One set of issues in the debate is of a more metacritical cast, in that both rhetorical studies and cultural studies come with quite significant methodological strengths. As Frentz and Rushing (Chapter 13) remind us, rhetorical studies has a "rich history" that has proven capable of dealing provocatively with issues relating discourse to society. As they describe it, rhetorical studies has always productively used case study analysis as its exemplar of critical practice, coupling that with the fluidity to move between sophisticated theoretical analysis and narration of local particulars through the disclosure of rhetorical texts. And, to Nelson's mind (Chapter 8), it is precisely this close reading and case study methodology that is the most important bond between rhetorical studies and cultural studies. He argues that this methodology has always been central and that linguistic evidence is absolutely essential in cultural rhetorical studies, if for no other reason than that it provides the only persuasive evidence most academics recognize.

On the other hand, the distinctiveness of case study analysis as a defining feature of cultural studies has also come under some scrutiny. Lately some have complained about cultural studies' supposed "falling away" from close readings to concentrate upon a critical practice that overemphasizes discourse as a theoretical system. Michael Billig, for one, has argued that cultural studies these days tends to deal with the larger structural issues of ideology, race, and gender without paying sufficient attention to specific cases. This practice tends to propel the cultural critique away from its context-bound, or "occasioned" or "rhetorical," aspects and often obscures the understanding that "utterances are not unproblematic reflections of wider discourses or internal states but their meaning is dependent upon their occasioned use" (208).

The case studies in *At the Intersection* make useful contributions to this general metacritical and methodological debate. Mailloux (Chapter 3) and Aune (Chapter 2) cite both classical sophistic writers on rhetoric and contemporary cultural critics in commenting on the contemporary condition of rhetoric, the "culture wars," and the "discourse of technology." In bringing these two traditions into the same discussion, they show how the two might be related. And Carole Blair and Neil Michel's essay (Chapter 1) demonstrates a form of analysis that explicitly relies upon "both rhetorical studies and cultural studies in a critical encounter."

In a way, this conjoining of the two disciplines might best be shown in relation to a condition I noted before, namely, the tendency of American culture studies to divide into "a tripartite approach to the study of culture" (Grossberg, "Toward," 140). This three-part division produces, it is claimed, a "diluted" form of cultural critique, one that cannot encompass the full cycle of cultural production, textuality, and consumption. But, contrary to this, Blair and Michel demonstrate that in practice a cultural rhetorical analysis does not necessarily favor one moment of the cycle over the others. In their essay they present evidence from the original legislation, the architect's conception, and decisions about the siting of the Astronauts Memorial. Not only that, they present a "textual" reading of the Memorial, its structure, and the mechanics that put it into motion. And they also attend to the reaction (or lack of reaction) of visitors to the Memorial. In this example, their full-bodied critique encompasses all aspects of the textual cycle, the circuit of production, textuality, and reception.[3]

In addition to such metacritical issues as these, this conjoining of cultural studies with rhetorical studies throws open for reconsideration four central topics of critical concern: context, text, readers and their power, and the relationship of critic to text.

Context

Rhetorical studies, as traditionally conceived, has a conditioned reflex to the question of context. Indeed, on one level rhetoric appears to lack a true sense of the broad social forces involved in producing discourse (Charland, "Rehabilitating," 262; Gaonkar, "Very Idea"), generally opting for more immediate or local definitions of "situation." Dilip Gaonkar asserts that "the rhetorical critic is so preoccupied with the immediate pragmatics of the text that s/he has not devised an adequate strategy for signaling the constitutive presence of the larger historical/discursive formations within which a text is embedded" ("Very Idea," 338). This narrowing focus upon the ever more specific local context results in what James Jasinski calls the "hypervalorization of the particular." The net effect, as he sees it, is to "sever the text and context from the flow of history" (201). Further, this tendency toward lopping off history has itself contributed to another diminution, namely, the perception that rhetorical studies are concerned exclusively with matters of textuality and indifferent to larger questions relating to ideology and society. In short, rhetoric seems predisposed to locate power in textuality, not material conditions. The inevitable result is what some see as a dim-sightedness at the horizons of analysis. As Maurice Charland concludes:

> Because it lacked a materialist foundation, and attributed too much to the power of words, and because it developed in an intellectual tradition where idealism and then positivism dominated, the study of rhetoric has not been characterized by the development of a fundamental political or cultural critique. ("Rehabilitating," 262)

Indeed, if rhetoricians need to consider larger "formations" more adequately the intersection with cultural studies suggests one model of how this might be done, in effect by holding in suspension the study of symbols and the historical forces that give them rise.[4]

Several of the essays in *At the Intersection* engage the issues surrounding the use of history and of social context, and of how a critic might, or ought to, define context. Blair and Michel, for example, take as the context for their study the whole of what they call a "South Florida Vacationscape." Such widening of the context far beyond what traditional criticism would allow seems authorized by their recognition of the shortcomings of using either a rhetorical or a cultural approach alone. Instead, they are determined to revise the stance taken so as to see the text within a culturally determined "experience rendered by [a] visitor's journey." Other contributors take context as intellectual and social. Aune (Chapter 2), for example, demonstrates how both political and popular discourses, taken together, begin to frame the social context of the late twentieth century, both reflecting anxieties about a new millennium and simultaneously shaping responses to it. For still other contributors, context is historical and broadly economic. Krips (Chapter 7) describes in some detail the social and cultural scene in and around the production of Holbein's masterpiece *The Ambassadors*. This leads him finally to consider how an encounter with the painting becomes a simulacrum to the viewer's "difficulties" in establishing a position in the new social space created by the expansion of trade, an increasingly capitalized economic system, and the formation of merchant capitalism emerging in sixteenth-century Europe. For Krips, only when Holbein's painting is placed into this "context" does it become useful as a way of understanding the social relations that were in play during this period.

But this attention to history is not without its problems and cannot be easily or simply glossed over. Condit (Chapter 6) examines the uses of "history" in both cultural studies and rhetorical studies and uses this examination both to differentiate between the two disciplines and to suggest a pre-scription for a more effective cultural critique. Within cultural studies, Condit argues, historicization means focusing on local conditions rather than on the flow of historical time, with a linking of particular practices to social forces rather than to past events or individuals. The inevitable result of this perspective is that history is always "short-term." Condit both warns against the danger of the absence of attention to the time streams of history and calls for a new practice that might have the potential to relate material events to cultural and rhetorical practices. History, she argues, must be rearticulated if effective critical studies are to be generated.

Text

There is equally energetic controversy over what "things" or "artifacts" or "texts" or "practices" should be studied, and the assumptions that underlie choices in this area are changing rapidly and dramatically. Once it might have been possible clearly and decisively to distinguish between cultural studies and rhetorical studies. For instance, cultural studies has always manifested a willingness to take on popular culture and media texts and to understand the connections or the intertextuality of these artifacts; while, traditionally considered, rhetorical studies has been chiefly interested in the genre of public address, often using platform oratory as the exemplar. The latter, what Condit calls "neoclassical" rhetorical studies, often concen-trates upon important or eloquent individuals, in large measure because the speeches of these "great men" are assumed to represent the motives of the past, to shape history, and to model aesthetic excellence in public address. As Condit points out, sometimes these "neo-classical" rhetorical studies had difficulty in getting beyond the discrete text, or conceptualizing in a systematic way how the process of creating and managing meanings hap-pens in a variety of texts across a variety of communicative forms, or in appreciating completely the insight that texts not identified as political are often those that are *most* political.

These days there is less a singular practice of rhetoric and public address studies than there is a more variegated volume of rhetorical work. In large part the contemporary discipline finds its inspiration in two sources. First, drawing from the abundant literature on social movements that dominated communication journals in the late 1960s and early 1970s, many working in rhetorical studies these days assume rhetoric is best stud-ied within a framework that includes collective and social dimensions, and it is best understood as the product of multiple voices contesting over power. These studies aim to reconstruct rhetorical action as collective, and they rarely take the single text as source. The second inspiration comes, as Condit notes, from the influence of feminism. These rhetorical studies adopt a long-term historical horizon and seek to understand the rhetoric of social change in such discourses as civil rights (Logue and Garner; Condit and Lucaites), abortion rights (Railsback; Vanderford; Lake, "Order"), women's place in the work force and the church (Jablonski; Foss), and so on.

In at least one other important way, rhetorical studies continues to move away from a preoccupation with platform oratory and the single discrete text. Intrigued by popular and media culture, invigorated by the interests of younger critics, this type of rhetorical studies strives to bring the insights of rhetoric to such current mediated practice as documentary news coverage (Rosteck, *See It Now*), television comedy (Dow, *Prime-Time Feminism*), and feature films (Rushing and Frentz, *Projecting the Shadow*). Though Sloop and Olson (Chapter 10) are surely right when they take care to distinguish the uses of the terms *culture* and *rhetoric* within such studies, it is nevertheless also true that these perspectives broaden what is considered "the text" in rhetorical studies and seek to draw out the social and cultural implications of historically situated discourses. These studies (Condit labels them "mediated rhetoric practice") represent a kind of mid-place between cultural studies and neoclassical rhetorical studies. Taken together with more "movement-oriented" perspectives, these rhetorical analyses of mediated culture reveal the ever closer relationship between rhetorical studies and cultural studies. In some ways, one insight we may derive from this volume is that, in contemporary practice, shifting assumptions about "textuality" might represent a most promising opening for a fledgling cultural rhetorical studies.

The studies in *At the Intersection* demonstrate how far such a cultural rhetorical studies might go in using insights from both fields. Aune (Chapter 2), for instance, shakes up assumptions about what is the "expected" domain of study of each discipline as he investigates futurists, conservative Republican politics, cyberpunk, and science fiction. In a sense, what Aune suggests is that the cultural critic in our increasingly interdiscursive culture has considerable latitude to tease out a "text" for analysis. And, as he makes clear, there is special urgency in doing so—in tracking what Aune calls "the circulation of social energy" that seems to flow between the popular and the overtly political. Such broadening of the concept of textuality or intertextuality is apparent in most of the other essays, as well. Mechling and Mechling (Chapter 5), for instance, propose new terminology—the concept of "shadowtexts"—that seeks to capture, in their study of popular films of the 1990s, the sense that textuality is for cultural rhetoric an intertextual "object." Similarly, Condit (Chapter 6) examines the way the discourse of genetic medicine is embedded in a longer-range "critical-historical" context to suggest how such a "text" must be reconceptualized to more fully reveal elements of local political critique.

Reader

Some of the most vexing issues at the intersection of rhetorical studies and cultural studies concern the relationship between texts and readers. On the one hand, texts are traditionally seen as "closed"—held to contain meanings immanent to themselves (that is, one cannot simply interpret them as one pleases); they are held to reproduce dominant ideological structures and thus exert preference for a particular reading or group of readings. On the other hand, texts do "play with signification" and give "pleasure" as an elaborate "writerly" game of producing meaning. Once again, the conventional mode of explanation places cultural studies and rhetorical studies at opposite poles. This explanation contends that, at least within the "neoclassical model" of rhetorical studies, rhetoricians have traditionally invested in the idea of a dominant text and the single "master" reading, while cultural studies more likely emphasized the affirmative power of readers over textuality.

But such stark antitheses, in this issue as in some of the others, are these days under modification. The issue may well be less one of different conceptions of the audience than one of different conceptions of the role and potential of discourse itself. Rhetorical studies seems comfortable with a more or less adversarial model of the social sphere, where competing ideologies, manifest in texts, strive to overturn others and to establish themselves as "common sense." This process involves a power struggle over comparative meanings of a social practice, with each "term" or "meaning" seeking dominance and hegemony over the other. So, rhetorical studies might logically trace the struggle over power as it developed in the abortion debate or in shifting definitions of African Americans in the United States. Cultural studies, on the other hand, has concerned itself mostly with struggles among different audiences or with a single discourse over multiple socially determined meanings or potential meanings of that discourse (Fiske, "Polysemy" and "For Cultural Interpretation"), or with the shifts or "ruptures" in discursive formations brought about by analogous shifts in the social formation (Stuart Hall, "Notes"). Both rhetorical studies and cultural studies may well address issues of power and interpretation, but far less apparent is what the most productive relationship between these two disciplines should be.

Some contributors to *At the Intersection* discuss this issue at length. Brummett and Bowers (Chapter 4) reject the immanent meaning of the text and instead work through in detail the (necessary) "rhetorical struggle over meaning." As they point out, traditional rhetoric, not so concerned with construction of subjects or objects, assumes an unproblematic treatment of audience. But what seems clear to Brummett and Bowers is that, when the critic looks at texts as a struggle over meaning, she or he is not necessarily impelled to choose either the polysemous text or the closed one. Instead, the agile critic recognizes that the management or negotiation of contradiction, both in texts and by audiences, is an inherently rhetorical process (Condit, "Polysemy"). We can see this perspective implicit in some of the other studies here. For instance, Mechling and Mechling (Chapter 5) argue for a new way of considering the weight of various material, institutional, and ideological contexts that might determine or circumscribe the range of possible meanings that a typical audience member in 1995 might discover in the film *Braveheart*.

Blair and Michel (Chapter 1) also acknowledge how traditional neoclassical rhetorical criticism has a tendency to treat the audience in a perfunctory way and to favor the "preferred" reading of the text. As a corrective, they demonstrate how one might engage the "real" audience and the kinds of meanings they might take away from a visit to the Astronauts Memorial, in effect, showing how the "preferred reading" generated in a traditional "rhetorical" approach might usefully be supplemented by the interpretations of actual visitors. In accounting for the "uniformly positive reading of critics and the negative or lack of reaction by visitors," Blair and Michel model what might be gained by applying cultural studies perspectives to rhetorical studies and vice versa. Again, the insight from the intersection of the disciplines is that the choice need not be polar, that is, either favoring the closed or open text. Cultural studies paired with rhetorical studies complicates the matter by assuming that audiences are never free floating ahistorical actors. Rather, the implication is that texts are subject to shifts in the contexts of their reception that can entirely change their specific meanings for specific audiences and thus their wider cultural significance. The insight demonstrated in both Brummett and Bowers (Chapter 4) and Blair and Michel (Chapter 1) is that texts both reflect conflict over meaning (and hence power struggles) in society and serve as the sites of these struggles. Therefore, the critic must ground in a specific material circumstance (historical, economic, political, social) the production of textuality and the kinds of readings that audiences might make. That is, between the extremes of text as completely open and completely closed is the space in which *active* audiences produce their own meanings but have to work on material that has been preselected and organized in particular ways by producers and that is governed by historical conditions, institutional decisions, and situational exigencies.

Critic

Closely allied to the text/reader dialectic is the set of questions concerning the text-critic relationship. In the wake of New Criticism and positivism, rhetorical studies has not been altogether reflective or candid about its own critical methodologies. It has not often brought to the foreground the way in which its own readings are influenced by other discursive and historical forces and how every critical reading bears traces of those influences. Sometimes rhetorical studies have been too quick to merely assume that interpretations are independent of the methodology that devises them.

Contributors to *At the Intersection* conceive of the method of criticism and the object of criticism relationally and seek to fully contextualize both the theories and methods used to study texts as well as the objects of the study.[5] No text is independent of the methodology that constructs it, because all methodologies themselves have social, political, and historical foundations. Again, the point is not that one studies texts or contexts, readers or readings, but that in these essays the hermeneutic categories are held always in tension—neither text nor context nor reader nor reading is conceivable as an entity separable from one another. Aune posits a "reflex-iveness of self" that stands quite apart from "objective" method; Blair demonstrate the questioning of the critic's role, and their essay is on one level a narrative of a critical engagement with a text. Sometimes this is manifest in the willingness of the critic to acknowledge personal assumptions and "subjective" values in the process of analysis and the rendering of the text (see Mailloux, Chapter 3, and Mechling and Mechling, Chapter 5, which considers the critic's stance more indirectly).

But to posit that the text is only and always "realized" in historically and contextually situated practices of reading does not require that we collapse these categories into one another. In the end what seems to come from these essays is that the method must "fit" the object/text or discourse, and, as Blair and Michel make clear, sometimes only the insights available at the intersection of these two critical disciplines can best reveal the various levels of influence and ideology within cultural practices. What this would seem to entail, of course, is a radically contextual approach to scholarship, one with no fixed theoretical or methodological program. But to others, this is not a viable option, in part because it runs counter to the assumption, reigning in cultural studies, that critique must be grounded in theory (see Sloop and Olson, Chapter 10, and Brantlinger, Chapter 12).

THE PROMISE OF A CULTURAL RHETORICAL STUDIES

As we imagine future intellectual and political work, the essays in *At the Intersection* are submitted as a proof of sorts of the type of subjects that cultural studies and rhetorical studies might jointly engage. One natural tendency, easy to arrive at after reading these essays, might be to conclude that they must inevitably glide toward one another, become conflated, each to become the other, or that one must provide institutional or academic "cover" for another. But such eliding cannot be done willy-nilly nor by happenstance. As Sloop and Olson (Chapter 10) point out, the two disciplines have come together in part because of the growth and popularity of cultural studies within the academy, because of its special affiliation with rhetorical studies, and because of their shared use of the term *culture*.

Sloop and Olson present the attractive vision of rhetorical studies serving the larger aims of cultural studies—of providing a space in which the political employment of the available means of persuasion is studied with a focus on how rhetoric works in any given situation, how change and exploration can be encouraged. In Sloop and Olson's conception, cultural studies will draw upon the findings and the discoveries of rhetorical studies as a way to empower itself politically. What is projected for the future, of course, is the image of cultural studies as interdisciplinary space, crossing and utilizing disciplines in pursuit of political intervention. Cultural studies "needs" productive disciplines, including the study of rhetoric, from which to draw upon in the implementation of its objectives.

This connection between the two seems a strikingly useful relationship. But there may be more and other ways to define it. For what seems urgent and surely striking in reading the essays contributed to this collection is how frequently they arrive at a compatibility, with rhetorical studies and culture studies seen as complementary. A second conclusion seems immanent in the first. While no contributor to *At the Intersection* suggests that the two metadiscourses should assimilate into one another, or should transform into the other in a sort of academic sleight of hand, these essays do seem to offer new ways of framing "old" problems. Indeed, the compelling idea here is not that one discipline should borrow theories or methods wholecloth from the other, but rather that because they engage such similar problems we might understand how each deals with parallel interpretive problems and intervenes in current practice. This will happen, I think, not by becoming the other, but rather by providing examples of how one might bring together production, textuality, consumption, history, and culture with the end of a more complete analytical practice.

The contributions to *At the Intersection* portray a rhetorical studies that offers to American culture studies a peculiar correcting lens emphasizing how the genre of political and institutional discourse might be usefully and oppositionally critiqued and how such discourse is not an adjunct to cultural understanding but is rather part and parcel of it. Also, a recurrent theme seems to be how rhetoric's insistence upon situatedness reopens questions of reference and reality and does not reduce them completely to language and textuality. In short, rhetorical studies is portrayed in *At the Intersection* as a discipline in retreat from the poststructuralist abyss—from an emphasis on the endless play of meaning, and as making an emphatic restatement of one of the original assumptions of culture studies, namely, that discursive meaning is fixed in and through particular contexts. Finally, it seems clear from these essays that rhetorical studies offers a mode of analysis for thinking about how texts are produced (intent), what they are (textuality), and what they do (consumption/effects). A more properly "rhetorical cultural studies" recognizes that the perspectives of rhetoric define an approach that holds in suspension text and producer, text and reader, text and society. It thus provides one solution to problematics of analysis encountered in culture studies work, and represents a sort of "middle ground" in contemporary cultural studies ameliorating the unacceptable retreat into either straight textual analysis or direct observation of audiences alone.

On the other side, cultural studies, as it is depicted in the essays here, delivers to rhetorical studies a richer and more fully realized model of how discourse is always a product of wider social formations and reflects necessarily the materialization of the ideology that gave birth to it. It offers a more sophisticated sense of the text-history-audience-critic relationship and also the crucial relationship between texts and critical methodologies, namely, how history and ideology shape readings and critical work. It emphasizes, once more, the insight that ideology and power attempt always to fix meaning in a particular direction and for particular ends and interests. It seems clear from these essays that the ideal relationship between rhetorical studies and cultural studies is one of mutual critique and transformation. Rhetorical studies and cultural studies can make each other more thoroughly and deeply historical. Indeed, as Nelson (Chapter 8) puts it, their intersection is, in a sense, a call for a "historicized linguisticality" and a return to "analysis that focuses on historically delineated struggles over meaning and form."

But just as an "intersection" suggests a coming together of ways that seem apparently bound for different destinations, it also is the case that at the intersection lie potential changes in direction, new perspectives, decisions, crossroads, and passageways to new futures. This collection is best seen as an intervention. In taking up rhetorical studies and cultural studies and putting them together, *At the Intersection* represents a challenge to business as usual and to the received condition of cultural and social critique. Of course, the real work remains, that of teasing out more in detail what might be exposed at the points of crossing, to see how they might develop over time and where this development might lead. It seems crucial that in these days alliances must be explored. As Frentz and Rushing (Chapter 13) argue passionately, these days it is of more import to confront fragmentation than structure and to craft lines of connection between institutions and their critiques rather than just to critique. Today, they continue, neither rhetorical studies nor cultural studies alone is adequate to the task. Nelson (Chapter 8) maintains that exploiting and developing points of contact between cultural studies and rhetorical studies is a paramount need for the two disciplines.

Cultural studies and rhetorical studies read together suggest a model of how discourse works in the late twentieth century and how one might intervene in that working. As Aune argues here, tracing "social energy" provides insights into the nature of "power as performance." Control and power are manifested today in a staggering array of discursive forms. Only a multidimensional critical practice can do justice to them. Cultural studies and rhetorical studies, while perhaps pursuing different paths, are driven by the same goal: understanding how discourse places and sustains relationships between people in society and how we might bring about positive changes in those relationships with the end of, as Stuart Hall has put it, "making the world a more humane place." These essays, written at the intersection of cultural studies and rhetorical studies, suggest complementary, interactive, and politically useful liaisons between rhetorical studies and cultural studies, and they exemplify the practice and the ends that Hall envisions.

NOTES

1. The forms and implications of this "globalization of rhetoric" are captured most cogently in Gaonkar's "The Idea of Rhetoric in the Rhetoric of Science"; this basic idea has been enunciated in many different forms, and its form here owes mainly to Stanley Fish, "Rhetoric."
2. The importance of cultural studies is further emphasized in O'Connor, "The Problem of American Cultural Studies," and Grossberg, "The Circulation of Cultural Studies."
3. This last phrase is borrowed from Richard Johnson, "What Is Cultural Studies Anyway?"
4. But John Sloop wisely cautions that defining and using the term *culture* within the literature of rhetorical studies are both complicated matters. For Sloop, culture has been variously defined in contrary ways, thus exhibiting a general lack of terminological rigor. Deciding upon a working definition of culture, Sloop seems to conclude, commits the critic to certain underlying assumptions and dictates the outcomes of the analysis in predictable ways.
5. Nelson, Treichler, and Grossberg, "Introduction," 14.

PART ONE

READING THE POPULAR AND THE POLITICAL
Converging Trajectories of Textuality, Method, Context

One of the commonalities of rhetorical studies and cultural studies is a commitment to anchoring critique in close case studies. This first section offers studies of popular or political artifacts that are also demonstrations of textuality, method, and context at the intersection of rhetorical and cultural studies. These essays engage difficult yet vital questions such as: Does the interest in how power is mediated via discourse provide a fruitful common ground for investigating the relationship between cultural and rhetorical studies? In what ways might the issues that drive cultural studies provoke renewed interest by rhetoricians in questions concerning the relationship of texts and context? of texts and readers? of texts and critics? How might rhetorical studies best contribute to our understanding of popular culture? What potentially useful approaches to the study of popular culture does rhetoric offer? Finally, taken as a whole, these essays offer models of what studies of communication acts in a cultural context might "look" like.

In their analysis of the NASA Astronauts Memorial, Carole Blair and Neil Michel (Chapter 1) illustrate how rhetoric and cultural studies might interact in critical practice. They discuss the thematics of rhetoric that have both enabled (through context, genre, the public) and disabled (through views of theory, audience, politics) this approach as well as how a linkage of rhetoric and cultural studies, albeit sometimes a strained one, has offered fruitful critical alternatives. Blair and Michel's essay repays close study. Its argument spirals outward, moving from a fairly standard (though perceptive) rhetorical reading of the aesthetics and meaning of the Memorial that invokes "textuality" and generic antecedents; and then, when faced with the unanticipated reactions of visitors to the memorial, the analysis "starts over," enhancing, deepening, and broadening the rhetorical reading by positioning the memorial intertextually with other central Florida "dreamscapes" and theme parks. Their essay demonstrates how one might accomplish a cultural analysis informed and influenced by an awareness of the politics of critical practice. Moreover, their essay may also be read on another level, as a monograph about the critical process itself.

In his essay (Chapter 2), James Arnt Aune reads together three sets of documents not usually conjoined: Newt Gingrich's speeches and interviews on the so-called Third Wave (or Internet "revolution"), the work of futurists Alvin and Heidi Toffler and George Gilder, and the cyberpunk fiction of William Gibson, Bruce Sterling, and Pat Cadigan. Taking as his central focus the rhetorical dimensions of the concept of "information" across these documents, Aune warns that these new technologies liberate the self, but not necessarily the community, and as a result they are the site of potential reorganization of class distinctions and power relations. Aune is most interested in the political/ideological dimensions of the "selling" of cyberculture as part of an ongoing capitalist strategy for deindustrializing the U.S. economy. Interestingly, Aune arrives at his conclusion via the crossing of traditional genres of discourse (traditional political policy statements, futuristic cyber-Republicanism, cyberpunk fiction, "vampire" stories) in a vivid and engaging demonstration of the practice of a cultural rhetorical analysis that is clearly aware of the inevitably porous divides between the political and the nonpolitical.

Steven Mailloux's "Reading the Culture Wars" (Chapter 3) is a careful case study that "illustrates one way rhetorical studies and cultural studies intersect." In presenting what he calls a "reception narrative" of how academic issues "travel" across discourses to debates over popular culture, he seeks first of all to revitalize the old dispute between philosophy and rhetoric in current cultural debates. Mailloux proposes a "cultural rhetoric study" that might reveal something about the wider fabric of culture in tracking the "rhetorical density of cultural conversation." He asserts that "technical, academic discussions have multiple and complex interconnections to debates in the mass media." Mailloux warns that cultural rhetorical studies must be sensitive to the way in which the "rhetorical density of cultural conversation" travels if they are to avoid the pitfalls on either side of the rhetorical studies/cultural studies issue. But Mailloux's essay is interesting on another level. It is both an account of the intervention of critique in academic cultural praxis and is itself an experiment in making this sort of intervention. So, in a way, the essay's personal tone makes it an essay on modes of reporting cultural rhetoric, and represents a paradigm of this perspective.

Barry Brummett and Detine L. Bowers (Chapter 4) take up the often vexing relationship between subjectivity and textuality. They argue that the familiar concept of the "subject position" has developed along parallel paths in rhetorical studies and cultural studies/film studies, even if under different rubrics (comparing the usages of Louis Althusser and Stuart Hall). Thus, Brummett and Bowers argue that the idea of subject position, or the stance offered to a reader by a text, already inscribes an intersection of cultural and rhetorical studies and is therefore a fruitful concept for scholarship linking the two fields. To develop this linkage and to use it critically and oppositionally, their essay proposes the novel analogous concept of the "object" position and argues that the subject positions offered to African Americans by many texts in American culture might better be termed "object positions." Going beyond the existing literature, Brummett and Bowers provide a more detailed theoretical structure for explaining different kinds of subject and object positions offered by a text, and point out that texts are sites of struggle over the positions offered rather than univocally suggesting just one stance. Finally, their theoretical argument is illustrated with analysis of the film *The Air Up There*. Brummett and Bowers provide a reading of the film that goes against a problematic racist (dominant) reading and that in the process reveals the emancipatory subversive potential within hegemonic discourse.

In their essay "American Cultural Criticism in the Pragmatic Attitude" (Chapter 5), Elizabeth Walker Mechling and Jay Mechling seek to revitalize a tradition of American cultural studies that has been under siege from various quarters for, among other things, its status relative to the discipline. Suggesting that both cultural studies and rhetorical studies arrive with traditions incompatible with the American experience, Mechling and Mechling argue for a new perspective on culture that is "founded neither in Marx nor Aristotle but in American pragmatism." They seek what they call the "lost tradition" of William James, John Dewey, G. H. Mead, and Kenneth Burke—to make clear an oppositional and critical alternative that they argue is necessarily more identifiable with American culture. This alternative, what they call a "pragmatic criticism," is a sort of middle ground, a theoretical tradition that draws on pragmatic and neopragmatic thought in order to ask about the connections between everyday commonsensical "local knowledge" and the knowledge embedded in the narratives of mass-mediated commodity culture. While this connection has been noted before, Mechling and Mechling both describe its assumptions and demonstrate how the approach might work. Taking up the recent film *Braveheart*, they demonstrate how a pragmatic criticism might in one instance confront power and dominance and render more pressing and urgent the gender conflicts inherent in what they call a "contemporary crisis of masculinity."

Celeste Michelle Condit (Chapter 6) begins her study of the character of "history" in rhetoric and cultural studies with the observation that, while neither body of scholarship is homogeneous, in general rhetoricians and cultural studies scholars "conceptualize history" quite differently as they situate human events in time. She argues for the need to combine the insights of cultural studies and rhetoric to produce a way of viewing human political action that is probabilistic and sensitive to the particularities of culture but that also incorporates macrohistorical concerns such as race, class, and gender in explicit ways. The results will be, Condit suggests, sensitivity to how historicity results in different readings, and thus she urges that more attention be given to context, which results in more and better readings of venerable texts. To illustrate the need for such a combination, her essay examines the problematic response rhetoric and cultural studies alone give to the recent explorations of the relationship between race and the genetic code. As an antidote, Condit offers an exploratory probe—what she calls "a progressive materialism"—based on an alliance of the historicity of rhetoric and the idealist premises of cultural studies.

The work of psychoanalyst Jacques Lacan, though exceedingly influential in Screen theory and in feminist theory, has not affected either rhetoric or cultural studies with the same force. In such circles, Lacan is typically understood as too much concerned with the private and the interior and too little interested in the public, the political, and the ideological. In his revisionist rhetorical reading of Lacan, Henry Krips (Chapter 7) argues that Lacan's concept "the gaze" may indeed be ideological. Krips accomplishes his recuperation of Lacan by analyzing a painting that appears to have preoccupied Lacan, Holbein's masterwork *The Ambassadors*. Krips's rhetorical reading of Lacan draws out the semiotic dimensions as well as the historical context of production of the work and, in investigating the "politics of the image," offers an alternative account of the gaze. Thus, Krips comes at the relationship between rhetorical studies and cultural studies by way of their shared attention to the image and their joint interest in questions of representation and signification. He concludes that such critique may serve the "interests of both cultural studies and rhetorical studies . . . without falling into the oversimplifying assumptions made by the Screen theory approach."

ONE

COMMEMORATING IN THE THEME PARK ZONE
Reading the Astronauts Memorial

Carole Blair
Neil Michel

I'm so glad to be leaving! What a week!

Me too. And anxious to see this site. From what I've read about it, this memorial seems pretty strange. Could you help me stow this bag? Thanks.

There. Yeah, I'm not sure what to think about a memorial with moving parts. But who knows? Maybe we'll like it.

Maybe. The mechanical thing is truly weird, but the idea of all that blank space to fill up the names of the future dead in the space program is what seems bothersome to me. I wonder if there's a movie on this flight.

Hey, speaking of movies, did you notice in that photo of the memorial that it looks kind of like the screen at a drive-in movie?

Ugh! Well, at least, we'll have plenty to talk about with this site. Oh, look, headsets on the way.

It's kind of interesting that this memorial wasn't put up in DC. After all the media saturation with the Challenger, it seems especially strange. Does anyone actually go to this place, aside from Star Trek or space program groupies? Washington seems like it would be a better place for it.

Well, at least there's probably an audience in Florida—for whatever reason—that's interested in space travel. Maybe it's a better place than DC for that reason. There are probably fewer distractions in Florida than there would be in DC. Besides—oh, the movie's starting . . .

Our essay relies on both rhetorical studies and cultural studies in a critical encounter with a significant cultural text—the Astronauts Memorial. We hope that our encounter might offer an example of rhetoric and cultural studies' capacity to converse as well as a demonstration of some of their different tendencies. This essay is our second attempt at the Astronauts Memorial. It has not proven an easy critical mark; our difficulties with it have led us consistently to points of contact between rhetorical and cultural studies, so we also intersperse here a narrative reconstruction of our attempts to grapple with those problems. Although rhetorical and cultural studies have much to offer each other, our purpose is to suggest ways in which some of cultural studies' best tendencies may serve as correctives to rhetorical principles. That is a prejudice of where we began: with an attempt to study contemporary U.S. commemorative sites, among them the Astronauts Memorial, as rhetorical.[1]

Our study of the Memorial began with two almost universally accepted premises of rhetorical study: (1) that rhetorical events are symbolic and (2) that they are more or less appropriate to their contexts. It is not so much that we *chose* these premises as our working assumptions; for rhetorical critics, these premises are as natural as breathing. Most contemporary rhetoricians take discourses to be definitively symbolic—containers of meanings that attract or secure the adherence of an audience.[2] That is, a text constructs or references a symbolic "world" that is more or less appealing to an audience. Rhetoric's capacity to exert influence or to have consequences is at least tacitly assumed among rhetoricians to be a result of its meaning; meanings are treated not only as the by-product of symbols but also as the connective tissue between discourse and audience.

Of course, it would be naive to presume that rhetoric is deployed in a vacuum; while rhetoricians treat meanings as the principal determinant of rhetoric's effects, they rarely study symbols and their meanings in isolation. Rhetoricians tend to contextualize rhetorical practice in terms of sociopolitical situations and/or generic antecedents or models. Both of these contextualizations offer the rhetorician grounds to judge the appropriateness of a text. "Rhetorical situation" is a broad notion, encompassing both the immediate setting of a discourse and the larger sociocultural milieu in which it is produced. The capacity of the discourse to fulfill the demands of a specific occasion as well as to accommodate the constraints of its context are considered vital considerations in its outcome.[3] Genre, too, as Jamieson has argued is "capable of imposing powerful constraints" ("Antecedent Genre" 414). Genres function as norms of memory; they specify what may be considered legitimate or appropriate discourse, offering precedent discourses as models against which to assess new discourses.[4] But a precedent discourse or genre also functions as a resource of understanding; it serves as an interpretive analogue, or set of instructions in cultural legibility. As

Carr et al. suggest, "In order for a space to be legible, particularly in the case of public areas, it must have recognizable cues that are understood by its potential users, cues that communicate what kind of place it is ... " (188). The recognizability of those cues is predicated on one's experience or familiarity with a genre or analogue.

These rhetorical principles at first seemed well suited to our critical needs. It is undeniable that the Astronauts Memorial is more than a little unusual, and so we were convinced that appropriateness would have to be raised as an issue. The Memorial also is rich in symbolism, and interestingly, responsive to its setting. On the grounds of our rhetorical reading of the Astronauts Memorial—as symbolic, and as situated within contextual and generic constraints—we became convinced that it held strong rhetorical potential.

THE SPACE MIRROR: ITS RHETORICAL POSSIBILITIES

The Astronauts Memorial (Figure 1.1) is located on the grounds of the Kennedy Space Center Visitor Center (KSCVC), on Merritt Island, between the Florida mainland and Cape Canaveral.[5] KSCVC consistently ranks

FIGURE 1.1. Astronauts Memorial, Kennedy Space Center Visitor Center. Photo courtesy of Delaware North Parks Services.

among the five most visited tourist sites in Florida, attracting approximately three million visitors each year (NASA Public Affairs, 182). The Astronauts Memorial was designated by congressional resolution shortly before its May 1991 dedication as the official national memorial honoring U.S. astronauts and test pilots who have died in the line of duty.[6] Funds for building and maintaining the Memorial were raised principally by Florida residents' voluntary fees for their choice of special *Challenger* automobile license plates. This fund raising effort secured funds sufficient not only for the Astronauts Memorial Foundation (AMF) to build and maintain a major memorial, but also for the construction and operation of a Center for Space Education, also located on the Memorial grounds.

The Space Mirror, the Memorial's focal commemorative structure, was designed by Holt Hinshaw Pfau Jones (now Holt Hinshaw, Architects) and was selected as the design of choice in a 1987 juried competition that attracted over 700 entries. It is located opposite the Center for Space Education on a six-acre landscaped site on the north side of KSCVC. The Space Mirror sits atop a raised landing modeled on a NASA launch complex platform[7] and accessible by means of a wide, ascending ramp (Figure 1.2). Standing on a turntable there is a polished black granite wall, 42.5 feet high and 50 feet wide. The names of astronauts and pilots killed in the line of NASA duty are cut through the granite surface and filled with clear acrylic.[8] The names are arranged by mission—the *Challenger* and *Apollo I* crews (Figure 1.3) are each listed together, for example—and these mission rosters are scattered over various panels of the granite face. Attached to the back of the wall are mirrors that direct sunlight back through the carved names. The mirrors are set on an immense apparatus, computer controlled to track the sun. The entire upper portion of the Memorial slowly and almost imperceptibly rotates and shifts its vertical tilt so that the sun will constantly strike the mirrors at the correct angle to light the names from the back. The mirror and light apparatuses, the huge slewing ring (which controls horizontal rotation), and the screwjack assembly (which allows for vertical movement) are all white and encircled by a white wall (Figure 1.4).[9] The fenced exit ramp is cantilevered out over the waters of the lagoon, and it turns back to permit visitors a clear view of the technical apparatus that makes the Memorial "work." Also visible through a door window at the base of the Memorial is the computer that controls the motion tracking.

Benches are located on the viewing platform so that visitors may sit and contemplate the Memorial's face at any time of the day. Opposite the Space Mirror on the landing is a dedication wall that bears this inscription: "Whenever mankind has sought to conquer new frontiers there have been those who have given their lives for the cause. This Astronauts Memorial, dedicated May 9, 1991, is a tribute to the American men and women who

FIGURE 1.2. The Space Mirror entry walk. Photo by Neil Michel.

have made the ultimate sacrifice, believing the conquest of space is worth the risk of life." Mounted on one of the railings that line the circumference of the landing is a placard that explains the workings of the Space Mirror noting in its concluding words that the granite surface "reflects the sky, thereby suspending the brightly lit astronauts' names among the clouds."

Public Commemoration: Genre and Symbolic Potency

Commemorative monuments traditionally have done rhetorical work similar to a eulogy. They mark death, declare particular relationships between the commemorated and the living, offer a space in which a community may gather to acknowledge its loss and reaffirm its sense of collectivity, and

FIGURE 1.3. The Space Mirror and inscribed names. Photo by Neil Michel.

suggest or even advocate a future for the community that is somehow linked to the lives or events commemorated (Karlyn Kohrs Campbell and Jamieson, 20). Given memorials' public character and their relative degree of material permanence, they also must remind audiences of the purpose and necessity of maintaining in memory those they commemorate, for the individuals commemorated were not intimates, nor even typically acquaintances, of most visitors.

Although the Space Mirror is unusual, it performs the eulogistic operations that any commemorative monument must. It not only acknowledges the deaths of the astronauts; it announces them. Like many traditional memorials, this one makes use of height to call attention to itself and its message of memory. It also invites the visitor to reflect on her/his relationship to the astronauts. The ramped approach to the black wall of the Memorial is marked by a stark color change in the sidewalk—to black—suggesting that the visitors are joining the commemorated astronauts in a special, elevated place (Figure 1.2). One can glimpse one's own reflection on the granite plane upon which the names of the astronauts are inscribed. The link between the living visitor and the deceased astronauts is explicitly forged, but the character of that connection is left open to interpretation. Visitors are invited to see their own images along with the astronauts' names, connected by their placement together on the black face of

FIGURE 1.4. The Space Mirror's technical apparatus. Photo by Neil Michel.

the Memorial, but the astronauts' names are inscribed above eye level, suggesting perhaps that the living must grow or reach to attain their ennobled position. The visitor is distanced from the black panels that bear the astronauts' names by the white open-mesh fence placed in front of the rotating mirror.[10] It is their names that are projected skyward by the reflected light of the sun, while the visitor and her/his reflected image remain earthbound. Whether one reads these gestures as marking the separation of the astronauts from the living by death, as enacting a symbolic elevation of their stature, or both, s/he remains linked to them by the mirror plane and by her/his entry onto the platform of the Memorial. The raised landing demands that visitors walk upward to enter the place set aside for the deceased astronauts; enter it they can, but only with such an effort. The commemorated astronauts inhabit space—now permanently—as their names are lit not only here for the visitor to see but also in the reflective projection of their names. They have returned to space and remain there in perpetuity.

The Memorial also invites reflection on the future of space travel, although this invitation too is less than definitive in its valuative valence. The upward and outward tilt of the Mirror (Figure 1.5), as well as its expansive reflection of the Florida skies, draw attention to space, to unexplored territory beyond our mundane earthly concerns. The mirror encourages the visi-

FIGURE 1.5. The Space Mirror. Photo by Neil Michel.

tor to look up and to think beyond the customary, to imagine outward, beyond the present. The inscription on the dedication wall connects space travel to other "frontiers," linking it to romanticized images of the West, of the sea, etc., and intimating the risk involved in confronting such unexplored territories. And, while the dedication wall also suggests that these astronauts believed that space travel was worth the risk, there is no explicit request for the visitor's agreement. If s/he reads the inscription together with the symbolic ennobling of the astronauts, s/he may be tempted to share their view. Their deaths are connected here not to the specifics of their individual missions, but to the larger objective—still residing very much in the future—of the "conquest of space."[11] But whether or not visitors acknowledge the objective's value, the Memorial suggests the astronauts are worthy of memory; at the very least, their sacrifice was consistent with their own values. The Astronauts Memorial, thus, does seem to do the rhetorical work of a traditional public memorial, but it does much more than that.

Commemorative monuments of the past twenty years have taken on additional rhetorical responsibilities that seem to have become, or are fast becoming, generic norms.[12] As we have suggested, contemporary public commemoration, when it is most effective, "solicits reactions of proximity and participation from its audience. It invites us to *confront* our own values. . . . If we take as prototypes recent efforts at successful commemoration, memorials *engage* us by asking us to think. Rather than telling us *what* to think, they invite us *to* think, to pose questions, to interrogate our experiences and ourselves in relation to the memorial's discourse" (Blair and Michel). These recent memorials invite critical reflection; they rarely reflect naive or romanticized visions of nationalism or righteous causes. They typically refuse application of a unitary hermeneutic principle of reading; they are polysemic, often offering competing or contradictory messages. In other words, they summon their audiences to *work* at reading and evaluating them, and to continue to reflect on the questions they raise. Their particular stylistic characteristics vary, but most reflect, and also inflect for their own purposes, features of the architectural language introduced by the Vietnam Veterans Memorial (Blair, Jeppeson, and Pucci, 281–282), for example, polished black granite, or the explicit naming of the commemorated individuals.[13]

The relationship between the commemorated astronauts and visitors to the Astronauts Memorial is rendered more as a question than as a declarative. So too is the issue of the future of U.S. space travel, whether or not we share the astronauts' view that it is worth the risk of life. Rather than inflicting emphatic, declarative views on the visitor, the Space Mirror raises questions and invites her/him to reflect on them. Although one is free to read the representation of the astronauts as a heroic one, there is no necessity to do so. Nor does the Memorial demand that the visitor value space travel to the extent they did, or even at all. Like its Vietnam Veterans Memorial predecessor, the Astronauts Memorial offers a space to honor the dead, even if the visitor chooses not to render their deaths as heroic or valorize the cause for which they died. On those issues, the Astronauts Memorial (like its predecessor) strikes an antinomic pose. As Kipnis suggests, the architects accept "the truth of undecidability, oxymoron notwithstanding" (142). The Space Mirror does not posture to achieve a particular meaning, but embraces, even takes advantage of, the "fundamental impossibility of knowing the meaning of any work" (79).

That is nowhere more evident than in its most prominently coded theme—a questioning of the relationship(s) between humans and technology.[14] The black stone, inscription of names, and highly polished, mirroring surface all are borrowed syntax from the language of the Vietnam Veterans Memorial, recognizable as elements to mark death, relationships with visitors, and the human cost of a cause or conflict. But this language is juxtaposed in the Astronauts Memorial with a highly unusual techno- mechanistic argot that creates a tension, virtually demanding that we examine humanity's relationship to technology. As Fisher suggests, "the work of [Holt Hinshaw Pfau Jones] forces such a confrontation with technology's 'dangers.' . . . If there is a faith here, it is the existential belief that salvation comes from facing the abyss" (72).

The black face of the Mirror may be read as symbolizing either humanity or mortality, in contrast to the white mechanism on its backside that can be taken to represent technology. But the white mechanism is not merely a symbolic reference *to* technology; it *is* technology. The dark-light symbolism and the representation-reality gestures together pose an interesting and engaging set of puzzles. Read most simply, death appears as the dark side of technology. That is, technology is not rendered here as an unquestioned good; it is represented as exacting a cost—the loss of human life. Alternatively, if the dark face of the mirror is taken to represent humanity rather than simply death, one might understand humanity as the Other of technology. The visitor is asked not only to consider her/his relationships to technology but also to evaluate that relationship. Has humanity become the negative Other of technology? Certainly the color contrast might suggest that. So too might the representation-reality double. Humanity is represented or reflected *symbolically,* but the technology employed in the Memorial is neither a symbolic representation or reflection; it is an *actual* working mechanism on the obverse of the merely referential humanity. Are humans assigned, then, to the realm of the merely ephemeral, somehow less real than their machines?

Or, should technology be understood instead as a burden on or counterweight to human experience? The visual dimensions of the black surface considered in opposition to the massive, heavy looking mechanism on its back might lead to such an inference (Figure 1.5). So too might the movements of the Mirror. During most of the day, the front of the mirror faces upward, with the mechanism seeming to weigh it down or to function as a ballast. Only in late afternoon does the human face of the Mirror reach its zenith, at a point perpendicular to the platform, and in apparent balance with its mechanistic other side. Does this zenith suggest a goal perhaps, of balance and harmony between technology and humanity? And what of the fact that the fences and railings, clearly installed to keep visitors at a safe distance from the working apparatus or from a fall into the lagoon, are the same stark white as the technological mechanism of the Memorial? Should that symbolic continuity linking visitors' safety back to technology be interpreted as a counter to the coded dangers of technology?

In whatever of these or other ways the relationships of death, humanity, and technology may be read, it seems apparent that the Memorial provokes questions about the character and value of the human's relationship to machine. It offers no clear answers; rather, it seems to maintain a studied ambivalence about the issues it poses, inviting visitors to decide for themselves. In that respect, the Space Mirror functions in much the same way as other contemporary memorials. It incites contemplation and thoughtfulness rather than decreeing preferred attitudes. It allows for different, even contradictory, answers to the questions it raises, but it indeed does raise compelling issues, about relationships of the deceased astronauts to the living, the future of the space program, and the values and dangers of technology. At the same time, it offers what all memorial discourses must—an acknowledgment and place of dignified tribute to the deceased. To the extent that the Space Mirror exemplifies these characteristics, it can be judged both generically appropriate and culturally legible. Though it is a relatively difficult text, demanding careful attention, so are most contemporary commemorative monuments. In fact, it is arguable that the popular success of some of them, the Vietnam Veterans Memorial being the most notable example, is due in part to the fact that they are *not* symbolically facile.[15]

Contextual Considerations

Generic dictates are complicated by the particularities of commemorative contexts. In the case of the Astronauts Memorial, numerous contextual factors impinge. The idea of building a memorial to honor astronauts took shape almost immediately following the *Challenger* shuttle accident in 1986. That alone posed an important problem. As Simons points out, prior to the accident, "NASA was perhaps the last unsullied American institution embodying American ideals of clean living, hard work, technological know-how and engaged in the business of conquering new frontiers" (261–262). It would be the task of the memorial to "rekindle a faith in the power of machines, of pioneers, and of collective social effort" (Hogben, 79), and, we might add, of NASA, in the aftermath of the accident. The Astronauts Memorial Foundation (AMF)—the group that would raise funds and sponsor the design competition—defused that difficulty to some extent by insisting that its memorial should honor all who perished in service to NASA, not just the seven *Challenger* astronauts. That decision, however, created its own problems, among them the demand that the memorial's design allow for, but "not bring undue attention to[,] the possibility of future space-related tragedies" (Astronauts Memorial Foundation, "National Design," 12), a potentially grim, if not overtly gruesome, symbolic gesture.

The AMF also decided that their memorial should be located in Florida. KSCVC was chosen as the favored site, mainly because of its proximity to a tourist population sufficiently interested in space travel to visit the complex and to the employee population of Kennedy Space Center (KSC). While the decision made a certain amount of sense, it also created a profound challenge for designers. In the design competition program, the AMF registered the rather understated concern that "Spaceport USA [later renamed KSCVC] is not a conventional setting for a memorial. Still, the design of this memorial is expected to have the same level of dignity, repose and timelessness that might be expected of any truly national memorial" (11).[16] KSCVC is an important public relations instrument for NASA, an agency that has been subject since its inception to the vicissitudes of public policy, shifts of national budgeting priorities, and occasionally wavering public interest and support.[17] Although KSCVC is managed and operated by a subcontracted recreational services firm, its rhetoric is NASA's, and it is universally positive.[18] Such positive messages would have to extend to any memorial located on NASA property. In a subsection entitled "Avoiding Negative Symbolism," in the design competition program, the AMF insisted that, while the memorial would "always be a reminder of tragic events, it is more important to be a reminder of positive and uplifting aspects of the astronauts and the space program" (12). Of all the contextual difficulties, this may have been the most significant. Although we will discuss KSCVC more later, a brief descriptive detour is in order here.

KSCVC is part history/technology museum, part window on a working launch facility.[19] Its overt objective is educational, to teach visitors about space travel and the U.S. space program.[20] But KSCVC is also promotional; most prominently displayed at KSCVC are the twin values of technological prowess and environmental friendliness. Technology is presented both as idol and as sponsor of improvements in everyday life on earth. And there are constant explicit reminders that KSC is situated on the Merritt Island National Wildlife Preserve; shuttle launches and endangered species coexist harmoniously, or so the message goes. KSCVC clearly serves an advocacy function for NASA, but that function is camouflaged somewhat by its buoyant atmosphere and educational mission.[21]

Visitors enter KSCVC through Spaceport Central, which houses two theatres, displays of rocket models, launch paraphernalia, and a wildlife exhibit highlighting "the stunning wonders of nature at the Kennedy Space Center, a 140,000-acre wildlife preserve that protects many endangered species" (*Spaceport USA*). A visitor may seek taped information about the various NASA facilities in the U.S. or about U.S. astronauts at one of the sets of interactive computer screens. Other screens offer her/him the chance to choose any year in the history of the space program and be treated to a program of space-related highlights of that year. The tapes are narrated by prominent individuals, most by television and film stars. Each segment begins with a popular song from the selected year, along with a review of contemporary events, before proceeding to the NASA achievements of the year.

Outside and behind Spaceport Central are ticket windows where visitors purchase admission to an IMAX film or a KSC bus tour. The Galaxy Center houses two IMAX theatres and a bi-level art gallery on the theatres' perimeter. Space shuttles and other space vehicles are featured in frequently sentimentalized renditions in the gallery. The IMAX films, *The Dream is Alive* and *Destiny in Space,* foreground the themes of space shuttle travel and space exploration. *The Blue Planet* is not about space travel, but its cinematography depends on it; this film is about the beauty of earth, the raw power of nature, and humans' impact on the fragile ecosystem.

Both tours echo the theme of technology's compatibility with nature. Each begins with the interpreter discussing KSC's status as a national wildlife preserve and pointing out with apparent pride that KSC harbors more endangered species than any other preserve in the United States. The Red Tour bus stops near the Vehicle Assembly Building, where visitors see a *Saturn V* rocket. Some tour groups (although not ours) are "lucky" enough to catch a glimpse of one of NASA's 6,000,000-pound Crawler Transporters, which move shuttles to the launch facilities. The guide tells visitors that the Transporter was designated in 1977 as a National Historic Mechanical Engineering Landmark by the American Society of Mechanical Engineers. The bus stops again near Complex 39A and 39B, the two shuttle launch pads. Visitors get a good look, although from a considerable distance, at the gigantic complexes and the intricate technology. On the Blue Tour, the longest stop is at the Air Force Space Museum at Cape Canaveral Air Force Station. Complex 26, site of the first U.S. satellite launch—the American response to Sputnik in 1958—is part of the museum complex. There, visitors see the restored mission control equipment in the "Blockhouse," now a National Historic Landmark. Located nearby is Complex 5/6, the launch location of the first manned space flight by Alan B. Shepard. Numerous missile, engine, antenna, radar, and rocket models are displayed in the exhibit hall and on the grounds. Each tour ends with a brief panegyric on the technological advances that have been made possible by the space program.

Back at KSCVC, visitors may choose the Gallery of Manned Spaceflight, where they see a moon rock as well as full-sized models of the *Viking* Mars lander and of the Russian *Soyuz* space vehicle that docked with an Apollo craft in 1975. Other displays chronicle advances in space suits worn and foods consumed by astronauts during their travels. The many exhibits are detailed and highly varied, but all emphasize and describe the technological achievements represented in the displayed items. Outside the Gallery is the Rocket Garden (Figure 1.6). Displayed there are authentic rockets and other flight hardware, representing various stages in the history of the space program. All of the apparatuses are stunning, in part because of their immensity. And many are striking not because they appear to be so advanced (although the visitor certainly has heard enough by this time to know that they are), but because they look like makeshift contraptions (Figure 1.7).

FIGURE 1.6. The Rocket Garden, Kennedy Space Center Visitor Center. Photo by Neil Michel.

Indoors again, visitors may attend an exhibit featuring a virtual (filmic) tour guide who leads them through displays featuring practical applications of the space program. Among the advances the space program can boast are improved insulin therapy, advanced breathing systems for firefighters, advanced wastewater treatment, enhanced weather forecasting, new flame-resistant materials, anticorrosive paint, and laser heart surgery. One of the NASA brochures informs the visitor that "It is difficult to find a facet of everyday life into which spinoffs have not penetrated, even though sometimes their origins in aerospace research are not easily recognizable" (*Information Summaries*).

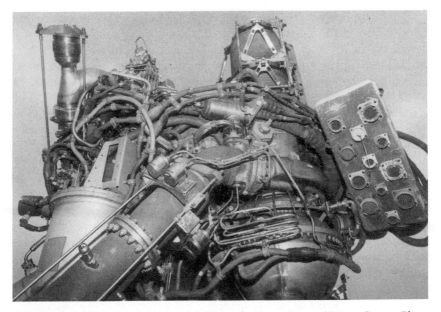

FIGURE 1.7. Flight hardware model, Kennedy Space Center Visitor Center. Photo by Neil Michel.

On one side of the Astronauts Memorial grounds is the Space Shuttle Plaza, where the visitor may walk through *Explorer*, a full-scale shuttle orbiter model, and later gaze at the imposing models of rocket boosters used to launch the shuttle. Inside a structure resembling a geodesic dome, visitors view exhibits that detail the preparations for a launch and the workings of the shuttle, and they may attend an hourly shuttle mission briefing (replaced by a lecture on the shuttle program when there is no mission to brief). On the opposite side of the Memorial grounds, near the Rocket Garden, is the AMF's Center for Space Education. Although most visitors apparently never venture there, it houses an educator's research facility as well as classrooms for the AMF-sponsored Educational Technology Institute, and the Exploration Station—a large area filled with entertaining and informative interactive activities.

Certainly, most visitors do not encounter *all* of these and other KSCVC offerings in a single day trip, but the park is compact enough for them to cover much of this ground in such a visit. Regardless, though, of how much of KSCVC they witness, it is certain that they have been baptized (as we have) in the warm, friendly (and entertaining) waters of NASA's public relations—messages about the wonders of technology and its compatibility with the natural environment are inescapable. Most visitors appear to find KSCVC interesting and cheerfully enjoyable. Indeed, the AMF was correct in pointing out that this is not an ordinary setting for a memorial.

Still, the Space Mirror seems to "fit" within its setting. Its most unusual feature—the exposed, pristine white apparatus—makes possible a continuity between the Memorial and other experiences at KSCVC. The Space Mirror itself is technology, another instance of technological achievement to be gazed upon and admired, like so many others at KSC. This continuity works against the possibility that a memorial on this site would introduce a somberness that might invalidate the KSCVC mood and message. The techno-mechanistic character of the Memorial connects the deaths to the technological marvels represented at KSC. It invites visitors to focus on death, but it *also* asks them to contemplate another fascinating technological achievement—the Memorial itself. In other words, it sustains the kinds of responses invited in other KSCVC locations, although it complicates them by naming those who have died in the service of NASA's accomplishments. The mood recommended by the Memorial certainly is more sober than in other KSCVC venues, but it is not grim. The Memorial creates a sense almost of inevitability; it is a reminder that NASA's accomplishments over the years involved such intense risk that such sacrifices were a virtual certainty. That sense of inevitability does not minimize the loss; it invests the loss with meaning. If one does not read the deaths as heroic sacrifices, s/he might view them as a seemingly inescapable price of the long-term technologically enabled mission of space exploration.

The blank space on the face (Figure 1.8), which accommodates the possibility of future losses, contributes to this message. While it surely might lead visitors to ponder the probability of future space program-related deaths, they might also contemplate how small the number of casualties has been in the space program to date. After touring KSCVC and seeing the hardware that has carried astronauts into space, the number of deaths seems impressively small. It seems quite remarkable that the vast space on the face of the Space Mirror is not filled with names. Instead, there are "only" 16, scattered over the face of the Mirror and reinforcing a message that NASA certainly would like to convey—that, while deaths in the U.S. space program may be virtually inevitable, they are at least *unusual*. The blank space also buttresses the impact of the Memorial's message about humans' ongoing tensive relationship to technology. As Adler suggests, part of the Memorial's "awesome power comes from the realization that it's unfinished" (69).

Finally, the Space Mirror cooperates with nature, another of NASA's publicly expressed values. As the visitor hears incessantly, much of KSC is a wildlife preserve. The Mirror conveys a respect for space in the reflection of its overwhelming immensity. The skies of Florida are reflected in the

FIGURE 1.8. The Space Mirror and its uninscribed space. Photo by Neil Michel.

Mirror and appear virtually continuous with it. The site is one of natural (and contrived) beauty. Alligators and sea turtles patrol the lagoon. Birds fly overhead and alight on the grounds and on the water. Most importantly, the technology of the Space Mirror is literally *dependent* on nature, for it tracks the course of the earth in its own movement.

The Space Mirror places at issue the emphasis on technology promulgated at KSCVC, but it also reproduces and reinforces the KSCVC messages in treating itself as a technological achievement that harmonizes with nature. It does so without sacrificing its commemorative function and without insulting the intelligence of visitors by insisting on an easily consumable, facile message in praise of heroic astronauts, NASA, and the U.S.

space program. In that way and others, it resembles and gains legibility from the Vietnam Veterans Memorial. Although the names are sparse here by comparison, and the profile of the granite wall quite different, it would be difficult to mistake the purpose or intended tone of this solemn symbolism. Like its predecessor, the Space Mirror does not dictate a singular or correct reading; it invites us to grapple with the issues it raises. The Astronauts Memorial is extraordinary, but neither its syntax nor its messages are so unusual as to be unintelligible. The verticality and dark-light images are pervasive in this culture,[22] and, as Rushing and Frentz argue, the theme of "humanity versus the machine" colors many popular culture products as well as social and philosophical critique. Our rhetorical reading suggests that the Astronauts Memorial draws from its generic predecessors in offering a culturally legible and appropriate commemoration, that it is symbolically rich and interesting, and that it bids for the kind of experience that appears to make contemporary commemoration "work" for its audiences.[23]

THE RHETORICAL PROBLEM
OR THE PROBLEM WITH RHETORIC?

These conclusions, as it turned out, simply could not be the end of the story. At some point during the first several days we spent at the Astronauts Memorial attending to its symbolism, its setting, and so forth, we also began to notice something else—other visitors. What was most apparent—and alarming—about them was that they did not appear to share our reaction to the Space Mirror. In three visits totaling eighteen days at KSCVC, we watched and listened to literally thousands of visitors, and the character and consistency of their reaction (or, more precisely, their lack of reaction) took us by surprise. We found ourselves on rather unfamiliar ground, witnessing firsthand what many rhetorical critics never attend to—a real audience.[24] We watched, we listened, and we took notes on visitors' activities and conversations day after day at the Memorial site—perhaps not typical activities of rhetorical critics, but very interesting ones.

Although we observed and overheard a number of different reactions, two dominant patterns emerged.[25] One was for visitors to be so distracted by other features of the scene that they ignored the Memorial altogether. The other was for visitors to wonder aloud to one another what this odd structure was, to figure it out (usually by recognizing one or more of the names—typically Christa McAuliffe, but sometimes one of the *Apollo I* astronauts), and then to move on without pausing for more than a photograph and/or a quick reading of the dedication wall or placard that explains the workings of the Space Mirror; many did not pause even that long. Some visitors were drawn to the mechanism of the Memorial, but even they stopped only very briefly for a look at it. The few visitors who sat down on the benches on the landing were more interested in discussing a film they had just seen, what time their tour bus was scheduled to leave, the weather, or their fatigue than to attending to the Memorial immediately in front of them. Many visitors remained on the viewing platform for less than two minutes.

Our interest grew as we concentrated even more on the visitors. Their reactions did not appear to be related to, or to vary much according to, differences of age, race, nationality, or gender categories—another surprise. In fact, the only clearly identifiable group that appeared to have a noticeably different reaction were KSC employees, recognizable because of uniforms or security badges. They seemed to respond in more attentive, engaged, and thoughtful ways with the Space Mirror. They spent more time there than most visitors, sometimes sat in quiet contemplation of the Memorial, and rarely spoke to others in their groups or to other visitors. The focus of their gaze was the Space Mirror. On their way to or from the Mirror, some of them would stroll slowly around the lagoon that the Memorial overlooks. It cannot come as a surprise that KSC personnel would be *more* attentive to the Memorial than other visitors are. What did surprise us, though, was the almost complete lack of interest and attention displayed by other visitors. And we were puzzled by the fact that the reactions were all so similar among a relatively diverse profile of people.[26]

After a time, we began to recognize a peculiar similarity among the visitors—their attire. Neither of us had ever seen so many Donald Duck shirts, Mickey Mouse ears, or Goofy hats in one place—except perhaps on the racks at Disneyland. George Meguiar, then Director of Marketing, confirmed what had become our suspicion—that the overwhelming majority of visitors to KSCVC travel there from Walt Disney World, approximately 40 miles away (Interview).[27] Although an at least mildly interesting piece of minutia, and the only apparent similarity among visitors, we were not immediately convinced that it could be related to our newfound problem—accounting for the fact that we and other critics responded so positively to the Astronauts Memorial[28] while most visitors did not. After all, we reasoned, Walt Disney World is *just* a Disney park. It seems worth remarking here that we were not being disingenous. We are Californians and, as such, neither unfamiliar with nor even completely immune to "the Disney magic." Trips to Disneyland were, for us, not frequent—but not unusual either. Although neither of us had ever been to Walt Disney World, we both were aware that it is bigger than Disneyland, that it includes Epcot and "some other stuff" that Disneyland lacks. And we had even read sparsely about the Florida park. But we were complacently close to the position of those Fjellman calls the "benighted few who think of Disneyland and Walt Disney World as interchangeable" and who are, as he suggests, "quite wrong" (395). So, we continued to look elsewhere for our explanation of the Astronauts Memorial's apparent rhetorical failure with its visitors.

In our first critical essay about the Memorial, we attempted to account for the visitor reactions by assessing the features of its most immediate context—its landscaped grounds (Blair and Michel). And there *are* serious design problems with the site. For example, alligators that prowl the lagoon area are a very popular diversion from the Space Mirror, and the Space Mirror simply is too proximate to, and missing any material or visual boundary from, other KSCVC venues.[29] Some of the site design flaws (e.g., the alligators' presence) aided us in understanding the very most detached reactions—when visitors are lured away from the Memorial altogether. Other design problems seemed important but not likely, even in combination, to produce the degree of aloofness we witnessed on the part of visitors to the Memorial. We certainly were convinced that the Memorial grounds could be improved to enhance visitors' experiences, but we simply were not satisfied that we had yet located the real problem of reception.[30]

We found it very difficult to ignore our reservations, not only because we were curious but also because it seemed so utterly dishonest to pronounce on a public memorial's appropriateness and symbolic virtuosity when we were perfectly well aware that it did not hold similar allure for its public. Although we seemed to be moving ever further out of our league as rhetorical critics, we finally decided to follow the only apparent lead we had in solving the reception puzzle. So, we started over, beginning this time where most KSCVC visitors begin—about 45 minutes away, near Orlando—at Walt Disney World.

MOVING IN ON THE MEMORIAL: WALT DISNEY WORLD

As we had learned already, the large majority of visitors to KSCVC travel there from the Orlando theme park district that encompasses Sea World, Universal Studios, and a host of smaller attractions.[31] By far the most popular and frequented attractions in this district are the major Walt Disney World (WDW) parks—the Magic Kingdom, Epcot, and Disney-MGM Studios. Although the other theme parks in the area resemble the WDW parks in important ways, it is WDW that lures most tourists to the area, and it is at WDW that most visitors spend most of their time. So, we concentrate our attention on WDW here.

To say that WDW took us by surprise would be to understate our response. Even if we had remembered more of what we had read about it, we could not have been prepared for what we encountered. Fjellman's description fills the void of our first inarticulate, rather stunned, reactions: "Walt Disney World is to Disneyland as the *Grundrisse* is to Theses on Feuerbach—a behemoth of an entirely different scale. . . . It's Mickey Mouse on steroids" (394). Our reaction was not just that of Disneyland-habituated theme park goers; it was practical too. How could we ever see enough of this place to get a sense of how it might be related to KSCVC or to the Astronauts Memorial? It is not "just" three theme parks in one, it is more like nine or ten. At 46 square miles, Walt Disney World is the size of San Francisco.[32] In addition to its three major components—the Magic Kingdom, Epcot, and Disney-MGM Studios—it contains three water parks (Blizzard Beach, Typhoon Lagoon, and River Country), plus a zoological park (Discovery Island). But there is also Pleasure Island, an entertainment complex of nightclubs, shops, and restaurants; the Disney Village Marketplace, a boutique shopping area; the Disney Institute; Disney University; seventeen (at last count) Disney resort hotels, many with themed venues and attractions; a wedding chapel; a campground; plus a plethora of on-property recreational venues for golf, tennis, swimming, fishing, skating, horseback riding, and so on.[33]

We certainly did not see all of WDW, nor does anyone else (we presume) who goes there for four or five days. However, aside from our perpetual note-taking stops, we tried to see it the way most other visitors would—by cramming as much as possible into a few days. Although our visits were necessarily selective, we began to see relevant message patterns forming as we visited more and more of the varied venues.[34] The "report" that follows collapses our observations of WDW into four related tropes: efficient fun, the safe (perilous) adventure, the anaesthetizing sanctification of technology, and the happy ending.[35]

Efficient Fun

Visitors to WDW are likely to know in advance that the parks are literally overloaded with a wide variety of enjoyable activities and attractions. If not, they would quickly conclude upon arrival that variety and enjoyment are almost directly proportional to available time.[36] Most area guidebooks suggest multiple-day passes as the best values and emphasize that visitors should allow plenty of time to visit the park(s) of their choice, and most visitors act on that advice. *Birnbaum's* recommends *at least* a five-day visit to enjoy "the best of Walt Disney World at less than a breakneck pace" (16).[37] The reasons for the advice seem clear; the visitor is literally barraged with choices of things to see and do. The WDW venues are packed with stimuli of inducement, with invitations for an overabundance of options for the visitor's next move. Because leisure time simply is finite for most people, there is a strong inducement to be efficient. It is very typical to overhear visitors urging one another to walk faster or to not waste time lingering over lunch. Complaints about long lines and waiting are rampant. Visitors are drawn to and plan according to the "tip boards" inside the entrances to each of the parks that tell which attractions have the shortest lines (Figure 1.9). Travel guides and planning books reinforce the need for efficiency. *Birnbaum's* warns the visitor that "the key to a successful visit to Walt Disney World is advance planning" (7) and cautions that, even during a five-day visit to Walt Disney World, "it is still necessary not to waste time in order to cover all the high points" (16).[38] The discursive economy of WDW graphs the imposing supply of things to do against the limited amount of time to do them.

The Safe (Perilous) Adventure

From the beginning of the visitor's venture into Walt Disney World, s/he hears or sees the message of safety linked to adventure incessantly. The long, winding drive through and around the Disney parks and resorts is a first adventure of sorts; it is very clear that we have entered a distinct and

FIGURE 1.9. The "Tip Board" at the entrance to Disney-MGM Studios. Used by permission from Disney Enterprises, Inc. Photo by Neil Michel.

"exotic" world.[39] The road signs are unusually colorful, and some have mouse ears, but they are numerous and helpful, guiding even first-time visitors safely and effortlessly to their destinations, whether one of the many resorts or one of the parks. Once inside a resort or hotel—many of which are themselves constituted by adventure themes (Disney's Polynesian Resort, Fort Wilderness Resort and Campground, Disney's Contemporary Resort)[40]—there are "cast members" that see to one's every need; everything reads as exceptionally safe and secure, even in the overcoded adventure-theme villages and restaurants.

Inside the theme parks, the safe adventure theme frequently gives way to the safe (perilous) adventure trope. Safety certainly is still a major part of the formula. Even though entering a seemingly alien world, the visitor is provided an easily readable map, from which s/he can find her way to a bank, a telephone, a maildrop, numerous and easily accessible restaurants and snack shops, lost and found locations, pet care centers, and lost children stops. Photo Spot signs thoughtfully point the visitor to picturesque backdrops for photos. There's always a helpful "cast member" nearby to answer a question or point to an attraction. Everything that one can imagine is provided; nothing could be safer.

Still, entry into one of these parks is marked clearly as "adventure," and the attractions range from the safe but fanciful (e.g., the Dumbo ride in the Magic Kingdom, the American Adventure in World Showcase at Epcot, or the Beauty and the Beast stage production at Disney-MGM Studios), to the extremely popular safe (perilous) adventures.[41] At Future World in Epcot, for example, visitors find themselves near disaster as they become stranded (as miniatures) inside a human body, in Body Wars. Still to come is Disney-MGM Studios' Twilight Zone Tower of Terror, a "thrill ride that's hurled you deep into a whole new dimension of terror," primarily as a result of its thirteen-story elevator drop (The Walt Disney Company, *Disney-MGM Studios Theme Park,* 1996). Disney-MGM Studios' Catastrophe Canyon, billed as "THE WORST THREE MINUTES OF YOUR LIFE" (The Walt Disney Company, *Disney-MGM Studios Theme Park,* 1994), subjects visitors to an earthquake, a tanker truck collision, and a flash flood. The ExtraTERRORestrial Alien Encounter in the Magic Kingdom features a "sinister experiment [that] brings a horrifying creature within a claw's reach of you!" Visitors may "ride on a runaway mine train" on Big Thunder Mountain Railroad, or travel through a haunted forest where they "dodge the Wicked Witch" in Snow White's Adventures (The Walt Disney Company, *Magic Kingdom*). In case the "perils" of these attractions are not sufficiently evident, WDW codes them as such, posting prominent warning signs at many of the attractions (Figure 1.10). Frank Wells, former CEO of The Walt Disney Company, described clearly what we mean by the safe (perilous) adventure trope: " 'Soft adventure' vaca-

FIGURE 1.10. Warning sign depicting the Witch in Snow White's Adventures, in the Magic Kingdom. Disney characters © Disney Enterprises, Inc. Used by permission from Disney Enterprises, Inc. Photo by Neil Michel.

tions are 'safe' versions of challenging or dangerous human undertakings. . . . Such contrived, engineered experiences, where safety is absolutely assured, indulge 'the yen for danger, adventure, new knowledge and out-of-the-ordinary experience' " (quoted in Adams, 180).[42]

The Anesthetizing Sanctification of Technology

The safety logarithm in the safe peril trope is not only underwritten by visitors' understanding that they are at WDW for fun and that all their needs will be safely fulfilled, but also reinforced by the third trope—the anaesthetizing sanctification of technology. Not only are the "perils" of these adventures made possible by technology, but so too is the relative safety of these attractions. Certainly the technology of the rides is typically well concealed, but there are two principal means by which the visitor is reminded of the technological surety, just in case s/he forgets that it has been the provident force of her/his safe thrills. First, a ride will be closed temporarily for maintenance on occasion, even while the park is open. Though a sporadic occurrence, it is a reminder of the conditions that enable both adventure and safety. Second, technology is coded explicitly as the "backstage" force in a number of attractions. "Backstage" moves to stage in Disney-MGM Studios' invitation to the visitor to see the behind-the-scenes dangers of Catastrophe Canyon, provided by a "safe, computerized special effect."[43] As Fjellman suggests, most of Disney-MGM Studios is about revealing the cinematic secrets "carefully kept from us at the Magic Kingdom and much of EPCOT Center" (283–284).

Even if the visitor never sees the "backstage" shows or witnesses a temporary closedown, however, the parks provide ample thematic witness to the virtues and powers of technology. Tomorrowland in the Magic Kingdom is almost exclusively encoded as a tribute to technology. It calls attention to its own technologically enabled coding, in "Circle-Vision 360" and *Audio-Animatronics®*, and it thematizes aviation and interplanetary travel. One of its older but newly updated attractions is Walt Disney's Carousel of Progress, in which one may "follow an *Audio-Animatronics* family through 100 years of electronic wizardry"[44] Many visitors to the Magic Kingdom end their days by viewing SpectroMagic, a parade that *Birnbaum's* describes as "a marvel of the computer age. Approximately 30 minicomputers are used and the audio is stored digitally on state-of-the-art microchips." SpectroMagic, we are told, "borrows from the prismatic holographic industry, military lighting developments, electro-luminescent and fiber-optic technologies, plus light-spreading thermoplastics, clouds of underlit liquid nitrogen, smoke, and some old-fashioned twinkling lights" (120).

Future World, composing approximately half of Epcot, provides an even more worshipful tribute to technology. Walt Disney's vision for the Experimental Prototype Community of Tomorrow was precisely to showcase new ideas and technologies "emerging from the creative centers of American industry" (quoted in Birnbaum, 123).[45] Interestingly, the possibilities for a new pavilion devoted to space travel have been discussed.[46] For now, visitors may ride through the history of communication technology in Spaceship Earth (presented by AT&T) or explore possibilities for the future in space, under the sea, and in the desert in Horizons. Or they may "[v]isit a house of the future, step into cyberspace, learn about and test the latest developments in computers, explore breakthroughs in virtual reality and communications for technology, [and] play the hottest new video games!" in Innoventions (The Walt Disney Company, *Epcot*), the latest "hands-on" experience in WDW's consecration of technology.[47]

The visitor literally may be overcome by the pervasiveness of the technological here; it has an otherworldly, almost narcotizing, effect. Even in one's hotel room, it is difficult to escape. A plethora of technological gadgetry and conveniences render the visitor's stay at a resort hotel safe and hypnotically luxurious, if sterile. The visitor is immersed in, and even becomes habituated to, a technologically constructed and controlled environment of whimsy and luxury. It is difficult to shake off the soporific effect after a few days at WDW. We experienced that effect, as have other commentators,[48] who have labeled it "sensory blanketing" (Alexander Wilson, 182), "stupefaction" (Adams, 147), "cognitive overload" (Fjellman, 23), "euphoric disorientation" (Fjellman, 254), and "peculiar enchantment" (Baudrillard, 171). The "immersion process" within the rhetorical world of Disney pacifies, "drain[s the visitor] of interpretive autonomy," and "blunt[s] visitors' powers of discrimination" (Baudrillard, 171; Fjellman, 13, 265). Visitors to Disneyland, interviewed by Real, sometimes compared their visit to a drug trip. And WDW provides a heavily intensified and much more sustained experience, because of its scope and the lengthier exposure most visitors have to its messages; there, technologically sustained control is the sacralized end and means of the experience. It may be difficult to emerge from the WDW-induced trance, but there is very little motivation to do so, given the final trope.

The Happy Ending

The technologically induced hypnosis is reinforced in the final trope—the happy ending. As the visitor witnesses over and over, nothing ever goes awry, and s/he increasingly relaxes and lets her/his guard down. It is difficult to get lost even in the gigantic parking lots at the parks, for the visitor is told at least twice in what section her/his car is located before disembarking the parking lot shuttle, and the sections are memorable anyway, because they're named after favorite Disney characters or theme park venues. No matter how thrilling or "perilous" the adventure of a park ride, one always emerges unscathed. In the simpler, fanciful attractions, the narratives always have fairy-tale endings. The themes of several new attractions (e.g., Jim Henson's Muppet™ Vision 3D, and the ExtraTERRORestrial Alien Encounter) have to do with technology run amok; however, the consequences of wayward or failed technology are always minimized or transmuted into comic effect—for a happy ending. Trophies to mark the success of the visitor's adventure are available from the pervasive gift shops, snack stops, and vendors.[49] All Disney adventures reach clear closure both narratively and spatially; the experiences are coded with clear symbolic endings and are segregated either by distance or physical enclosure from others. Nothing ever gets confused, goes wrong, or ends unhappily, from the visitor's experience of the thrill rides to her/his return in the evening to a luxurious dinner and the perfectly (technologically) controlled private space of her/his hotel room. One can have perfectly safe (perilous) thrills all day (or all week), but, thanks to technology, there is no real danger or threat; all the narrative conclusions are at least cheerful, sometimes ecstatic, celebratory, or carnivalesque.

These four WDW tropes work together as a rhetorical brief to situate the visitor's experience. The efficient fun trope does its work by reinforcing the need for sustained exposure to the other three tropes. Should visitors comply, their experiences for the next few days will be saturated with the intertwined messages of those three tropes, which work together to create and sustain a very specific message and subject position for the visitor. The sanctification of technology permeates; technology is explicitly coded as the singular means of securing human progress and comfort. But technology also fuels the other two tropes. The possibilities for a WDW adventure—whether fanciful or full of peril—are vouchsafed by technology. The visitor's experience is rendered as absolutely dependent upon technology; without it, there is no adventure. Technology also underwrites the safety of the visitor and hence a seemingly inexhaustible supply of happy endings. To the extent that these tropes work to interpellate the visitor, s/he escapes the bounds of her/his mundane existence, transported to a world of passive, hypnotic fantasy.

The approximately 45-minute drive to KSCVC seems utterly insufficient to recover from the seductive effects of the "Disney magic" in any case. But when the visitor arrives at KSCVC, s/he will simply encounter another set of texts, slightly different, but largely repeated and reproduced from WDW. KSCVC perpetuates WDW's rhetoric, coaxing visitors to remain immersed within the vista of efficiently fun, safe, technologically enabled happy endings.

FROM THEME PARK TO . . . THEME PARK: RETURNING TO KSCVC

Only after returning from Orlando did we recognize the extent to which the theme park syntax is repeated at KSCVC. The reproductions are multiple and clear, explicitly extending the boundaries of the theme park zone to encompass KSCVC.[50] The parking lot sections at KSCVC are marked by names of the space shuttles (Figure 1.11), paralleling the character and venue namings in the lots at WDW (Figure 1.12). KSCVC, though tiny by

FIGURE 1.11. Sign in parking lot, Kennedy Space Center Visitor Center. Photo by Neil Michel.

comparison with WDW, provides a similarly broad array of visitor services, listed helpfully in its brochures, just as they are in the WDW Guide Maps. Intermittent appearances by the Spaceman (Figure 1.13) are KSCVC's answer to the Disney characters that occasionally surface in the WDW parks and resorts (Figure 1.14). Like WDW (Figure 1.15), KSCVC offers its own photo spots (Figure 1.16). KSCVC has added themed topiary (Figure 1.17), clearly aping that at WDW (Figure 1.18). "Satellites and You," a 45-minute exhibition detailing the applications and values of satellite technology in everyday life, uses animatronic effects and functionally serves as KSCVC's own "Carousel of Progress." Play areas for children have analogues in Sensory Funhouse (Wonders of Life) and Image Works

FIGURE 1.12. "Grumpy" parking sign, Walt Disney World. Used by permission from Disney Enterprises, Inc. Photo by Neil Michel.

(Journey into Imagination), both in Epcot. The Space Shop, Orbit Cafeteria, Mila's Roadhouse,[51] and Space Dots stands (Figure 1.19) parallel WDW's themed gift shops, restaurants, and gift and snack booths (Figure 1.20). Visitors may purchase t-shirts that display cartoon characters alongside a space shuttle.[52] All signs portend a simple extension of the theme park experience.

Indeed, KSCVC's tonal differences from the Orlando theme parks are minor, if not elusive. KSCVC's educational motif certainly made it distinct from the other parks, until Epcot, complete with research facilities, opened in 1982 (Figure 1.21). KSCVC is located on an operational space launch facility, so visitation activity sometimes is disrupted by a scheduled rocket

FIGURE 1.13. The Spaceman posing for photographs, Kennedy Space Center Visitor Center. Photo by Neil Michel.

or shuttle launch. Even that boundary between real and fictive place, however, has been eroded by the presence of actual experimental research programs at Epcot and by the addition of Disney-MGM Studios, which is explicit in its self-references as a "real" working film studio. Like the larger theme parks to the west, KSCVC is blithely cheerful, and it offers an abundance of choices and inviting stimuli. Nothing at KSCVC breaks the mood or the themes of WDW; if anything, KSCVC seems to make every effort—down to the finest semiotic detail—to convince visitors they never left WDW.

Our rhetorical reading had hinged on understanding the Astronauts

FIGURE 1.14. Walk-around character Goofy signing autographs at the Magic Kingdom. Disney characters © Disney Enterprises, Inc. Used by permission from Disney Enterprises, Inc. Photo by Neil Michel.

Memorial as a discrete, independent, unproblematic text, bounded by the context of KSCVC. The continuities between WDW and KSCVC, however, prompted a shift in perspective. We revised our stance so as to understand a text as a landscape (or, more properly in this case, a "dreamscape"), a geographically and culturally determined *experiential* habitat rendered by the visitor's journey.[53] That is, this text or landscape is forged by a series of intertextualizations on the part of the visitor. What s/he reads together composes and orders the landscape, offering specific "rules for reading" that will construct and constrain her/his reading of its components (Stock,

FIGURE 1.15. Picture Spot at the Magic Kingdom. Used by permission from Disney Enterprises, Inc. Photo by Neil Michel.

318).[54] What constitutes this landscape for the visitor, of course, is wholly dependent upon her/his experience. But, as Mechling and Mechling suggest, we can at least hypothesize a "home society" within which a particular discourse is likely to be read: "Society, in this view, is a vast network of structures of signification, of verbal and nonverbal narratives. People perceive and remember these narratives not in isolation but as part of a system. . . . Texts refer to each other, the ability to understand some texts depends on experience with others, vocabularies from one text bleed into others, and so on" ("Campaign," 109). Surely, if there can be a "bleeding of vocabularies" between two apparently discrete places, WDW and KSCVC are prime examples. KSCVC not only reproduces the syntax and tone of WDW but also repeats its major tropes.[55]

Technology obviously is the reigning deity at KSCVC.[56] All the other tropes that compose the tourist experience near Orlando are also present, but reconfigured in emphasis. At KSCVC, efficient fun retains its place; although the pitch of the experience is slightly less frenetic, it is clear that the supply of activity outstrips the available time for most visitors. Added to the mix is a strong environmentalist theme that, while readable in the WDW parks, is not featured quite as prominently there.[57] The vital difference, though, is that there are *no* attractions at KSCVC that pretend to

FIGURE 1.16. Photo spot sign at Kennedy Space Center Visitor Center. Photo by Neil Michel.

place the visitor at risk; quite the contrary. Visitors are reassured repeatedly that their movements are restricted for their own safety, *never* that they are embarking on perilous journeys. They are positioned as spectators of the space program, not participants, and they are consistently kept at a safe distance from its operations. They are surrounded by space hardware, but the hardware is decontextualized, pried loose from the scene in which it has functional value . . . and within which it carries a risk. While the visitor is exposed to extreme "dangers" at the other parks, only to be reassured at each juncture that s/he is safe, KSCVC reproduces the safety trope but voids it of any element of threat or hazard.

If the visitor has no need of being "saved" from peril by technology at

FIGURE 1.17. Astronaut topiary at Kennedy Space Center Visitor Center. Photo by Neil Michel.

KSCVC, s/he reads the multiplicity of its wonders, accessing information about technology by means of technology. The coupling of technology to safety actually becomes tighter and more focused than at WDW, because the suggestion of peril drops out of the textual matrix almost altogether. As for space travel itself, the perils are not denied, but they *definitely* are not foregrounded. Adventure is depicted as safe—protected by increasingly advanced engineering. The only overt marker of the space program's dangers is a film about Apollo 13 now playing in one of Spaceport Central's small theatres.[58] But even that was added to the KSCVC roster of attractions only after the Hollywood version had effectively reminded the public of the happy and heroic outcome of that near-disaster. Risk, to the extent it appears at all, is deferred; it is either "back then," or "out there," not here and now. Happy endings, the accomplishments and successes of NASA, are clearly marked for the visitor, and everywhere they are achieved by the provident force of technology.

KSCVC demands very little from the visitor in terms of altering the position already constructed for her/him by WDW. The same tropes are

FIGURE 1.18. Dumbo topiary at the Disney Village Marketplace. Walt Disney World Resort. Disney characters © Disney Enterprises, Inc. Used by permission from Disney Enterprises, Inc. Photo by Carole Blair.

present, reiterating in only slightly altered form the messages to which the visitor has already been conditioned by overexposure. Visitors are aware, of course, that they have entered a real, working space launch facility, but that awareness carries with it few, if any, entailments for their experience. The KSCVC messages may be about "reality," but the extraordinary character of the reality represented here certainly must resemble the fantastic adventures of Disney more than that of everyday life for most visitors.[59] Here, as at WDW, the visitor is asked to submit her/his experience to the control and direction of the "lessons" the park has to offer. Visitors need be only passive recipients of messages; they are asked to expend little effort to reap the rewards of education and enjoyment.

FIGURE 1.19. Space Dots vendor at Kennedy Space Center Visitor Center. Photo by Neil Michel.

This lack of effort demanded from the visitor already places her/him in a problematic position vis-à-vis the Space Mirror. After days of exposure to texts that essentially ask visitors not to think, or that at least excuse them of the responsibility, they are confronted suddenly and unexpectedly with a text that is readable, but not without effort. The Space Mirror poses questions rather than answers of its visitors, and it demands that visitors not submit passively to a message but expend contemplative effort to understand it. In contrast to the effortlessly readable discourses that constitute the visitor's experience of both WDW and KSCVC, the Space Mirror confronts her/him with a difficult text. The Space Mirror demands not dependence but effort on the part of its visitor. In that respect, it is alien to virtually every other experience of visitors who travel the route from WDW to KSCVC.[60]

But the effort the Space Mirror demands from the visitor is not the only problem. The particularity of the Space Mirror's questions also render it an alien, perhaps even unwelcome, interloper in the theme park perimeter. To the extent that the Memorial poses questions of the visitor with respect to her or his relationship to the deceased astronauts, the visitor must acknowledge that they *are* deceased. But in the theme park dreamscape she or he has just traversed, symbols of death are virtually nonexistent, perhaps even unthinkable. Even when Disney characters or visitors are placed in seemingly mortal dan-

FIGURE 1.20. Rainforest Cafe in the Walt Disney World Resort. Used by permission from Disney Enterprises, Inc. Photo by Neil Michel.

ger, the peril is averted so that the adventure may continue.[61] At the Astronauts Memorial, though, the visitor encounters perils that have not been averted, ones that end unhappily. If this alien symbol—death—is readable at all after days of theme park adventures, it certainly must be an awkward one to read within the otherworldly and reliably safe texts that have composed the visitor's experiences.

That awkwardness is intensified to the degree that the Space Mirror codes any questioning of technology and its relationship to humanity. Space exploration is not posed as an unquestioned good, as it is everywhere at WDW and KSCVC. Nor is technology portrayed here as guaranteeing safety; the Astronauts Memorial distances safety from technology, displaying both danger and safety as technology's companions. The Space Mirror's coding of the representation–reality double with respect to humanity and technology places at issue the visitor's vacation-constructed experience, which has been permeated by messages about the safety and virtues of technology. It might place visitors in the very uncomfortable position of examining their own experiences with regard to technology; it might even invite them back from fantasy to reality, with all of its unhappy as well as happy endings.

If visitors were to consider themselves in relation to the astronauts, as

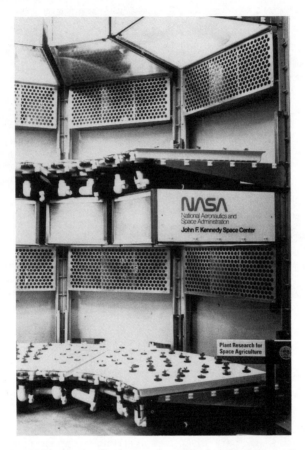

FIGURE 1.21. NASA cosponsored research at The Land exhibit in Epcot. Used by permission from Disney Enterprises, Inc. Photo by Neil Michel.

the Memorial might ask them to do, they are positioned again in conflict with the theme park messages. Within those conjoining texts, the visitor's experience is paramount; her/his enjoyment is the whole reason for being of those texts. While situated as a passive spectator, the visitor is central; it is her/his happy ending that composes the motivational structure of the text. At the Memorial, though, the visitor might be led to read her/his role as small, unheroic, or unextraordinary with respect to the astronauts. At least, her/his power and position are placed at issue, for the generative authority of the visitor's happy ending fails against the perils of space travel.

To the extent that the visitor has read and allowed herself/himself to be read into the discourses of the theme parks, the Space Mirror can offer little more than a source of discomfort and discord. To read it seriously entails that the visitor question the other texts that have rewarded her/his temporally contiguous experience. The most comfortable position for visitors is to simply avert attention, to retain the considerable rewards offered by the other attractions, and to allow themselves to be distracted or distanced from the text of the Space Mirror. The efficient fun trope prevails; there are so many other (more amusing) sights to see at KSCVC . . . and so little time.

CONCLUSION

Concluding our study of the Astronauts Memorial by painting implications for the intersection of rhetorical and cultural studies is not a task that comes easily, in part because we think our study remains far from "complete." But concluding this way is difficult too because we have not done a lot of thinking about rhetoric and cultural studies as *necessarily* distinct or opposed categories; we have been more interested in appropriating from both discursive fields in whatever ways happened to suit our critical interests. It is not an easy task to identify the moments at which our perspective shifted from rhetoric to cultural studies, because those moments blurred together and never seemed marked by a border crossing. But promises to speak about the intersection of rhetoric and cultural studies, and to pose one as a corrective to the other, oblige us to articulate at least what we see as their different tendencies, if not a distinctly marked or insurmountable frontier between them.

When we stepped onto the plane to travel to Florida, we were "being" rhetoricians. If we replay our conversation, reproduced at the beginning of the essay, what we "hear" in that conversation are largely the rhetorical concerns of symbolic, situational, and generic adequacy.[62] More important, though, what we hear is a conversation that foregrounds the Astronauts Memorial itself. As one of our colleagues observed astutely, after reading an earlier draft of this essay, "How many regular tourists stand around for hours looking carefully at inscriptions, thinking about the angle of the object, noting its placement, geography [and] cant . . . ? Face it, you two are odd viewers." That we were thinking about the Memorial at all on the way to Florida already had set us apart from the vast majority of other soon-to-be visitors, most of whom probably are not aware of the Memorial's existence, much less concerned about it as a more or less symbolically interesting or rhetorically appropriate instance of contemporary commemorative art.

Neither of us has any recollection of when precisely we began to notice the other visitors to the Astronauts Memorial or their reactions to it, but that moment certainly seems to have marked the point at which our work began to shift to a cultural studies frame. That is not to suggest that it shifted *from* rhetoric, only that we began to pose questions that rhetorical study typically would not. Rhetorical study seems to us unnecessarily impoverished by its tendency to treat audience experience in only perfunctory or assumptive ways. In that respect, cultural studies offers rhetoric a corrective.[63] We share Condit's concern that an exclusive concentration on audience reception may be understood or used to invalidate a critic's reading "on grounds that the popular audience would not share the critic's response" ("Interpellating," 244). We remain convinced that the written, critical performance resulting from a critic's "odd viewership" is important. It performs a service, what Benson suggestively describes as doing a "part of society's homework." That homework is an intervention; it works, as he points out, "in aid of shared social knowledge—monitoring our institutions and practices and encouraging critical reflection" ("Rhetorical Structure and *Primate,*" 185). It recommends the critic's particular reading of a text as one to which we should attend. It promotes a possibility of reading differently, and perhaps more productively or responsibly.[64]

Still, rhetoric often seems to stray to an extreme of not attending to other audiences' experiences. What difference did it make for us to consider audience reaction to the Astronauts Memorial? A lot. Because we paid even just a little attention to an audience's reactions and its peculiar characteristics—neither very difficult in this case to detect—we believe we were better able to account for the rhetorical failure of a discourse that we believed ought to be a success. Had we not paid attention to that audience, we might have promoted, however inadvertently, the compellingly naive assumption that, since the Space Mirror *ought* to provide a fulfilling commemorative experience, that it actually *does*. To the extent that rhetorical study retains its almost exclusive focus on the context of production and the meanings generated symbolically in the product, and its inattention to experience and reception, it will be trapped in the dilemma of either rendering such a dubious conflation or having little or nothing to say about what discourse does.[65]

Since rhetoric typically does not address the material presence or practices of audiences, we believe it misses two marks that cultural studies has taken up and explored productively. First, if we fail to deal with audiences as real, material beings and their experiences as significant, we almost certainly will overlook differences that *make* a difference in how discourses are used, consumed, and redeployed. Cultural studies often parses such differences as those that organize themselves around differences of race, gender, and/or class. We do not remember focusing on the fact that we were "doing" cultural studies when we posed the question of how different segments of the Memorial's audience seemed to respond, or when we sought out answers according to the race-gender-class (as well as age) markers that so often figure in the cultural studies matrix.[66] We did not find any answers about race, gender, class, or age, but we found some answers. Had we never asked these questions, we never would have noticed that there indeed were differential reactions to the Memorial, but that they divided most overtly along the line between visitors and KSC employees. This was not the answer we expected, but it was a useful one nonetheless. Certainly less affected by the codes of the tourist landscape, the KSC personnel seem both able and willing to engage the Astronauts Memorial as a place of commemoration. Their different reactions suggest that it is not so much the Space Mirror itself, but what visitors read it *as* or what they read together *with it,* that renders the visitor's experience so apparently distinct from what we had led ourselves to expect.

The notion of different conditions, contexts, and practices of reading leads us to the second missed opportunity in rhetorical studies. Rhetoric tends toward the naturalized, (too) easy gesture to take "text," or "discourse," as an unproblematic container, to see its borders as given in the activity of production and its character designated by its naming (e.g., as a memorial). We began our study of the Astronauts Memorial assuming that it *was* a memorial, that is, that it was an identifiable, bounded rhetorical product that would, in some way and more or less successfully, play out its generic identity as public commemorative art. What we finally recognized was that the Astronauts Memorial is, for many, an anomalous landmark in a vacation dreamscape. Its borders are not the memorial grounds but a tourist zone, and its degree of cultural legibility is predicated less in a commemorative genre than the extent to which visitors have consumed and been interpellated by other textual components of their vacation journey.[67]

This different understanding of the text rendered our earlier judgments of the Memorial's contextual appropriateness hollow-sounding, at best. However, we began to realize that our first critical account of visitor inattention—based on flaws in the design of the Memorial grounds—was not wrong but incomplete. Those flaws do divert and distract, and perhaps on occasion they even work independently to do so. But, read back into the larger text, the ways in which those landscape design features work on visitors make more sense. The problematic features of the Memorial site offer the visitor precisely what s/he requires to escape the difficulties and dissonances s/he might confront in the Space Mirror—diversions and distractions. The visitor need not confront the discomfort of reading death or its connection to technology, if s/he simply attends to the alligators, gazes at the Explorer, or sees Mila's and decides to go have lunch. What appear to be (and are) site design errors actually *contribute* to the larger text, by helping to forestall its infringement by unwelcome, discordant, or incompatible messages (e.g., the symbolism of the Memorial). At least some of the site design flaws could be corrected, but we are not convinced that such changes would enhance reception. The site design flaws work altogether too well as consonant parts of a larger and more forceful text; but they remain minor components in the experiential landscape. In any case, they currently work together with other components of that text to render the Memorial as unreadable or, at least for the most part, unread.

We do not mean that the Astronauts Memorial should receive the kind of rejection-by-inattention response that this textual re-bordering seems to generate and even to reward. Instead, we are suggesting that critics be attentive to different reading practices, their conditions, and their contexts. Reading a text through the lens of a rhetorical theory—rhetorical criticism's usual tendency—is not wrong, but it is only *a* way of reading,[68] and it will not necessarily bring us any closer to understanding how primary audiences read the same text, or even what counts for them *as* "the text." We believe critics—including rhetorical critics—ought to be concerned with reception, not exclusively the reception of texts by professionally trained academic critics, but the readings, reactions, and responses of others as well. To not be concerned with audience is to effectively deny the character of rhetoric as doing work beyond itself (Bitzer, 3).

Characterizations of rhetoric as definitively and exhaustively symbolic contribute to that denial. Discourse *does* construct meanings symbolically; that is one kind of work that it does, but only one. If we limit critical effort to a focus on meaning, we will miss the additional work that a discourse does, not only on audiences but on other discourses. Discourse includes and excludes, rewards and punishes, promises and denies, constructs and undermines privilege, and so forth, work that cultural studies has probed advantageously.[69] What discourse appears to do in the Florida vacation landscape, among other things, is to construct a subject position for the visitor and reward her/him for occupying it.[70] Certainly not all visitors are interpellated by the WDW (or any other) discourse; but this discourse does work to reward them for occupying the "preferred" subject position. The theme park rhetoric works not only to interpellate; it also subverts virtually any messages besides its own. It creates what Morse has called the "fiction effect," a *distraction* from the "here and now," by promoting a "liquidity of words and images" that undermines a sense of "different levels of reality and of incommensurable difference between them" (213).[71] Those activities of the discourse are not "meaning" that it generates, but other things it does *in addition to* generating meaning. Such consequential effects are ones we think should not be overlooked.

Perhaps the most significant of the issues cultural studies raises has to do with the political character of discourse (Bennett, 23). We have touched here only in the lightest way on the political imbrication of the WDW,

KSCVC, and the Astronauts Memorial. For the record, we have been alternately fascinated, astonished, and appalled by the macro-political dimensions of the vacation discourses we encountered in central and coastal Florida and their relationship to the reception of the Memorial. For example, although we have not taken it up directly here, we could not help but notice what appears to be NASA's callous disregard and disrespect of the national memorial that occupies its grounds. We are intrigued as well by the fact that both the discourse of KSCVC and of the Memorial lack any reference to the U.S. space program's initiation and maintenance within the motivational context of the Cold War, that space "exploration" and its everyday technological "spinoffs" both happen to be mere by-products of the military uses that inspired the establishment of the program to begin with. And we are interested in the recent controversy about the non-inclusion on the Memorial of the name of an African American officer who was assigned to the Pentagon's Manned Orbiting Laboratory, rather than to NASA, when he was killed (Oberg). In offering only a passing salute to those issues (and others) here, our focus certainly has been less overtly macro-political than it might be (and than we hope it will become in a "spinoff" from this essay).

However, our view, and one supported by the developing tradition(s) in cultural studies is that attending to the cultural practices of everyday life and their reception (e.g., vacation texts) is always already political.[72] Here, as in many instances of cultural studies, the practice of criticism itself is challenged at the level of assumption (Fiske, "Cultural," 159). What counts as the text that will be read? Whose readings of a text will be considered authoritative? Should we read texts in their contexts of production or of reception (to the degree that it is possible with various media to distinguish those contexts)? Will we attempt to understand not only the meanings generated by texts but also the work that texts do when they are deployed in various spaces and conditions of praxis? These issues, ones not frequently even raised much less answered to satisfaction in rhetorical studies, are crucial, ones that cultural studies thrusts on rhetoric, advantageously in our view. If we have left aside for now the "big" political questions, we hope that we at least have managed to demonstrate the value of addressing these "smaller" ones about the politics of critical practice.

ACKNOWLEDGMENTS

We would like to acknowledge the insightful readings and helpful suggestions of Jay Mechling, Kent A. Ono, and John L. Vohs, all at the University of California, Davis. We owe a debt of gratitude as well to: James R. De Santis, President, Astronauts Memorial Foundation; George Meguiar (TW Recreation Services), former Director of Marketing, Spaceport USA; the NASA Educators Resource Center, Kennedy Space Center; Gailyn Simpson, former Director of Finance Administration, Astronauts Memorial Foundation; and Melissa Tomasso (Delaware North Parks Services), Marketing Representative, Kennedy Space Center Visitor Center; for the time they granted us for interviews as well as materials they supplied us. We appreciate the efforts of Margaret Adamic, of the Disney Publishing Group and of Peter Wissoker at Guilford, for their help in the process of securing copyright permissions. And we are very grateful to Marc Hinshaw, Dwight Ashdown, and Paul Holt, of Holt Hinshaw, Architects (San Francisco), for their time and their insights, as well as for their great generosity in giving us open access to their files on the design, planning, and construction of the Astronauts Memorial.

NOTES

1. That is, we understand these public memorial sites as partisan, meaningful, influential discourses or texts. Although some traditional rhetoricians would exclude nonlinguistic forms as legitimate objects of rhetorical criticism, it has become commonplace in the past twenty-five years for rhetoricians to study media products, advertisements, artworks, etc. By "text" and "discourse," we mean here simply instances of rhetoric, as most rhetoricians would refer to them. As we shift our assumptions to a more cultural studies–oriented frame later in the essay, our understanding of those terms also will shift.
2. See, for example, Bitzer and Black, particularly the sections of the report by the Committee on the Scope of Rhetoric (208–219), and by the Committee on the Advancement and Refinement of Rhetorical Criticism (220–227).
3. For general discussions of appropriateness, see Bitzer; Gronbeck; and Rosteck and Leff. These authors deal with the issue in very different ways, but they certainly are in agreement that appropriateness is an important and widely accepted judgment standard among rhetorical critics.
4. This is not to suggest that genres are historically stagnant categories; they are, as Jamieson argues, "evolving phenomena" ("Generic Constraints," 168). She suggests that particular rhetorical events may even "shatter generic expectations" (168). That would not render those events necessarily inappropriate or ineffective. But, as Blair, Jeppeson, and Pucci suggest with respect to memorials in particular, generic "violations" are not gratuitous either. A departure from generic resources or norms "typically signals a peculiarity of situation calling for alteration of type and/or the inadequacy of a generic norm to appropriately respond to a situation" (276).
5. Our reading of the Astronauts Memorial reproduces portions of our rendition of it in Blair and Michel. We appreciate the willingness of Joachim Wolschke-Bulmahn and Dumbarton Oaks to allow us to use brief sections of that essay. There are some changes here because of our different purpose and because some changes have been made to the site. That earlier essay was based upon visits in 1992 and 1994, while this one is based on those plus a September 1996 visit. We will note sections that resemble or reproduce the other essay at the points they appear in this essay.

6. House Joint Resolution 214 (House, April 30, 1991; Senate, May 6, 1991) passed just days before the May 9 dedication. There had been an attempt in 1986 to build an astronauts memorial in the Washington, DC, area. Although its supporters received the necessary congressional support in Senate Joint Resolution 372, the project appears not to have progressed much beyond that point. By designating the Florida site a national memorial, Congress essentially eliminated any possibility of an astronauts memorial in Washington, DC (see United States, Congress).

7. That this was the intention of Holt Hinshaw Pfau Jones was borne out in an interview with Marc Hinshaw and is also supported in correspondence between the architects and contractors (Ashdown).

8. At the time of our most recent visit in 1996, there were sixteen names inscribed in the Space Mirror, specifically: Theodore C. Freeman, killed in 1964 in a T-38 crash; Charles A. Bassett, II, and Elliott M. See, Jr., both killed during an instrument landing in 1966 at McDonnell Aircraft's St. Louis plant; the three *Apollo I* astronauts (Roger B. Chaffee, Virgil "Gus" Grissom, and Edward H. White, II), killed in a ground simulation in 1967; Clifton C. Williams, Jr., killed in a T-38 accident in 1967; Michael J. Adams, killed in a 1967 X-15 crash; the crew of the *Challenger* (Gregory B. Jarvis, S. Christa McAuliffe, Ronald E. McNair, Ellison S. Onizuka, Judith A. Resnik, Francis "Dick" Scobee, and Michael J. Smith), killed 73 seconds after launch in 1986; and Manley Lanier "Sonny" Carter, Jr., killed in a plane crash while on NASA business in 1991.

9. Our descriptions of the Space Mirror's mechanisms rely on those provided by Hinshaw, Holt, and Ashdown, of Holt Hinshaw, as well as an undated information sheet entitled "Facts About the Astronauts Memorial, Kennedy Space Center, Florida" that was included in the Astronauts Memorial Foundation press kit.

10. This physical separation of the visitor from the wall was not part of the original design. The barrier in the architects' design was a mechanical handrail designed to allow the visitor access to the turntable upon which the granite face of the Memorial rotates—whenever such access was safe. The mechanical handrail was deleted from the design by the AMF, apparently because of cost overruns and safety concerns (Hinshaw, Interview). The result was predicted by the architects, the loss of some of the power of the visual experience: "[T]he real effects of the glowing names are almost supernatural—but only if you are close enough for the reflected sky to fill your entire field of vision" (Holt, Letter, 2). The stable barrier also denies visitors sufficient proximity to touch the wall.

11. We find the "conquering" and "conquest" language gratuitous and inappropriate. If there is a single symbolic gesture in the structure that we believe detracts from its commemorative messages, the language of this dedication is that gesture. According to Hinshaw, this smaller structure was originally supposed to be a "mission wall" that inscribed each of NASA's individual missions into space, not a dedication wall for the AMF (Interview).

12. Abramson suggests that the Vietnam Veterans Memorial's "polished black granite and list of names quickly became clichés in American monument building" (680). Both certainly have become common practices, but we think it

more useful to see them as interesting departures from tradition than to dismiss them as clichés.

13. We take the Vietnam Veterans Memorial as both exemplar and prototype. The design demands thought on the part of the visitor. While it is not particularly cryptic, it is polysemic; that is, it accommodates and supports an array of (sometimes contradictory) readings. That is arguably the most important of its rhetorical dimensions. Blair, Jeppeson, and Pucci make that argument explicitly. Both the scope and depth of reaction to the piece further attest to the Memorial's polysemy and to its almost unbelievable success as public art. The Vietnam Veterans Memorial changed public commemoration's language and shifted its emphasis. Not only did it set in motion a boom in commemorative building, but it also seems to have served as a model for much of the commemorative work that followed in the 1980s and 1990s. Among the memorials that reproduce various elements of its design language are the NAMES Project AIDS Memorial Quilt, the Salem Witch Trials Tercentenary Memorial (Salem, MA), the National Law Enforcement Officers Memorial (Washington, DC), the Civil Rights Memorial (Montgomery, AL), the Korean War Veterans Memorial (Washington, DC), as well as countless local and state Vietnam veterans memorials.

14. Other critics agree that the technology-humanity theme is the Astronauts Memorial's most crucial one. Fisher claims that the Space Mirror is, "at once, a paean to the power of our technology and an essay on its existential danger" (Thomas Fisher, 74). McCoy suggests that it "represents the poignant myth of the limit of technology. . . . [It] alludes to the fallibility—as well as the infinite promise—of technology. . . . While it illuminates the doomed trajectory of Icarus it also traces the outlines of a more sensitive and positive direction for technology and architecture" (107). McCoy goes on to suggest that the work addresses our relationship of "love, hate, and reconciliation" with technology (107), and both he and Hogben (79) link it to Mary Shelley's *Frankenstein.* Our reading of the technology theme is approximately the same as in Blair and Michel.

15. This seems to be at least implied in others' arguments about the Vietnam Veterans Memorial in particular (see Blair, Jeppeson, and Pucci; Griswold; and Sturken). It also seems to be the assumption of many recent memorial designers, whose works have been complex and difficult collages of designs and materials. The California Vietnam Veterans Memorial (Sacramento), as well as the U.S. Navy Memorial, the Korean War Veterans Memorial, and the Franklin Delano Roosevelt Memorial, all in Washington, DC, are excellent examples.

16. The AMF made the distinction explicitly between monumental Washington and touristic Florida: "[KSCVC] is a busy tourist facility with many contemporary, non-traditional structures. By way of contrast, many of the memorials in Washington, D.C. are located within an urban environment of monumental and classical architecture where national memorials are an expected, almost natural occurrence" (6). We do not mean to suggest that a memorial to astronauts, or specifically this structure, should have been placed in Washington, DC. However, we are convinced that it should have been sited differently at KSCVC or removed to a different locale altogether.

17. The wavering support for NASA has been a result of a number of issues: the degree to which the space program can contribute to defense or foreign policy; the capacity of the economy to sustain a program that, to many, appears expendable; and so forth. One of the best indicators of NASA's fickle fortunes is its wildly fluctuating employment rolls at KSC: "Employment at KSC peaked in 1968, with 26,500 people working on the Apollo program. But by July 1970, national priorities had been realigned and, in the harsh light of reduced funding, KSC's work force was pared to 15,000. . . . Following Skylab, employment at the Center dropped to around 8,000, where it remained until Shuttle activities edged it up to a 1981 complement of 12,000, and 15,000 by 1985" (NASA Public Affairs, 182). In addition to reflecting economic and budget issues, these figures follow a consistent pattern that reflects defense and foreign policy priorities. NASA was established in 1958, in the wake of the Soviet Union's successful Sputnik launches. The Mercury, Gemini, and Apollo programs were the U.S. entries in the midcentury "space race" to beat the Soviet Union to the moon. The mid-1980s resurgence was due, in no small part, to Ronald Reagan's announcement and support of the "Strategic Defense Initiative." Employment slumped again after the *Challenger* accident but "rebounded," probably due to SDI imperatives, from a low of 13,700 to 17,000 in the late 1980s (182).

18. In our conversations with AMF representatives, KSCVC marketing personnel, and the Memorial's architects, it was never volunteered but frequently confirmed that virtually no message produced at KSCVC could remain if NASA disapproved of it. And there is every reason for NASA to want to cultivate an exceptionally positive public image. KSCVC is operated by Delaware North Parks Services. That firm replaced the prior subcontractor—TW Recreation Services—in May 1995, between the times of our second and third visits to KSCVC.

19. Some of KSCVC's exhibits are quite similar to those in the National Air and Space Museum in Washington, DC. As Michael L. Smith points out, KSCVC is an expanded version of the U.S. Space Park exhibit at the 1964 World's Fair in New York City, cosponsored by NASA and the Defense Department. While most of KSCVC's venues, like those of the NASM and Space Park, represent the past, the principal messages are about the present and future. Visitors are reminded everywhere that they are touring a site where history continues to be made.

20. Most of the displays, tours, films, and so forth have to do only with U.S. efforts and achievements in space. The few exceptions are those having to do with cooperative international efforts, such as the Apollo–Soyuz mission, and an occasional mention of the U.S. presence on the Russian space station Mir or preparations for the international space station project.

21. The following discussion of the Memorial's appropriateness to its context is similar to that in Blair and Michel.

22. That dark-light images both draw attention and serve specific rhetorical functions of denoting "good and evil" is argued convincingly by Osborn. Whether they are "archetypal" in the sense that he suggests, drawing on universal human experience, or culture-specific remains an open question, in our view.

Still, for the majority of visitors to KSCVC, it is a virtual certainty that the black-white imagery is no mystery.

23. Our critical reading is aimed simply at demonstrating the rhetorical possibilities of the Astronauts Memorial—its symbolic richness, its alignment with the genre of contemporary commemorative architecture, and its responsiveness to its context. We do not view our reading as exhaustive of the symbolism of the Space Mirror, nor would we expect other visitors necessarily to read it the same way; certainly they might find other meanings in it, or they might read the same themes in more fragmentary ways. That is not a critique of visitors' reception ability or the readings themselves. Our observations at various memorial sites have led us to the conclusion that many visitors render extremely insightful readings of the commemorative messages.

24. Of course, ethnographic and rhetorical work are not utterly opposed or incompatible. See, for example, Conquergood; Ellis, especially 3–10 and 327–337; and Van Maanen. Still, the large majority of critical work in rhetoric is devoid of accounts of actual audiences. Some rhetorical criticism hypothesizes an audience or identifies audience demographics, but few rhetoricians deal with audience groups directly. Of course, we have a rather "unfair advantage" in pointing to that lack, given rhetoric's traditional focus on the spoken or written word. It is almost impossible to visit a public memorial site without encountering other visitors; it is, however, quite possible to watch a televised news conference or read the text of a speech in virtual solitude.

25. Our observations are based principally on watching and eavesdropping on visitors. Both are relatively easy to do unobtrusively at the Memorial site because of its size, the openness of the platform and landscaped areas below, and the steady flow of visitors. Both of us also conversed with other visitors frequently. There is considerable stranger interaction at KSCVC, but we did not initiate conversations (and we tried to follow rather than lead in their substance) because of our concern about intruding into others' experiences. We recorded the substance of those conversations as well as our other observations in field notes and photography. We also mapped patterns of visitors' movements to and from the Memorial. When it was feasible, we timed the stay of a visitor on the viewing platform. We made similar kinds of observations at other KSCVC venues, although not as extensively at any one of them as at the Memorial site. Still, our observations on the tour buses and on visits to the other KSCVC attractions suggested to us that visitors were generally more attentive than when they visited the Space Mirror. They conversed about displays, asked guides and one another questions, shared information, and so forth.

26. We mean *relatively* diverse. The majority of visitors are white, and most are from the United States, Canada, or western Europe. Most visitors of color are from other countries. Most visitors, it appears, are middle class. Genders are represented in approximately equal numbers, and the age range is quite broad. Although the diversity here is limited, there are sufficient differences among the visitors to expect that we should observe at least some differences of response. Had we conducted interviews, we certainly would have found some. But visitors' primary response—of attention—seemed not to vary much at all.

27. Meguiar did not make the actual percentages available to us, but he did say

that, when Disney came to Florida, millions more visitors descended on KSC's visitors complex. Melissa Tomasso, a marketing representative at KSCVC, confirmed that Walt Disney World is KSC's "largest feeder" and that the majority of visitors to KSCVC travel there from Orlando area theme parks (Telephone Interview).

28. Other critics have made assessments at least as positive as our own. Adler labels it "brilliant" and a work of "awesome power" (69). McCoy says that it "speaks poetically of a need for harmony between technology and nature, exploring the possibilities for a responsive architecture" (107). And Fisher calls the Memorial "an absolutely brilliant work—provoking, disturbing, and moving" (Thomas Fisher, 74). The Memorial was honored with a P/A (Progressive Architecture) award in 1989.

29. The AMF's design competition program suggested that wildlife access to the lagoon could be blocked (14). However, the AMF and its landscape architects apparently decided against that. The original site plan called for more distance between the Space Mirror and the other KSCVC venues. But the planned siting of the Space Mirror would have disrupted NASA telemetry lines (Gailyn Simpson, Interview), so it was relocated. Still, a visual or physical barrier between the Memorial and the remainder of KSCVC—a wall or a stand of leafy trees—certainly would have enhanced the site.

30. Our conviction that the flaws of the Memorial grounds offered an insufficient account of visitor disengagement was strengthened by the fact that some of the design problems we had noted were corrected between our 1994 and 1996 visits to the site—with negligible impact on visitors' reception.

31. It is clear that the WDW population is actively sought out by KSCVC. Brochures readily available in the hotel lobbies of Orlando-area resorts promote KSCVC's virtues and emphasize that admission and parking are free—a welcome anomaly amidst the jumble of theme parks lining the corridor between Orlando and Tampa (*Kennedy Space Center Visitor Center*). KSCVC is not unique in being understood as a side trip from WDW or in being read together with the texts of the theme parks. As Mairston suggests, "Comparing an amusement park with a national park may make as much sense as comparing a discotheque with a museum, but tourists seem to do exactly that. The [Everglades National] park attracted 1.8 million visitors—an all-time high—in 1972, which happened to be Disney's first full year of operation. Since then, annual attendance hasn't topped 1.4 million." Quoting Garry Sabbag, former general manager of the Flamingo Lodge, Marina and Outpost Resort, he continues, "If people go to Orlando and visit Universal Studios and Disney World, they get excitement, fireworks, lasers. Then when they come down here, it can be very boring to them." Sabbag says that "We call it the Mickey Curtain. . . . People go to Orlando and think they've seen the spectacular stuff in Florida" (12). Addressing the same issue but less directly, Fjellman observes tellingly that "The average tourist stayed in Florida for five days, so even the four-day pass [at Walt Disney World] left other central Florida attractions to scramble for a share of the fifth day" (149). We visited and have mentioned here only the largest and most proximate of the parks. West of WDW is Cypress Gardens, and Busch Gardens lies further to the west, in Tampa. Several smaller parks, like

Wet 'N' Wild, are located near Orlando. Many smaller attractions have been put out of business since 1971, largely as a result of the Disney competition (see Sehlinger, 7–11).

32. Most commentators on WDW list its total area as 43 square miles; *Birnbaum's* puts it at 45 square miles (43), while the 1997 *Walt Disney World Vacation Planning* video uses a figure of 46 square miles. The discrepancy, relatively minor in any case, probably is accounted for by recent land acquisitions for the addition of the sports complex.

33. This, like all descriptions of WDW, is dated before it reaches print. According to The Walt Disney Company's *1996 Annual Report,* the Marketplace and Pleasure Island are being expanded (roughly doubling in size), and they will be merged and renamed Downtown Disney. The *Cirque du Soleil* was set to open in 1997, as were Disney's Coronado Springs Resort and Disney's Wide World of Sports. Anticipated in 1998 were the Disney Cruise Line (and its terminal conveniently located near WDW) and Disney's Animal Kingdom (27–28).

34. For example, we skipped the recreation (tennis, golf, etc.) areas, and we missed a few of the resort hotels as well as the Disney Institute and University. We spent by far the greatest amount of our time in the three primary theme parks, and we parceled out the remainder to Pleasure Island, the Disney Village Marketplace, and some of the more popular Disney resorts.

35. Our identification and description of these four tropes is based exclusively on our own reading of the theme parks and of travel brochures and literature about the parks. We were aware, of course, that a great many critics have written on WDW. However, we did not believe at the times of our visits, nor do we now, that our purposes would have been well served by simply echoing their conclusions. We were looking for something very specific and fundamentally different from any other critic's work that we know of—how visitors to KSCVC might be influenced by their prior visits to WDW. Moreover, we find Bryman's view virtually unassailable: "[T]he parks are not inert texts. . . . Consequently, just as the Disney theme park attractions are continually undergoing change, interpretations of the parks need to shift" (83). Only after conducting and organizing our own reading did we consult other critical accounts of the theme parks; they have been quite useful in bolstering certain positions or filling in certain blanks. Most of these accounts are generally consistent with our own, although their goals are quite different. For example, we agree with commentators who read the parks in terms of ideological and political-economic positions (see Fjellman, 15). Moreover, we are sensitive to specific differences among the parks, which some of these critics' readings emphasize (see Fjellman, 317). We have focused on neither of these (or other) legitimate readings here not because we disagree or consider them unimportant, but because they are not pertinent to our purpose.

36. Of course, time at the parks is, in turn, dependent upon disposable income. Adult admission to any of the major parks in the Orlando area for one day was between $30 and $40 in the fall of 1996 (our most recent visit).

37. *Birnbaum's* is designated as WDW's "official guide" and even is distributed free to guests of the WDW resorts, but other area guidebooks make essentially the same point.

38. Other guidebooks and travel brochures concur; in fact, some are organized around the theme of maximizing efficiency by visiting particular attractions on particular days or at specific times of the day (see Sehlinger).

39. Commentators often mention or even focus upon the entry of tourists into the seemingly alien environment (see, for example, Adams, 40; Fjellman, 11; and Shaw and Williams, 170). A number of textual codes are explicit in this segregation of the tourist from his or her everyday experience. As Sorkin points out, the visitor encounters a "customs-like barrier, thence to relinquish one's car to hotel, campsite, or daytripper's parking lots and enter the system. The toll booth is also the limit of a monetary zone; within [Walt] Disney World, visitors can pay either with conventional instruments or with 'Disney Dollars'" (223). This coding is not purely an illusion. WDW *is* an independent administrative/governmental unit, because of its 1967 designation by the Florida State Legislature as the Reedy Creek Improvement District. See Fjellman, 12; Kurtti, 27; and Sorkin, 225.

40. These resorts are thematically and architecturally connected to sections of the theme parks, as Findlay notes (111). For example, Fort Wilderness is a parallel to Frontierland, the Polynesian Village to Adventureland, and the Contemporary Resort to Tomorrowland. The resorts are very much part of the whole theme park experience. As Fjellman points out, "Walt Disney World is in the hotel and restaurant business just as deeply as in the amusement park business" (132). Restaurants that reflect or reproduce WDW themes, for example, the Rainforest Cafe and Planet Hollywood, are now admitted to WDW territory as well (Figure 1.20).

41. This distinction is similar to Mechling and Mechling's identification of the BIG/EXPENSIVE/DANGEROUS coding they found to be characteristic of Great America's attractions and less descriptive of Disneyland's ("Sale"). As they predicted in 1981, many new Disney attractions have since followed the Great America model, although they retain a much stronger narrative component.

42. What we have in mind by this safe (perilous) adventure trope is found also in Adams's description of Space Mountain in the Magic Kingdom: "[Its] race through the blackness of an interplanetary void is for riders a conquering of fear and danger. As riders reach the exit, they are convinced of their own bravery and fortitude. There is a tangible feeling of having risen to meet a challenge" (145).

43. Unnamed Disney-MGM Studios guide, quoted by Dunn (49). A number of commentators discuss the implications of the transformation of backstage to stage at WDW (see, for example, The Project on Disney, 46).

44. Walt Disney Company, *Magic Kingdom Guide Map*. The Carousel of Progress was created by Disney for the 1964–1965 New York World's Fair. Fjellman calls it the "pivotal hinge between the mythological history at the Magic Kingdom and the corporate view of technological empire at Future World [in Epcot]" (80). We should neither forget that the Carousel is "presented" by General Electric nor neglect Wallace's observation that it is a "paean to Progress—defined as the availability of consumer goods" (140). Wallace surely is right to emphasize the commodity theme, but it is also essential to remember

what kinds of consumer goods are sacralized in the messages of the Carousel—technological ones.

45. Walt's vision, of course, was altered substantially after his death. Epcot is decidedly not a "community," but an amusement park (see Kurtti, 81–89). Its model, as a number of commentators have pointed out, is the world's fair (see Steve Nelson). The promotion of centers of American industry remains as a crucial component, however. Major attractions in Future World at Epcot are sponsored by (and arguably promote the self-serving messages of) Exxon, AT&T, United Technologies, General Motors, Nestle, Met Life, and Eastman Kodak. Innoventions features displays of products from a host of corporations. While sponsorship (and corporate interests) may be most evident in Future World, it is present at other WDW venues as well. For example, "It's a Small World" and Space Mountain in the Magic Kingdom are "presented" by, respectively Mattel Toys and Federal Express (The Walt Disney Company, *Magic Kingdom*). Disney-MGM Studios' Star Tours is sponsored by Energizer, and its Great Movie Ride by Coca-Cola (The Walt Disney Company, *Disney-MGM Studios*, 1996).

46. Kurtti, 97. As it is, space travel is featured prominently in a number of Disney venues. Fjellman goes so far as to call it the "compulsory advertisement for NASA" (364), noting that a number of films and exhibits in WDW depend on NASA photos or film footage. One wonders if the "advertisement" for NASA ultimately may become KSCVC's commercial downfall. If Disney realizes its plans for a pavilion on space travel, it could undermine KSCVC's tourist market. It would not be the first time WDW offered what Fjellman calls a "spoiler attraction": "Although the same would be said of the Living Seas at EPCOT Center (a potential threat to Sea World), Typhoon Lagoon (a threat to Wet 'N' Wild), and Pleasure Island (a threat to Church Street Station in downtown Orlando), the Disney-MGM Studios park was particularly galling for Universal [Studios]" (144).

47. Although the language of sacred icons comes rather easily in discussing Epcot, we take as our source an anonymous but very insightful child whom we overheard remarking to his parents prior to one of the Future World presentations: "It's just like church."

48. Although critics and commentators go to the theme parks with their critical compasses fully functional, they too report the parks' effects on them personally. Dunn says of his visit to Disney-MGM Studios, "The longer I stayed on Hollywood Boulevard, the more an atmosphere of cinematic unreality flooded over me" (39). And Fjellman reports that "It always takes me a few days after I return home from WDW to get used to opening my own doors again. As I often get bruised once or twice before I readjust, I have the opportunity to get mad at a world that makes me do things for myself" (456n). (Also see The Project on Disney, especially 106–109.)

49. Mechling and Mechling make the equation of commodity and trophy: "[T]he notion of subjecting oneself to the DANGER of these rides and *surviving* them is an important clue to [their] meaning. . . . Moreover, the survivor returns not simply to safety but to *reward* as well. The safe zones are filled with *consumer goods* . . . " ("Sale," 407).

50. Although the visitors complex at KSC predated WDW, it has been expanded and updated several times. That it continues to add syntactic features resembling WDW's has been evident to us even over the course of our three visits. The topiary, play areas, and outdoor photo spots were all added, for example, between the times of our second and third visits.

51. Mila stands for Merritt Island Launch Area (Tomasso, Interview). Its menu and decor are reminiscent of the early 1960s, the heyday of the U.S. space program.

52. They are not Disney characters. Those we saw portrayed Snoopy and Woodstock in the foreground of a shuttle, with a text reading "Kennedy Space Center Shuttle Command." Although KSCVC does not incorporate Disney's cartoon characters in its products, the connections between WDW and KSCVC run deep, no doubt usually beyond the perceptions of most guests but still helping to construct the experience. NASA's licensed products are sold at WDW (Meguiar, Interview), Disney's space travel films are borrowed from NASA, and Disney sometimes provides entertainment for special events at KSCVC. For example, the Walt Disney World Singers provided the music for the dedication ceremony of the Astronauts Memorial in May 1991. Conversely, astronauts Jim Irwin, Gordon Cooper, and Scott Carpenter were the first riders of Space Mountain at its opening ceremony in January 1975 (see Fjellman, 134–135). During our most recent visit to Florida, *Apollo 11* astronaut Edwin "Buzz" Aldrin appeared for book signings at both KSCVC and Epcot. References to NASA and the space program are everywhere at WDW. In addition to the more obvious cases—footage of shuttle launches and oceanographic photos from space—NASA's cosponsorship of botanical experiments is also marked in Living with the Land and The Land Backstage Tour at Epcot (Figure 1.21). Other relationships between the two sites and people's readings of the connections are described by Haden-Guest, especially 300–305.

53. This habitat is a provisional one, generally in harmony with Mitchell's understanding of landscape "not as an object . . . but as a process by which social and subjective identities are formed." His project is to ask "not just what landscape 'is' or 'means' but what it does, how it works as a cultural practice" (1). But Clifford's notion of a contemporary ethnographic culture as a traveling one, as distinct from a situated one, is also vital to what we have in mind.

54. As Jonathan Smith suggests, it is "the question of how the visible landscape might structure our regard of elements in that landscape" (82).

55. Warren strengthens our case for reading the theme park journey as the "home society" of the Astronauts Memorial. She argues that "landscapes of leisure" (e.g., theme parks) "were once treated as separate, self-contained places within which one could escape from the rigours of daily life now are seen as not so much segregated sites but modes of representation that permeate virtually all landscapes and hence are inseparable from our daily lives" (173).

56. Collins suggests provocatively that technology is itself a character in the television series *Star Trek: The Next Generation* (141). The same seems to be true at KSCVC, but in perhaps an intensified way. As Blair and Michel point out, there are almost no references to humans at all at KSCVC: "Here the techno-mechanisms of space travel . . . supersede, indeed efface, the labor and accomplishments of the makers and users of the mechanisms."

57. We do not mean to imply that the environmental theme is *un*important at WDW. Discovery Island, is a member of the American Association of Parks and Aquariums, and as Fjellman points out (345), it is a species manager for a number of categories of waterfowl. Nonetheless, Disney's coding of the natural environment is at best ambivalent. As Alexander Wilson suggests, the nature evoked at Walt Disney World "is always a nature that has been worked and transformed; subsumed by the doctrine of progress" (180). (Also see Mechling and Mechling, "Sale," 410.)

58. Of course, visitors can make the effort to seek out additional information, for example, from the interactive programs that offer presentations about years in the space program. The 1986 program, for example, certainly could not avoid mention of the *Challenger*, since the January accident effectively forestalled the possibility of any "highlights" for that year. But the program symbolically transmutes the accident into another heroic NASA achievement—the addition of numerous and rigorous new safety features and checks for shuttle launches.

59. Visitors to KSCVC from WDW may already have been explicitly encouraged to view space program activity as just one more Disney fantasy. At SuperStar Television in Disney-MGM Studios, an audience volunteer holds up Neil Armstrong's cue card for his famous line when he made the first moon walk (see Dunn, 44). This attraction, like most in WDW, blurs any distinction between reality and cinematic fiction.

60. It seems worth noting one other difference in degree at this point between KSCVC and WDW. Visitor movements are more tightly controlled and monitored at WDW. If the Astronauts Memorial were at WDW (however unlikely that scenario), visitors would be practically forced to see it, they would gaze on it for precisely the length of time the Imagineers thought appropriate, and they would be told what to think about it—all in friendly, congenial ways, of course.

61. Adams concurs, suggesting that "The possibility of death . . . could never be allowed to intrude on Disney's 'perfect,' carefree world" (151).

62. That reproduced conversation is an approximation of the actual conversation we had on our first trip from California to Florida. We do not mean to imply that it is an exact recording of what we said to each other.

63. Radway's work on romance novels and Jenkins's on fan communities come immediately to mind as cases of cultural studies work that fixes its attention on audience, certainly to a far greater extent than we do here.

64. See Nothstine, Blair, and Copeland, 4. To argue for the value of a professional critic's reading is not necessarily elitist, although it is sometimes understood as such. In our view, it is the professional critic's job to be an "odd viewer." Typically, if not always, our (often public) university educations and positions grant us the luxuries of (1) time for attention and reflection necessary for extended critique and (2) a sanctioned voice that allows us to speak and write about those things we have attended to and reflected about. Such a position becomes elitist, for example, if professional critics' responses to rhetorical practices are the *only* ones that are granted legitimacy, or if they are taken to be self-evidently *more* legitimate than the responses of other audiences.

65. We are not by any means suggesting that rhetorical study should always or nec-

essarily focus on issues of reception, nor would we enjoy being held to such a stricture ourselves. However, we believe that rhetorical study would benefit by looking to cultural studies on this score and by working harder to theorize and analyze reception and social/cultural effects of discourse.

66. Giroux not only points to the race and gender emphases in cultural studies, but adds youth—an age-marked culture—as well (16). Also see Nelson, Treichler, and Grossberg, 12.

67. Such considerations of intertextualization are consistent with other work in cultural studies, for example, Bennett and Woollacott. Also see Barthes, "Work."

68. Perhaps we could even go so far as to say that rhetoric's fascination with theory, as distinct from what Rosteck notes as cultural studies' resistance to grand theory ("Cultural Studies," 396), has contributed to its lack of commitment to the concrete, particular, and political. The difference in emphasis on theory between rhetoric and cultural studies certainly is lodged in rhetoric's goal for its criticism to construct or refine theory (Blair), as opposed to cultural studies' goal in its critical practice to be "responsible to its situation" (Nelson, Treichler, and Grossberg, 6). Largely as a result of appropriations of cultural studies by some rhetoricians, there are some exceptions to this opposition. See, for example, Brummett, "How to Propose"; Brummett, *Rhetoric*, especially 78–88; McGee, "Text"; and Solomon, "Things."

69. Fiske makes the point quite clearly: "Discourse can never be abstracted from the conditions of its production and circulation. . . . The most significant relations of any piece of discourse are to the social conditions of its use, not to the signifying system in general, and its analysis exemplifies not an instance of that system in practice, but its function in deploying power within those conditions" (*Media*, 3).

70. What we have in mind here partakes of both the Gramscian notion of hegemony, which thematizes consent, and the Althusserian concept of interpellation, or production of an ideological subject. For an exceptionally clear articulation of both, see Eagleton (*Ideology*, 112–121; 149–157). Jonathan Smith suggests even more exactly what we have in mind when he argues that readers of a landscape "are offered opportunities to act and to have their act defined. It may be a technical goal of any landscape to control this response, and to limit interpretive play. . . . [T]he landscape defines our actions in two ways: it tells us what we can do and what we may or ought to do" (89).

71. Morse describes the "fiction effect" as arising from a matrix of experience formed by shopping malls, freeways, and television. Since she makes occasional comments about theme parks as well, we think it appropriate to consider the vacation journey as an additional, if less everyday, addition to the matrix she identifies.

72. See Fiske, "Cultural Studies"; Grossberg, Nelson, and Treichler, 4; and deCerteau.

TWO

CATCHING THE THIRD WAVE
The Dialectic of Rhetoric and Technology

James Arnt Aune

Prolog 2018

3Jane Wichelns is awakened by the soft vibration of the computer chip implanted behind her left ear. To the accompaniment of Satie's Gymnopédies a rather soothing voice quietly whispers: "It's 700 hours, 17 November 2018. Point your right index finger to the menu on your telescreen to select further options." 3Jane points to the small screen on the side wall of her bedroom and orders a pot of freshly ground Monsooned Malabar coffee to begin brewing in the kitchen. She then clicks on her daily schedule:

> 800: Videoconference with the Dean; click here for a list of rhetorical options
>
> 900–1200: Finish SCA paper, "The Most Significant Passage in 'The Rhetorical Situation' "; send knowbot to check the Net for any new references since yesterday
>
> 1200–1300: Videoconference with students in Argumentation class, Alpha C Community College
>
> 1300–1430: Lecture on visual tropes, Interplanetary Business Machines Executive Collective
>
> 1430: Pack for SCA convention in Chicago; click here for current weather information
>
> 1500: Leave for airport, NW Flight #486; click here to order your meals, movie, and companion

We now discreetly leave 3Jane to her morning rituals.[1]

There is no rhetorical mode so powerful or so fallible as prophecy. 3Jane may be waking to a joyous technoutopia or to a nightmarishly nomadic life as an overworked adjunct professor. 3Jane may work in a truly democratic university-without-walls or may herself be a cyborg designed to serve a power elite she never sees face to face.

Projecting the future has become a growth industry, both inside and outside of academia. Desire and anxiety about new communication technologies circulate in a steady flow from popular culture to government to big business to the university. Not coincidentally, the new world information order is an ideal site for the very different research strategies of rhetoric and cultural studies to meet. Each of these has its own concomitant skills and incapacities. The rhetorical tradition, adept at analyzing political strategy, has been less skilled in mapping the trajectories of popular desire, while the cultural studies tradition, rightly drawing attention to issues of gender, performance, and desire in popular media, has been less skilled in analyzing conventional political discourse.

This essay is an attempt at combining the research strategies of the two traditions, at observing what Stephen Greenblatt calls the "circulation of social energy" (6) among literary, popular, academic, and political discourse about the cultural impact of the new technologies of communication.

Greenblatt's new historicist cultural poetics rejects a focus on single texts isolated from contemporary social practices and proposes instead that we ask "how collective beliefs and experiences [are] shaped, moved from one medium to another, concentrated in manageable aesthetic form, offered for consumption" (5). He further attempts to determine how pleasure, interest, and anxiety—"social energy"—circulate among different cultural zones in a particular time period.

Tracing the circulation of this social energy—"power, charisma, sexual excitement, collective dreams, wonder, desire, anxiety, religious awe, free-floating intensities of experience" (Greenblatt, 19)—provides important insights into the nature of *power-as-performance*, which I take to be the chief point of intersection between traditional rhetorical studies and the newer vocabularies of cultural studies. Yet, what both traditional rhetorical studies and cultural studies have tended to neglect is the way in which "power" is in the last instance *class* power. As Fredric Jameson tirelessly reminds his postmodern academic audience, all human cultural expressions are simultaneously utopian yearnings and attempts to manage the intolerable contradictions of a world in which, as always, "the underside of culture is blood, torture, death, and terror" (*Postmodernism*, 5).

Following Greenblatt and Jameson, I try to practice a new sort of rhetorical-cultural analysis in which I "transcode" differing forms of cultural and political discourse (Jameson, *Political Unconscious*, 40). I examine how particular rhetorical forms (composed of stock arguments and narratives) interact with audience desire and anxiety in particular historical conjunctures. The political thrust of such analysis involves locating key points of strain or contradiction in rhetorical arguments and narratives as they try to map historical change. Locating contradictions is an essential tool for advocates seeking ways to respond to a dominant discourse.

I will proceed in this essay to analyze the more conventional political discourse of Alvin Toffler, George Gilder, and Newt Gingrich and compare it to the literary discourse of the cyberpunk novelists William Gibson and Bruce Sterling and the avant-garde communication scholar Roseanne Allucquère Stone.

In this case, the dominant discourse that circulates with surprising frequency among the various texts I examine is a libertarian ideological one that is at the same time a discourse of inevitability. The simultaneous celebration and denial of human agency in the face of "the Third Wave" is a theme shared by figures who would normally be viewed as occupying different sides in what has come to be called "the Culture War." This shared ideological theme, I will argue, is the effort to cope with social anxieties about the reconstitution of class boundaries in the late-twentieth-century industrialized world.

We thus have an opportunity, under the sign of an "articulated" rhetorical-cultural studies, to examine the interplay of division and mediation as political strategists and cultural workers attempt to name and tell stories about "When It All Changed"—the alleged transition to an "information" economy. As we shall see, the very hypertrophy of "information" as a governing norm for ideal communication seems to generate anxiety about the nature and uses of the "body."

PART I: THE STRATEGIES OF CYBER-REPUBLICANS

While academic postmodernists were proclaiming the death of master narratives and neo-Marxists were arguing for a "Marxism without guarantees," the most influential theorists of the computer revolution ironically were reinventing the dialectical materialist view of history.

Shortly after the conservative Republican victory of 1994, Ted Turner's Turner Publishing issued a short book by Alvin and Heidi Toffler, with a foreword by Newt Gingrich, that summarized their three-stage theory of history (*Creating a New Civilization*). The Tofflers believe that we are experiencing a "system crisis," as the United States moves from a Second Wave industrial economy to a Third Wave information economy. As they see it, the "master conflict" of the industrial economy was the battle between agrarian interests defending the First Wave and industrial-commercial advocates of the Second Wave (a battle represented clearly by the American Civil War). The new master conflict will be between those (like Pat Buchanan on the right and the AFL-CIO on the left) who resist the transition to a global information economy and those who understand how the new system will work.

The Third Wave is marked by the following changes:

1. Knowledge becomes the chief factor in production.
2. Work, politics, and entertainment become less centralized, meaning that large organizations are doomed.
3. Work will become more interesting and flexible.
4. Bureaucratic uniformity will be replaced by sophisticated tools of system integration and information management.

These changes will require significant economic investments and political change. For the Tofflers, the United States, for example, should take the lead in developing the international information infrastructure. Further, alternative political institutions based on the values of minority power, semidirect democracy, and decision division will facilitate peaceful transition to a Third Wave civilization.

The Tofflers lament, however, that our political imagination lags behind our technological imagination. Traditional Republicans, as the Tofflers put it, are still dreaming of "Ozzie and Harriet," while traditional Democrats are still dreaming of "River Rouge" (the giant auto plant in Detroit) (77).

George Gilder, the author of *Sexual Suicide* and *Wealth and Poverty*, two very influential books among conservatives, takes a slightly different slant on the Third Wave in his *Life after Television*. While, like the Tofflers, Gilder contends that large organizations are in jeopardy, he also asserts that police states simply cannot work after computerization, since computers "increase the powers of the people far quicker than the powers of surveillance" (61). Gilder picks up the theme of cultural politics that entered mainstream Republican rhetoric after Dan Quayle's "Murphy Brown" speech of 1992 and asserts that "the most dangerous threat to the U.S. economy and society is the breakdown of our cultural institutions" (56).

What will cure this breakdown? In Gilder's view it will be the death of television (caused by what media analysts call the "convergence of modes") and the accompanying restoration of the home and family as the center of society. Very soon, radio, TV, the Internet, as well as books and newspapers will enter the home on a single cable (with the telephone becoming wireless). Then, no longer will a centralized media apparatus dictate tastes and values to a mass audience.

Gilder invites his audience to imagine creating "a school in your home that offers the nation's best teachers imparting the moral, cultural, and religious values you cherish" (55). Unlike the Tofflers, who are sympathetic to single-parent and gay families, Gilder argues that "The PC is a supply-side investment in the coming restoration of the home to a central role in the productive dynamics of capitalism, and the transformation of capitalism into a healing force in the present crisis of home and family, culture and community" (215). In Gilder's view the computer makes possible both telecommuting and home schooling, and will no doubt restore a traditional gender-based division of labor as well.

The Toffler historical dialectic and the Gilder concern for traditional values are merged in an important speech delivered by Newt Gingrich shortly after the 1994 elections. The speech, originally given to the Washington Research Group, has been widely circulated on the Internet by *Washington Weekly,* which appends the following editorial comment:

> The following speech has been largely ignored by the media. You may find it a compelling vision for America's future. It may become a historic speech, setting a new course. Bypass the media by distributing the speech widely, and let an informed people decide. (1)

This call to bypass "the media" is a recurring theme in libertarian rhetoric about the Internet: one can now "pull" from many sources rather than having centralized media "push" information to passive audiences (Negroponte, 84).

In Gingrich's speech he relies heavily on his credentials as an academic historian to tell a story about American civilization. Gingrich first invokes what rhetoricians call *kairos,* a sense of speaking at the "right time," in this case on Armistice/Veterans Day. This day, Gingrich begins, reminds us of the political failures of the Great War, which led to "Nazism and the Soviet Empire, the Gulag and Auschwitz," as well as of the sacrifice of "those who believed enough in freedom to have died for it."

The memory of wartime sacrifice also is appropriate, Gingrich says, because we are at another turning point in history comparable to World War I. Our very civilization is at stake:

> I am a history teacher by background, and I would assert and defend on any campus in this country that it is impossible to maintain civilization with twelve-year-olds having babies, with fifteen-year-olds killing each other, with seventeen-year-olds dying of AIDS, and with eighteen-year-olds ending up with diplomas they can't even read. And that what is at issue is literally not Republican or Democrat or Liberal or Conservative, but the question of whether or not our civilization will survive. (1)

Gingrich then notes the surprise felt both by the Democrats and "the Washington elite" at the Republican victory, and compares it to the surprise felt by the Germans at D-day.

Gingrich, like the Tofflers and Gilder, next speaks within a rhetorical form that has exploded in popularity in recent years: the management guide, an offshoot of the traditional advice manuals often associated with the rhetorical tradition. Gingrich first says that he follows the planning model used by Eisenhower, Marshall, and Roosevelt during World War II, "the most complex large human activity ever undertaken."

> This planning model consisted of a hierarchy of four layers: the top of it was vision, and after you understood your vision of what you are doing you design strategies, and once you had your vision and strategies square, you designed projects which were the building blocks of your strategies, and inside the context of those projects, you delegated dramatically, an entrepeneurial model in which a project was a definable, delegatable achievement. . . . At the bottom of the model is tactics, what you do every day. (2)

Gingrich then combines this planning model with a leadership model ("listen, learn, help, and lead") and explains how the "Washington elite" cannot understand the 1994 Republican revolution, because they have ceased to listen to the people.

Somewhat abruptly, Gingrich then characterizes himself as a "conservative futurist," something that "obviously doesn't fit anybody's current word processor." His canon of recommended works on planning and leadership are the Tofflers' works, Peter Drucker's "Effective Executive," Deming's "Concepts of Quality," the *Federalist Papers,* and de Tocqueville's *Democracy in America.*

Gingrich's study of these works has led him to conclude that there are five large changes "we have to go through" in order to get to the twenty-first century.

First, "we have to accelerate the transition from a Second Wave mechanical bureaucratic society to a Third Wave information society." Gingrich contrasts the speed and ease of using an ATM card with the process of communicating with the federal government. He proposes that government must get up to date with information systems and help to develop distance medicine, distance learning, and distance work, all of which "could revolutionize the quality of life in rural America." Government must provide all documents of the government on the Internet so that the ordinary citizen has the same access to them that "the highest paid Washington lobbyist" does.

Second, we have "to recognize the objective reality of world market, to realize that we create American jobs through world sales, and to make a conscious national decision that we want to have the highest value-added jobs on the planet with the greatest productivity, so you can have the highest take-home pay and range of choices in lifestyles." Such a world market requires rethinking our current view of "litigation, taxation, regulation, welfare, education, the very structure of government, the structure of health."

An important step in coming to terms with the world market is "that every child in America should be required to do at least two hours of homework every night," not by government, but as the result of "a level of civic responsibility we are not used to."

Third, "we have to replace the welfare state with the opportunity society," eliminating the culture of poverty created by the Great Society.

Fourth, we have to reassert "the deeper, underlying cultural meanings of being American," and say to "the counter-culture: 'nice try, you failed, you're wrong.' "

Fifth, Americans have to exercise more individual and civic responsibility in order to make sure that downsizing the federal government will work. Gingrich here cites the authority of the Brown University historian Gordon S. Wood to demonstrate that Jefferson's great insight was "that you had to have limited but effective government in order to liberate people to engage in civic responsibility" (4–6).

The rhetorical structure of Gingrich's address thus includes a mythic narrative of a transition from feudalism to industrial capitalism to information-based capitalism, a stock set of characters—Washington elites, counterculture types, pregnant teens, wise military and business leaders, the Founding Fathers, and the ideographs of "government," "civic responsibility," "happiness," and "information."

Since Gorgias, rhetoricians have taught that persuasion is accomplished when audiences hear messages at the right time and are enabled to forget about the contradictory aspects of political practice. The rhetorician promotes an illusion of harmony until the rhetorical situation matures and dies; some illusions persist and become recognizable "ideologies," or what Pocock and others (e.g., Fallon) call "political languages." As McGee has taught us, the power and vulnerability of a given rhetorical practice often can be located in the peculiarly nonreferential characteristics of ideographs.

The contradictions in Gingrich's rhetoric are not difficult to locate: How can one promote civic responsibility while proclaiming that government is evil? How can one promote the work ethic while maintaining that consumption and "lifestyle choice" represent happiness? How can one promote individual liberty while constrained by world-historical shifts in the mode of production? How can we make government more local without a corresponding shift in business and financial organizations? How can we proclaim American exceptionalism while committing ourselves to a global economy and the rule of multinational corporations? How can we commit ourselves to unlimited access to "information" when information includes words and images that are destructive of civic responsibility?

It is not surprising, really, that the Gingrich coalition of 1994 should have fallen apart so swiftly, since the forces concerned with restoration of family, local government, and traditional values inevitably conflict with forces committed to a world market, unlimited access to information, and increased consumption. As Jefferson and de Tocqueville themselves recognized, there is an inherent tension between civic virtue and the demands of commerce, a tension that their "biggest fan," Professor Gingrich, seems to have forgotten.

The Republicans came to power in 1994 largely by redefining popular economic anxiety as created by excessive government control and by decline in traditional values; as economic anxiety declined and as President Clinton skillfully stole Republican symbols, the Republican redefinition seemed incoherent, at best, or mean and backward-looking, at worst.

Perhaps most important, Gingrich's speech ignores the body-based, so-called social issues that had energized participation by the Christian Right in the 1994 election. When pressed on issues such as abortion and homosexuality, at least among elite audiences, Gingrich typically echoes the argument of his friends the Tofflers, namely, that the Third Wave will radically restructure family life, sexual attitudes, and personal morality (Toffler and Toffler, 9, 25). The freedom of the unattached self in the global marketplace overrides traditional moral concerns, as Gingrich's opposition to the Communications Decency Act demonstrates.

The old split between traditionalists and libertarians in the Republican Party, temporarily healed by Ronald Reagan's powerful ethos, has reopened, as Reagan's heirs compete for legitimacy (see Aune, *Rhetoric and Marxism*, 135–142). The anxious concern for personal morality and religious transcendence, which tends to increase in times of rapid economic change, is reflected in popular and journalistic anxiety about pornography on the Internet (Peter H. Lewis, "New Concerns"). It is an anxiety easily channeled against economic elites as well as against so-called cultural elites, as the success of Patrick Buchanan with some traditional Democratic constituencies suggests. Under pressure, cyber-Republicans like Gingrich propose to salve popular anxiety with appeals to the historical dialectic and "the invisible hand of the market." Such appeals, however, are ideally better suited to audiences of intellectuals than to mass audiences.

PART II: ARISTOCRATS SLUMMING
IN THE CYBERCULTURE

Around the time that Professor Gingrich was lecturing his comrades, the counterculture he demonized in those lectures was discovering the Internet as well. It was as if poststructuralist French theorists—with their arguments about the priority of writing over speech, the body-without-organs, the decentered subject, the simulacrum, the Panopticon, and the floating signifier—had called a whole material infrastructure into being that verified their most far-out theories.

The personal computer and Internet revolution also proved to be a cure for a certain exhaustion in the academic practice of the humanities. Soon scholars were designing their own Web pages, literary research centers were using hypertext to integrate the study of text production with traditional literacy criticism, and technologues and computer geeks of all sorts were following the pronouncements of Baudrillard, Foucault, and Derrida. After 1994, job announcements in "computer-mediated communication" or "new technologies" began to appear. Students who for years had avoided library research found it easier to locate and read rhetorical documents on the Web. I, like many of my colleagues, suddenly found it easier to "keep in touch" via e-mail, and my sense of community often extended further in cyberspace than within my own academic institution. I also spent countless hours on IRC (Internet Relay Chat) and MUDs (Multiple User Dimensions or Dungeons) communicating with others (largely undergraduates, it seemed) and trying on various identities (the precise details of which had best be left to my therapist).

Shortly after my introduction to e-mail, USENET, and later MUDs, I felt as if the texture of my everyday life had changed and that all the persons, groups, and institutions around me were struggling to make sense of a future that had somehow arrived ahead of schedule. For Raymond Williams, one of the tasks of cultural studies is to understand "a felt sense of the quality of life at a particular place and time: a sense of the ways in which the particular activities combined into a way of thinking and living"—what Williams called a "structure of feeling" (*Long Revolution*, 48). Williams's concept is helpful in making sense of the rhetorical and literary representations of the Third Wave.

Williams first develops the concept of "structure of feeling" in an analysis of the communicative forms and narratives of 1840s England. According to Williams, by the 1840s the dominant social character included

> The belief in the value of work, and this is seen in relation to individual effort, with a strong attachment to success gained in these terms. A class society is assumed, but social position is increasingly defined by actual

status rather than by birth. The poor are seen as the victims of their own failings, and it is strongly held that the best among them will climb out of their class. A punitive Poor Law is necessary in order to stimulate effort. . . . Thrift, sobriety, and piety are the principal virtues, and the family is their central institution. The sanctity of marriage is absolute, and adultery and fornication are unpardonable. (*Long Revolution*, 61)

These views make up the "dominant social character" of the dominant group of the time: the industrial and commercial middle class. Williams points out, however, that there was also a residual aristocratic social character that believed "birth mattered more than money; that work was not the sole social value and that civilization involved play; that sobriety and chastity, at least in young men, were not cardinal virtues but might even be a sign of meanness and dullness" (*Long Revolution*, 61–62).

It is interesting that many of the major reforms of the period were accomplished by Disraeli's successful rhetorical strategy of using aristocratic ideals to temper middle-class ideals. Class anxiety was often coded in the literature of the period, as Williams writes, as "a pervasive atmosphere of instability and debt," with characters being rescued by an unexpected legacy or by emigration (*Long Revolution*, 65).

The structure of feeling of the late 1980s and 1990s in academia consists of another sort of anxiety: a sense that knowledge has in fact become capital, but that knowledge workers remain doomed to enjoy the fruits of their knowledge in "psychic" rather than real income. This anxiety has resulted in a valorization of the "body" as a theme in cultural and literary analysis, and in a turn toward the popular as a revenge against the holders of capital.

Good representatives of this structure of feeling are the works of Roseanne Allucquère Stone, Bruce Sterling, and William Gibson, which unite an ecstatic sense of language and performance, a sense of body-anxiety and sexual transgression, and a critique of corporate capitalism that ends in a defense of radical libertarianism.

The genre of what came to be known as "cyberpunk" fiction began with the 1981 publication of William Gibson's *Neuromancer*, a novel that coined the term "cyberspace," and contributed a number of other terms that recur in the discourse of cyber-culture, including "jacking in" and "the meat" (to refer to the body).

Cyberpunk had its own literary precursors, notably William S. Burroughs (whose descriptions of "the Interzone" in *Naked Lunch* bear an uncanny resemblance to some aspects of the Internet); Thomas Pynchon, with his black-comedic blending of high science and low popular culture; and Samuel R. Delany, whose poststructuralist science fiction, notably in *Flight from Neveryon,* is both intellectually more complex and better science fiction than any work of the cyberpunks.

What was distinctive about cyberpunk, however, was its ability to continue the modernist project of representing the city in crisis. Gibson's Sprawl is as much a depiction of present-day Houston or Los Angeles as it is of a future dystopia: a city of rampant crime, drug use, medical experimentation, governmental collapse, and corporate control. Unlike the modernist hero of hard-boiled fiction—say Sam Spade or Marlowe—Gibson's heroes possess no fundamental moral code that can serve as a basis for opposition to the existing order. Plot movement takes the form of a quest, but it is a quest driven more by addiction to information—or, better, to the act of being "jacked-in" to acquire information—than by a quest for truth.

Later versions of cyberpunk seem to try to address the problem of human agency that dogs the earlier novels. Neal Stephenson, for example, in *Snow Crash* and *The Diamond Age*, creates plucky, street-smart young women who learn to use technology effectively and seem to possess a Marlowe-like moral code. Still, as David Brande has noted, the achievement of cyberpunk in general lies in its symbiotic or "parasitic" relationship to the post-Fordist, globalized capitalist economy (99).

But what of the general political stance of cyberculture and its inhabitants? Gibson and Sterling's coauthored novel *The Difference Engine* seems to provide an ideological underpinning for the Third Wave that rests on a return to nineteenth-century Radicalism. Gibson and Sterling invite us to imagine Victorian England as it might have developed had Charles Babbage's plan for a "Difference Engine," or computer, been realized. The Difference Engine makes possible immense economic productivity, but at the cost of increased air pollution ("the Stink") and extensive invasion of privacy. The ideological basis of this society is "Radicalism," in which knowledge alone serves as the basis of social mobility and entry into the aristocracy. The Radical Lords (successful scientists and engineers) are also allied with the working class, which is organized into guildlike unions.

Although at one level *The Difference Engine* reads like a dystopia, Gibson and Sterling have clearly captured the political utopian fantasies of the professional-computing class. The novel, like other cultural representations of new communication technology, serves an invaluable cognitive function. The reason why popular narratives should be studied side by side with conventional political rhetoric is, as Fredric Jameson writes, following Althusser, that ideologies inevitably take the form of narratives that invent a place for the subject in history, and that artistically interesting or successful narratives inevitably bring ideological contradictions to the surface:

> What art makes us *see*, and therefore gives us in the form of "*seeing*," "*perceiving*," and "*feeling*" (which is not a form of *knowing*), is the ideology from which it is born, in which it bathes, from which it detaches

itself as art, and to which it alludes. (Althusser, quoted in Jameson *Wyndham Lewis,* 21)

The core political narrative being revised in *The Difference Engine* is Disraeli's Victorian novel *Sybil, or The Two Nations* (from which several of the characters' names are derived), which proposed an alliance between the aristocracy and the working class to solve the political problems of England (Sussman). The negative elements of the new Victorian England notwithstanding, the implied reader of *The Difference Engine,* like the implied reader of Gibson's Sprawl trilogy or Sterling's *Islands in the Net,* is one who possesses knowledge or computer expertise as his only capital and feels caught between the older ruling class and the working class into which he fears he may fall.

A recurring theme in political, journalistic, and fictional representations of the Third Wave is a heightened awareness of the importance of play. What the older working class, like the backward-looking parts of the capitalist class, do not understand is that *work* and *play,* rather than being the antinomies they are in the old capitalist work ethic, have now been brought together by the new technologies.

My own fieldwork for the past three years among participants in Internet Relay Chat groups as well as various MUDs confirms the observation that work and play appear to constitute a continuum for the digerati. Fascination with role-playing games such as Dungeons and Dragons, with the novels of Anne Rice, and interest in sex-magick, wicca, sadomasochism, and gender-bending are common cultural characteristics of avid Internet users.[2]

Roseanne Allucquère Stone, a transgendered former audio engineer for Jimi Hendrix and now professor and director of the Interactive Multimedia Laboratory at the University of Texas at Austin, most accurately reflects the cultural sensibility of the participants I have observed over the past three years. Stone's *The War of Desire and Technology at the Close of the Mechanical Age* (1995) emphasizes the element of play in human-computer interaction, the role of the computer as an arena of social experience rather than a "medium" or "tool." Stone is absorbed with the fantasy of escaping the body and reinventing one's identity—in the form of the cyborg or the vampire—and she places at the center of her cultural criticism the social behavior on the Internet that has occasioned so much puzzlement, namely, the chat rooms, Internet relay chat, and MUDs and MUSHs that have occasioned anxious discussions of computer addiction by college administrators.

Stone artfully weaves together chapters on multiple-personality disorder, the oft-told tale of the cross-dressing psychiatrist on CompuServe, phone sex, the Vampire Lestat, and corporate crisis at Atari. The recurring image in her writing is boundary-crossing.

> We are no longer unproblematically secure within the nest of our location technologies, whose function for us (as opposed to for our political apparatus) is to constantly reassure us that we are without question ourselves, singular, bounded, conscious, rational; the end product of hundreds of years of societal evolution in complex dialogue with technology as Other and with gender as an othering machine. (182)

Stone urges us to go beyond the disruption of current body definitions by androgyny and cross-dressing. In a performance entitled "What Vampires Know: Transsubjection and Transgender in Cyberspace" she holds up the image of Fakir Musafar hanging by ropes through slits in his pectorals as having more potential for disrupting our gender structures.

The sadistic hunger of the Vampire Lestat gives him a perspective on human bodies that others lack:

> He sees people trapped, stuck in their particular gender positions, in their particular subjectivities, not able to make the jump to seeing subject position as a boat that's momentarily at anchor, but that can actually move through a sea of possible subject positions. The vampire would like to make more of that visible. He talks about it in terms of the Dark Gift that turns one into a vampire. (9–10)

Stone is concerned that "power is most powerful when it's invisible, and in the new social spaces of communication technology is as yet quite invisible" ("Vampires," 11). The radicalism of the privileged spectator position of the Vampire Lestat and the practices of sexual role-playing and sadomasochism lies in their willingness to make the process of power exchange visible rather than invisible. It is one thing if people play at dominance and submission games as consenting adults, with clearly defined rules and "safewords," but quite another when the participants are, say, students at the Citadel. Gender-bending, consensual sadomasochism, and role-playing are, in Stone's terms, political acts because they make structures of power visible.

Now all of this is fine as far as it goes. Transgender liberation may be one of the last steps in the fulfillment of the liberal project: the removal of all artificial barriers to participation in the public world. On the other hand, the seemingly boundless variety of "lifestyle choices" and the seemingly boundless plasticity of the human body itself are but variations on the traditional libertarian capitalist theme of the individual being left free to maximize utility in any way that does not infringe on other individuals' freedom. The message of the transgendered cultural radical Sandy Stone is essentially the same as that of the conservative economists Milton Friedman and Deirdre McCloskey: liberty means unlimited self-expression in rhetoric and other forms of cultural performance. The new technologies liberate the self, not the community.

And in this respect, at least, Newt Gingrich and the cyberpunk cultural radicals strangely share the same political imaginary: detached from the production of anything real, detached from any location in traditional communities or cultural practices (other than occasional nods to the Framers), the liberated subject is free to commune with like-minded subjects on a Net that exists in "real time," but not in space. And if you don't like what you see rolling across your screen, you can always log off, and then log on with a new identity.

While the cyber-Republicans and the cultural radicals have thought that they are discovering the new country of the Third Wave, they have instead reinvented the mythology of the frontier, where unlimited extension in space is the basis of the freedom to invent oneself. That such freedom should be the cause of tremendous anxiety among rust-belt workers, inner-city youth, or newly divorced mothers is but a sign of their failure of imagination, curable with distribution of free laptops or subscriptions to *Wired*.

As Christopher Lasch, whose untimely death came just as the ideology of the Third Wave was consolidating its successes, wrote in his last work, *The Revolt of the Elites and the Betrayal of Democracy*:

> The thinking classes . . . live in a world of abstractions and images, a simulated world that consists of computerized models of reality— "hyperreality," as it has been called—as distinguished from the palpable, immediate, physical reality inhabited by ordinary men and women. Their belief in the "social construction reality"—the central dogma of postmodernist thought—reflects the experience of living in an artificial environment from which everything that resists human control . . . has been rigorously excluded. (20)

But the reinvention of the Three-Stage Dialectical Theory of History (which, to borrow a phrase by Marx, has now occurred twice, the first time as tragedy, the second time as farce), however reassuring to nervous academics, computer professionals, and capitalist entrepreneurs, cannot wish away the Second Wave-like effects of a computerized economy. What of Superfund environmental disaster areas in Silicon Valley (belieing the myth that computing is somehow a "clean" industry), the dramatic increase in repetitive stress disorders and other computer-related illness, the exploitation of Third World women and children in computer manufacturing, the role of computerization in the reduction of middle management, the role of investment in computer equipment as a cause of inflation in educational and business costs (without accompanying increases in productivity), and the coming crash of overinflated technology stocks? For all the energy, desire, and anxiety expended on promoting fantasies of the Third Wave, the real world appears to be founded on the same class divisions, regimentation, and environmental degradation as the Second Wave.

PART III: BRINGING "CLASS" BACK IN

Two features of the Third Wave represent positive opportunities for political organizing and rhetorical mediation of the contradiction between information and body. The first lies in the role of what can only be called "proletarianization" of the professional-managerial class under the impact of computerization of information (Aronowitz and DiFazio). Physicians subjected to "medicine by the numbers" in health maintenance organizations, managers faced with downsizing, and professors threatened with the loss of tenure are now facing the kind of economic restructuring and anxiety that blue-collar workers experienced in the early 1980s.

The second lies in the ideology of "information" itself, which in the "hacker ethic" ("Information wants to be free": Steven Levy, 26–36) serves both to reinforce the individualism of the capitalist order but also in turn to undercut the ability of capitalism to enforce privacy and property rights. Critical social scientists have had trouble understanding what the late Alvin Gouldner meant in *Against Fragmentation* (1985) when he asserted that the "New Class" of humanistic intellectuals and technical intelligentsia represents a potential "universal class" in the way that the working class was for Marxism. The positive moment in the Third Wave lies in its creation of technical opportunities for bridging the "Two Cultures" gap as well as in uniting the "New Class" against the old capitalist elite.

* * *

The rhetoric of cyberculture does not yet know itself as a class-based rhetoric. It has so far proceeded by reaching out to two of the available "languages": the rhetoric of the 1960s counterculture and sexual revolution, with its valorization of the desiring body and its complicity in the commodification of that desiring body by the culture industry; and the rhetoric of liberty and the free market, the capitalist ideology most congenial to the financial wing of the ruling class.

If my analysis in this essay is correct, the avant-garde of the technical intelligentsia and of cultural critics share the following characteristics: first, a rejection of tradition, whether modernist narratives of liberalism, social democracy, or communism, as well as older religious or classical humanist narratives; second, a sense of distance both from the working class and from the capitalist class, and a conviction that "information," whether defined in technical or cultural terms, is the fundamental resource of the new world order rather than land, capital, or labor power; third, a valorization of cultural "play" as a quasiutopian fusion of technology, labor, and the arts; fourth, a sense of blocked ascendancy, in part because of the defunding of higher education and of basic scientific research, and also in part because of the instability of employment in the new technologies sector; and fifth, an absence of any genuine politics, in the sense either of a political party or a social movement (although the environmental movement remains the one site of potential unification of the two halves of the New Class). Even the politician most savvy about the political hopes of the technical intelligentsia, namely Newt Gingrich, has been unable to provide an effective voice for them, given his dependence on the highly volatile Christian Right for part of his power base.

If it is true, then, that a way into reading the cultural narratives about the Internet revolution lies through understanding them as coding class anxieties and utopian fantasies, as well as enacting the contradictions of a split New Class, what political alternatives remain? Is the New Class potentially an agent of liberation, whose essential libertarianism could be turned as easily against Big Business as it has against Big Government, and thus preparing the way for "the withering away of the State" foretold by Marx? Or does the proletarianization of scientists, engineers, and college professors under the constraints of capitalist globalization represent an opportunity for a new alliance with the working class in a new configuration of the traditional socialist or social-democratic project?

The solution to the New Class's thus far limited bid for hegemony is either, like Christopher Lasch, to launch a neopopulist critique of the revolt of the elites, or, like Alvin Gouldner, to help the information class develop a sense of its possibilities as a universal class. In any case, the new technologies of communication represent sites of class struggle as significant as the dark satanic mills of "the Second Wave." May the union of rhetorical and cultural studies be equal to the task of naming the structures of domination and the possibilities of struggle as the Third Wave continues to be born.

Epilog 2018

After the convention, 3Jane Wichelns and her former graduate student 2Phaedrus walk to the El stop named for the Haymarket Square Martyrs, and ride along the South-Side Skyway to the end of the line, passing newly rebuilt steel mills, bright greenhouses full of exotic fruits and vegetables, and the holographic text monuments to Native Son *and* Studs Lonigan.

They stop at a quiet spot by Lake Michigan, where they sit and watch the autumn leaves blow by, listen to the waters of the lake, and quietly read to each other from a real book, translating from Greek into English, the text that begins: "I went down to the Piraeus yesterday with Glaucon, son of Ariston, to pray to the goddess . . . " (Bloom, 3).

NOTES

1. Fans of cyberpunk will note that I have appropriated my heroine's first name, 3Jane, from the Tessier-Ashpool clone-daughter in *Neuromancer*. Fans of cultural studies undoubtedly will not know that I have appropriated her last name from the founder of the American tradition of rhetorical studies, Herbert Wichelns (see Wichelns).

2. In fact, a more thorough analysis of the rhetoric and culture of the professional-computing class would probably need to pay more attention to the work of Rice or Anne McCaffrey than to the cyberpunks, who, in my experience, are seldom read by MUDders and IRCers.

THREE

READING THE CULTURE WARS
Traveling Rhetoric and the Reception of Curricular Reform

Steven Mailloux

In fall 1986 I arrived at Syracuse University as chair of an English department that had already decided to revise its undergraduate curriculum. But the precise content of that revision was far from clear, as evidenced again and again during the year-long series of faculty meetings and the near constant flow of memoranda proposing new curricular models. (Later, the *Chronicle of Higher Education* reported that some called this period at Syracuse "The Memo Wars" [Heller, "New Curriculum"].) Early on I proposed using "rhetoric" (and later "cultural rhetoric") as the organizing term for rethinking the relationships among the different activities organized under the English Department at Syracuse: literary history, critical theory, cultural studies, linguistics, creative writing, English-as-a-second-language, and rhetoric/composition. At the end of my first semester, I sent to the Dean of Arts and Sciences a collection of faculty memos, attempting, I suppose, to give him some sense of what I believed to be an interesting curricular debate going on in our department. The Dean, a philosopher by trade, handed me this and only this response: a Gahan Wilson cartoon from the *New Yorker* that pictures a bailiff swearing in a witness with the words "Do you swear to tell the truth, the whole truth, and nothing but the truth, and not in some sneaky relativistic way?"

I was tempted to interpret the Dean's response as (among other things) a repetition of that age-old conflict between Philosophy and Rhetoric, more exactly a replay of Plato versus the Sophists, with the Philosopher viewing the Sophists as relativists partly because of their preoccupation with rhetoric. This take on the Dean's response made it unintentionally ironic, given the fact that even at this early point the supposedly relativistic theorists in the English department were in the process of rejecting *rhetoric* as the organizing term for the new curriculum. In the end, the department adopted the name "English and Textual Studies" (ETS) for a reconceptualized major organized not by literary historical coverage (Medieval, Renaissance, Modern, etc.) but by clusters of courses categorized by mode of inquiry (historical, theoretical, political).[1]

The Dean's response (or, more accurately, my reading of his response) prefigured the later reception of the ETS major within the so-called Culture Wars. In this essay I will examine that reception to illustrate one way that rhetorical and cultural studies can intersect. In what follows I trace the cultural rhetoric of this interpretive history within local and national contexts through various media in the late 1980s and early 1990s.

Let me set the stage for my rhetorical analysis with two citations from the institutional history of curricular reform at Syracuse. The first statement comes from the Cultural Right. In winter 1986 I visited Syracuse as a candidate for the chair of the English department. During that visit I asked for an open faculty-student forum so that I could hear negative as well as positive views of my (at that point) rather vague proposals for curricular change. I remember giving a little campaign spiel in which I said something like "I hope to lead us into a discussion in which we reconceptualize the relations among literary criticism, cultural studies, critical theory, rhetoric and composition, creative writing, and other parts of traditional English departments." At the end, I asked my audience for responses and called on the first raised hand I saw. This future colleague stood up and declared, "It took fascist tactics to bring someone with your Althusserian ideology here as candidate for chairman," and then sat down. This declaration was a one-sentence foreshadowing of the rhetorical politics to follow when I accepted the offer to join the Syracuse faculty as department chair, a faculty that did in fact reconceptualize English studies in its new ETS major three years later.

The second statement comes almost a decade after the first. It is almost as brief and was written by another Syracuse colleague, but one who might be seen as representing an extreme Cultural Left position: "The analytic banality and political complicity of . . . [rhetorical] analysis can best be seen in the narratives that Steven Mailloux is producing about the institutional changes at Syracuse: social change, in his analyses, is the effect of 'persuasion' not the contradictions of forces of production and social relations of production—trope not class—is the dynamics of history" (Zavarzadeh, "Stupidity," 12, n. 5).

These two statements name the rhetorical parameters of verbal persuasion and ideological coercion that reappear as motifs throughout the narrative to follow. Within the temporal frame of these two declarations, 1986 through 1995, I will situate the Syracuse ETS major and its reception as part of the ongoing debates over the future of the academic humanities. To carry off this rhetorical analysis, I will resort to some shorthand: for example, I have already used two such terms, "Cultural Right" and "Cultural Left." I want to acknowledge from the start that this shorthand terminology is not innocent; it is, in fact, an important part of what I call the *rhetorical politics of naming* that plays such a constitutive role in curricular and other contemporary debates. By "Cultural Right and Left," I simply mean two opposed stances within current educational and disciplinary controversies. One topic within these debates is whether and how to change the structures and practices of humanities schools and their departments. In my rhetorical shorthand, "Cultural Right" names those who tend to resist major changes within the academic humanities; and "Cultural Left" refers to those who promote significant changes. Of course, what counts as "significant" or, for that matter, what counts as "change" is often itself a point of contention, as we will see in the case of Syracuse's reforms.

I should also note in passing that these designations do not coincide exactly with the terms referring to the right and left in national party politics, though there is often an important, at least symbolic, overlap. The two critical statements from my ex-colleagues at Syracuse with which I began are comments from people who were both on the political Left—indeed, at the moment of enunciation they both labeled themselves Marxists, albeit of very different stripes. The first in 1985 was a pre-Althusserian unreconstructed Marxist, while the second continues to be an Althusserian postmodern Marxist.[2] Ah, the politics of naming.

Indeed, these names I'm giving to agents of change and their opponents and the more technical characterizations I'm using for particular positions on both sides are further examples of the rhetorical politics to which I will continually return. For the moment, let me say again that I will be constantly oversimplifying—for example, there are certainly more than two positions within the Culture Wars—but I will try to oversimplify in a complicated way. I want to claim that stereotyping and caricaturing are rhetorical strategies defining the curricular and more general educational debates. They apparently can't be avoided, but perhaps they can be understood rhetorically in more useful ways.

Now let me turn to the reception of the ETS major. Several members of the original group pushing for curriculum reform left Syracuse in the early nineties, but the great advantage of institutionalizing new disciplinary movements is that a program like ETS is less dependent for its survival on specific individual professors and, in the short run, can rely upon institutional inertia to prevent an immediate abandonment of progressive reforms, the same inertia ironically that in other departments helps traditionalists defend outworn curricula. The first full year of ETS course offerings (1990–91) resulted in positive evaluations from students, and the number of department majors, which had grown dramatically during the previous five years, remained stable despite a sudden drop in total university enrollment.[3]

Outside Syracuse University, the diverse reception of ETS was symptomatic of wider cultural debates. The local newspapers published accounts of the curricular changes, ranging from rather straightforward news stories with a slightly positive slant (primarily because department administrators were given the most space in explaining the theory and practice of the ETS major) to polemical opinion pieces condemning the changes for all manner of cultural, intellectual, and political sinning. In summer 1990 when the national discussions, dubbed "the Culture Wars," often focused on reading lists and canon debates, the Syracuse *Post-Standard* published two articles, Fred Pierce's "SU Curriculum Challenges 'Classics' " and James McKeever's "SU Takes a New Look at the Classics." The overall tone of the first can be gleaned from the opening sentences: "Starting this fall, you won't have to read Shakespeare, Chaucer or Milton to be a Syracuse University English major. You might, however, have to dig through tomes on Marxist theory, obscure feminist texts, or even Stephen King's horror novel, *Carrie*" (Pierce, A1). Pierce quotes Charles Watson, the English department's director of undergraduate studies, as claiming that "what you read is not now as important as how you read it."[4] Instead of explaining Watson's comment, Pierce quickly moves on. He gives a bit more space—but not much—to John Crowley, the chair who succeeded me and who saw the curricular reforms through the school and university curriculum committees. But Pierce takes a passing reference by Crowley as an opportunity to connect the Syracuse reforms with the Western Civ controversy at Stanford University, where two years before "similar—but less extensive—curriculum changes" brought forth from then Secretary of Education William Bennett the charge that those changes amounted to " 'an attempt to junk Western civilization.' "[5]

A month later a second *Post-Standard* article on ETS seemed to be a direct reply to worries expressed by the first reporter and the few "dissenters" he identified. Speaking of the majority, James McKeever reports how many Syracuse English faculty "say those who respond to the changes by focusing on the 'fate' of the classics are trivializing the new curriculum" (McKeever, C1). In the new ETS curriculum "literary classics will still be read, but in a different light." They "will be studied not only for their artistic merits, but in the context of the political, cultural, and historical forces that shaped their work—and the work of lesser known writers" (C1). Other faculty quoted in the article note the way that ETS reflected changes in the humanistic disciplines, and they remark on the inevitability of controversy as such intellectual transformations take place.

But the nature of that controversy as represented in the national media had shifted by the following year, with the emphasis in the Culture Wars moving from struggles over the canon to battles over "political correctness." Beginning in late 1990 and continuing through President George Bush's June 1991 commencement address at the University of Michigan, PC-bashing remained a topic of passionate debate within the cultural conversation about the present and future of U.S. higher education. This impassioned rhetoric registered on the local scene in November 1991, when the Syracuse *New Times* ran a piece entitled "The Corruption of SU English: New Curriculum Discourages Independent Thinking," which claimed that multiculturalism had "infected the Syracuse University Hall of Languages," home of the English department. The professors there—"primarily refugees from the frustrated neo-Marxist flower child movement of the 1960s"—were abandoning "the idea of inspiring students to think in favor of telling them what to think." Traditionally, the article explained, "courses were primarily concerned with introducing students to the evolution of literature, the difference between art and rhetoric, and how to speak and write clearly, accurately, even honestly." Now, "a new breed of English professors" was changing all this—presumably with the agenda to ignore literary history, collapse the distinction between art and rhetoric, and encourage unclear, inaccurate, and dishonest (sophistic?) speaking and writing. "Joining the deconstructionists, these dedicated followers of fashion prepared the department for the political correctness . . . that was already stifling independent thought in some of the nation's other colleges."[6]

These local receptions near the university were not unimportant for the wider reception of ETS within the broader Culture Wars. I turn now to that larger context not only to illustrate the rhetorical interconnection of local and national debates over the humanities but also to suggest again that the philosophy/rhetoric and Plato/Sophist oppositions remain significant in understanding contemporary cultural politics.

The more general reception of ETS involved as many understandings and misunderstandings, compliments and insults, careful articulations and silly caricatures as other episodes in the Culture Wars of the last few years. One of my favorite misinterpretations of the Syracuse ETS major came from the ex-chair of a more publicized stronghold of Cultural Leftism, Duke University. In the *Journal of Advanced Composition* the editor entitled one interview "Fish Tales: A Conversation with 'The Contemporary Sophist,' " a title quite appropriate to the story I'm telling. When asked about the future of disciplinary reform in English departments, Stanley Fish commented in this interview: "If the change, when it comes, goes in the same direction that Syracuse has pioneered, then it might be just as accurate to call the department 'the department of rhetoric,' with a new understanding of the old scope of the subject and province of rhetoric" (Olson, "Fish Tales," 256). I would like to think Fish was historically accurate here, but in fact, as I have mentioned, the Syracuse English faculty specifically rejected the name of rhetoric, and the unit most sympathetic to rhetoric as an organizing term, the Writing Program, slowly separated from the English department during and after my tenure as chair.[7]

More historically convincing than Fish's interview comment and my wishful thinking are some remarks by Gerald Graff in *Beyond the Culture Wars: How Teaching the Conflicts Can Revitalize American Education*. Graff interpreted the ETS major as an illustration of his "teaching the conflicts" model. To a certain extent I agree with this assessment, but I should also note that the ETS curriculum contrasts with Graff's model in some important ways. For example, ETS juxtaposes differences (in modes of reading) throughout the curriculum as a whole but does not necessarily thematize those differences in department-wide conferences or in a single course as in Graff's proposals. Thus, ETS emphasizes performing the conflicts in recognizable ways rather than explicitly teaching them, though such teaching might also occur in individual classrooms and advising sessions.[8]

But to learn more about current debates over the academic humanities and about the ETS major's reception within those debates, we need to look at less sympathetic readers of the Syracuse curriculum. In the *New Criterion*, a journal of the Cultural Right if there ever was one, James Tuttleton wrote a review of Graff's *Beyond the Culture Wars* in March 1993. Near the end of the review, Tuttleton takes up Graff's discussion of the ETS major at Syracuse. First, Tuttleton gives a long quotation from Graff's book: Graff writes that "No teacher at Syracuse is *forced* to enter the departmental dialogue. . . . Because the program is organized as a dialogue, any teacher's refusal to enter can be interpreted by students as itself a meaningful choice (not necessarily a discreditable one)" (emphasis in original). Graff then includes and Tuttleton reproduces part of a letter to Graff, in which I said:

> Under the Syracuse plan . . . "a faculty member simply continuing to teach his course in a traditional, isolated way does not undermine the curricular 'conversation' because the curriculum causes his action to be read as a move in the conversation. Since students will be helped to 'read' their courses side-by-side, when they take a traditionalist course they will be able to read it through the grid of the new major." (Graff, 187, quoted in Tuttleton, "Back to the Sixties," 33)

I think my rhetorical point here was simply that the ETS grid of courses helped students to understand the different ways of reading within the department and that the grid allowed them to interrelate these different interpretive rhetorics more easily than they had been able to do in the old curriculum. Be that as it may, Graff followed the quotation from my letter with the realistic comment: "It remains to be seen how well the conception [of a curricular conversation] will translate into practice, but the principle seems to me sound."

Then Tuttleton comments in his turn:

> Sound? It is a recipe for punishing the independent thinker. First, the department boss tells the lone professor that he is not *forced* to collaborate; then his non-cooperation is noted as intentional; then there is the insinuation that his non-cooperation is possibly discreditable; students are then instructed by the cooperators in how to view the traditionalist and his non-cooperative course. I have no doubt about the fate of the lone non-cooperator: first, the salary cut, then discriminatory course assignments, then the impossible schedule—and before and above all else, chairmanly and departmental contempt. (34; emphasis in original)

Tuttleton ends his hypothetical scenario about the probable results of the new Syracuse ETS curriculum: "Since the Department is now a Commune for promulgating left-wing sociological arguments, with a view to politically correct indoctrination, the lone professor can be expected to undergo group 'Re-Education' and 'Rehabilitation' " (34).

There is something of the same anti-PC rhetoric in a 1990 article called "Syracuse University and the Kool-Aid Acid Curriculum," which combines Tuttleton's vehement political censures with its own blunt theoretical objections. Taking all his information about ETS from Pierce's Syracuse *Post-Standard* article, Nino Langiulli attacks what he calls the "Marxist, relativist, and historicist" assumptions of the new curriculum and argues that, given those assumptions, "there could be no basis for preferring Shakespeare, Milton, or Chaucer, to Alice Walker, Roger Rabbit, or, indeed, the Simpsons. The added implication for anyone addicted to the habit of drawing inferences," Langiulli continues, "is that there are no great authors, no issues which are transhistorical or transcultural. Still further, there is no human nature and no civilization; only books and authors captive of their times, only issues which are transient and culture-bound, and, therefore, only the vagaries of race, gender, and ethnicity" (Langiulli, "Syracuse University," 5). Langiulli's fear of relativism is typical of the Culture Wars, as is his reductive move in the politics of naming, where all advocates of the ETS curriculum get indiscriminately lumped together under the label "postmodern Marxist." But his particular version of the move becomes more meaningful when seen in relation to some of his more scholarly work.

In the Syracuse article, Langiulli facetiously writes: "We must be excused for raising the issue of consistency and non-contradiction, when we have been told by post-modern Marxists that they have learned to live with ambiguity—not to say contradiction" (6). Then he follows this up with the claim that, for "our blessed postmodern Marxists" at Syracuse, "anything means everything and everything means anything" (7). Langiulli attributes this "doctrine" to Derrida (7) and then repeats it, using exactly the same phrase in his book *Possibility, Necessity, and Existence*, on the Italian philosopher Nicola Abbagnano. Comparing Abbagnano's and Derrida's interpretations of possibility, Langiulli notes the ambiguity of the central concept: "Aristotle's classical treatment recognizes this ambiguity. After attempting to defend the principle of noncontradiction (the principle of meaning, the basis of truth, and the starting point of 'first philosophy') against the Sophists especially, Aristotle says, 'It is possible for the same thing to be *potentially* two opposites, but not actually' (emphasis added)."[9] As Langiulli explains, Abbagnano builds on Plato's and Aristotle's notions of existence and possibility to establish a primary sense of the latter term, an originary, univocal level of unambiguous meaning that Langiulli requires of a successful philosophy of possibility. In contrast, Langiulli sees Derrida as coining the term *différance* to describe the "otherness and dis-connection" at the very "bottom of things," an otherness and disconnec-tion "so absolute that there is never univocity but only equivocity—no ori-gins and no ends." Whereas Abbagnano "looks into the face of possibility and sees finitude," Derrida "looks into the face of possibility and sees infinitude." Using the phrase he used to condemn the Syracuse ETS curric-ulum, Langiulli says of Derrida's *différance*: "Distinctions dissolve into one another so that anything means everything and everything means any-thing" (*Possibility*, 52).

But the rhetorical echoes of Langiulli's diatribe against the ETS major do not stop here. In the very next paragraph, in "a digression on a digres-sion," Langiulli wonders why "many literary critics claiming to be disciples of Derrida and the deconstructive method do not follow him into the abso-lute free play of sense/nonsense but stop short in their interpretations of 'writers' and 'texts' at the banalities of race, ethnicity, sex, and, of course, class" (*Possibility*, 52). In his Syracuse article, Langiulli makes a move anal-ogous to that in his book, first criticizing the curriculum's purported inter-pretive relativism—anything means everything, everything means anything—then condemning its reductive imposition of a single political meaning and value. That is, as Langiulli goes on at great polemical length about the ETS major, he shifts his target from the philosophical relativism he sees in its structure and content to the political indoctrination he deplores in its pedagogical process and educational effects. He notes at one point that the new ETS courses "are curiously reminiscent of those given as 'reeducation' in such places as Kampuchea, Ethiopia and, until its deliberate demise, Jonestown, Guyana" (Langiulli, "Syracuse University," 6). The article ends sedately: "As the students of Syracuse imbibe this sweet new curriculum, laced as it is with the poison of multiculturalism, let us hope that the body count remains low. If we do not find the will to resist this suicide of the West being carried out in the labyrinths of America's academe, our students will find themselves on line to drink from the vats of a Kool-Aid acid curriculum—one that is intellectually trivial and ethically lethal"(8).

Langiulli's rhetorical move here is typical not only of the Cultural Right within curriculum debates but also, as we will see, of the Left as well. Michael Bérubé has usefully characterized this foundationalist gambit that transforms charges of epistemological and ethical relativism into attacks on intellectual intolerance and political correctness. Bérubé writes: "Here's the strategy in a nutshell. First, accuse the academics of relativism. When the academics reply that they don't actually consider all opinions equally valid, that they take strong exception to student-goons, who demolish shanties, hold mock slave auctions, and scrawl swastikas on university structures, then follow the accusation of relativism with the accusation of political correctness" (Bérubé, 130).

Relativism leads to nihilism, which leads to fascism—this logic appears often in current debates over teaching the humanities and originates at several different points on the political spectrum. I am especially interested in how it appears to be a contemporary repetition of ancient and modern attacks on sophistic rhetoric. I realize that a reduction of the Culture Wars and curriculum debates to a restaging of Plato versus the Sophists might be among my most blatant oversimplifications, and I am cognizant of various warnings that these ancient debates are simply not pertinent now. But it seems to me that it is precisely a perception of the impertinence of postmodern sophistic rhetoric that seems to be causing a good deal of the intellectual and political controversy within today's heated public discussions. Obviously, the current Culture Wars differ from debates in classical Athens, but differences as well as similarities can be usefully assessed by demonstrating the way restagings of Platonism versus Sophistry are both continuous and discontinuous with their ancient antecedents (see Mailloux, *Rhetoric, Sophistry, Pragmatism*).

This rhetorical fact—of repetition with a (sometimes radical) difference—can be seen both in the explicit namings that go on in the more popular cultural debates as well as in the less obvious connections these debates have to the sometimes technical and specialized arguments made by participants in their scholarly work directed at more restricted professional audiences, as I have just tried to show in the case of Langiulli. Let me expand this claim into two points important for a fuller understanding of what might be called the rhetorical density of any cultural conversation.

First, technical academic discussions have multiple and complex interconnections to debates in the mass media outside the university. We might figure these connections as rhetorical transfers from one cultural site to another, movements of arguments, narratives, tropes, phrases, and names from one medium (department memos), through others (catalogue course descriptions, scholarly journal publications), to others (daily newspapers, radio interview shows, weekly monthly news magazines), to still others (television documentaries, national party platforms, congressional hearings), and back again. It would be odd indeed if during such travels the cultural rhetoric on any side of a particular issue did not become radically transformed in various ways for various purposes as it moved from one site to another, from one medium to another. Whether such transformations clarify or distort, oversimplify or purify, these translated pieces of cultural rhetoric play prominent roles in the debates at the sites of their destination. Thus, and this is my second point, cultural rhetoric study cannot simply dismiss caricatures of theoretical or political positions by either the Cultural Right or Left if such translations play significant roles in determining the dynamics or outcomes of various cultural confrontations. What such study can do is clarify the rhetorical interconnections, for example, between academic and popular levels of debate. Out of such clarification comes not necessarily a solution to conflict but at least an opportunity for intervention. Such rhetorical analysis is another form of reception study, in this case the reception of academic theories and vocabularies in the more general cultural conversation outside the university (cf. Foucault, "Archeology"; and Said, "Traveling Theory").

To again make my rhetorical point concrete, let me return to the reception of ETS. I have tried to suggest that behind Langiulli's condemnation of the Syracuse curriculum is the same Platonic-Aristotelian suspicion of sophistic relativism that fueled his rejection of "the extreme consequences of the thought of Derrida, Deleuze, Foucault, and Lacan" in his scholarly book.[10] Similarly, Tuttleton's condemnation of ETS relates to an appeal made in his literary scholarship to this identical tradition within Western philosophy. The appeal is explicit and emphatic in the final chapters of his recent book *Vital Signs: Essays on American Literature and Criticism*, "Jacques et moi" and "Some Modern Sophists." In order to ground his attack on the contemporary Nietzschean claims of "a number of pontificating Sophists" (338), he argues for "the ancient analysis of truth and how it can be linguistically represented" (326). For Tuttleton, "there is no better account available than that in Plato and the *Metaphysics*, the *Posterior Analytics*, and the *Peri Hermeneias* (*On Interpretation*) of Aristotle" (326).

Just as the ancient Greek Sophists were refuted—"I regard them as sufficiently eviscerated in the great dialogues of Plato, in Socrates' innocent questions, and in the stunning *Metaphysics* of Aristotle" (314)—so too does Tuttleton see himself as extending the Platonic-Aristotelian tradition in a vigorous refutation of "the contemporary Sophists," who "have it that the inevitable gap between word and the thing itself, between signifier and the signified, proves that reality is inaccessible through language" (322). This linguistic skepticism is "the latest form of nihilism" (318) and, combined with a tendency "toward interpretive chaos" (340), constitutes a form of sophistic relativism: "Once the critic breaks with essentialism, anything goes" (348, cf. 330). But—and here we approach a more direct connection between his foundationalist philosophizing and his political objections to the ETS curriculum—for Tuttleton all this postmodern sophistry leads, as with Langiulli, from absurd theory to dangerous politics. "Once we verbally invert everything—by saying that black is white, up down, central marginal, aberrational normative, and so on—perfection will arrive," according to Tuttleton's contemporary Sophists. "This seems hopeless and a desperate counsel" to Tuttleton, who argues further that the politics of these Sophists is not simply that of emptying out the theory supporting the moral and social traditions of the West but of filling up that emptiness with whatever personal or ideological agenda they see fit (339).

Even more specifically, Tuttleton resorts to the once tried and true rhetoric of the Cold War to make his case against "the current academic Sophists" (349), whose "deconstructionism has proved immensely fruitful to the political left in trying to foment that chaos in the domain of values that is said to be necessary to launch the supposed forthcoming revolution" (344). Tuttleton thus sees himself exposing this "covert intention" (345) of poststructuralist sophistry, which opens the way for political opportunists with a Marxist agenda and encourages "a sinister assault on liberty" (346). Tuttleton claims this potential assault is actualized in the Syracuse ETS curriculum, which, to repeat, he sees as "promulgating left-wing sociological arguments, with a view to politically correct indoctrination" (Tuttleton, "Back to the Sixties," 34).

It is ironic, of course, that some of the strongest attacks on the Syracuse reforms have come from exactly those ideological positions both Langiulli and Tuttleton identify with ETS itself. Soon after the department formally accepted a general description of the changes, a *Chronicle of Higher Education* article ran with the title "New Curriculum at Syracuse U. Attacked by 2 Marxist Professors."[11] Contending "that the planned curriculum is 'part of the crisis management of late capitalism,' " Mas'ud Zavarzadeh and Donald Morton are reported to "have beaten the traditionalists to the punch—call it a left hook—arguing that the changes are superficial and not radical enough." Many of Zavarzadeh and Morton's 1986–1987 Syracuse department memos had already expressed the grounds for their objections, and these later became the basis for the critiques of

ETS published in their essays and books of the 1990s. Like those on the Cultural Right, these postmodern Marxists from the Cultural Left found the supporters of ETS to be woefully wanting in their theories and politics. But, whereas Tuttleton and Langiulli worried about sophistic relativism leading to leftist ideological indoctrination, Zavarzadeh and Morton complained about relativistic rhetoricism maintaining the wishy-washy liberal pluralism of the traditional humanist status quo.

"Like all 'new' transforming curricula in U.S. universities," write Zavarzadeh and Morton, the Syracuse ETS major "is a 'transformation' that does not transform anything; it simply meets the educational needs of the changing (post)modern labor force of late capitalism" (Zavarzadeh and Morton, *Theory as Resistance*, 136). The authors argue that "among the most important strategies for absorbing the opposition and maintaining the system is the strategy of pluralistic inclusion: the institution assimilates the discourses of its adversaries." And this was exactly the strategy "that was deployed to ward off radical change in the Syracuse English Department," according to Zavarzadeh and Morton (149). Furthermore, a pluralistic leveling of discourses that explicitly *included* led to a coalitionist politics that covertly *excluded*. Or, as Zavarzadeh and Morton put it, in a rather incisive rhetorical analysis:

> What happened in the Syracuse English Department happens all the time: the radical thinker is situated on an axis of alternatives such that she has the "free choice" either of working from within the system or being marked as an "extremist" who can therefore be "legitimately" excluded because she can be regarded as "self-excluding." In other words, the options come down to either being "persuaded" of the legitimacy of working within the system and thus accepting the existing structures, or finding that there is no space for radical change. "Persuasion" (the model of democratic conversation) is, in other words, an alibi for a pernicious system of surveillance and punishment built on the principle: "Be persuaded, or else . . . " (149–150)

I suppose I am being rather disingenuous in attributing to Zavarzadeh and Morton an "incisive *rhetorical* analysis," since "rhetoric" is the last thing with which they wish to be associated, as we will see. But "rhetorical" is exactly what their talk of persuasion amounts to, and, furthermore, the claim of their analysis illustrates precisely why rhetoric and politics go hand in hand and need not (even should not) be separated in theory or practice.

Nevertheless, a separation of rhetoric and politics is what Morton and Zavarzadeh insist on—in their depoliticized notion of rhetoric and in their limited representation of contemporary rhetorical study. For example, in their distinction between "ludic (post)modernism" and their own "resistance (post)modernism," they give rhetoric over to an apolitical formalism, under the guise of a reactionary postmodernism with its view of the "unending 'playfulness' (thus the term 'ludic') of the signifier in signifying practices." As with Tuttleton and Langiulli, the rhetorical Derrida becomes the pivotal theoretical figure where poststructuralism goes wrong: in contrast to ludic (post)modernism's Derridean "understanding of *différance* as an effect of rhetoric," Morton and Zavarzadeh's resistance (post)modernism "articulates difference in the social space of economic exploitation and labor." But, whereas Tuttleton and Langiulli see *différance* as providing the theoretical excuse for imposing a repugnant Marxist agenda upon the humanities, Morton and Zavarzadeh see *différance* as a strategic device for taking away the ground of the "real" necessary for any liberatory political project like Marxism.[12]

Morton and Zavarzadeh's persistence in depoliticizing rhetorical study extends from their theoretical formulations to their historical narratives. In their story, "the rhetorical turn in the humanities has successfully diverted inquiries from the politics of intelligibility to the tropics of knowledge" (Zavarzadeh and Morton, *Theory, (Post)Modernity, Opposition*, 205). Such an account is misleading but instructively so. Shouldn't the authors have recognized that contemporary rhetorical studies often resists separating rhetoric and politics, language use, and social materiality? Weren't they aware of proposals for Marxist and materialist rhetorics (McGee, "Materialist's Conception," Wess)?

In their critiques during the 1990s, Morton and Zavarzadeh have continued to demonstrate an antirhetorical bias already apparent in their earliest published attacks on ETS. In "War of The Words: The Battle of (and for) English," these authors criticized initial proposals at Syracuse and assumed (mistakenly it turns out) that rhetoric would organize the revised major. "Syracuse's 'new' curriculum is similar to many other 'new' curricula in that it is part of a concerted political effort by conservatives to contain change by recycling traditional educational ideas and practice by updating 'literary studies' as the study of rhetoric" (19). Their complaints against such study raise once again the specter of relativism:

> The study of "rhetoric" actually represents all existing discourses as automatically legitimate by virtue of their very existence and thus by implication as "equal." A rhetorician can be as much interested in the rhetoric of the Ku Klux Klan as in the rhetoric of imprisoned black South Africans: for the rhetorician all social phenomena are occasions for cognitive inquiries. And, of course, this fits right into the dominant picture of what the academy is and should continue to be: a place where all inquiries are equally urgent. (19)

Morton and Zavarzadeh are both right and wrong here. They are right in that rhetorical study has no built-in ideology; it can be effectively adapted to various political agendas. They are wrong in that no interpreter can treat all inquiries equally. Any rhetorician is situated within particular social, disciplinary, and institutional networks, acting within specific webs of desires, beliefs, and practices; and this situatedness makes some inquiries more urgent than others. Unsituated relativism is an impossibility, and thus it is not a danger that Morton and Zavarzadeh need worry about, for rhetorical study or any other inquiry.

Differences in ideology are, of course, another matter. Rhetoricians do come in various ideological flavors, and it is quite possible that rhetorical theorists currently tend to be more liberal than radical. Still, this need not be the case, evidenced by the many recent proposals of critical rhetorics.[13] Moreover, the topic of language and ideology has gained increasing attention in contemporary cultural study and political theory. To pursue such topics within the human sciences, we need more rhetorical studies, not less. And, finally, as I have tried to demonstrate in this essay, readings of today's Culture Wars make it obvious how important the relationship of rhetoric to politics continues to be, both as a part of the analytic frame and as an issue within the debates analyzed. These reception narratives can play a prominent role in a cultural rhetoric studies wishing to avoid the pitfalls of various orthodoxies on both the Cultural Right and Left. Avoiding such pitfalls remains a significant challenge for those combining rhetoric with cultural studies in the years ahead.

ACKNOWLEDGMENT

Portions of this chapter appeared in Steven Mailloux, *Reception Histories: Rhetoric, Pragmatism, and American Cultural Politics* (Ithaca, NY: Cornell University Press, 1998). Copyright 1998 by Cornell University Press. Reprinted by permission.

NOTES

1. See Mailloux, "Rhetoric Returns to Syracuse," for a rhetorical history of these local curricular discussions. Also see Steven Cohan, John W. Crowley, Jean E. Howard, Veronica Kelly, Steven Mailloux, Stephen Melville, Felicity Nussbaum, Bill Readings, Bennet Schaber, Linda Shires, and Thomas Yingling, "Not a Good Idea: A New Curriculum at Syracuse," unpublished essay, December 1987 (copy available on request at sjmaillo@uci.edu). In the ETS curriculum, courses listed under the History Group include Literary Histories (e.g., Literary History to 1800), Histories of Symbolic Forms (e.g., History of Ideas), and Discursive Histories (e.g., Reception Aesthetics); those under the

Theory Group are Theories of Representation (e.g., Semiotic Theories), Poetics and Formal Analysis (e.g., Theory of Genres), and Rhetoric (e.g., Discourse Analysis); and under the Politics Group are included Culture, Power, Knowledge (e.g., Ideology), Resistance and Power (e.g., Race and Discourse), and Gender and Sexualities (e.g., Feminisms).

2. Certain interpretations and misinterpretations of Althusserianism played a peculiarly prominent role in some episodes of the Syracuse debates. See, for example, Weissman; and Morton and Zavarzadeh, "Nostalgia." For a recent assessment of Althusser's more general influence, see Kaplan and Sprinker.

3. For a detailed account of the general university situation, see Kenneth Shaw.

4. Pierce, A8. Pierce limits Watson to that single sentence. Carol Parlin was a bit more generous in her report three days earlier, when she quoted Watson on the same topic: "The purpose of a literary education is no longer to have a student get a sort of Regents-exam familiarity with the standard classics. . . . We're much more interested in the process of interpretation and in the literary and cultural status of texts than in taking for granted and mastering a list of so-called literary classics. In a general sense, the new curriculum will refuse to take for granted the status of a classic just because it has traditionally been called a classic" (Watson, quoted in Parlin, 1).

5. Pierce, A1. For accounts of the Stanford controversy, see Lindenberger; and Pratt.

6. Rybaak, 8–9. As the nineties progressed, the reception of the ETS curriculum was often tied explicitly to the controversies over "political correctness." Shortly before the publication of the New Times piece, the Syracuse English Department had been visited by a documentary crew from British television, and the ETS major became a prime exhibit for a rather sensationalist "exposé," about U.S. universities, aired in London as "War of the Word" on Channel 4 during December 1991. See the appropriately titled commentary in the London Observer: Simon Hoggart, "All Present and Incorrect on Campus," 15 December 1991; and Hugh Hebert, "Inside the Universities of Uniformity," 18 December 1991. For a less negative local account of PC and ETS, see Renée Levy. On the debates over political correctness more generally, see Jeffrey Williams; Newfield and Strickland; Bush; and John Wilson.

7. In spring 1997 the Writing Program's new PhD in Composition and Cultural Rhetoric was officially approved. For a full description, see Syracuse University Writing Program, "Proposal for a Doctorate of Philosophy in Composition and Cultural Rhetoric" (spring 1996).

8. For a fuller discussion of ETS in relation to Graff's model, see Mailloux, "Rhetorically Covering Conflict."

9. Langiulli, Possibility, 51–52, quoting Aristotle, Metaphysics, 1009a35.

10. Langiulli, Possibility, 53. Also see Langiulli, "On the Location of Socrates' Feet," where he interprets a line from Plato's Phaedo as a reply to "the ancient liberal view of the Sophists—the view that reality, morality, and esthetics are only matters of opinion since there are no transcendent points of reference" and then uses this interpretation as "a reply to contemporary sophists, a.k.a. anti-foundationalists or contemporary liberals" who "in order to vindicate

humanity . . . maintain that there can be no foundations and philosophy as the search for them . . . is either futile at worst or poetry at best" (143).

11. This article appeared alongside a longer piece by Heller, "Some English Departments Are Giving Undergraduates Grounding in New Literary and Critical Theory," which described curricular and pedagogical reforms at Carnegie-Mellon, Syracuse, and other universities.

12. Zavarzadeh and Morton, *Theory, (Post)Modernity, Opposition,* 107; see also Zavarzadeh and Morton, *Theory as Resistance,* 7. This view of Derridean deconstruction should be contrasted to Derrida's explicit rejection of rhetoricism (Derrida, "Afterword," 156, n. 9; and Olson, "Jacques Derrida," 18–19).

13. There have been calls for "critical rhetorics," "radical rhetorical studies," and "materialist rhetorics"; see, for example, McKerrow; Reed, 174, n. 5, and 176, n. 20; Bernard-Donals, 159–178. Also see Aune, *Rhetoric and Marxism*; Berlin; and Cain.

FOUR

SUBJECT POSITIONS AS A SITE OF RHETORICAL STRUGGLE
Representing African Americans

Barry Brummett
Detine L. Bowers

Who are "we," late-twentieth-century Americans? The question invites a recitation of demographic categories, of groups: we are male or female, old or young, rich or poor—and we are of certain races. The meanings of these categories are socially, symbolically created and charged with political and social import. That is especially true of race. We are not created equally, nor with the same expectations, nor the same prospects, when it comes to race.

How is race symbolically created? How are whole racial groups relatively empowered or disempowered by exposure to the messages comprising the cultures in which we live? How are people recruited to participate in their own oppression and devaluation?

These are questions about *rhetoric,* because they ask how people are induced to accept racial categorization and valuation. Yet they are also *critical* questions, because they begin to ask how social *structures* are created, beyond the impact of particular messages and isolated decisions. For centuries, the hegemony of race in America has been fueled primarily through rhetorical strategies hidden in the texts of everyday experience—but how? This essay suggests a way to fuse rhetorical and cultural studies in the service of better understanding of how texts construct race. First, we turn to the work that has been done in cultural studies on subject position. We expand and develop that work by explaining the potential rhetorical effects of three categories of subjectivity. But we argue that an explanation of racial politics requires a further theorizing of how what we call *object positions* might also be offered rhetorically by texts. As a consequence, we propose a method for understanding texts as sites of struggle between subjectification and objectification of racial identities, and we illustrate that struggle with a rhetorical analysis of the 1994 film *The Air Up There*.

SUBJECT POSITION THEORY

One important concept that recurs across the range of critical studies—Marxism, feminism, and so forth—is the idea of *subject position.*[1] A subject position is a stance, role, or perspective one takes in relationship to a text so as to read or engage the text. From that engagement, as Hayden White suggests, "a specific subjectivity is called up and established in the reader" (193). Bill Nichols argues that "the self-as-subject or ego will be precisely a term in a relationship," either with another, with a text, or with others as mediated through texts (31). Texts "interpellate," or call to readers to accept certain stances, roles, or interpretive strategies. The verbal and nonverbal texts in college lectures and classrooms call forth the subject positions of *students*; the students will assume the contrasting positions of *employees* later on in response to the texts of business and office. These are stances taken in relationship to those texts: "All the viewer need do is fall into place as subject, an easy step yielding the pleasure of recognition as identity is once again confirmed" (38). As Stuart Hall puts it, "We are hailed or summoned by the ideologies which recruit us as their 'authors,' their essential subject. We are constituted . . . in that position of recognition or fixture between ourselves and the signifying chain . . . " ("Signification," 102).

It would be useful to specify here three kinds of subject positions that texts offer to readers (although we will have space to develop a discussion of only one of them). First, a reader might take an *identified* subject position. This reader finds characters, themes, or images in the text with which he or she identifies, or desires to identify. The child who imagines himself Shaquille O'Neal while watching his hero on television is accepting an identified position from which to read the text. The identified subject position is our focal concern below. Second, the reader might take an *implied* subject position. Here, the reader does not identify with a character or image in the text, but is nevertheless called to and constructed as a subject in order to read it. Ironic or satiric texts often encourage this stance. *In Living Color*'s "Men On . . . " recurring sketch did not encourage a viewer to identify with the two effeminate men portrayed; rather, the text calls to a reader that recognizes "in jokes" about sexual preference. The text calls to us to take the position of a knowing ironist. Third, the reader might take a *subversive* subject position, in which a subjectivity is assumed that is at odds with, and often directly opposed to, the call of the text (e.g., Owen). For example, the feminist viewer of television's *Martin* will most likely find nothing to identify with, and may well refuse even the complicity with the text that an ironic stand would demand; such a viewer constructs for herself an active subjectivity that takes shape as it wars with the text's insensitivities toward women. Subversive subjectivities are never free of textual relationship, however. They take shape both in response to the offending text and on the basis of a subject position constructed by other texts. Subversive subject positions are always intertextual. A subversive feminist subjectivity is made "elsewhere" and then crystallized in the moment of opposition to *Martin*, for instance.

The three types of subject positions described above are not quite the same as the useful scheme of three decoding positions presented by Hall ("Encoding," 136–138). We note some differences and similarities. Hall's scheme is keyed to the reader's relationship to power structures as mediated through a text. Our scheme is keyed to the reader's relationship to a text that has an effect on power structures. A dominant position, for Hall, decodes messages "full and straight," as the empowered encoders intended it. That stance may or may not be our *identified* subject position; someone might identify with a character or action and yet interpret those signs in ways not intentionally encoded by an author. A negotiated position alters the terms of a hegemonic sign for particular circumstances, saying in effect, "we'll read this differently here," as in a deficit hawk who nevertheless reads Medicare cuts as pernicious, adopting a negotiated subjectivity when that issue arises. This has little or no correspondence with our *implied* subject, who does not see herself in a text but nevertheless sees for herself a stable and "invited" way to read or understand the text, as with an ironic reader. Hall's oppositional decoder and our *subversive* subject are very much the same. In general, Hall sees texts more as channeling meanings and positions already offered in society. We see texts more as sites of struggle that generate meanings and positions present in society.

Several implications of subject position theory will be of particular relevance to our argument here. We argue that subjects today are decentered and changeable, that those subjects are socially created, that socially created subjects are defined by their group identities, and that distribution of power among groups makes subject creation a matter of political struggle.

First, because subjects are constructed in relationship to discourses and because the discourses to which people are exposed are changing and fragmented, postmodern subjects today are often described as *decentered*: changing and changeable, malleable, and disconnected. John Fiske attributes this condition to our experiences of myriad everyday texts: "The necessity of negotiating the problems of everyday life within a complex, highly elaborated social structure has produced nomadic subjectivities who can move around this grid, realigning their social allegiances into different formations of the people according to the necessities of the moment" (*Understanding the Popular,* 24). There is, as Susan Sontag argues, a "plurality of meanings" in texts and images, some of which call pluralistically to subjects (109).

Second, such a decentered and changing subject is socially created because the discourses that call it into momentary existence are socially held and controlled. Bill Nichols says that "the self-as-subject is a social construct whose place will vary according to the construction process. . . . In each case, the individual is called into being as a subject by the other; his or her identity hinges upon the other by whom she is objectified and to whom she is subjected" (30, 34). People assume subject positions in relationship to texts, but also to others as mediated through texts. People are called to in such a way that they are socially defined and situated subjects. Thus, whole groups of people, such as blacks, are socially defined by the texts of popular culture.

Third, the process of subject creation is geared to group identities. We are called to not by individual name, but by the kind of person we are, according to the categories deemed most relevant by any culture. Lorraine Gamman and Margaret Marshment claim that discourses call to us to become subjects with group characteristics as defined by race, class, gender, sexual preference, age, and so forth: "The structuring of dominance through processes of identification and objectification in narrative fictions can be applied with equal pertinence to power relations organized on the basis of class, ethnicity, or generation" (7). Or as Teun van Dijk puts it, "To control other people, it is most effective to try to control their group attitudes and especially their even more fundamental, attitude producing, ideologies, because in that case the others will behave out of their own 'free' will in accordance with the interests of the powerful" (37). van Dijk notes correctly that the creation of subject positions along the lines of social groups is often occluded; those most oppressed by the positions offered to them by social discourses are recruited to participate in those very discourses. bell hooks describes that recruitment as the process of "colonization," (*Art,* 4) and seconds van Dijk's claim that the process is hidden, "a process of overt colonization that goes easily undetected" (*Rage,* 111; *Yearning,* 155; *Outlaw,* 168–169). As Bill Nichols explains, "Ideology uses the fabrication of images and the processes of representation to persuade us that how things are is how they ought to be and that the place provided for us is the place we ought to have" (1). Much of the ideology of categorization is the creation of disempowered groups as object or Other: "Within white-supremacist capitalist patriarchy, images of power and freedom are symbolically personified by the white male 'subject' in relation to whom all other beings are constructed as unfree 'objects'" (hooks, *Art,* 163).

A fourth implication is that the construction of subjects in social relationships, through culturally held discourses, puts us squarely in the arena of ideological struggle, for, as Nichols asserts, *"how* we are termed as selves can therefore be defined as an ideological question" (30; emphasis in original). The creation of subjects becomes an issue of power and social control; people will be created as the empowered interests of a society want them to be, *or* in subversive resistance to and refusal of those empowered interests. Creation of subjectivity is a means to the end of political power. The question of subjects is therefore a question of rhetoric. The creative power of texts is struggled over because that power, to determine meaning, is so valuable.

Struggle takes place over how groups of people are textually represented because those representations are the raw materials for constructing subject positions: "Representation is a crucial location of struggle for any exploited and oppressed people asserting subjectivity and decolonization of the mind" (hooks, *Art,* 3). The textual relationships that power and privilege call us to take may often seem natural and obvious, but not always. They can always be refused, and sometimes are. Some texts contain within themselves signs that facilitate refusal. Fiske claims this is true of all texts of popular culture (*Understanding the Popular,* 25). Sometimes resistance is empowered through turning to other, subversive texts. In either case, what it means to be of a certain race, gender, class, or sexual orientation is not determined and dictated; it is struggled over.

Of the several group identities through which our subjectivities are called into being, race particularly is a discursive, social, ideological creation (e.g., Hacker, 3–16). To name people as black, white, Asian, and so forth is both to assert within each category a unity that is biologically indefensible as well as to assert among categories distinctions that are biologically inaccurate. Yet, the construction of race, *and of racially inflected subjectivities* through rhetorically strategic representation, has been a major discursive preoccupation of American culture for centuries, creating what Clifford Staples has called "the hyperreality of racial politics in postmodern America" (11). People have been called to become "en-raced" subjects in specific ways so as to perpetuate racism, which is, as Joel Kovel argues, itself "a symbolic product, a set of fantasies . . . insofar as the symbols and fantasies of racism have been themselves generated by the history of race relations and sustained by the rest of an organically related culture" (5). Both verbal and nonverbal "socio-cognitive representations" of all sorts comprise the texts that call us into racial being (van Dijk, 27).

The discourses that create Americans as en-raced are, of course, filling the mass media. Jannette Dates and William Barlow argue that "in American society, by reproducing the ideological hegemony of the dominant white culture, the mass media help to legitimate the inequalities in class and race relations" (4). van Dijk identifies media texts and images as the site of racial ideological struggle: "The media have the ability to contribute the shared elements that define the ethnic situation and that develop or change the ideological framework used by white people to understand and control ethnic events and relations" (39).

But media also contain the rhetorical resources for refusing oppression such as sexism (Kuhn, *Women's Pictures*, 31) and racism. As hooks puts it, "the field of representation remains a crucial realm of struggle" (*Art*, 57–58). Dates and Barlow note that there has always been both the hegemony of racist images and resistance to that hegemony by African Americans, resulting in a "split image" of what it means to be black in the United States (3–4).

How people struggle over the subjects they are called to become can be clearly seen by studying struggles over racial ideology conducted through texts and images of the mass media. When we watch televised sports and situation comedies, attend the cinema, and read the daily newspapers, these texts of our everyday experience call to our racial identity. We accept or refuse those calls according to the levels of our awareness, politicization, and access to discursive resources.

Insufficient attention has been paid to the intersection of two concerns: (1) some subject positions, especially those concerning race, are constructed in so damaging and repressive a manner that they are best understood instead as *object positions*. Whole classes of people may be created for others *and for themselves* as objects, not as subjects. Some social critics, for instance, have observed that this is what happens with pornography, the texts of which offer women only a stance as objects, and encourage others (males) to view them in that way as well (e.g., Kuhn, *Power of Image*, 11). Similarly for blacks, hooks maintains that "assimilation and participation in a bourgeois white paradigm can lead to a process of self-objectification that is just as dehumanizing as any racist assault by white culture" (*Art*, 39). Indeed, hooks goes on to say that there is a "struggle of oppressed and exploited peoples to make ourselves subjects" ("Postmodern," 11). We believe that insufficient attention has been paid to the ways that object positions, as well as subject positions, may be discursively created, especially for blacks. Stuart Hall ("Encoding") has no such concept. Nakagawa, however, comes close to our idea of object positions with his notion of "deformed subjects" ("Deformed Subjects"). Thus, (2) the specific discursive and textual practices and characteristics that underlie and facilitate either subjectification or objectification have not been adequately explained. Many studies have noted, for instance, that blacks are depicted by the media in demeaning and dehumanizing ways.[2] But too few studies specify the discursive resources that contribute to the creation of object or of subject positions. Texts need to be seen as resources for, rather than simple determinants of, either subjectification or objectification. We need to understand how signs might be appropriated toward either end, for, as hooks notes, "acts of appropriation are part of the process by which we make ourselves.... The 'use' one makes of what is appropriated is the crucial factor" (*Art,* 11). That will be the goal of this paper, because, in the absence of an understanding of specific textual dynamics, one can point only to the most obviously racist texts as dehumanizing or objectifying. A concern for specific textual resources and dynamics is rhetorical; we want to explain the rhetoric of some concepts (subject and object positions) that have been in the domain of cultural studies.

An understanding of how texts create subjects or objects can also create more awareness of how the discursive construction of race is *struggled over* rather than simply dictated by discourse. We will suggest some answers to the questions: What symbolic means do people have to refuse a text that calls to them as objects? What textual resources enable the active and subversive construction of subject positions in response to that racism? Fiske notes correctly that texts may be used in either hegemonic or subversive ways, and that through "excorporation" people may actively "make their own culture out of the resources and commodities provided by the dominant system" (*Understanding the Popular,* 15, 37). How both textual oppression and resistance operate specifically needs to be explained, then. In short, we take up Cornel West's call for

> inquiry into the discursive conditions for the possibility of the hegemonic European (i.e., white) supremacist logics operative in ... the West and the counterhegemonic possibilities available ... [and] a microinstitutional (or localized) analysis of the mechanisms that inscribe and sustain these logics in the everyday lives of Africans, including the hegemonic ideological production of African subjects. (21–22)

Racism is perpetuated by many mechanisms. Here we propose a focused analysis of the textual means by which people are encouraged to see themselves and others as objects, or the means to refuse an object position by reclaiming a subjectivity. We undertake that analysis by theorizing two broad classes of subjectification/objectification and then using that structure to analyze a recent film that clearly exemplifies popular culture as a site of struggle over racial ideology, particularly in connection with media images of Africans and African Americans, namely, the film *The Air Up There.*

A THEORETICAL PERSPECTIVE
ON SUBJECTS AND OBJECTS

What is needed for a text to call to, or facilitate, a subject position? In contrast, what do texts do to encourage object status for some of their readers? We organize our discussion of these textual characteristics under two broad headings, *authority* and *narration* (see Figure 4.1).

A reasonably "complete" analysis of the subject positions suggested by a text would attend to the resources offered for construction of identified, implied, and subversive subject positions as well as object positions. Due to space limitations, here we can only model what such an analysis might look like by contrasting one sort of subject position to object positions. For purposes of narrowing our focus and creating a manageable essay, we will compare resources within the text for creation of an *identified* subject position and of an object position. Analysis of the resources for implied or subversive subject positions is a fruitful matter for further research.

Finally, although we do not have the space to review it here, our analysis is informed by a well established literature in narrative studies, of which Walter Fisher, Dennis Mumby, and Hayden White are good examples.

Authority

To create a *subject* position, a text must depict a person or group of people as having authority. The term *authority* has at least two senses that are germane to our discussion. Authors have authority in that they are the origin of the thoughts and language of a text. And those who are in charge of some enterprise have authority. These two senses of authority overlap to create two specific textual characteristics that together constitute the authority of a subject position.

First, a text will call to an identified subject as one having authority if it identifies the subject as an *origin of motive,* an initiator, a chooser, as one

Subject positions encouraged by:	Object positions encouraged by:
Authority	Anonymity
Origin of motive	Commodification and the body
Voice	Voicelessness
Narration	Noise
Plot maturity	Isolation and acontextuality
Fully realized characters	Otherness

FIGURE 4.1. Textual characteristics supporting object or subject positions.

responsible. An authorial subject position is a locus and source of thought, decision, and control over one's self and, if appropriate, over others. To create subjects, then, a text will say (to a subject, or about a group of subjects) "you do what you do because of the decisions you have made. You are responsible for what you do because you initiated that action. You cause things to happen for yourself and for other people."

Second, a text will call to an identified subject position as one having authority if it presents the subject as having a *voice*: "the human subject is a speaking subject" (Kuhn, *Women's Pictures*, 46). An identified subject position with authority would be the author of its own stories and history, and we would know those narratives to proceed from the subject because we literally hear the subject's voice. That voice has a distinctive style that marks the subject as "real," as personal, as individual. A subject's voice reflects a distinctive verbal and nonverbal style; it may include a vocabulary or argot reflective of the subject's connectedness to larger groups in his or her culture or history.

This characteristic of voice is particularly appropriate in identifying what might constitute black subject positions. A number of critics have noted that European culture has, since the invention of the printing press at least, privileged sight as the sense that conveys knowledge and information primarily (e.g., Altman; Ong). And other scholars have noted that African cultures are more heavily grounded in orality, *nommo*, and the power of the spoken word (e.g., Asante; Gates). Dick Hebdige indicts Western culture's "bankruptcy of the gaze." Instead, he develops an intriguing argument noting the spiritual linkage of the soul with the breath, and of the breath with voice, and concludes that celebrations of "soul" in the rhetoric of racial liberation of the 1960s were also celebrations of the spoken voice (125–127). An African subject is thus not only an author but a speaking author, literally with a sounding voice.

Anonymity

Now that we have considered a reading that creates a subject position, we turn to textual characteristics that support an *object* position. What do texts do so as to deny subjectivity to individuals or whole groups of people? Let us consider the "opposite" of authority. It will be useful to oppose authority to the idea of *anonymity*; one with no name has no authority. "In whose *name* do you cast out demons?" we ask, because the name says who one is and by what right or power one has authority.

If, as Marxist theory would hold, social relationships are influenced by economic conditions, we should not be surprised to find that the objectifying correlate to the creation of a subject position is *commodification* (e.g., Fiske, *Understanding the Popular*, 11, 14). A commodity in capitalism is a good to be bought and sold. Action in the economy is always about, or directed toward, commodities, but of course they themselves are never the source of action. Commodification therefore creates an object position when it denies active agency to people. Commodities must be reducible to the terms of a common denominator, specifically, money, the currency of the economy. We can assess automobiles, for instance, in terms of how much each one costs. Furthermore, commodities must be reduced to common dimensions that provide a basis of comparison, so that one knows *what* one is buying and how it measures up to other goods. Automobiles are defined, then, in terms of horsepower, cubic feet of cargo or passenger space, gasoline mileage, and so forth. Note that a major tool of commodification is quantification; that which cannot be quantified becomes difficult to treat as a commodity. Quantification allows the existence of a stable medium of exchange, such as capital, without which there can be no commodities.

The commodification of whole groups of people through media images follows that same pattern. hooks notes that people are objectified when their authority to act or to make a difference is removed: "Mass media continually bombard us with the images of African Americans which spread the message that we are hopeless, trapped, unable to change our circumstances in meaningful ways" (*Art,* 57). People are offered a position only as objects, they are commodified, when they are reduced to *parts* that can be equated with or compared to other parts, in other words, when they are assigned an exchange value. Of course, a crucial historical fact of African *American* experience is that people were once legally and economically regarded as commodities during the period of slavery. The "slave trade" linguistically and legally legitimized the exchange of bodies as a capital venture. Disconnected facets of black culture (music, fashion) continue to be a way to objectify through commodification: "Contemporary commodification of blackness creates a market context wherein conventional, even stereotypical modes of representing blackness may receive the greatest reward" (hooks, *Art,* 58, *Yearning,* 2). That pattern of commodification has continued to link capitalism and racism; Kovel argues that capitalism requires the reduction of the world to the quantifiable and thus the objectifiable, and is for that very reason crucial for racism (xlvi–xlvii). Capitalism legitimates the market appropriation of black culture, which commodifies it and makes mere objects of black people. As hooks states about the 1990 film about an interracial heart transplant, "Films like *Heart Condition* make black culture and black life backdrop, scenery for narratives that essentially focus on white people. Nationalist black voices critique this cultural crossover, its decentering of black experience as it relates to black people, and its insistence that it is acceptable for whites to explore blackness as long as their ultimate agenda is appropriation" (hooks, *Black,*

32). In sum, the anonymous object is similar to Michel Foucault's idea of the "docile body," which is always subordinated and controlled ("Afterword," 212).

People are offered object positions when media images call to them in terms of their parts, specifically in terms of parts that are quantifiably comparable to other, similar parts. Objectification occurs because parts are not active agents. An example of such commodification would be the reduction of athletes to statistics of height, weight, speed, strength, and the whole panoply of sports "trivia." Reduction of an athlete to these lowest common denominators among athletes makes them commodities; speed in the 100-meter race, or earned run average, or arm reach for a boxer is the equivalent of horsepower, torque, or price among cars. Moreover, the reduction of exchange to the act of "trading" reduces the individuals to goods, as parts, with sharp parallels with the African slave trade. The trading of athletes from one team to another is much like the auction of slaves that moved them from one plantation to another.

A person or a group of people offered a position as a commodity will have no authority. Automobiles do not decide to whom they will be sold. Nor have they a *voice*. They are talked about, they do not talk. The creation of an object position for people, then, will involve suppression (although elimination may be impossible) of voice, literal and figurative, in the images that are being used to induce object status. The image will be more talked about than talking. It will do what it is told more than it will decide what to do. It will be moved (by the authority of others, such as a coach or a game plan) more than it will move of its own volition.

A shift of images to the body is always an ideological move, Fiske contends: "though the body may appear to be where we are most individual, it is also the material form of the body politic, the class body, the racial body, and the body of gender" (*Understanding the Popular,* 70). Annette Kuhn identifies this objectification in media images that focus on women's bodies, creating woman, for both women and men, as nothing more than "an object of desire" (*Women's Pictures,* 11) A focus on the *bodies* of blacks has been a major resource of racist ideology and of the imposition of object positions upon them for centuries: "The black body had always received attention within the framework of white supremacy, as racist, sexist iconography had been deployed to perpetuate notions of innate biological inferiority" (hooks, *Art,* 202). West notes that historically, in the West, "Africans are associated with acts of bodily defecation, violation, and subordination. Within this logic, Africans are walking abstractions, inanimate things" in short, commodities ("Marxist Theory," 23). Historical contributions in the American media to the ideological creation of blacks has included images of them as animals, for example, apes and baboons, beasts, and sambos with grossly exaggerated lips, noses, buttocks, whites of eyes, and so on, in other words, as mere bodies uttering mindless dialogue.[3] Kovel reviews the familiar and dismal history of racist myths that equate Africans with mere physicality, sexuality, dirtiness, and so forth (xlv–xlvi, 51–92; also Hacker, 61–62). So a major resource of objectification of blacks in particular is a reduction of images to body images, to those "parts" that are not authorial, that are moved by external forces rather than the locus of internal motivation, units that cannot speak for themselves.

Why would a reader not simply refuse an object position? The question is not so simple: texts contain symbolic resources that may facilitate construction of both object positions and several kinds of subject positions. We intend to show that *The Air Up There* is such a site of struggle. But these are some reasons why an audience might be disposed to construct an object position rather than any kind of subject position: if most of the signs within most of the texts available are more conducive to object positions, as in a relentlessly racist culture; if previous exposure to objectifying texts creates in a reader the habit of assuming an object position, as in a reader whose self esteem has been damaged by a racist culture; or, if extratextual rewards seem linked to object positions, as in an apartheid culture that assigns secure if degraded roles in the economy to those willing to accept objectification.

Authority and Anonymity in *The Air Up There*

The Air Up There positions white institutions—St. Joseph's College, a traditional Catholic college, and Jimmy Dolan, the assistant basketball coach for the school—as primary initiators of motive from the outset of the film. Dolan is competing with another white assistant coach to replace Head Coach Fox (also white) upon his retirement. *All* leadership at St. Joseph's is white: the Alumni Banquet shows a mixed but voiceless audience, yet an all-white head table of speakers. Dolan mishandles a recruiting effort and is sent as punishment on a scouting trip to Idaho. Yet, he is evidently an authorial originator of motives, for he disobeys and travels instead to Africa, hoping to win the coaching job by recruiting a basketball player (Saleh), whom he has seen in a video of a Roman Catholic missionary school in Winabi, Kenya. Dolan discovers that Saleh is the son of a tribal headman who intends for his son to someday take over the leadership of the tribe. Dolan wins the trust of the tribe, the Winabi, by aiding them in keeping their land from falling into the hands of a greedy land developer, Nyaga, from the neighboring town and tribe, Mingori. The differences between the Winabi and the Mingori people are settled through a basketball game that Dolan helps the Winabi win. He gets the prized Saleh for his efforts. St. Joseph's then chooses Dolan to replace the retiring head coach as a reward. Thus, things happen for the Winabi *because* of Dolan's entree into the society, and his access to Saleh is through the work of a Catholic missionary. Like the missionary Father O'Hara, Dolan becomes *the* agent for igniting constructive change in the Winabi.

Much of *The Air Up There*, in short, seems to be not only calling to white subject positions but also to identify whites as the locus and authority of motivation, even for the Africans. The potential effect on a black audience is to reduce chances for an identified subject position, to offer that audience no reading role to "be." Indeed, there seems to be symbolic material in the film actively offering the object position of anonymity to a black viewer.

The commodification of Africans is especially striking in the movie. Dolan has come to Africa to *get* a black man—glimpsed only as the image of a body making spectacular slam-dunks in a grainy movie—and bring that man back to the United States, in a parody of the slave trade. Dolan's first sight of Saleh in the flesh emphasizes that flesh: Saleh dives off a cliff and into a lake, then walks out of the lake, like Venus rising on the half-shell, to Dolan's rapturous and coveting gaze, Saleh's muscular and nearly naked body dripping with water. "Saleh!" Dolan breathes, almost erotically. The moment parallels hooks's interesting claim that "the quintessential symbol of the fetishized eroticized black male body as an object of spectacle is the image of Michael Jordan" (*Art*, 207).

Saleh resists running right off with Dolan, but does not explain why; at first, he seems to have no voice of his own. It is the white nun, Sister Susan, who speaks for him in telling Dolan, "Saleh's royalty, like a prince," and must stay to help his people face "adversity." Later Dolan is told that his commodification of Africans has offended Saleh's father, for Dolan is "trying to buy his son with a herd of cattle." (Note that this is a fleeting resource for black authority in an African's refusal of commodification.) When the offer of cattle does not work, Saleh becomes the prize if a basketball game with the neighboring Mingori is won. If the Winabi win, "I get Saleh," demands Dolan. The game is won in the final seconds by Saleh's execution of a spectacular play, but Saleh is not the origin of it. We see that it is exactly the same play Dolan was famous for, complete with Dolan's own taunting words that accompany its tricky moves.

This material offers to a black audience a role, a reading position, of passive objectivity. It says to such an audience, "You are commodities and will wait for others to act upon you, to speak for you." On the premise that texts are often sites of struggle over subject and object positions, however, we must note the resources within *The Air Up There* for construction of an identified black subject position with authority. Black audiences can find offered to them within this film a stance that does grant them motive and voice.

The idea of *voice* is an important source of black authority. The Africans have much fun at Jimmy Dolan's expense by ridiculing him in their own language; translations in subtitles are run across the bottom of the screen. These are African people subverting White authority with an authority of their own, and black American audiences can make use of those voices to construct authorial positions for themselves. Thus, Jimmy smilingly and unknowingly thanks his fellow bus riders, who announce in their own language, "This albino fool is traveling to Winabi," and who tell him, "You are stupider than you are white." Arriving at the Mingori bus station, Jimmy launches into an execrably voiced attempt to ask about transportation to Winabi. The agent bides his time, mastering and discomfiting Dolan with his voicelessness—then reveals that he commands more voices than does Dolan by speaking in perfect English. The agent is clearly the source of motivation here, controlling the interaction.

Dolan must walk to get to Winabi, and by luck encounters some of the Winabi themselves. They are far less Westernized than were the Mingori, dressed in tribal clothing; they wear African clothing by their own choice and motive. They are voiceless on the journey to Winabi because *they* choose to be, while Dolan prattles on to his own embarrassment. Once there, his guides reveal that they, too, speak English and have mastered more voices than has Dolan.

Once in Winabi, Dolan fails to win Saleh's father's favor. Dolan decides to do anything to ingratiate himself, but this determination puts him on the terrain of Winabi motivation. Now he does what *they* do, following *their* plans. He herds goats, disastrously, to the hoots and heckling of the tribal elders. He is given goat's milk by the Winabi, who know it will cause diarrhea. He helps haul water from the river in a bucket brigade. When he tells Saleh that technology could make that job easier, Saleh objects, "But then we cannot visit with each other," firmly replacing Western techno-motives with African social ones.

The bet that pits the Winabi against the Mingori in a basketball game that will determine ownership of Winabi land is pointedly made, not by Dolan, but by Saleh's own father. Dolan acknowledges African authority in this case: "They made a decision for themselves, I'm just helpin' 'em out." During the game, Dolan and Saleh release each other from the terms of the agreement, under which Saleh will return to America if the Winabi team wins. "This isn't about you goin' back with me," Dolan says, "You do whatever you want," releasing authority to Saleh. A decisive move in the Winabi's victory is that when Dolan is injured, it is Saleh's father who makes the authoritative decision to allow his older, errant son back into the good graces of the tribe as well as the game itself. In these ways, a black audience can find an identified subject position with authority of motive and voice in *The Air Up There*.

Narration

A text that creates a subject position will provide for the subject a fully realized *narration*. Images generating a subject position will be of people situated within a complete story, or story-like discourse. The narrative will be *of* the subject-creating images, rather than *about* passive and acted-upon objects. Narration provides an *explanation* for why people are doing what they are doing, how they got "here," and where they are going: "Only that which narrates can make us understand" (Sontag, 23). Situating images of a people within a narration therefore offers those people a subject position, specifically in two ways.

First, a subject position is engendered by a narrative that features *plot maturity*. The subject is enmeshed in a fully developed narrative that provides explanation. There is a *context* for action that grounds motives and reactions of subjects. There is evidence of beginnings, development of action, and resolution of dilemmas. The story that a subject is the *author* of is also *autobiography*; subjects tell their own stories, or they take up a relationship to stories about them. Indeed, Hayden White notes that narratives require "central subjects"—without one, you do not have the other (*Tropics*, 16).

Second, a subject position is created by a narrative that features *fully realized characters*. A subject is someone who stands in relationship to others and who gains meaning from those relationships. Thus, subjects are enabled to come fully into being only in connection with fully realized textual characters. Images that create subjects will show people linked in community, love, even enmity, with others. Out of such networks steps the reading subject. John Berger expresses this idea in claiming that "the better the photograph, the fuller the context which can be created" (*About Looking*, 61). The idea of fully realized characters situated in meaningful connection with others is expressed almost poetically by Hebdige's call for more "soul" in media images. By "soul" we think he means the depth of fully developed characters in relationship to which subjects find community: "Soul is a means of articulating a new community of affect. . . . Soul as a way of making sense—personal and collective sense—in a way that is active, and actively opposed to the kinds of sense that are dominant and given. Soul as a way of building back a sense of ground and holding that ground against a sense of weightlessness" (131).

Noise

What do texts contain that offer object positions to people? What is the "opposite" of narration? It may be useful to think of *noise* as the opposite of narration, noise in the sense of random, disconnected, disjoined information. The connections among descriptors and predicates is what makes a narrative. An object is a thing with no story to tell. Stories are told about it, but it has no story of its own. When people are objectified, they are stripped of their own story, and their descriptors disconnect entropically. We see noise as comprising at least two elements: *isolation and acontextuality*, and *otherness*.

An object in and of itself is *isolated, out of context* and relationship. It seems not to be connected to anything, anybody, any community, nor can a story be constructed to lend plausibility to its being there. The reader of the text does not know why it does what it does, how it got to be where it is, or where it is going and why. Hayden White notes that having a history is the same as having a narrative (*Content*, 9). Objectification is really what Berger complains of in saying that "the contemporary public photograph . . . offers information . . . severed from all lived experience" (*About Looking*, 52).

A second element of noise is that an entity is defined largely in terms of its strangeness, its lack of place in "our" story, its *otherness*. A major resource of racism, particularly with regard to black Americans, has been construction of them as "the Other," as objects "over there" about whom one might whisper stories, anecdotes, and scandals, but who stand mute with no tale of their own to tell. Laurence Thomas argues that blacks have suffered more from discrimination than have Jews because Jews were better able to maintain control over the narratives of and about their culture. Kovel and others maintain that this discursive stance is fundamental and endemic to racism in the West: "The dominant institutions of Western society are shaped according to white interests and organized symbolically about whiteness. In this order the black can only be Other" (xxxvii). In other words, texts objectify blacks when the stories they tell are only white stories, and whites' stories. The black person "will still be defined by an order whose power and dominion are white. And in this order, blackness is Otherness" (xxxviii). Hacker locates this work of objectification even in the moment-to-moment texts of everyday existence; he argues that the frequent experience of blacks as the only one of their race in a classroom, office, on a jury, and so forth creates an object feeling, of being that which everyone looks at or regards as strange and as Other (39). In sum, we might expect objectifying texts to be impoverished with regard to blacks: to treat them as bit players, as scenery, as being grounded in no story of their own, as isolated from context and relationship.

Narration and Noise in *The Air Up There*

With narration, as with authority, much of the material in this film offers an identified subject position for white audiences that may leave the black reader an uncertain place to stand. The film begins with narrative revealing the history of Jimmy Dolan, his tenure at St. Joseph's, his rocky relationship with Head Coach Fox. The narrative of Dolan's struggle to replace Fox is the overarching narrative of the entire movie; at any given moment, the question "What is all this about" would shift the narrative to one concerned with white people. Only gradually is the Winabi narrative unfolded. We are simply told that Saleh cannot leave, that there are problems. Reasons for the actions of the Winabi, their history, and their personal character lag far behind the development of white narratives. Whites can identify with Dolan, but blacks are only gradually given the African story and African characters with which to identify.

One result is the creation of many symbolic resources that would encourage the creation of an *object* position keyed to *noise* for a black audience. There are only two speaking parts granted to African *Americans*, and they show up early in the film: two young men who run up to Dolan to show him that they have shaved the jersey numbers of their favorite St. Joseph's players into their hair. But *why* they have done so is never made clear; this bizarre act, marking them as strange and Other, is not connected to any clear motive, nor is there any character granted to these two men at all. Dolan further disconnects them from the narrative context by ignoring them.

Dolan is off to Africa, which is treated as wholly Other. The film in which he first sees Saleh describes St. Joseph's African mission as located in "the farthest reaches of the Third World." This sense of the African as the Other is echoed by the subtitle over the first African scene: "Northern Frontier District—Kenya," marking the place as distant frontier to the more "central" West. The West is the point of reference for the key sign of basketball itself, for the Winabi and the Mingori alike have learned it from watching American satellite television. Nevertheless, they cannot have mastered it, for Dolan tells the chief, "You probably don't even know who the Final Four are." The influence of the West is shown in that the tribal elders of the Winabi are clothed in cast-off ratty Western clothing that contrasts with the African garb of most of the other Winabi.

As the standard of success, the West, specifically St. Joseph, is centered. Rather than ask what business Dolan has in Winabi, Saleh asks, "Am I good enough to play for you?" Rather than express his allegiance to Saleh, Dolan responds, "Are you with me?" Saleh agrees. It is Saleh who later says, "I believe in you, Jimmy Dolan. I would like to be your brother," positioning Dolan as the center toward which he moves. Even some indigenous Winabi customs are recast in Western terms: Dolan refers to an initiation ceremony as "the part with the rap music and the large knife."

Three scenes deserve special mention as suggesting an African surrender to Western narrative. Early in the film, one African refers to Saleh as "the boy"—despite the fact that he is an adult and well over six feet tall. The self-destroying racist implications of that term are echoed later when Saleh calls a fellow African basketball opponent "flat-nose." Finally, the celebratory African music that rises up with the Winabi basketball victory segues into American rock and roll, and we see Saleh run onto the court at St. Joseph's sporting an American haircut, wearing the St. Joseph's uniform. He can be seen as having given himself over totally to the Western narrative offered by Dolan. For a black audience, this material says that African subjects should and inevitably will merge into a Western narrative. It isolates the African subject from African contexts, history, and narrative, inserting that subjectivity instead into the European context. In that way, it makes the African Other and creates an object position for black audiences.

As with authority and its opposite, anonymity, *The Air Up There* also contains within it the resources for refusal of a white subject or a black object position keyed to narration and noise. A black audience can look to some signs as ways to construct a black subject position keyed to plot maturity and fully realized characters.

The Air Up There contains a number of scenes that can easily be read as positioning whites as Other, typically represented by Dolan. Arriving in Africa, Dolan is obviously out of place and cannot bend the Africans to his own narrative of helping him get to Winabi. He sets out on foot across the grasslands to try to find it, and is passed by a busload of Africans who both ignore his pleas for a ride and laugh at him in his distress. Once in Winabi, Dolan confidently makes his pitch to Saleh to accompany him. Saleh politely refuses and then simply walks away, leaving Dolan with no further story, no place to go, no position to take. "Don't leave me here with the goat," he pleads to Saleh's disappearing back. The next morning it is Dolan who is object and Other: awaking, he finds he is being stared at by a large crowd of children, who laugh at his sudden, flustered arising. Afflicted by diarrhea because of goat's milk, Dolan, with his pants down in the bush, is suddenly surprised by the appearance of a wild boar. The boar is killed by a Winabi who will not shake Dolan's soiled hand, Dolan in this instance representing the physically repulsive Other. More frequent, and more supportive of a subject position for black audiences, are scenes in which an African narrative seems to be primary. Saleh questions Dolan's motives and sanity in coming to Africa for recruitment purposes: "Are you healthy up here?" he asks, pointing to the head, rewriting Dolan's narrative as one of potential mental illness. Dolan's first encounter with Saleh's playing is disappointing, because Saleh plays with sheer incompetence at basketball; the other Winabi enhance Dolan's first impression by mugging disgust at Saleh's bumbling performance. The moment Dolan turns his back in sorrow, Saleh flies through the air to land a perfect slam dunk. "I played a good joke on you!" he tells Dolan; the whole episode has been an African plot, not Dolan's.

Although the film begins with the white narration of St. Joseph's, which encases the whole text in one sense, in another sense the film moves toward an increasingly Africanized plot. What began as an effort by Dolan to "win" Saleh turns into an effort to help the Winabi win their land through the basketball game; the terms of the narration shift from the United States to Africa. This shift is facilitated by the major development within the plot of Dolan's initiation into the Winabi. One of the Winabi point guards is injured and cannot play. Dolan is about to leave, but Saleh initiates the crucial plot turn: "You must become one of us," he tells Dolan, since only Winabi can play on the team. Dolan would then be enabled to play.

The process of Dolan's initiation can be read as a process of his entering the Winabi narrative. The tribe sends him on a quest up the side of a mountain, a dangerous and grueling adventure. Once on top, he sees tribal garb and gear that he is to don. He does so, but in an important symbolic move he also throws his beloved NCAA championship ring into the abyss below. He has become Winabi, positioning the tribe as center. He returns to play the game in tribal dress with tribal markings on his skin. That narrative follows Saleh and Dolan back to America. Although, as noted above, Saleh is seen entering the St. Joseph's fieldhouse looking thoroughly Americanized, we see his Winabi bodyguard standing watch in the shadows dressed in full tribal costume and even carrying a spear. Africanized plots and characters are there "in reserve," even within the context of the Western plot. In these ways, an identified black audience can find the symbolic resources for creation of a subject position for themselves.

CONCLUSION

We cannot say that any given text representing Africans or African Americans generates only a subject or object position, for, as hooks reminds us, "margins have been both sites of repression and sites of resistance" (*Yearning*, 151). In that regard, the balanced symbolic resources of *The Air Up There* may be atypical. Instead, we hope to have shown how texts may be analyzed to show the resources of signification within them, the raw materials that might be used to encourage object or subject status, and the work of racism in slanting available signs of blacks toward the work of objectifying.

Finally, we contend that this study could not have taken the shape it has were it not for the conjunction of cultural studies and rhetorical studies. A traditional rhetorical approach alone would not have been so much concerned with the construction of subjects or objects—indeed, the traditional conception of audience assumes stable subjects already "in place," ready to be swayed by a text that moves but does not constitute them. Traditional rhetoric does not usually allow itself to think as structurally as we have here. And critical studies is only lately emerging from a preoccupation with the alleged determinisms of class, race, or gender to grasp the essentially rhetorical concept of texts as sites of struggle, in which signs and reading strategies are used by people toward competing suasory ends. Both traditions need to be tapped to explain how texts make people and societies what they are.

NOTES

1. Subject position is explored in Althusser; Fiske, *Understanding*; Foucault, "Afterword"; and Stuart Hall, "Encoding/Decoding," "Signification, Representation."
2. See Husband; Roach and Felix; and Dates and Barlow, 4–5.
3. The stereotypical images are well documented in the video documentary *Ethnic Notions*.

FIVE

AMERICAN CULTURAL CRITICISM IN THE PRAGMATIC ATTITUDE

Elizabeth Walker Mechling
Jay Mechling

As a consequence of the postrationalist "linguistic turn" away from the scientistic objectivity of the Enlightenment, there is in cultural criticism today an urge to make explicit the underlying assumptions of our intellectual work. This impulse is gaining momentum in contemporary studies of culture and of rhetoric. For instance, Gene Wise provides an admirable response to this urge in his essay that recommends an interdisciplinary "American cultural studies." Further, this same goal and spirit animate both the recent volume of rhetorical criticism edited by William Nothstine, Carole Blair, and Gary Copeland and a series of rhetorical criticism seminars held at the annual meetings of the Western States Communication Association from 1991 through 1995.[1] In all of these settings, rhetorical critics have attempted to make visible the most basic assumptions underlying their critical practices. In response to helpful prodding from seminar organizers and from the editors of *Critical Questions,* some critics have been forced to consider in public such crucial interpretive issues as: how they select the "texts" they choose to study; what role theory plays in their work; how they develop interpretations; how they construct a critical essay; and the history of getting a piece of criticism into print. In many cases, these editors and critics have turned their own critical methods back on their own work, resulting in revealing reflexive cultural studies of the everyday practices of workers in what Barbara Ehrenreich, hoping to wrest the concept of the New Class from the hands of neoconservative critics, calls "the professional middle class" (10), also conceptualized as the knowledge class.

We have participated in the projects mentioned above, and we want to use the present essay to draw together something like a comprehensive description of our own critical practices. We have no intention of promoting these as a new paradigm for the conduct of American cultural criticism. Indeed, since we practice criticism "in the pragmatic attitude," it would violate our own principles to advocate a fixed theory or method. We merely want to open our assumptions to public scrutiny and say why writing criticism in this attitude brings us so much pleasure, even when the topic of a given piece of criticism is painful in some of its aspects. Becoming explicit about the consequences of working out of the pragmatic attitude leads us to deal with such questions as: Why practice criticism in the first place? What motivates our criticism, and who benefits from whatever knowledge our criticism creates? These are crucial questions that link rhetorical criticism to the various species of cultural studies, which share (if nothing else) a commitment to a critical stance toward contemporary cultures. Put differently, cultural studies makes value judgments in ways that violate (some) people's views about whether objectivity is as desirable (or possible) as rhetorical criticism, working out of the ideas of the Enlightenment, says it is. Rhetorical criticism has a complex and sometimes contradictory intellectual history involving the Enlightenment, structuralism and poststructuralism, modernism and postmodernism, and so on. We see nothing to be gained by rehashing that history beyond the fact that our pragmatic position suggests that we ask, "What are the consequences of this intellectual history for particular critical practices?" Most important for us is that questions of motives and consequences, all dictated by the pragmatic attitude, connect the goals of our criticism with the goals of those who would identify themselves as practicing American cultural studies.

In what follows, then, we present first a sketch of our understanding of philosophical pragmatism as it guides our criticism. This sketch leads to our positing that there are seven working assumptions guiding the critic working in the pragmatic attitude. We then demonstrate this approach to criticism by offering a critical reading of the 1995 film *Braveheart,* which happened to have won five Academy Awards, including Best Picture and Best Director (Mel Gibson). Finally, we offer some concluding observations on the connections between our professed goals and our actual practices.

THE PRAGMATIC ATTITUDE

When John Dewey, George Herbert Mead, and colleagues published a collection of essays reflecting the diversity of their work, they called the book

Creative Intelligence: Essays in the Pragmatic Attitude.[2] The phrase "the pragmatic *attitude*" fits their philosophy, for pragmatism is a more flexible approach than the usual sort of paradigm that neatly lays out a plan for the conduct of science. Scholars of intellectual history have noticed this about American pragmatic philosophy for quite some time. Cornel West entitled his history of pragmatic thought *The American Evasion of Philosophy* precisely because so much American thought has worked apart from traditional European concerns with epistemology and metaphysics. "American pragmatism," explains West in his introduction, "is less a philosophical tradition putting forward solutions to perennial problems in the Western philosophical conversation initiated by Plato and more a continuous cultural commentary or set of interpretations that attempt to explain America to itself at a particular historical moment" (*Evasion,* 5).

Indeed, the genealogy of American pragmatism varies from historian to historian. For West, the tree begins with Emerson and includes Charles S. Peirce, William James, John Dewey, Sidney Hook, C. Wright Mills, W. E. B. Du Bois, Reinhold Niebuhr, Lionel Trilling, W. V. Quine, and Richard Rorty. Giles Gunn focuses more on the line connecting William James, Henry James, Sr., John Dewey, and Richard Rorty, but it should interest rhetoricians that he counts Kenneth Burke in this company. Charlene H. Seigfried recovers the women philosophers such as Jane Addams in the pragmatic tradition. But what stands out clearly is that, while some authors see other histories (e.g., John Diggens) as relevant, most eventually lead to Rorty.

When rhetoricians talk of pragmatism (or neopragmatism), they tend to talk exclusively about Rorty. John Nelson, Allan Megill, and Donald McClosky chronicled Rorty's involvement in the 1984 University of Iowa Humanities Symposium on the Rhetoric of the Human Sciences and the reactions of the rhetoricians to what Rorty had to say. The response injected Rorty permanently into the conversations of rhetorical critics. Janet Horne later made the case that Rorty, despite his critics, has a great deal to offer rhetoricians, while John Lyne took the occasion of a long book review essay in the *Quarterly Journal of Speech* to offer a more critical view of Rorty's usefulness for the practice of rhetorical criticism.

This narrow focus on Rorty, both celebratory and critical, seems to us a mistake. Certainly Rorty has a great deal to offer the American cultural critic, both in his pragmatic attitude and in the vocabulary he offers for talking about communication and community. But Rorty's critics have made some solid points about the gaps in Rorty's understanding of the American social order, and we find Cornel West's outline for a "prophetic pragmatism" an attractive alternative that builds on Rorty but that has an important dimension for dealing with ethical questions in the postmodern intellectual and political landscape. Briefly, and to be elaborated later in this essay, we would say that we find Rorty's "liberal irony" an unsatisfying ethical and political position from which to write American cultural criticism. The following working assumptions in our critical practices, then, rest upon the pragmatic tradition so well described by Rorty, but the assumptions also lead us beyond Rorty in the direction of West and feminist pragmatists.

OUR WORKING ASSUMPTIONS

We can describe our practices best by naming and discussing seven working assumptions.

1. THE PRAGMATIC CRITIC ASSUMES THE SOCIAL CONSTRUCTION OF REALITY.

Pragmatism holds a theory of truth and of reality that forms the orientation commonly called "the social construction of reality." Let us look, first, at what pragmatism says on these issues and then at how this approach gets enacted in cultural criticism.

Pragmatism was born in a period of radical change in American culture, on the cusp of grand transformations of the American economy, social structures, and belief systems. Part of what Thomas Cochran calls the "inner revolution" at the turn of the twentieth century was a loss of faith in our ability to know absolute reality. William James and other pragmatists laid the philosophical groundwork for American social and psychological thinking that, through George Herbert Mead to the symbolic interactionists in sociology, saw our immediate, everyday reality as something we humans create through our ongoing communication (e.g., Erving Goffman). Peter Berger and Thomas Luckmann's treatise *The Social Construction of Reality* still stands as the best summary statement of the constructionist position. Although both Berger and Luckmann steep this and their other work in European as well as American theory, there is a strong connection between the authors' conceptualizations and pragmatic thought, a connection made through the work of Alfred Schutz (e.g., Schutz; J. Mechling, "Jamesian").

In some ways, the neopragmatic philosophers like Rorty were simply playing catch-up with the sociologists and others who were already practicing a cultural criticism based on the pragmatic approach to experience and reality. Thus, when Rorty "shocked" philosophers in the late 1970s by announcing "the end of philosophy," by which he meant the collapse of the Enlightenment view that our minds were like mirrors to nature, sociologists were already into their second generation of studying the social construction of reality. Kenneth Burke plays an important role in this history, for we agree with Gunn's view that Burke worked out of the pragmatic tradition and helped that tradition see the role of literary and other rhetorical texts in the social construction of everyday reality. In a way, then, pragmatism has been with us in rhetorical criticism for quite some time, through Burke.[3]

The social constructionist tradition's attitude toward reality is consistent with pragmatism's controversial understanding of "truth." William James claims pragmatism offers an understanding of "truth" that rejects correspondence theories of truth, and he proposes, instead, an approach that sees truth as something that "happens" to an idea (*Pragmatism*, 97). Rorty, for example, sticks with James and Dewey, elaborating a narrative-based understanding of how communities work on telling truths. Rorty's understanding of the pragmatic tradition, therefore, is that

> it is the doctrine that there are no constraints on inquiry save conversational ones—no wholesale constraints derived from the nature of the objects, or of the mind, or of language, but only those retail constraints provided by the remarks of our fellow inquirers. . . .
>
> I prefer this . . . way of characterizing pragmatism because it seems to me to focus on a fundamental choice which confronts the reflective mind: that between accepting the contingent character of starting-points, and attempting to evade this contingency. To accept the contingency of starting-points is to accept our inheritance from, and our conversation with, our fellow-humans as our only source of guidance. (*Consequences*, 165–166)

Accepting "the contingency of starting points" calls upon the critic to exercise the will to live and to work in a world continuously in the making. Doing criticism in the pragmatic attitude, therefore, probably takes a certain personality "type," a person grounded in such a way that he or she can bear the constant tension of uncertainty. Christianity grounds West's "prophetic pragmatism" (*Evasion*, 232), while Rorty's atheism (*Contingency*, 68) leads him to have a "faith" in free conversation. It is absolutely essential that the pragmatic critic be clear about what sort of faith grounds her ability to accept pragmatism's socially constructed world.

Our second working assumption proceeds from the assumption of the social construction of reality:

2. THE PRAGMATIC CRITIC PRIVILEGES EVERYDAY EXPERIENCE, FOLKLORE, AND LOCAL KNOWLEDGE.

The pragmatic attitude privileges cultural practices of the everyday sort. As William James says, in our favorite passage from his work:

Our minds thus grow in spots; and like greasespots, the spots spread. But we let them spread as little as possible: we keep unaltered as much of our old knowledge, as many of our old prejudices and beliefs as we can. We patch and tinker more than we renew. The novelty soaks in; it stains the ancient mass; but it is also tinged by what absorbs it. Our past apperceives and cooperates; . . . it happens relatively seldom that the new fact is added *raw*. More usually it is embedded cooked, as one might say, or stewed down in the sauce of the old.

New truths thus are resultants of new experiences and of old truths combined and mutually modifying one another. (*Pragmatism*, 83; emphasis in original)

A person encounters a new cultural text, familiar or unfamiliar, and cooks that text in the stew of previous knowledge. The intertextuality between the new text and the old and between the old texts themselves becomes our topic, such that the objects of our study are not the texts but the relationships between texts (relationships are real but not empirical). Both the texts and their relationships are socially constructed through verbal and nonverbal communication. There may be private meanings and idiosyncratic ways in which an individual "cooks" a text, but our criticism can examine only what is made public.

Clifford Geertz's talk, borrowed from Max Weber, about "the webs of significance" (5) suggests a grid metaphor for visualizing the relationships between texts. Wise visualizes a series of concentric circles: the critic begins with the "dense fact" at the center and moves outward to increasingly broader fields of texts related to the center and to one another. William James's metaphor of the grease spot suggests a much messier relationship between the new and the old, and that metaphor probably serves us best for discovering the surprises in the ways texts modify one another in the dialectic of the stew.

The pragmatic attitude suggests that we gather the particular details of actual human practices in order to make a persuasive guess about how an audience might incorporate a new experience into the stew of the old. The ethnographic approach lies at the center of pragmatism, even if that means figuring out how to do historical ethnography. Elizabeth's early study of the rhetoric of the free clinic movement was ethnographic because it was crucial that she see whether and how the discursive practices and organizational practices of a clinic interacted (E. Mechling, "Paradox"). For historical periods, such as our work on persuasive campaigns and resistance in the 1950s, we have had to do the historian's equivalent of ethnographic "thick description," looking for connections between our more traditional rhetorical texts and the nonverbal and verbal texts that suggested the contours of existing beliefs in the 1950s (Mechling and Mechling, "Hot Pacifism"; Mechling and Mechling, "Youthful Citizenship").

Interdisciplinary historians, anthropologists, and sociologists over the past twenty years have been developing ways to do historical ethnography. This interdisciplinary endeavor has had some jolts and changes of its own, as both history and the interpretive social sciences over those same decades have made the linguistic turn into poststructuralist, postrationalist ideas about the relationships between our languages and the ways we know the world (a point made long ago by the pragmatists). We view it as a good sign that some rhetorical critics have joined this project. Too often, though, critics take a narrow view of what counts as a historical text, so that contextualizing takes place between two or more overly similar (i.e., written, preserved, canonized) texts.

The privileging of everyday experience, therefore, suggests that the critic be familiar with the work of folklorists. Folklorists are the ethnographers of everyday life, showing in detail how people construct meaning and consent in their oral, face-to-face cultures. In our experience, the work by folklorists, rhetorical critics, and cultural studies critics converges in pragmatic criticism. Some years ago, for example, Roger D. Abrahams introduced folklorists to the work of Burke and demonstrated the possibilities for "a rhetorical theory of folklore." We see our work as helping return to this agenda.

3. THE PRAGMATIC CRITIC BEGINS WITH A DENSE TEXT.

The pragmatic, social constructionist assumption suggests a strategy for choosing a text to study. All texts are created equal. If cultures are the connected webs of signification that we think they are, or (to change the metaphor) if cultures really are like biological systems, then any single text is connected in some manner to every other text in the web or system. In theory, the critic should be able to begin with any text and follow the web of connections to every other text. Those connections and the relationships among texts and among systems of texts constitute the "contexts" for texts.

In practice, though, critics do not seem to consider all texts as equal. We must say "seem" because we see in print only the successful exegeses of texts. Unlike natural scientists, cultural critics do not publish the negative result, the failure to find significance in a text. Among the successful cases, the selection of texts does not seem as arbitrary as the theory allows. Burke assured us that he could find the representative anecdote in a postage stamp, but it is difficult to find many examples of such tours de force. Published criticism features "important" texts, "central" texts, "neglected-but-important texts," and so on.

Why in theory should we be able to get as much meaning out of any text, while in practice we consider a minuscule set of classes of texts? In formulating his own axioms for an American culture studies, Wise begins with this: "*Inquiries in American culture studies should not look for facts in experience, but for 'dense' facts—facts which both reveal deeper meanings inside themselves, and point outward to other facts, other ideas, other meanings*" (529; emphasis in original). Is it simply dumb luck that has led us to some especially productive "dense" texts? Do we have some sort of intuitive sense that signals when we are in the presence of "dense" texts? Or have we learned somehow, somewhere, what distinguishes a dense text from a "lean" one, a "thick" text from a "thin" one? We like to think our success in finding productive, dense texts, like Great America (Mechling and Mechling, "Sale") or books attacking sugar (Mechling and Mechling, "Sweet Talk"), has not been dumb luck, nor do we believe in mystical intuition.

We are alert to a potential paradox here, for the notion of "the dense text" suggests that there are qualities of a text apart from the critic's making a text "dense" through the act of interpretation. The pragmatic attitude might better say that density "happens" to a text, just in the same sense that truth happens to an idea, when the critic's goals and some qualities of the text come together such that the critic sees the text as "relevant" to her or his interests. We must be careful to see that the pragmatist's position on the independent reality of texts is not the relativist's; Rorty (especially in *Consequences*, 166–169) quite nicely dispatches the charge of relativism often leveled at pragmatists. But it is still true that no text is dense absent the critic's making it so. Beginning with a "dense text" comes down to beginning (if there *is* a "beginning" in pragmatic criticism) with a text that seems to the critic "relevant" to the world the critic wants to help create through the act of criticism.

How does the critic recognize relevance in a text, especially when (in our own experience) so many "trivial" or "irrelevant" texts turn out to be so relevant to our goals? We believe that our "playful" spirit has helped us test whether a trivial text is relevant, after all. Hence our next assumption.

4. THE PRAGMATIC CRITIC PLAYS WITH THE DENSE TEXT.

We notice that the texts we have chosen over the years have been very common, familiar texts that we have lived with in the natural attitude of everyday life.[4] To paraphrase the anthropologists, if the trick in studying another person's culture is to make the strange seem familiar, then the trick in studying one's own culture is to make the familiar seem strange.[5] How does this happen?

First, let us note that the familiar/strange dichotomy varies according to the breadth of the phrases "another's culture" and "one's own culture." The hegemonic processes of American public culture work to naturalize certain people's cultures as belonging to us all. Not belonging to the "American" culture portrayed by the naturalized images in public culture may help make that naturalized culture seem strange. Women are in a position to find strange the masculinist assumptions in cultural texts and arrangements. Similarly, race, ethnicity, social class, sexual orientation, religion, and any number of particular social locations have the potential of making the familiar (i.e., naturalized, hegemonic texts and their assumptions) seem strange, of making problematic the heretofore unproblematic.

But there is a catch here, because none of these positions (gender, race, class, sexual orientation, etc.) is privileged in cultural studies. A feminist scholar may be able to make problematic the masculinist bias in an institution or a theory, but she then may be taking as unproblematic a new set of assumptions that, themselves, could be made problematic. This puts us into the infinite regress of positions that, finally, leaves us no privileged position from which to launch cultural criticism. This may be the postmodern condition of the cultural critic, but most of us continue to write even after having made "the linguistic turn."

So, is there some more proactive strategy for making the familiar seem strange, beyond depending on marginality and difference? Here's where the interdisciplinary project and its playful character come in.

The critic's task is to step outside the naturalized, commonsense, taken-for-granted attitude toward a text. This is not so easy. Our dreams do this without our willing it, but so do some of our jokes (more on dreams and jokes in a moment). We humans seek intoxication for various reasons, not the least of which is the new perspective intoxication brings to familiar objects. Artists are able to accomplish having a different perspective somehow, and we call it creativity. We have quite a confusing list, so far: dreams, jokes, intoxication, creativity.

Gregory Bateson saw clearly what the members of this list have in common. In his classic essay "A Theory of Play and Fantasy," Bateson employs Whitehead and Russell's Theory of Logical Types to develop his theory of *frames* and, especially, of the frame created by the metacommunication "this is play" (*Steps*, 178–179). The metacommunication of play presents the players with a restricted set of rules and procedures for interpreting all messages within the frame. Play is fundamentally paradoxical. The play frame stands against everyday life and draws its power from the differences. The play frame assumes the subjunctive "what if?" mood. The play frame doubts what the everyday frame affirms. The play frame performs operations on the everyday frame, often through symbolic inversion and other decentering strategies. One can never return wholly to the naturalized attitude toward the texts of everyday life once one has played with them (Handelman, 186–187).

Having established a theory of play, Bateson extends his argument to fantasy, and now we discover the list that puzzled us earlier. Humor, dreams, art, poetry, creativity—the Theory of Logical Types and frame analysis open up what these human gestures have in common (see also

Koestler). To be creative is to be able to jump frames and levels of abstraction. And, warns Bateson, creativity and madness resemble each other in this regard (*Steps*, 278).

We must raise here the problem of volition. We are reminded of the classic example of the paradoxical injunction "Be spontaneous" (Watzlawick, Beavin, and Jackson, 199–200). Can critics will themselves to be creative? Yes and no. Bateson's theory of the double-bind suggests that some people (e.g., schizophrenics, humorless people) lack the ability to play, that is, to move easily and comfortably between frames and between levels of abstraction. But these people are few. Most people already know how to play, and one form of play is the interdisciplinary game.[6] Anybody can begin the game in formulaic ways, with faith that enough practice may lead to the spontaneous play of interdisciplinary thinking.

Here's the game. Take a text and begin to play with it. Step outside your normal, everyday way of thinking about the text and consciously assume the frames associated with disciplines. Wallace Stevens's wonderful poem shows us "Thirteen Ways of Looking at a Blackbird," so find thirteen different disciplines and play at what approach each might take to the text. Then shift frames again. Ask what difference gender makes, both in the production and consumption of the text. Ask similar questions relating to race, social class, ethnicity, sexual orientation, age, religion, region, and any other human particularity that might make a difference. Shift frames again, asking how this text may "migrate" from one context to another, from folklore to popular culture, from literature to film, and so on. Each of these moves does more to deconstruct the natural attitude toward a text and to open new meanings.

There is nothing wrong with doing this mechanically, formulaically. To be sure, playing the interdisciplinary game takes some courage and knowledge, but knowledge of a special sort. Defining knowledge as accumulated information dooms the project; defining knowledge as the ability to work at the metacommunicative level solves the problem. Practicing at playing the interdisciplinary game eventually may develop habits of thinking, a cognitive style, that bleeds over into taken-for-granted, everyday life. Thus, what we were calling "intuition" before, in recognizing some texts as "dense," is a learnable cognitive style.

5. THE PRAGMATIC CRITIC LOOKS FOR INTERTEXTUAL CONNECTIONS AND FOR PATTERNS IN THOSE CONNECTIONS.

As his second axiom for an American culture studies, Wise explains that "*IN AN ONGOING CULTURE, EXPERIENCES ARE INTER-CONNECTED ONE WITH ANOTHER. A distinctive task of American*

Studies is to trace those interconnections through cultural experience, con-
nections which the compartmentalizing of knowledge into discrete aca-
demic disciplines has tended to obscure or block" (530; emphasis, capital-
ization in original). For us, a dense text is implicated in many cultural
narratives. The first attempt to connect the text with another leads to
branching possibilities, with the implicated texts and their stories multiply-
ing almost geometrically. The dense text almost makes connections for us.

Again, Bateson offers sound wisdom on the matter of making connections. As Bateson puts it, we understand the "meaning" of a text by understanding "the pattern which connects." Taking gross anatomy as the field
and the anatomy of a crab as his "text," Bateson explains that the parts of
the crab have relations to one another that provide "first-order connections." The comparison of crabs with lobsters or of humans with other
mammals reveals "similar relations between parts (i.e., . . . second-order
connections)" (*Mind and Nature,* 11). Then comes Bateson's characteristic
leap, drawn from his central interest in the stochastic nature of systems
(including human thought) and in Russell and Whitehead's Theory of Logical Types: "The *comparison* between crabs and lobsters is to be compared
with the comparison between man and horse to provide third-order connections. . . . The *pattern which connects is a metapattern.* It is a pattern of
patterns" (*Mind and Nature,* 11; emphasis in original).

Bateson urges us to think about crabs and humans and societies and
redwood forests as stories, and once we make that leap the cultural critic
can think about individual texts as stories, about cultural systems as stories, and about the metapatterns as stories. Bateson defines "context" as
"pattern through time," and without contexts there is no meaning. Even
definition by function (his examples are a leaf and an elephant's nose) necessarily finds meaning in temporal context (*Mind and Nature,* 5–6).
Bateson provides a useful way to think about the connections between the
parts of a text, between the patterns of connections in comparing texts, in
the patterns of connections in comparing comparisons of texts. In our
experience, dense texts lead easily to connections.

6. THE PRAGMATIC CRITIC LOOKS FOR ARTFUL TEXTS OR AT THE ARTFUL DIMENSIONS OF TEXTS.

Folklorist Alan Dundes makes a useful distinction among texture, text,
and context. The "texture" of a folk act and genre, for example, consists of
"the language, the specific phonemes and morphemes employed," along
with other linguistic, paralinguistic, and nonverbal features of a communicative act we might want to call folklore (254). The texture of a folk communication is what makes it artful, and a commonly accepted definition of
folklore is "artistic communication in small groups" (e.g., Ben-Amos, 13).

Dense texts tend to be artful, though the aesthetic principle governing the text might not be apparent in the natural attitude. Rhetorical critics might be employing too narrow a definition of artfulness in the texts they study. In any case, we must always ask what the texture of a text has to do with seducing our attention. Critical essays themselves often achieve artistic communication, so a suitable question of inquiry would be into the ways the textural decisions made by a critic contribute to the essay's persuasiveness.

It is on this matter of the art of persuasion that the folklorist has something to show the rhetorical critic and the cultural studies critic, for the folklorist deals with expressive culture (as opposed to instrumental culture) and communication. The folklorist understands the folk aesthetics of oral and visual cultures and can recognize those aesthetic structures and processes when they appear in other media, such as print or film. For example, in our analysis of some of the central texts in the mythopoetic men's movement (Mechling and Mechling, "Jung and Restless"), we drew upon Robert Plant Armstrong's distinction between "synthetic" and "syndetic" aesthetic principles to show the orality of those printed texts. Many texts in mass-mediated culture are "familiar" to viewers or readers because they follow the aesthetic principles of oral composition and performance, but few cultural studies critics see these connections. If everyday experiences provide the primary material for "cooking" the new experience of a text, then the relationship between the aesthetic structures and processes of the new and old experiences are relevant for the act of criticism.

7. THE PRAGMATIC CRITIC WANTS TO MAKE A DIFFERENCE IN THE WORLD.

We note that in our own critical scholarship we are drawn to texts with moral and therefore political consequences. That one of us (Elizabeth) has been drawn to the study of social movements and that the other's (Jay's) interdisciplinary home, American Studies, calls itself a "movement" are not incidental to what impels our selection of texts. Taking cultural criticism as a social movement practice means that the critic is alert to the moral and political implications of texts, including the texts created by critical practice. *Cui bono?* (who benefits?) is a question we pose both about the texts we study and about the critical texts we generate.

Making the familiar strange is in many ways a profoundly radical political act. Radical sociologist C. Wright Mills argued in the 1950s that the goal of a critical sociology was "to connect private troubles with public issues," and the women's movement of the late 1960s quickly adopted the motto that the private is political. Symbols and narratives become "naturalized" through processes of cultural hegemony, and it is when the merely contingent seems natural that we modern humans get into the most trouble. Cultural criticism brings doubt where, before, there was affirmation and trust.[7] The autonomous individual eventually returns to affirmation but does so with the new awareness of choice. This new consciousness, of course, makes our beliefs contingent and tentative, but, having willed these beliefs, they are far preferable to the beliefs we hold involuntarily.[8]

All this suggests that the best texts to study are the ones that appear most natural to the critic. Disneyland is seductive and compelling, so we made it a text and drew normative comparisons between that park and Great America (Mechling and Mechling, "Sale"). We felt it would be irresponsible to write and publish our essay on sugar without drawing the moral and political lesson we learned in constructing that analysis (Mechling and Mechling, "Sweet Talk"). Our criticism of the civil defense debate of the 1950s and early 1960s originated in our retrospective astonishment that the bomb and civil defense practices had become so natural to us and our families (Mechling and Mechling, "Civil Defense"). In fact, we see in every case of our own work (individually and in collaboration) the political and moral practices common to social movements (Mechling and Mechling, "Hot Pacifism"). In our minds there is only one reason for writing criticism, and that is to make a difference in the world. This makes criticism in the pragmatic attitude completely and unashamedly political. Every pragmatist since William James has aimed at writing cultural criticism that searches for a better community, without believing that the community's understanding of what is "better" will remain unchanging.

In *Contingency, Irony, and Solidarity,* Rorty lays out a political agenda of resuscitating liberalism. In writing about "the contingency of language," Rorty reiterates the familiar pragmatic views of the conversational basis for our knowledge, of the processual and contextual understanding of truth, and of the role of poets and artists in fashioning reality through their special acts of making metaphors and other symbolic practices (94). On "the contingency of a liberal community," Rorty observes that "the institutions and culture of liberal society would be better served by a vocabulary of moral and political reflection" that favors metaphor and self-creation over the Enlightenment's misguided notions of truth, rationality, and moral obligation (44). What a liberal society needs, in this view, is "an improved self-description rather than a set of foundations," and that self-description emerges (never complete) out of public conversations, led by the strong poet and others who use language to broaden our view of what is possible (52). "To see one's language, one's conscience, one's morality, and one's highest hopes as contingent products, as literalizations of what once were accidentally produced metaphors," writes Rorty, "is to adopt a self-identity which suits one for citizenship in such an ideally liberal state." Rorty calls citizens of such a state "liberal ironists," and he examines in detail how he aims at steering a middle course between Foucault, "an ironist who is unwilling to be a liberal," and Habermas, "a liberal who is unwilling to be an ironist" (61).

Rorty is quite explicit about the actual practices of liberal ironists, and we might look upon these as a description of the critic's practices in the pragmatic attitude. To be a liberal ironist is to make common sense problematic. The ironist is a nominalist, that is, "she thinks nothing has an intrinsic nature, a real essence." An ironist is a historicist who "spends her time worrying about the possibility that she has been initiated into the wrong tribe, taught to play the wrong language game." The ironist views the historical sequence of ideas "as gradual, tacit substitutions of a new vocabulary for an old one," so one task of the culture critic (as ironist), we would say, is to show how one vocabulary supplants another. "The ironist's preferred form of argument is dialectical in the sense that she takes the unit of persuasion to be a vocabulary rather than a proposition. Her method is redescription rather than inference." Moreover, "ironists are afraid that they will get stuck in the vocabulary in which they were brought up if they only know the people in their own neighborhood, so they try to get acquainted with strange people ... strange families ... and strange communities ... , " primarily through books of all sorts. Literary criticism has come to assume the "cultural role once claimed (successively) by religion, science, and philosophy" (80–82).

Thus, the only "social glue" that a liberal society needs is a consensus that everyone gets "a chance at self-creation to the best of his or her abilities" and that everyone gets to participate in the public, free discussion. What helps strengthen the "social glue" is a consensus that we can hold hope for increasing human solidarity, but this is not the Enlightenment's solidarity based upon positing a universal human nature. Rorty rejects both the hope of metaphysics and of religion that there is a definition of "the human" (and, therefore, of right and wrong) that "stands beyond history and institutions" (189). Rather, the liberal ironist knows that solidarity is contingent, and she can only hope that "progress toward greater human solidarity" will come from "the ability to see more and more traditional differences (of tribe, religion, race, customs, and the like) as unimportant when compared with similarities with respect to pain and humiliation—the ability to think of people wildly different from ourselves as included in the range of 'us' " (192). The liberal ironist turns to novels and ethnographies, especially, to help her think about such solidarity.

This sounds remarkably like Peter L. Berger's argument for an ethnographically informed approach to "relativizing the relativizers," that is, to choosing, finally, how to act in the world even though we see the social construction of all beliefs, including our own (47). But, as anyone familiar with Berger's book knows, Berger's search for anthropological constants is framed by his Christianity, indeed makes no sense outside the search for a transcendental reality in judgment of our realities. Thus, Berger's approach strongly resembles West's proposed correction to Rorty's neopragmatism, though both might be surprised to hear this. Strongly sympathetic to most of Rorty's argument, West believes that "Rorty's limited historicism needs . . . a more subtle historical and sociological perspective" (*Evasion,* 209). West proposes the outline of a "prophetic pragmatism" that "confront[s] candidly the tragic sense found in Hook and Trilling, the religious version of the Jamesian strenuous mood in Niebuhr, and the tortuous grappling with the vocation of the intellectual in Mills" (212). Disagreeing with Rorty on the necessary role of religion, West situates his own version of prophetic pragmatism within the Christian tradition, feeling affinity with James, Niebuhr, and Du Bois in thinking about pragmatism in religious terms. Christianity is not the only tradition through which one might exercise a prophetic pragmatism, but there are notable elective affinities between the two. Clearly, West has issued more of an invitation than a marching order for intellectuals. Neopragmatism is no paradigm delineating a normal science. Rather, it is an attitude that expects no final vocabulary to define itself.

West's prophetic pragmatism comes closes to describing how we see our own work, especially as he describes the element of tragedy (not to be confused with irony) in taking the pragmatic attitude. Our description here probably raises far more questions than we have answered, but we intend what we have said here (understood against the body of cultural criticism we have written together) to be an invitation for rhetorical critics of American culture to consider adopting the spirit, practices, and goals of criticism in the pragmatic attitude.

Having laid out the seven working assumptions that inform and motivate our criticism in the pragmatic attitude, we wish to demonstrate this criticism with a critical "fragment." By calling it a fragment we mean that our reading of a particular "dense" text—in this case, the Academy Award-winning film *Braveheart*—is contingent, emerging, and never finished.

A CRITICAL FRAGMENT: *BRAVEHEART* (1995)

The credits began rolling, and the Oakland, California, audience with which we had just finished viewing *Braveheart* applauded appreciatively. Jay's was the lone hiss amidst the din, and as the lights came up Elizabeth turned to him to ask, "What's the matter with you?" "I've already seen *Spartacus,*" replied Jay, in a snippy way meant to convey his put-down of the film we had just seen. As we strolled out of the theater complex and to our car, Elizabeth pressed Jay on his reaction, as she thought the film not terribly different from other films Jay had liked. She allowed that the film was highly formulaic, driven by the requirements of the historical romantic epic genre, but that it was still possible to take pleasure from that formula without giving it much power. Jay explained that he was bothered by the politics of the film, coming so soon after the Oklahoma City bombing. The film, it seemed to him, endorsed the American militia movement's position that it was morally right to take up arms against a national government. He was also disturbed by the audience's laughter when the king (Charles I) threw his son's gay lover through a window to his death. Elizabeth agreed that the homophobia of the film and the audience's reactions were troubling, but she thought Mel Gibson's male chauvinism and homophobia are well enough known. She argued for an equally plausible, alternative reading of the film, one that celebrated the opposition and resistance to the absolutist state. "This film was completed long before the Oklahoma City bombing," she noted, "and the film better supports the radical left's opposition to government." Our ensuing conversation continued along these lines, with Jay expressing inflated claims against the film ("Timothy McVeigh—isn't that a Scottish name?") and Elizabeth arguing just as energetically that the film was an "open text" that could as well entertain a liberal, left reading as a reactionary one. We knew we had to write about the film to sort out our own readings and, most of all, to figure out what it was about this "dense text" that made possible and plausible both readings.

Meanwhile, in the course of our year-long talking and early writing about this film epic about Scotland's thirteenth-century national hero, William Wallace, the film garnered five Academy Awards—including Best Picture and Best Director (Mel Gibson)—and the Golden Globe Award for Best Director. Given the Hollywood community's view of its own reputedly "liberal" political values, the harvest of awards would suggest that the Hollywood establishment favored the "liberal" reading of the film, a reading that saw Wallace as a romantic freedom fighter against English colonialism. It is difficult to know what to make of the huge audiences the film enjoyed, both in its theatrical runs and in its video rentals and sales. Initial critical responses recommended the film as an epic love story; none commented extensively on its politics, except perhaps to characterize it as a film about the fight for freedom against tyranny. We have no audience response analysis to see to what extent viewers went along with the filmmakers' and critics' claims that the film was "about" the love story set against the fight for freedom, an historical romance of sorts.

Braveheart is a very political film, in our view, one that draws its power from the conflation of two discourses in American public culture in the 1990s. Through the familiar genre of historical epic romance, the film proposes a grand narrative linking discourses about masculinity with discourses about nationalism. Just as American culture was experiencing twin "crises" in masculinity and nationalism at the end of the nineteenth century, so the culture is experiencing those same twin crises at the end of the twentieth. And, just as a few "dense" texts in the 1890s attempted to solve the twin crises by bringing them together—very dramatically in discourses about the Spanish-American War, for example—so *Braveheart* connects and attempts to resolve the two crises in a single narrative.

We have just announced our thesis, our "conclusion," in advance of our analysis of the film, a move that follows the scholarly conventions of the critical essay but that gives the false impression that criticism follows a simple, linear evolution. Criticism in the pragmatic attitude knows that even our perceiving *Braveheart* as a "relevant" or "dense" text already implicates "what we know" from prior experiences (viewing *Spartacus,* for example). Moreover, once we have viewed *Braveheart* and thought about it in relationship to other texts, such as the Oklahoma City bombing, those texts now have a different meaning for us. Thinking about the conflation of discourses of masculinity and nationalism in *Braveheart,* in other words, makes us "see" anew in the Oklahoma City bombing the parallel discourses implicating nationalism and masculinity. For the pragmatic critic, distinguishing between a "text" and its "context" makes sense only as a temporary move, as a strategy meant to begin the inquiry someplace; danger lies in coming to believe that texts really have an existence apart from contexts. But we have to break into the dialectic somewhere to begin.

Even though the film's great success makes it a likely candidate for cultural criticism in anyone's hands, it is our own experience working on the discourses of masculinity (Mechling and Mechling, "Jung and Restless") and on the discourses of nationalism (Mechling and Mechling, "Youthful Citizenship") that incline us to read the film in those two contexts. And even if we weren't critics, we and millions of other Americans are immersed every day in folk and mass-mediated discourses about both crises. We "see" the film in a particular way, and our critical practice, this essay, is meant to persuade the reader that the film is doing certain sorts of cultural work, much of it dangerous. Thus, our choice of the text, our critical approach, our analysis, and our motives for doing cultural criticism are all linked. But, as we said, we have to begin somewhere, so let us begin by taking notice of some things about the text.

One way to play with the text is to play the structuralist's game. Although structuralism and formalism belong to the Enlightenment project that poststructuralists and pragmatists are supposed to have abandoned, the interdisciplinary, pragmatic critic should not be afraid to play with the structuralist's methods if that exercise leads the critic to useful truths. We employ these methods with a different "attitude," seeing the structuralist method as one tool among many to create knowledge about a text. We do not privilege the knowledge generated by the structuralist method as "true" in any sense other than the pragmatist's, but we do not discard it, either. We could "announce" some of our claims about how *Braveheart* works to make meaning, but we would be more honest in saying that, when we are "stuck" about how to begin interpreting a text, we fall back upon some structuralist methods to get us unstuck. Thus, for example, it was seeing the character of and the relationships between the two carousels at Great America that got us "unstuck" and helped us "see" how the whole park arranges a narrative alternating between the clusters of values represented by those two carousels (Mechling and Mechling, "Sale"). Similarly, the structuralist ploy helped us to get started with *Braveheart*.

Years ago Lévi-Strauss distinguished between the diachronic and synchronic structures of a mythological narrative, and it is useful to begin with these two structures in *Braveheart*.[9] The diachronic structure (or plot) moves across time in a sequence of events. Most popular films follow recognizable narrative formulae, and one of the "pleasures" of viewing such a film lies in its fidelity to a familiar formula. *Braveheart* tells the story of the coming of age of a national hero—a narrative form typical in many (if not most) modern nation states with heroic personae ranging from George Washington to William Wallace. Often the national hero does not seek the role history bestows upon him (or, rarely, her). The folklorist familiar with the work of formalist critic Vladimir Propp recognizes this formula common to many European folktales: the hero suffers from a "lack" (in this case, freedom from oppression, but also the lack of a father), embarks on a quest to find what he is lacking, faces several tests of strength, courage, and cunning, and succeeds in most of those tests, though the hero may meet a martyr's fate.

In these features, the plot of *Braveheart* resembles the classical tale type from European sources. The filmmakers "Americanized" the story, however, by adding elements of what Jewett and Lawrence call "the American monomyth." In this American narrative formula, a community in harmony faces a threat. The community is unable to deal with the threat, and so it must rely upon the special skills of an outsider. The outsider resolves the threat, but his special skills make him a risk for the community, so he must move on. The monomyth usually employs what Burke called the "representative anecdote" of the Fall, a narrative formula requiring innocence, pollution (fall), guilt, purification (mortification or victimage), and redemption. This narrative within the American monomyth legitimates the violent acts used by the monomyth hero to restore the community. The monomyth hero's violence is a "redemptive violence" (e.g., Slotkin, *Regeneration*; Slotkin, *Gunfighter Nation*) that serves good, moral social ends. *Braveheart* borrows pieces of the monomyth, showing a community of

Scottish nobles unable to do anything about their internal dissension and the external threat from England. Wallace arrives with his spectacular physical and mental skills, and for a while he is able to turn back the external threat and unite the squabbling Scottish nobles. His capture and martyrdom arise from the returning pollution of Scottish dissent and betrayal (by Robert the Bruce and other Scots nobles at the Battle of Falkirk), which makes possible the return of the external threat. Wallace's sacrificial death (there is Christ imagery in his first act of redemptive violence—the killing of the sheriff—and at his execution) becomes the redemptive act for Scotland.

The romantic narrative formula in *Braveheart* follows the monomyth in one important respect, namely, the monomythic hero cannot settle down with a wife, as he wishes. In many cases, his love cannot be consummated; thus (as in other versions of the myth), Shane cannot marry the farmer's wife, Rambo's love interest is killed, and Superman cannot marry Lois Lane.[10] William Wallace consummates his love with Marion, but she is murdered shortly thereafter, denying him the wife and children he desires. Similarly, William's love with Isabelle lasts only one night.

The diachronic structure of *Braveheart,* then, follows familiar formulae from both folklore and mass-mediated culture. The mythology the screenplay taps into legitimates William's violence, making it redemptive violence, and we are led to understand William as a hero who must stand apart from the society he is trying to protect.

The synchronic structure of *Braveheart* lies in the simultaneous symbolic relationships it poses. Lévi-Strauss's useful analogy sees the diachronic structure of a myth as its musical melody and the synchronic structure as its harmony. He believed that humans think primarily in terms of binary oppositions, and this film helps the audience think that way. The film establishes a clear opposition between WILD and TAME, which stands for related oppositions, such as uncivilized/civilized or rural/urban. The film values the wild. Thus, the first scenes of William depict him as a dirty, unkempt, almost feral boy, and the adult William returns with the same wild man's hair and dress, despite his supposed civilizing under the tutelage of his uncle Argyle. Dialogue establishes early that William belongs to the land (his very first act of return is to look at the old homestead and breathe deeply the air of home). He assures Marion's father that he wants to stay away from "the troubles" and settle down as a farmer, as a husband, and as a father of sons. This wild man stands for Scotland, in opposition to the tame/civilized/urban English, but he also stands for a peasant class of Scots, as opposed to the Scots nobles, who aspire to the tame/civilized/urban values of the English. It is important to the film that William actually has tasted of both clusters and prefers the wild. We know that uncle Argyle has taught William how to read, has taught him languages (including French and Latin), and has taken him to Rome and other cities of Europe. So there is a civilized side of William beneath the uncivilized exterior; he can operate in both worlds and he prefers the wild, in part because he sees how corrupt is the tame/civilized/urban side. So encoded in this opposition of wild/tame are other parallel pairs of values, including good/bad, pure/corrupt, and kind/cruel.

There is another aspect of William's wildness worth noting. William's dreams and final vision (of Marion walking through the crowd gathered at his torture and execution) wed the wild and the mystical. As a mystic, William has special access to types of knowledge others do not possess. This is a knowledge belonging to the "wild," natural side of the binary oppositions.

Father/son dyads constitute the crucial central set of oppositions in the film. In the order in which they appear in the film, the four father/son dyads are Malcolm/William Wallace, Edward/Edward Plantagenet, Robert/Robert the Bruce, and Campbell/Hamish. The film provides a discourse about fathers and sons through these four very different relationships.

William's father, Malcolm, doesn't last long in the film. He and the older son, John, return as dead bodies from battling the English. The father dies a warrior-patriot's death. It is significant that it is his uncle, Argyle, his father's brother, who rides up on a white horse and takes William. William dreams that night of lying next to his dead father, who turns to look at William and says: "Your heart is free. Have the courage to follow it." Anthropologists take note of the role of uncles in socializing boys into manhood in certain societies, even when the natural father is present. Argyle plays that role for William, promising to teach him how to use the sword after he has taught him how to use his mind. William is motivated by his absent father and empowered by his uncle.

The English king, Edward I (Longshanks), and his son Edward II provide a stark contrast with the Malcolm/William dyad. The early scene in which Edward supervises the wedding of his son to Isabelle, the daughter of the king of France, his rival, establishes Edward's displeasure with the homosexuality of his son, who glances back at his lover, Philip, during the wedding ceremony. Philip is always with the prince, and the two pay more attention to fancy dress than the prince does to the princess. The prince looks increasingly feminine in each successive scene, up to the scene where Edward throws Philip out a tower window to his death and the prince attempts a weak and failed physical attack on his father. The prince's homosexuality also provides a motivation for Isabelle's infatuation with William, first in the abstract as she hears that William fights to avenge his slain Marion, and then in the concrete as she meets, kisses, and eventually beds William. The prince is a feminized man who can satisfy neither his father nor his wife.

The Bruces, father and son, provide yet a third model of the relationship. The elder Robert, who hides in the castle at Edinburgh to conceal his progressive rotting with leprosy, is the unprincipled realist, who advises his son in the machinations and treachery that the father thinks necessary to get his son the Scottish throne against a number of claimants. The younger Robert is an idealist who is manipulated by his father. Despite his nobility, the son is a weak man. He submits to his father's plotting, which finally includes his betrayal of William at the Battle of Falkirk. Late in the film, Robert also unwittingly helps his father set the trap in which William is captured. Confronting his father, Robert says:

> "I want you to die."
> "Soon enough I'll be dead. And you'll be king."
> "I don't want anything from you. You're not a man. You're not my father."
> "You're my son, and you've always known you're mine. At last you know what it means to hate. Now you're ready to be king."

In telling his father "you're not a man," Robert is rejecting one patriarchal definition of manliness. He aspires to the manliness of William and does not know how to be that sort of man.

Hamish and Campbell are the fourth dyad, and they are all physicality. Hamish and Campbell perform a traditional masculinity, including some fireside joking that "some men are longer than others." They are the ultimate masculine bodies, but lacking the wit that Malcolm and William would have had together had Malcolm lived. Hamish is like a brother to William, and Campbell is like an uncle. So they exist as a model of father/son comaraderie that William misses, but they still do not have William's ideal balance of mind and body.

The four father/son dyads, therefore, provide four different relationships and five or six different ways of being a man, from the extremely physical masculinity of Hamish and his father to the feminine masculinity of the prince. In these relationships lie the material for the film's both posing the "crisis of masculinity" and for offering a solution, a point to which we shall return shortly.

Gender provides yet a third major binary opposition in the film. As a romance, *Braveheart* foregrounds Marion and the Princess Isabelle, the two women William loves and loses. But perhaps we should begin not with the presences but with the absences, with the women who are erased in the film. None of the father/son dyads has a mother present. William, who was probably born in 1272–1273, has no mother in the film, even though James Mackay reports that the historical record shows she survived her husband; he was slain in 1291, while she died in exile in 1297 (60,

112–113). The only mother in the film, actually, is Marion's, and she exists to make the point that women need mothers as role models and that fathers cannot (or should not) raise daughters alone. William's lack of a mother also erases his mother's family, so that it is his father's brother and not his mother's brother (as is most common in other societies) who initiates William into manhood.

Both Marion and Isabelle are women suitable for the monomythic hero to love but lose. The loss of Marion impels the narrative's action, for her murder is the turning point that motivates (in the film's terms, at least) William's rebellious action. Both are strong, intelligent women, but both also want to marry William and have his children. (Isabelle taunts the dying Edward I that she is bearing a child not of "his line," implying that she is pregnant with William's offspring.) The women function in this narrative to define the sort of man a woman wants—not a man like Hamish, not a man like Robert the Bruce, not a man like Edward, but a man like William.

A fourth binary opposition also reminds us of what is missing in the film and how the film codes that absence. Reading the film as a text about 1995 rather than about 1295, the critic must ask how race and ethnicity are coded in this film. The characters are all white and British, so the main conflict appears to be over social class issues, but the wild and uncivilized nature of the Scots could be coding race in an odd way. This is where the 1992 film *The Last of the Mohicans* comes into play as an earlier text that helps contextualize *Braveheart*. The central character of that film, Nathaniel, is a racial anomaly; he is a white man raised by Native Americans, and he has the long hair and dress that mixes signals about his race. The father/son relationship between Chingachkook and Nathaniel lies as still another possibility and best resembles what Malcolm and William would have had. Moreover, the politics of *Mohicans* pits five groups—a "good" Native American group, a "bad" Native American group, the American settlers, the English army, and the French army—against one another, and in this narrative the Americans are more like the Natives than they are like either the English or the French. As uncivilized "wild men" standing against the English, then, the Scots resemble both the American settlers and the Native Americans, and the anomalous figure of William (in this case, raised as a savage and later civilized by whites) strongly resembles that of Nathaniel. Indeed, there is a scene in *Braveheart* where William is running along a mountain trail, his long hair waving behind him, that is almost identical to a scene in *Mohicans*.

Our textual analysis would not be complete without noting how much the diachronic and synchronic structures of *Braveheart* depart from the historical narratives upon which the screenplay by Randall Wallace relies. The screenwriter and director took the historical record of a legendary Scots hero and rewrote the history, turning Wallace into projective material for a narrative about the United States in 1995 rather than about Scotland at the end of the thirteenth century. The problem for any historian writing about William Wallace, notes biographer James Mackay, is that the record is so sparse and that most of what is known or thought to be known about Wallace is based on an epic poem written by Blind Harry in the fifteenth century, 150 years after Wallace's execution in 1305 (14). MacKay shows, for example, that Wallace's father, Malcolm, was no mere peasant or commoner; he was a minor lord of whom there is historical record. William's mother was no commoner, either; her father, Sir Ranald Craufoord (Crawford), was the sheriff. William was the middle son (between Malcolm and John), not just the younger of two sons, as the film has it. As the second son and unable to inherit his father's property, William probably was trained for the priesthood, so he received a classical training, but not from a warrior-like uncle Argyle; William took his clerical training from a clerical uncle, his father's younger brother. In fact, so far from being a commoner was William that, in the confusing swirl of bloodlines and claimants to the Scottish throne at the end of the thirteenth century, he could have made a plausible claim through his great-great-grandfather, Richard Wallace (18).

Moreover, as we have said, William was at least eighteen years old when his father was slain by an English knight and twenty-four when his mother died. Marion Braidfute was no commoner either; she was the daughter and heiress of Hugh Braidfute. She was murdered in 1297 by the sheriff for concealing the (by then) outlaw William, and she may have had a daughter by him (Mackay, 105–113).

The film also simplifies a much more complicated relationship between the younger Robert the Bruce and William. It is probable that it was Robert who knighted William in 1297, and for three hundred days William was the Guardian of Scotland, in effect the ruler. The Battle of Falkirk ended that government. "A quarter of his life lay before him," writes Mackay, "but never again was he to exercise any meaningful influence on the course of affairs" (200). Thereafter, Sir Malcolm Wallace and Sir John Wallace, William's brothers, served with Robert the Bruce.

We see, then, that the filmmakers rewrote Scottish history in several strategic ways. They chose to have William appear a commoner, a "wild child" left fatherless and motherless and raised by a wise warrior uncle. They chose to picture him as an outsider hero in contrast with the bickering Scottish nobles. They chose to portray him as a master military tactician who lost only when betrayed by "friends" (though there is some evidence of his having made blunders at Falkirk). All of these changes enable us to read the film by connecting the film's narrative to American society in 1995.

The film engages in one additional layer of invention to the extent that it promulgates a Scots highland tradition that was largely "invented" in the first place. As historian Hugh Trevor-Roper shows, the "highland tradition of Scotland" actually was the conscious invention by Englishmen in the late eighteenth and early nineteenth centuries as part of the romantic movement that looked to more "wild" roots for "authentic experience." The kilt is an eighteenth-century invention by an English Quaker from Lancashire, for example, and the tartan plaids never were used to distinguish clans. Similarly, the bagpipe was not part of the highland tradition. But the film needs these invented traditions, these claims to an authentic Scots identity being squashed by the English. Uncle Argyle tells young William at his father's funeral that the bagpipe music is the sound of "outlawed songs on outlawed instruments," and the kilt makes possible the masculine display of contempt as the Scots army bares its genitals and then its "arses" to the English at the Battle of Sterling. The biographers of Wallace, moreover, say that his weapons would have been the pike and the double-edged broadax, the latter a formidable weapon in the hands of a man with Wallace's height and reach. But the film arms Wallace with a sword, so much more phallic in its meanings.

Having established the analysis of the text's diachronic and synchronic structures, we now turn our pragmatic criticism to the contexts that help determine the range of the text's possible meanings for the U.S. viewing audience in 1995. We need to construct an inventory of the kinds of experiences the audience would have had prior to seeing the film. We have not done an audience response analysis with viewers, so (like the historian) we need to lay out those historical experiences that best resemble in their structures and content the diachronic and synchronic structures of the film. Moreover, just because we have not done an audience response study does not mean that we cannot make calculated guesses about the likelihood that some sorts of viewers might have different readings of the film. (We, after all, have a reading that is different from the filmmakers' intentions, we assume.) Condit suggests, for example, the constraints on an audience's freedom to interpret a text, such that some texts are relatively open or closed.

Recall that our thesis is that *Braveheart* does its cultural and ideological work by conflating discourses about masculinity with discourses about nationalism. So we begin our contextual analysis with a brief description of the experienced "crises" in both realms in 1995, and then we look at the other sorts of texts that speak to these crises and that the viewer might juxtapose with *Braveheart* when viewing and thinking about the film.

There are many signs of a felt "crisis of masculinity" in the 1980s and 1990s. Among the causes cited are the women's movement, the failure in Vietnam, social and economic forces changing the nature of the family, the gay rights movement, and grand scale changes in the nature of work in

Late Capitalism. Signs of the felt crisis range from the backlash against feminism (Faludi) to trends in mass-mediated narratives about masculinity (e.g., Jeffords). The symptoms of this crisis strongly resemble the symptoms historians such as Gail Bederman have noted in American culture at the end of the nineteenth century, another period of intense change in the nature of work, as the economy moved from a stage of capitalism emphasizing production to one emphasizing consumption. Scholarship on "masculinities" has burgeoned in the past ten years, both as a symptom of the crisis and as a discourse about the crisis.

Likewise, there are also plenty of signs of a "crisis of nationalism" in the United States. The end of the cold war, ironically, ended one traditional source for national identity, and public discourse about the "globalization" of the American economy (made concrete in combative trade talks with Japan and in the debate over U.S. participation in the North American Free Trade Agreement) has made American nationality highly problematic. The increasingly harsh debates over immigration and over the value of multiculturalism are symptoms of the crisis, as are the books written for the general audience and proposing various sorts of nationalism, from the nativist (e.g., Brimelow) to the liberal (e.g., Lind). Cultural studies scholarship is also taking up the topic of nationalism and its construction through mass-mediated discourses (e.g., Eley and Suny).

In 1995, *Braveheart* was not the only text available for Americans to think about the experienced crises. These are what Brummett calls the "shadow texts" that " 'follow' other texts, ever present, rarely if ever consciously noted, dependent on other texts for their existence, yet providing reassurance of the fundamental 'reality' of the meanings embodied in other texts" (*Rhetorical Dimensions,* 46). The texts of the mythopoetic men's movement, for example, offer discourse conflating masculinity and nationalism. Books such as Robert Bly's *Iron John* and Robert Moore and Douglas Gillette's *King, Warrior, Magician, Lover: Rediscovering the Archetypes of the Mature Masculine* diagnose the "crisis of masculinity" in American society, variously blaming women, the mass media, and men themselves for abandoning the traditional roles and values of men (Mechling and Mechling, "Jung and Restless"). As spokesmen for a revitalization movement, these authors call for a return to strong male role models such as those found in "the old stories." Men should reassert their rightful role as fathers, modeling both male strength and love for their sons and daughters. The Promise Keepers, the Million Man March, and various books (e.g., Blankenhorn) tell men that they must atone for their surrender of the father role and restore the whole family. To the great extent that American public discourse constructs a reigning metaphor of the nation as a family (Lakoff), this solution to the crisis of masculinity also promises to solve the crisis of nationalism.

The films *Robin Hood* and *The Last of the Mohicans* also propose a solution to the twin crises, though not as coherently as *Braveheart*. (We should note, parenthetically, that the film *Spartacus*, with its narrative about imperialism for the audience of 1960, is both a visual and narrative shadow text for *Braveheart*.) William, Robin, and Nathaniel combine precisely the Jungian archetypes—king (political leader), warrior, magician, lover—that Moore and Gillette describe as constituting "the mature masculine" type for the 1990s. These authors argue that men are as much victims of patriarchy as are women, that our modern civilization has made men weak. A harsh and punitive patriarchy is the expression of "immature masculinity," so their solution is to call men back to a mature masculinity. The four father/son dyads in *Braveheart* help make clear the qualities of the "mature masculine."

The 1995 film *Rob Roy*, about another Scottish national hero of a later period, poses an interesting contrast with *Braveheart*. Whereas the critic might ask what is to be made of the fact that we had two films about Scottish heroes in so short a time in the mid-1990s, these are very different films. Both offer a discourse on Scottish nationalism, but their treatment of masculinity differs. *Rob Roy* foregrounds the romance, and Rob Roy models a masculinity that combines the best features of masculine strength and caring. Class conflict almost disappears as the conflict becomes one between personalities, with the main antagonist as a seeming fop who turns out to be a brutal, skilled swordsman suffering from his own family history (born a bastard of a prostitute mother and an English noble who would not recognize him). There is not much of a crisis of masculinity in Rob Roy, so the main character does not work as well as does William Wallace in condensing the two crises.

Another shadow text for *Braveheart* was the April 19, 1995, bombing of the federal courthouse building in Oklahoma City. The film opened in theaters a few months after the bombing, by which time the American public knew well the story of the alleged bombers and of their affiliation with racist, anti-government right-wing militias. The militias see themselves as freedom fighters in the style of colonial militias fighting for American independence against English rule, and we have no doubt that militia members would identify strongly with the Scots (there is an important Scots-Irish element in American history) and with Wallace's final cry, "Freedom," as he is about to be beheaded. The militias defend their right to bear arms, and the film establishes early that the Scots have to train with rocks because the English will not let them have weapons. The burning of the highland village, then the burning of English assassins trapped by William, may even echo the burning of the Branch Davidian compound, the first anniversary of which event the April 19 bombing in Oklahoma City marked.

Braveheart is not "about" the militias and the Oklahoma City bombing in the literal sense; but it is about these events in its metaphorical connections. The film captures a present cultural tension and contradiction. One way for Americans to "read" the film is as a patriotic narrative, identifying with the Scots against the English oppressors. In this reading, the Scots stand for the American revolutionaries who fought for freedom against tyranny. But another way to read the film is as a moralistic diatribe against the federal government, a diatribe that legitimates violence in the name of freedom and white nationalism. The "Freemen" and other militia groups are a symptom of the felt twin crises of masculinity and of nationality, and the acts of the militias offer a "solution" that legitimates violence in the same way that *Braveheart* legitimates violence. The use of these narratives of masculinity and nationalism to describe a morally justified violence pokes at the heart of the contradiction between a society born in revolution and yet committed to the peaceful, lawful resolution of differences. As Slotkin puts it in *Gunfighter Nation,* the "problem of reconciling democratic values and practices with the imperatives of power is both the central contradiction of American Cold War ideology and the classic problem of democratic politics" (353). The end of the cold war and the rise of threats of domestic terrorism have relocated this contradiction and helped put the force versus consent dilemma at the heart of the twin crises of nationalism and masculinity.

Another sign of the reactionary politics of *Braveheart* is its treatment of homosexuality. Mel Gibson has earned the wrath of gay rights groups with earlier public comments about homosexuality, and the homophobia in *Braveheart* does little to change minds on Gibson's position. We were quite shocked that the theatrical audience with which we first watched *Braveheart* actually laughed at Philip's being thrown out the window by King Edward. We could excuse the laughter as a nervous reaction to a horrifying sight, but the audience did not laugh at other equally horrifying scenes in the film. The audience clearly thought that gay Philip deserved the death Edward delivered; and this was in a large audience in a place (Oakland, California) normally progressive on social issues. The project of solving the twin crises of masculinity and nationalism has no place for feminized men, as is evident in other 1995 discourse about gay men in the military. But the film does have to solve the problem of distinguishing between the spiritual and physical intimacy of heterosexual men and the intimacy between homosexual men. The film, like the mythopoetic men's movement, makes clear the possibility of strong homosocial bonds that are not sexual.

Two symbols in the film that unify the themes of a mature, heterosexual masculinity and nationalism are the embroidery by Marion and William's (Gibson's) body itself. At Malcolm's funeral, where Marion and William are both children, she picks a thistle and gives it to him to comfort his sorrow. Upon his return as an adult, William shows Marion that he has kept the thistle all this time. Marion embroiders a handkerchief with this-tles, and it is used to wrap their hands together in their secret marriage cer-emony. It is this same piece of embroidery that the sheriff uses to wipe clean the blade with which he has slit Marion's throat, and which William finds after killing the sheriff. William keeps this embroidered cloth throughout the film as a remembrance of Marion, but the thistle does dou-ble symbolic work, both as a national symbol of Scotland and as a tradi-tional symbol of love. The nationalism condensed in the embroidered cloth is confirmed in the final scene, where Robert the Bruce carries the cloth tucked in his glove as he leads his Scottish army against the English and wins "their freedom."

William's body itself is the second symbol that condenses the twin themes of mature masculinity and nationalism. As Jeffords shows in her analysis of several films from the 1980s, including the *Lethal Weapon* films with Mel Gibson, the bare-chested "hardbodies" of the masculine heroes of these films come to represent the nation. Sometimes these hardbodies are battered and wounded, but their ability to recover reassures the audience that America is strong. Throughout *Braveheart,* William's (Gibson's) body represents Scotland, and in the penultimate scene of his torture and beheading this body suffers the ultimate humiliation. But William is defiant to the end, when he "sees" Marion in the crowd (he will join her in heaven) and he grasps her embroidery to the end. The film is true to the period's custom of treating a traitor to a hanging, disembowelment, beheading, and "quartering" (that is, cutting the body into quarters and distributing the parts afar). Strangely, for a film filled with explicit may-hem, including several beheadings in battle, we do not see William's beheading, nor does the film include the more gruesome customs. Accord-ing to Mackay, the traitor would be mutilated (that is, his penis and testi-cles would be cut off and put into his mouth) and he would be "drawn," that is, he would be cut open from breast to pubis, his intestines and other organs drawn out and burned in a fire (265–266). The film accords Wil-liam's body a special privacy in its destruction, and he is never literally emasculated. Thus, even his quartered body serves as a unified symbol of mature masculinity and nationality.

At the outset of this analysis we called the politics of *Braveheart* "dan-gerous." The film legitimates violence against the government as a means to solve felt crises in masculinity and nationalism. It valorizes a narrow def-inition of good masculinity and legitimates the murder of a homosexual. It is little wonder, as the press reports, that *Braveheart* was "the all-time favorite movie" of conservative Republican presidential contenders Pat Buchanan, Robert Dornan, and Steve Forbes (Garchik). But that the film is also a favorite among so many people who would otherwise call themselves "progressive" is what motivates this analysis most. There has been much scholarly heat over the summer 1996 blockbuster film *Independence Day* and its narratives about nationalism, internationalism, and patriotism. (It even has something to please the militias, in its blowing up of the White House and its confirmation of a conspiracy story that the government has been hiding the existence of aliens from the American people since the 1950s discovery of a crashed alien craft in New Mexico). But *Independence Day* is so cartoonish, so transparent in its politics, that it seems a waste of good time to level pragmatic criticism at its text. It is films like *Braveheart*, films that disguise so much of their politics, that require our critical attention. Such films seduce even otherwise critical intellectuals, so good are these films at telling a story that speaks to unspoken worries, doubts, and personal ambivalences. As we have argued before (Mechling and Mechling, "Jung and Restless"), there are unintended consequences of embracing a mythopoetic men's movement, for the Jungian assumptions carry ideology dangerous to both men and women. *Braveheart* invokes a "mature masculinity" with "a friendly face" to argue for a brand of nationalism that ought to be debated for what it is.

CONCLUSION

This essay announces through orienting principles and by example the practices we call "criticism in the pragmatic attitude." We have meant to be descriptive of our own practices rather than proscriptive for those who would call themselves cultural critics, though we recommend the attitude. We cannot locate the pragmatic attitude on any current map of rhetorical theories or "paradigms," as it shares features with other common practices in rhetorical criticism. The pragmatic attitude shares certain postpositivist philosophical assumptions with poststructuralist theories, but the attitude is well over a hundred years old and seems to flourish quite independently of both modernist and postmodernist ways of thinking. The attitude is America's most original contribution to social thought. The attitude embraces the "principled opportunism" that Henry Nash Smith some forty years ago said constitutes the "method" of American Studies, which means that the attitude borrows promiscuously from methods that work for generating "truths" relevant to the inquirer. The promiscuously playful proclivities of the attitude also mean that all sorts of phenomena may become "dense texts" for making knowledge; in other words, no text cannot count as a "rhetorical text." The attitude asks that we have the folklorist's respect for peoples' meaning-making in their everyday lives.

The attitude refuses to separate fact from value. The attitude is profoundly political, but it implies no particular politics. Thus, while our own politics might tempt us to see the pragmatic attitude as having an affinity for the leftist politics of cultural studies and ideological criticism, the attitude does not necessarily lead there. Consider the complexities of a Reinhold Niebuhr or a Peter L. Berger and one sees how the attitude carries with it no necessary destination on the political spectrum. Indeed, the pragmatic attitude interrogates all positions, including those of cultural studies critics and of rhetorical critics practicing ideological criticism. But a difference is that the critic working in the pragmatic attitude knows, with William James, that we must cultivate the "strenuous mood" in moral life and act upon our hypotheses "while waiting" for the final truth in ethics ("Moral Philosopher," 306, 294). Deconstructing all positions, showing the social construction of all knowledge, amounts to only one moment in the critical act; the consummate moment lies in asserting truths that imagine a better world. That is why we part company with Rorty's irony and embrace the tragic sensibility where many other pragmatists land. You can hear that sense of tragedy through the optimism of both William James and Cornel West. "Only trust a sad soldier," Peter Berger once observed in recognition of the sense of tragedy that must accompany action in a world of contingencies, uncertainties, and incompleteness.

These final thoughts hardly constitute an attractive case for joining the party of pragmatists, and we do not want to leave the reader with the impression that only manic depressives need apply. Rather, as we hope our published work conveys, we have great fun writing criticism. And just talking about our criticism, just arguing and laughing on the way to our car after seeing a film, feels like we are living life in the strenuous mood James recommends. And it feels good.

NOTES

1. William Nothstine and Harry Sharp, Jr., organized the 1991 seminar on "The Question of Questions"; Harry Sharp, Jr., and Carole Blair organized the 1993 workshop on "Choosing the Artifact(s)"; Anne Pym and Harry Sharp, Jr., organized the 1994 workshop on "The Spirit of Criticism"; and Philip Wander and Wen Shu Lee organized the 1995 workshop on " 'Critical Questions' In and About Criticism." We wrote a position paper for each of these workshops, and the present essay contains revised portions of those essays. Thoughtful criticism of the earlier essays and of the present chapter from a number of friends has forced us to articulate and defend our practices, so we thank our colleagues in rhetorical criticism, Jay's colleagues in American Studies, and the fellows at the University of California Humanities Research Institute at the fall 1996 residential seminar on "Post-National American Studies." Tom Rosteck provided gentle, acute criticism that helped us have our say.

2. Rochberg-Halton adopted this usage for the subtitle of his book *Meaning and Modernity: Social Theory in the Pragmatic Attitude*, and the phrase seemed so apt that we have used it ever since.

3. Barry Brummett's *Rhetorical Dimensions of Popular Culture*, for example, draws upon Burkean criticism to outline what we consider an approach to popular culture "in the pragmatic attitude," even though Brummett never connects his method to pragmatism.

4. The language we adopt here is that of the phenomenologically informed sociology of knowledge (see Schutz).

5. Please note that historical texts may appear "strange," so the historian's task resembles the anthropologist's. Because the two of us tend to study contemporary American texts, we have posed this principle as the problem of making the familiar seem strange. Of course, this easy division begs the question of what constitutes an historical event. How old and out of our experience does a text have to be in order for it to strike us as unfamiliar? Nor does this division warn us sufficiently against those cases where an historical event (e.g., our own childhood) seems familiar but amounts to, in fact, social constructions by narrated memories. In any case, separation in time is one way a seemingly familiar text becomes strange.

6. Our friend Stanley Bailis uses this phrase, which we borrow from him.

7. This doubt is a crucial element in play, and the contrast between doubt and affirmation is a key dimension of the relationship between play and ritual (see Handelman).

8. Berger's *A Rumor of Angels* still offers the best advice for moving through the moment of radical doubt to the moment of affirmation ("relativizing the relativizers," he calls it). The notion of a "will to believe" is, of course, William James's.

9. Some of the best-known criticism in American cultural studies has adopted this distinction (see Wright and Radway, for examples).

10. At the start of the 1996 television season's *Lois and Clark: The New Adventures of Superman,* Lois and Clark did get married. In violating the formula of the monomyth, the writers of this series may have had in mind a 1990s marriage of equal partners, as opposed to the cold war's romantic asymmetry between Lois and Superman. The writers paid a price for this violation of a principle of the monomyth; the show was cancelled the next season.

SIX

THE CHARACTER OF "HISTORY" IN RHETORIC AND CULTURAL STUDIES
Recoding Genetics

Celeste Michelle Condit

> How else could we articulate the word "history," now, except in speech marks, under the sign of vocative instability, outside of any assumed consensus?
>
> —David Simpson, in honor of Raymond Williams

Rhetoric and cultural studies are situated differently with regard to "history," for we understand these two intellectual practices to have had different pasts. Both practices are transdisciplinary, even transacademic, and each concerns itself with the role of discourse in the processes of change and stability in the social formation. Rhetoric, however, configures itself as having been a field of inquiry and action for over 2,500 years. Cultural studies, in contrast, values its own youth, and dates itself within the contemporary period, indexing its founders and formative events at less than three or four decades. Rhetoric has the variable and complex ties to "history" that one might expect from millennia of accretion, whereas cultural studies, if not resolutely presentist, at least operates with a truncated historical horizon.

For those interested in the intersections of critical rhetoric and cultural studies, the apparent magnitude of this difference in historical stance makes the exploration of the significance of "history" a pressing question. The urgency of the question is further heightened by the increasing dehistoricization of critical rhetoric itself. Before "history" disappears altogether as a mode of critical discursive practice, an interrogation of the historical seems appropriate. This essay moves only a little distance in addressing the multifaceted questions regarding the status of history in critical discursive studies. It sojourns in search of answers by three simple forays. First, it characterizes the stance of cultural studies toward history. Then, it describes the stance of two different rhetorics toward history. Finally, it asks whether rhetoric and cultural studies need attend to "history" and, if so, in what manner.

HISTORY AND CULTURAL STUDIES

Both rhetoric and cultural studies find themselves embedded in continual exercises in self-definition.[1] For cultural studies, this definitional angst is probably related to the youth of the field. Moreover, as cultural studies becomes "successful" as an academic and institutional practice, harboring resources to distribute, there is growing contestation over what "counts" as cultural studies. The resolution of these contests is not self-evident within an antidisciplinary matrix that has always appropriated earlier theorists and new intellectual ground.[2] For present purposes, I take as "cultural studies" that which so names itself, leaving the turf fights over authenticity and ownership to those so minded.

In general, the self-identified advocates of cultural studies define their field as "devoted to understanding the specific ways cultural practices operate in everyday life and social formations" (Grossberg and Radway, ii). Or, as it is put by Bill Schwarz, the goal of cultural studies has been "the transposition of the qualitative—aesthetic and ethical—co-ordinates associated with literary criticism to the practices of lived or popular cultures" (380). Within this project, the forces encouraging presentism are evident. The scene of the everyday and the "social" stand in some ways as opposite to "history," understood as an academic practice of recounting the great individuals and events that have shaped the nation states of the world (e.g., Chakrabarty; David Simpson).[3] Thus, though cultural studies scholars see their efforts as focused on "the particular" and as being "historicized" (e.g., Grossberg and Radway; Schwarz), this "historicization" generally means focusing on local conditions and concerns rather than relating one historical moment in time to a narrative of prior events or even practices.

Rather than placing particulars and the local in a time stream of past-present-future, cultural studies encourages linkage of particular practices to social forces, such as capitalism, patriarchy, racism, colonialism, and so on. This linkage to present social forces rather than to past events or individuals is evident in the publications accumulating in both readers and journals. Work in cultural studies is diverse, but it most often includes topics such as rock music, crime dramas, AIDS, *Hustler,* James Bond, shopping centers, "1968," and *Dallas.* A casual census of the journal *Cultural Studies* and of essay collections identifying themselves as cultural studies suggests that less than five percent of the work in cultural studies attends to "historical" concerns, understood either as an extended time stream of events or as construction of a disciplinary identity through a history of the founding and development of the field. The exceptions occur in the work of Stuart Hall and in feminist cultural studies, where there is more often a classically political focus, a phenomenon that will be used as a guidepost later.[4]

Even in those instances where cultural studies ties back into the event stream of the nation state, the time horizons of this linkage are distinctively short-term, confined to the decade or so surrounding the events, and almost (but not quite) uniformly embedded in contemporary frames. The same short-term frame is applied to accounts of the (sub/trans/anti)disciplinary formation of cultural studies. Almost all accounts trace the formation of the discipline to the early 1970s with the publication of three books by three founding fathers—Raymond Williams, Richard Hoggart, and E. P. Thompson.[5]

The relative presentism of cultural studies does not arise from ignorance or neglect, but from a series of intentional commitments.[6] The first of these commitments is to maintaining the "fluidity" of cultural studies practices. As Grossberg and Radway note, "Cultural studies is in fact constantly reconstructing itself in the light of changing historical projects and intellectual resources" (ii). Such fluidity would be weighed down by the need to maintain an extended historical lineage (e.g., Steedman). Similarly, Ioan Davies insists that cultural studies "is not at the top of a pyramid in creating a new academic 'discipline,' rather, it is a guerrilla warfare against all such appropriations" (170).

The preference for adaptation and shifting of terrain over extended historical linkages is related to the focus on everyday life, which cultural studies sees as intimately bound up with aesthetic activities such as the consumption of rock music, movies, and televised fiction and nonfiction. This attention to popular culture is in turn linked to a sense that the contemporary era is radically different from all previous eras. Work in cultural studies tends to presume that there is a sharp discontinuity between that which happens in the contemporary period and that which happened before the rise of the electronic mass media. Because of this radical break, it is assumed, long-term histories cannot be of much use or interest. David Morley articulates the sense of the fissure between the present and the past by noting the character of the postmodern era in which cultural studies finds itself. Morley asserts that "All discussion of postmodernism implies an attempt to suggest some kind of watershed or transition from an earlier period, or way of understanding or acting in, or on, the world. . . . To say post- is to say past; some kind of shift is signaled in the term itself" ("Postmodernism," 50). Stuart Hall echoes this message with regard to the disciplinary history of cultural studies itself. He suggests that "what is important are the significant breaks—where old lines of thought are disrupted, older constellations displaced, and elements, old and new, are regrouped around a different set of premises and themes" ("Two Paradigms," 520). Long-term histories appear irrelevant if one views each time period as fundamentally discontinuous with other historical moments.

This commitment to the new, the present, and the future over the past and its "history" is intricately and ironically tied to a desire to be free of the oppressive institutions, relationships, and vocabularies laid down in the past.[7] "History," as Dipesh Chakrabarty notes, has a fundamentally Eurocentric orientation. To escape the privileging of the (mis)universalized Eurocentric orientation and to legitimate and free the local cultures of the world from the dominant nation states of the West thus requires a series of dehistoricizing efforts. One of the key moments in this "escape" is a flight from the state or nation, theorized as a series of oppressive institutions that serve the interests of Europeans, capitalism, and patriarchy. Chakrabarty argues that "so long as one operates within the discourse of 'history' produced at the institutional site of the university, it is not possible simply to walk out of the deep collusion between 'history' and the modernizing normative(s) of citizenship, bourgeois public and private and the nation state" (350). The shift toward attention to "culture" and "the social" that is central to cultural studies is thus simultaneously both a move to delegitimate the state and therefore necessarily a rejection of the constructions of "history."[8]

These basic tensions between the past, history, and the projects of cultural studies can be traced to the discourses of the "founders" of cultural studies themselves.[9] Although the work of Williams and Thompson was in some senses profoundly historical, as Hall has argued, this work simultaneously constituted a reaching toward a different form of intellectual practice ("Two Paradigms"). Moreover, Williams himself discoursed at some length on the problems of historical consciousness (e.g., R. Williams, *Marxism*). The rejection of history has, moreover, been argued more radically as a foundational doctrine by the American "founding son" of cultural studies, Larry Grossberg ("And/in New Worlds"). Grossberg suggests that to do cultural studies requires a replacement of the temporal frame of modern European culture with spatial and machinistic frames. From its basic foundations, therefore, cultural studies established a relationship to history that was distinctive in two ways. Cultural studies focused on relatively short time spans and gave relatively scant attention to classically political phenomena of nation states such as leaders, wars, and elections. Rather than tying cultural phenomena to "history" in the classical sense, cultural studies emphasized links to social and economic formations and relationships. Rhetorical studies has related to history in somewhat different and more diffuse ways.

HISTORY AND RHETORICAL STUDIES

Because it has been a marginal academic practice for over 2500 years (in the West), there is no singular practice of rhetorical studies, and rhetorical work can be located at widely disparate sites. In daily life, every human being practices rhetorics of some sort, on a regular basis. Moreover, advertising, public relations, and political consulting firms fill the skyscrapers of major cities. On the academic plane, rhetoric can be located today in departments of (Speech) Communication and English, as well as in transdisciplinary formations such as the Iowa Project on the Rhetoric of Inquiry. My focus will be on the rhetorical practices of (Speech) Communication departments, from which I hail.

Two streams of rhetorical studies dominate the journals and conferences of (Speech) Communication. The first, "neoclassical," approach is deeply entwined with traditional historical practices, in some cases even placing History as a role model (e.g., Lucas). The second approach, dubbed "critical rhetoric" by its most significant practitioner, Michael Calvin McGee ("Fragmentation"), has crafted new approaches to historicity without becoming presentist or localist altogether.

Neoclassical rhetorical studies assume that rhetoric is important because public discourse serves as a major factor in the event streams of time or because of its aesthetic qualities. It is presumed that great individuals of the past have created the world in which we live through their words and actions. The words of great individuals are therefore of interest and significance both because they represent the motives and meanings of the past and also because they serve as levers that have created futures. They are also of interest to the extent that they constitute standards of aesthetic excellence. Consequently, neoclassical studies focus on examinations of speeches by persons whom the critics take to be great individuals or particularly eloquent speakers, such as Abraham Lincoln, Theodore Weld, and Dwight Eisenhower (Leff, "Rhetorical Timing"; Stephen H. Browne; Medhurst, "Reconceptualizing"). Linked to this neoclassical approach to public address is a strong tradition of studies of the history of rhetorical theory itself (Poulakos; Bizell and Herzberg). This neoclassical tradition has expended its energies preserving and interpreting a series of textbooks and theoretical treatises on rhetoric within the Western tradition that stretches back to before Plato.

Neoclassical rhetorical studies have exhibited modest growth during the twentieth century, both in quantity and in internal development. In the late 1960s and early 1970s, however, a new sort of rhetorical practice began to develop in (Speech) Communication departments in the United States. Primarily as a result of the civil rights and antiwar movements (and eventually, feminism), a new vision of rhetoric began to surface.[10] Rather than focusing on individual speakers, these scholars began to frame the study of rhetoric within collective and social parameters. Increasingly, public rhetoric began to be understood not as the intentional production of great individuals but as the product of multiple voices, in contest over power, and partially overdetermined by the nature of language itself.[11] The most recent culmination of these trends is "critical rhetoric" (McGee, "Fragmentation"; McKerrow). While heavily influenced by theoretical perspectives from "outside" American rhetorical dialogue (in general, the same interdisciplinary theoretical matrix drawn on by cultural studies), critical rhetoric also draws on its internal experiences and studies, which have consisted of a sustained critical practice examining multiple public and social discursive phenomena ranging from women's issues to "nukespeak."

Critical rhetoric has not completely disengaged from history, but it has rearticulated the character of history and its relationship to history in a variety of ways. One of these projects has been the challenging and reconstruction of rhetorical histories. Projects of this sort have included Carole Blair's creative and reconstructive critical interpretation of the histories of rhetorical theory ("Contested Histories"), Karlyn Kohrs Campbell's rewriting of public address both to include women and to revise the standards employed in the canonization of texts, and Martha Solomon's rewriting of portions of U.S. history to draw attention to such indicative and problematic moments as the Tuskegee Syphilis Project ("Rhetoric of Dehumanization").

A second manner in which critical rhetoric has redefined history and the relationship between rhetoric and history is through the production of a body of studies that portray rhetorical action as a collective phenomenon. Inaugurated primarily, but not exclusively, by feminists, these works chart the ways in which multiple voices participate in constructing the rhetoric involved in social change processes such as the quest for the ERA (Foss, "Equal Rights"; Solomon, "Positive Woman"), the development of abortion rights (Lake, "Order and Disorder"; Railsback; Vanderford), and the civil rights movements (Logue and Garner; Proctor). Research on these central social issues has been joined from time to time by a variety of other pressing social topics (Charland, "Constitutive Rhetoric"; Hasian; Lake, "Enacting Red Power"; Schiappa). Such work is methodologically demanding, because it requires defining a large group of relevant texts, interpreting the cross-cutting themes within these texts, and placing these texts within other social forces (such as economics, gender, and race). Such work also entails a continual reengagement with the historical questions regarding the force, influence, and relationships of discourse and other social elements.

The components relevant to collectivized models of discourse and social change have been partially theorized by a third version of critical work, exemplified by the scholarship of Michael Calvin McGee. McGee postulated that discourse was material ("Materialist's Conception"), that its force/meaning was determined by its usage ("The 'Ideograph' "), and that its reception was complexly shaped not only by the mass media but also by a fragmentation and reconstruction process actively participated in by its multiply situated audiences ("Fragmentation"). Studies fulfilling McGee's agenda would attend to both the diachronic and synchronic development of public vocabularies (e.g., Condit and Lucaites), but also to the way in which these were appropriated by ordinary agents. That last agenda item is difficult to fulfill in a historical study, given the limited records left by ordinary agents. McGee's latest agenda thus moves the field further from a long-term historical horizon. Such is also the case with the fourth version of critical rhetoric, which focused on television and film.

Rhetorical studies of television and film merge with those offered by cultural studies. It is often not clear to which academic subject position an author would claim allegiance (Brummett and Duncan; Cuklanz; Vaughn). Critical rhetoricians working in these areas share many of the theoretical antecedents of scholars in cultural studies, and the research agendas of both sets of scholars are shaped by the distinctive characteristics of their objects of study and by the politically activist identities of most of their practitioners. One might identify some differences of degree between the two practices. Rhetorical studies have been somewhat more single-minded in their use of textual analysis and less oriented toward audience studies, though much of cultural studies is also firmly textual. Differences in style and political philosophy were originally apparent (Charland, "Rehabilitating Rhetoric"), but styles and political philosophies have changed, become more complex, and more interrelated.[12] For the purposes of this essay, however, the most significant difference is that major rhetorical studies have maintained some degree of overt linkage between the rhetorical and the historical (understood as the political events of the nation state), even when focusing on film and television. Bonnie Dow, in *Prime-Time Feminism,* for example, describes the ways in which situation comedies about single women have developed in relationship to political events and social trends, such that the treatment of these character types can and should be linked to different moments of feminism in the sociopolitical realm. Similarly, Janice Rushing has shown the ways in which the evolution in film of the "frontier" thesis in society is both linked to and appropriated by Reagan in his "Star Wars" addresses ("Ronald Reagan" and "Mythic

Evolution").[13] As with cultural studies, however, this historical orientation is both attenuated and markedly different in character from the heavy and conventional historicism of neoclassical rhetoric. One is tempted, therefore, to consider whether the movement away from history by these two progressive intellectual practices constitutes a trend that, by its shared assumptions and convergence, justifies a complete abandonment of history in favor of presentist orientations.

DO CULTURAL STUDIES
AND RHETORIC NEED "HISTORY"?

There can be little doubt that attending excessively to the past can involve neglecting possibilities for the future. If one's attention is directed primarily on that which has been, one leaves little space for imagining that which might be different. Further, focusing exclusively on the political events of nation states may tend to draw attention toward leaders and the powerful and away from the masses and their ordinary lives. Finally, critical scholars are irremediably savvy about the constructedness of all histories. While the past may have, indeed, existed, critical scholars are wary of the ability to provide accounts of the past that carry any authority, that represent anything more than the ideological agendas of the storytellers who pose as historians.

These reasons clearly justify the decentering of modernist history according to the projects of progressive politics. I wish, however, to suggest that there is an equal danger lurking in an absence of attention to the time stream, even for progressive scholars. While the recounting of the past is indeed subject to the ideological interests of the teller, the past exists, all the same, as one of the material forces that has shaped the material constructions in which our present is bound, and therefore the past continues to exert influence on the practices of the present. Thus, Western postcolonialism is constrained by the specific geographies carved out by colonialism, as are efforts to transcend postcolonialism. These constraints rest in multiple material practices ranging from language distributions to the particular placement of dams and roadways to complex interactions among gender, race, and religious institutions. However attenuated our temporal frame, the past and its accretions cannot be dismissed as immaterial. Liberation therefore requires coming to terms with that past.

The material bindings of the present by the past cannot be negated merely by the suggestion that history be seen as a series of "discontinuities." The need for sustaining attention to history is recognized even within Grossberg's argument for a radical reframing of cultural studies away from temporality and toward spatiality. Grossberg qualifies his claims by noting that "To begin to try to think of power spatially does not mean that we erase history; it means that we see history as singular events or 'becomings' (in the terms of Deleuze and Guattari, 1987) rather than as continuity or reproduction" ("Cultural Studies and/in New Worlds," 7). To portray history with regard to new becomings rather than as continuities does not mean that the past is irrelevant, because discontinuities are always partial, not total. The sunrise of a becoming is always delimited in some ways by the horizon of the previous sunset. Grossberg recognizes this and indicates that therefore history has power. His argument is consequently attenuated, suggesting not a complete displacement of time by temporality, but a reframing of time within spatiality as a "placed time" (7). The task for cultural studies, as for critical rhetoric, is therefore to construct a new theory and practice relating the material encrustations of the time stream to cultural and rhetorical practices.

It is not clear how such a research project might proceed. As the fragment from the Simpson essay that opens this article suggests, a predominant assumption of contemporary scholarship, a legacy of structuralism, is that history can be nothing more than false tales constructed by ideologically interested narrators. We need, therefore, to perform an operation that specifies the relationship between the material time stream and the "histories" that are constructed about that time stream.

I begin this effort by distinguishing between the term "time stream," referring to the material, unsayable series of interrelationships and movements that have come before us, and "history," by which I hereafter mean to denote our speech and symbolism about that time stream. This distinction is basic to understanding that we are affected by the past (part of the time stream) in two distinct ways—both through the stories we tell about the past (narration and accreted symbolism—our "histories") and through the inevitably unspeakable multidimensional accretions of the time stream (of which we may or may not be aware). This distinction, however, runs contrary to some of the most popular contemporary theories of language, which have portrayed "all reality as socially constructed," a view that suggests that the material world is only of social consequence insofar as it is mediated by language and symbol systems (Brummett, "Some Implications"). I want to sponsor, however, a view of linguistic materialism, as opposed either to objectivism or relativism.[14]

To do this, begin by noting that the linguistic relativist view of language suffers from the errors of structuralist thought, which dematerialized language, conveying language as "mere words," with meanings "arbitrarily" determined by the formal structure of language alone. As McGee ("Materialist's Conception") and others have argued, this a-material account of language is errant. Language and its meanings are constructed through a history of usages. Liberty has the particular meanings it has in different times and places not because it is some inherently "structural" opposite of equality, but because speakers and writers have used the term in compelling ways, and these usages have both legitimated social institutions and left accreted meanings to the next generation of language users.[15] As I have suggested further, these usages have material links to the lived experiences of the peoples who employ them (though these links are not simple ones [Condit, *Decoding*]). Language thus cannot be, as Baudrillard suggests (in *Fatal Strategies*), endlessly and effortlessly recycled, with meaning dependent solely on the whim of the message constructor (though Baudrillard is correct that advertisers treat it in this fashion). Instead, reconstructing language requires work, persuasive effort on the part of rhetorical agents. This work must account for both linguistic elements—the audience's experiences and the accumulated usages of the symbols at issue—as well as nonlinguistic elements (e.g., the particularized characteristics of the media being used, the distribution of power to speak, the distribution of would-be audiences, etc.).

Both critical rhetoricians and students of cultural studies should find themselves more sympathetic to a materialist account of language than to the linguistic relativist account. A materialist account of language does not deny that language shapes the particular meaningfulness of the material world in which we live, but it does not presume that the meaningfulness of language can be independent of material constraints. The materialist view thus accepts neither the naive concept of reference employed by the objectivists (in which language simply mirrored or conveyed reality) nor the equally naive stipulation that there is no relationship between the nondiscursive material realm and language, the view which has been characteristic of linguistic relativists.

A materialist account of language thus recognizes that the past has existences and consequences that are not and cannot be fully articulated (language being an inherently reductionist and displacing medium). These material consequences are never independent of the meaning-making function of language and other cultural symbol systems, but they exert a force that is not solely a product of those systems. Consequently, linguistic materialism specifies that historical narratives are more than simply products of the ideological agendas of narrators. They are complex interactions among the narrators, the audiences living in the present, and the artifacts of the past (including discursive material artifacts such as documents, the lived language bequeathed to the agents of the present, and other nondiscursively articulated material conditions). Each of these components constrains historical narratives. History thus has an irreducible ideological component, which is itself material, but it also has other material components. Critical rhetoricians and students of culture thus can and should relate to historical narratives in the same way that they ought to relate to other cultural practices—treating them as substantive cultural phenomena with material force and presence, a presence manifested discursively. Historical narratives, in other words, should be treated by critical scholars as meaning-full. They are not merely a tissue of meaningless fabrications, though they are not simply objective portrayals of the past. History can be and must be engaged, examined, and reconstructed. Because the past is materially present in the languages and institutions in which we live, and which we seek to alter, and because history is our language about that past's presence, history must be struggled over. It cannot be ignored or left to the definition of others. Progressives who would be activists ignore these material constraints at the peril of impotence, or of doing unintended, naive damage.

I offer the case of genetic medicine as an illustration of why and how critical scholars must engage with the time stream to do future-oriented work. Critical scholars in genetics have examined public discourses on genetic medicine, arguing that these encourage an asocial biological determinism and discriminatory attitudes with regard to both class and disability. Dorothy Nelkin and Susan Lindee, for example, have argued that "charged with cultural meaning as the essence of the person, the gene appears to be a powerful, deterministic, and fundamental entity" (126). They find this problematic because they believe that "the idea of genetic predisposition encourages a passive attitude toward social injustice, an apathy about continuing social problems, and a reason to preserve the status quo" (101).

Ruth Hubbard and Elijah Wald agree, arguing that "the myth of the all-powerful gene is based on flawed science that discounts the environmental context in which we and our genes exist. It has many dangers, as it can lead to genetic discrimination and hazardous medical manipulations" (6; see also Lippman). Hubbard and Wald further describe genetics as inherently discriminatory, arguing that "tests that emphasize inborn genetic differences as the causes of potential disabilities are by their very nature discriminatory, because they sort people on the basis of factors that are beyond their control" (135).

Most of the critical studies in genetics are situated in the recent contemporary period, and they are guided by a now standard idealist-oppositional framework. Such an approach is not historically comparative but rather sets as the critical standard a nonmaterial ideal defined simply by reversing (opposing) that which currently exists. The discourse of genetic medicine is thus compared to an ideal public discourse that would assign no role to human biology whatsoever and that would make no distinctions between material states that are better and worse for people (e.g., sickness vs. health). This ahistorical work implies, and has been taken to imply, that the discourse of genetic medicine is bad and that funding of genetic medicine should cease. Hubbard and Wald, for example, argue that the Human Genome Project "promises major benefits that in reality add up to little" (67), and they assert that "quite aside from the waste of money and scientific personnel, the human genome project will have unfortunate practical and ideological consequences" (55). They conclude that "it would be better to educate everyone about the importance of diet and exercise and to work toward providing the economic and social conditions that could enable more people to live healthily, rather than spending time and money trying to find 'aberrant' alleles and to identify individuals whose genetic constitution may (but then again, may not) put them at special risk" (77).

Situating the discourse of genetic medicine in a critical-historical framework gives it a dramatically different cast from this idealist, dehistoricized critique. Comparative historical analysis indicates that the discourse of genetic medicine did not replace an ideal discourse in which social accounts were assigned sole causal status and biology was ignored, nor did it replace a discourse in which there was no discriminatory talk. Instead, the discourse of genetic medicine replaced a long-standing and highly problematic set of discourses about human heredity. In these older hereditarian discourses, biology was equally determinative. The *New York Times,* for example, declared in 1958 that "genes determine the traits of man from generation to generation" (Springer, 15), while *Parent's Magazine* noted in 1953 that "everything a child inherits is determined by the genes" and that "it's now possible to predict quite accurately various traits of an expected baby; and where exact predictions can't be made, we can state the odds for and against the appearance of specific traits" (Scheinfeld). Articles of this era were often explicitly discriminatory in their attitudes, as for example the article in *Today's Health* in 1952, which declared that because "somewhere around 80 to 90 per cent of his brain power is inborn," that "children sometimes slide down the family tree because of men's inclination to marry women of less intelligence" (Laird, 32). Moreover, these discourses assumed a moralistic cast in which "the sins of the father" were visited on his progeny for multiple generations. Genetic disease was, implicitly and often explicitly, the product of the moral failings of families. Genetic diseases, were, therefore, to be kept "secret." On a comparative basis, the discourse of medical genetics is no more deterministic and is less discriminatory than that which preceded it (Condit, "Contribution"; Condit and Williams).

There are other important ways in which the discourse of medical genetics needs to be historically situated. The idealist-oppositionalists portray genetic medicine as a luxury of the rich. They argue that, globally, infectious diseases are far more significant than genetic diseases and that it is only in privileged places where genetic disease is of concern (Lappe, 78, 81). A recent research report sponsored by the World Health Organization (WHO) and the World Bank called *Investing in Health Research and Development* (Garrett), however, suggests that this is a far too presentist notion. By the year 2020, WHO indicates, infectious diseases will drop to 40 percent of the international health and disease toll, and diseases with genetic components will rise correspondingly, increasing globally, not merely in rich nations.[16] The presentist oppositional framework has led critical scholars studying genetics to miss this material component of the future because they assume that whatever is of utility for the rich (now and here) must always be of disutility for the poor. However, this is clearly not the case for genetic medicine. Genetic disease does not allocate itself by social class in a permanent transhistorical formation—in Venezuela, even today, the poorest of the poor suffer from Huntington's disease. Serious genetic diseases tend to lead to downward social mobility in all known social formations, not simply due to stigmatization but also because long-term serious disease inherently interferes with resource accumulation and usually requires unusual expense. Moreover, ethnic minorities are hard-hit by specific genetic diseases: persons of western African origin are much more susceptible to sickle cell disease than are other ethnic groups; Ashkenazi Jews are susceptible to Tay-Sachs and other genetic syndromes; certain Mediterranean groups to thalasemmia; and Caucasians are more likely to get cystic fibrosis. Genetic diseases are thus not the exclusive concern of well-to-do whites. Poor people and minorities in substantial numbers are materially harmed by genetic diseases, and to ignore this pain merely because it is shared by those who are economically and socially advantaged seems perverse. Revising the conditions of the social system in the other ways that Hubbard and Wald suggest is surely desirable, but it is not incompatible with treating genetic disease.

These linkages to class and race, while manifesting themselves distinctively as a product of various sociocultural conditions, nonetheless are material in themselves, not "caused" by a particular social system, though they might be partially cured by one, and though they are certainly given particular meanings by the social systems in which the embodied subjects who carry these genetic codes live. The fact that the meaning of genetic medicine is constructed by the intersection of genetic codes and social codes (rather than being constructed solely by social codes) accounts for the tendency of activist groups of persons susceptible to, or victimized by, genetic diseases to support greater funding for research in genetic medicine (Kolata; Greenough). Representatives of the groups concerned have good reason to differ from the disembodied oppositional voice.

Critical scholars who have failed to attend to the material and historical dimensions of genetic medicine have chosen the wrong goals and the wrong targets. Guided by a presentist, idealist-oppositional framework, they have sought to stop "genetic medicine" in favor of a purified social formation in which a commitment to equality effaces all attention to the body and its materiality or in favor of other health interventions. Instead, critical scholarship—whether addressed from the standpoint of cultural studies, rhetoric, or other disciplinary formations—needs an historically informed perspective attending to how the body and its genes have been related to the social system in the past, as well as what that relationship might be in the future. Such a perspective sets an alternative goal—to ensure that in the future genetic medicine, along with all other health-supporting factors, will be available to all of the bodies who need them. Public funding and support are essential for this to occur. If private companies take the lead in genetic research, they will produce tests and treatments for those who have the money to pay for those treatments (Lappe, 77). If genetic medicine is a public commitment, then there is the possibility for tests to be produced on the basis of public health imperatives (i.e., "need") rather than on the basis of market dynamics (i.e., who can pay the most). Public statements insisting on equity are a preferable way to ensure that sickle cell research (which affects blacks predominately) gets as much attention as does cystic fibrosis research (which affects whites predominately). In contrast, stalling public research on genetic medicine today will only ensure that, as the year 2020 approaches and the need for genetic medicine as a health priority becomes more equally shared on a global basis, the private research format will have formulated the practice of genetic medicine on the basis of market imperatives. Scholarship that resists public funding of genetic medicine thus encourages a future world wherein only the rich have access to genetic medicine, while the relative needs of the poor for this medicine have become equally substantial. Critical discourse scholars should thus not oppose public funding of genetic medicine but rather argue that such public funding is grounds for insisting that all human bodies receive the medical care they need.

The case of genetic medicine provides one example where critical discourse scholarship goes wrong when it does not attend to the time stream in which cultural practices are situated. This example should suggest that to be free from the problematic institutions of the past requires that we understand a broad range of things about what that past was, as well as attend to the future material components of the time stream. This requires that critical scholars find methods for building their own histories and for formulating historical components in their studies even when those studies are resolutely about building better presents and futures.

HOW SHOULD WE DO HISTORY?

It should be obvious that critical-historical work is different from traditional historical work. The critic's goal is not to produce a grand narrative that articulates a series of causes and effects focusing on decision making and action by a few great individuals in the context of a nation state. However, neither can critical discursive work be a shallow ideological mirror simply "opposing" the discourses of the present. Work pursued in an oppositional frame falls prey to conservative forces because it allows conservative discourses to set the agenda, define the territory, and provide the vocabulary. To seek to be a politically progressive intellectual is different from seeking to be a political activist in the conventional sense. A political activist is present-bound. She has a particular agenda—"pass the ERA," "stop the welfare reform bill," "prevent offshore drilling." Such political activism is essential, and its tools are those ready at hand—the vocabulary of opposition and the hand-me-down ideologies of the recent past with which the activist immediately identifies. Politically progressive academics, however, while linked to the activism of the moment, are also charged with larger time horizons and with the formation (and/or formalization) of new ideologies. Such ideological work cannot afford to let the agenda be set only by the immediate moment, by the opposition, nor by previous ideologies, even when those ideologies were formulated by those on "our" side. The incorporation of critical history into the intellectual productions of progressives is therefore important.[17]

A variety of scholars have already described various components for the construction of critical histories. Historians have dealt at some length with the issue of social history, and media scholars have already given some attention to "cultural memory." Michel Foucault has both produced such histories (*Madness*) and described the rationales of their production (*Archaeology*). Closer to our immediate fields of attention, Carole Blair has recently argued that there are three key features of critical historiographies. She has suggested that critical histories, as opposed to traditional and systems-oriented histories, treat the past not as monument or relic but rather as a "text," that critical histories adopt an attitude that is neither sacralizing nor optimistic but, rather, "critical," and that historical accounts should be constructed that are neither singular nor plural but particular ("Contested Histories").

In spite of the utility of these and other formulations of the projects of critical history, the goal of much cultural and rhetorical studies should not be directed at the production of critical histories but rather at the incorporation of critical history into the study of present rhetorics and cultures. There are two important ways in which history might be incorporated into cultural studies and critical rhetorics.

First, rhetorical and cultural studies ought to be conducted in an historically comparative frame rather than an idealist-oppositional frame. That is, rather than assuming some totalistic, timeless ideal ("a public discourse free of attention to biology," "the end of patriarchy," or "the fall of capitalism"), against which the present is held up as an inevitably failed moment, the critique of the present should be framed by a consideration of the character of the past and the possibilities and concerns of the future. The goal is to be materialist by placing present practices within the time stream of past-present-future rather than to be idealist by positing each moment as a failure of a perfection located out of human time in some transcendent ideal space (a game always too predictable in its outcome and which, though often of utility in the politics of the moment, is not a sufficient guide for political-intellectual action long term). The orientation of such critical historicism is different from classical history not only because it attends equally to future and past but also to the extent that it takes account of the critical historiographic suggestions offered by Blair.

There remains, however, the question of what about the time stream is of importance. Here, feminist work is instructive. Feminists working on abortion and other social issues have shown an admirable tendency toward the integration of the concrete political policies of the present with examinations of cultural practices (Franklin, Lury, and Stacey). They have recognized that cultural practices are related not only to broad social forces such as class dynamics and immigration patterns but also to the formal laws of the state. The reproductive practices of various groups of women, for example, cannot be situated solely with reference to discourses of femininity on popular soap operas; they must also be situated in the birth rate, immigration patterns, and the surrounding laws regarding availability of contraception, abortion, and child care. The same is true for all popular culture. It is instructive to link rock and roll, for example, to the dynamics of youth and to race and class. It is also important, however, to tie these dynamics to the development of copyright laws that enable the transfer of "popular" culture from local indigenous groups to mass corporations by making the marketing of "popular" culture feasible. Thus, while there can be no singular model for rhetorical and cultural studies, the existing feminist work suggests the importance and the practicability of incorporating the state back into the reflections on local rhetorics and popular cultures. These studies illustrate that to focus on the state is not inherently to privilege "great individuals." Once history is reconceived as a struggle among multiple forces, rather than merely as the imposition of a few "dominant" individuals, attention to the state can be reconceived not as a deflection from the practices of daily life but as an interaction with those practices.

Both critical rhetoric and cultural studies have sought to "break from the past" by disavowing the notions of continuity, individual heroism, and the singularity of the events of the nation state. There are good reasons for these departures from modernist visions of "history." There are excessive costs, however, in evolving a scholarly political practice that is exclusively presentist, and the space may now exist for those "devoted to understanding the specific ways cultural practices operate in everyday life and social formations" to attend more thoroughly to and to theorize the connections between the everyday rhetorical and cultural practices of the immediate moment and their pasts and possible futures. Whatever one's disciplinary "identity" (or, preferably, whatever one's disciplinary position of the moment), history needs to be rearticulated if effective critical studies are to be generated. "History," indeed, does not constitute a simple set of objective facts. The past does, however, constitute a set of material forces by which we have been bound and to which we should attend.

NOTES

1. In rhetoric definitional essays are available in Lucaites, Condit, and Caudill; in cultural studies see Grossberg and Radway; Grossberg, Nelson, and Treichler, *Cultural Studies;* and Munns and Rajan.
2. See Munns and Rajan; Stuart Hall, "Cultural Studies and Its Theoretical Legacies"; Grossberg, Nelson, and Treichler, *Cultural Studies.*
3. There are, of course, branches of academic historical practice that have concerned themselves with "social history," and these have become more central to history in recent decades. However, the event and great individual focus of history remains its central identifier, and it is these features against which cultural studies reacts.
4. See, for example, Stuart Hall and Jacques; Stuart Hall et al.; and Franklin, Lury, and Stacey.
5. For critical commentary on these formulations, see Steedman; and Jones.
6. I employ the concept of "intention" in a bracketed way, aware of the ways in which intentions are strongly influenced by a variety of factors. For example, one is struck both by the material conveniences offered by a doctrine authorizing the "forgetting" of thousands of years of history and also by the fit of the psychological force, identified by Harold Bloom (Aune, "Burke's Late Blooming"), by which young academics are compelled to commit intellectual parricide in order to advance their own careers.
7. The fact that cultural studies sees itself as deliberately constructing a break with the past at the same time that it argues that it is discontinuous with the human past is one of those discursive seams that reveals a rhetorical project and the ideological contradictions inherent in all such projects.
8. I do not endorse this dichotomy, and prefer the efforts to reintegrate notions of the state with cultural studies and/or rhetoric (see also Lloyd and Thars).
9. For further, more poetic, elaborations of these tensions, see David Simpson.
10. This revision can be observed in an exchange over "black power" and appro-

priate standards for public rhetoric that occurs among multiple authors in the *Quarterly Journal of Speech* between 1968 and 1974. See, for example, Burgess; Ehninger; described more fully in Lucaites, Condit, and Caudill.

11. In this transition the earlier, similar concerns of the general semanticists were reframed in a Burkean manner.

12. Rhetorical studies tend to recognize linkages to cultural studies explicitly, whereas cultural studies tends to appropriate rhetorical vocabularies without crediting their academic sources (e.g., Bennett).

13. An example of a scholar self-consciously blending cultural studies and rhetorical studies to produce such a historicizing of cultural products is Shome.

14. This view is more fully articulated in Condit, "The Need for a Materialist Rhetoric."

15. This is not to deny that the meaning of language is *in part* a function of language's basic characteristics (i.e., its "structure" [see Condit, "Burke"]).

16. These computations are fraught with complications and uncertainties relating to antibiotic resistance and the evolution of new infectious diseases. Global health problems are caused by infectious agents, environmental/nutritional factors, genetic predispositions, and behavior (tobacco use will account for as much as 15% of all global death and disability). My point is not to endorse one of these four factors as central in order to marginalize the others. My point is to emphasize that all of these factors are important for the health of all human beings, regardless of class position. Health research debates should not, therefore, be conducted on a basis that assigns particular technologies to one group rather than another. Rather, we need to make our goal the equitable distribution of and access to all health technologies.

17. I use the term "progressive" for lack of any appropriate and broadly unifying term to indicate those seeking social change that would liberate oppressed groups and construct social structures with greater commitment to justice, freedom, and mutual care. I understand the critique of "progressive" thought for its tendency toward "inevitability" and its ability to be appropriated by the Right for business purposes. However, any term can be so appropriated (the terms "revolution" and "change" have both been employed ideologically by the Right recently), and to hope for "social progress" is not at all to see that progress as inevitable or linear.

SEVEN

RHETORIC, IDEOLOGY, AND THE GAZE
The Ambassadors' *Body*

Henry Krips

Since Aristotle the question of texts' influence on their audiences has been a central concern of rhetoric. In recent times the terms of this concern have broadened, in that the work on semiotics by Charles Sanders Peirce and the Russian formalist school has permitted a radical expansion of the concept "text" to encompass a variety of nonlinguistic sign systems. In particular, the field of images was opened to semiotics, drawing visual representations into the fold of rhetoric.

The impact of images has also been the concern of another more recent academic discipline, namely, cultural studies, specifically in its intersection with Screen theory. Screen theory developed in the late 1960s from the work of a group of French and English film theorists including Christian Metz, Jean-Louis Baudry, and Stephen Heath.[1] In the form in which it came to influence cultural studies, it combined elements of an eclectic range of theoretical perspectives, including the early semiotic work of Roland Barthes, Louis Althusser's conceptualization of ideology as a process of *méconnaissance* (misrecognition), and Jacques Lacan's seminal work on the mirror stage.[2] In particular, the Screen theory approach treated images as semiotic systems in need of decoding as well as mirrors in which viewers (mis)recognized themselves. One of its major strengths lay in its semiotically driven techniques for uncovering ideological messages encrypted in images. In the context of the 1970s, this aspect of the theory contributed importantly to the development of a politics of the image.

Judith Williamson's classic work *Decoding Advertisements* exemplifies the Screen theory approach to cultural studies.[3] Following Barthes in *Mythologies,* she treats advertising images as semiotic systems—syntactic combinations of visual elements, each carrying a meaning. By occupying particular positions within a system of oppositions and equivalences, these meanings are constituted prior to and independently of the act of viewing. Further, she thinks of advertisements as sites of images in which the viewer misrecognizes him- or herself. As in Screen theory more generally, the medium or apparatus within which the images are created and circulate is treated as a device—in Foucault's sense, a *dispositif*—for encrypting and projecting images onto the viewer. The image is taken as the site of a so-called gaze, a place where, by seeing a picture of themselves, viewers experience a reflexive form of self-scrutiny. These ideas dovetail well with the popular "sender-message-receiver" model characteristic of traditional communication theory, a feature preserved in the subsequent work of John Fiske and others, which allows for the possibility of viewer resistance as well as the overdetermined, contradictory, and indeterminate nature of the message (*Television Culture,* 169–178).

From its inception, however, a major flaw became apparent in Screen theory. As Lacan had already emphasized in his earliest writings, the accession to subjectivity is not merely a matter of imag-inary self-(mis)recognition.[4] The human subject additionally must enter the symbolic order, that is, fall under the law of the signifier, which, following Freud, Lacan identified with the Oedipal triangle and law of the father. The subject must also come to terms with what Lacan later calls "the Real," those paradoxical points of "rupture between perception and consciousness" at which the system of perceptual symbolic categories falters (Lacan, *Concepts,* 56). Thus, if images are to have a constitutive impact upon subjects, then their interaction with viewers must involve not only a process of imaginary identification but also entry to the symbolic order and negotiation with the Real. In his *Four Fundamental Concepts of Psychoanalysis,*[5] Lacan responded to this requirement by developing a theory of the impact of pictures, specifically paintings, upon their viewers. In particular, he offered an account of the gaze as involving the destructive assault by light upon viewers' visual fields, an assault that precipitates subjects into direct confrontation with the Real.

This Lacanian account of the gaze seems to entail that ideological factors play no role in the constitutive effects of images upon viewing subjects, thus vitiating the element of ideology critique so important to media and film theorists of the 1970s as well as more recent critics. In her book *Male Subjectivity at the Margins* (1992), Kaja Silverman criticizes Lacan exactly along these lines. She accuses both Freud and Lacan of taking a conception of human subjectivity characteristic of contemporary, white, middle-class European males and generalizing it to all times and places:

> Not surprisingly, given the ideological thrust of his essays on sexual difference, we can see the same kind of universalizing project at work in Freud's account of the symbolic father as we find in Lévi-Strauss's account of the exchange of women. . . . Freud consequently made it impossible to conceptualize the incest taboo outside the context of a phallocentric symbolic order. . . . Lacan also equates culture with the Name-of-the-Father. "In all strictness the Symbolic father is to be conceived as 'transcendent' " . . . he [Lacan] observes. (Silverman, *Male,* 36–37)

The point here is not merely that Freud's and Lacan's views are themselves ideological, and specifically patriarchal, but also that, by universalizing a particular conception of human subjectivity and thus denying that mechanisms of subjectification have culturally and historically specific effects, Freud and Lacan make ideological critique impossible.

The agenda of this essay will be to respond to these criticisms by showing how Lacan's views can be supplemented to acknowledge the ideological nature of the gaze, thus framing it as an object for political critique. In particular, I argue that a painting to which Lacan returned again and again in his writings, Hans Holbein's masterwork *The Ambassadors* (see Figure 7.1), is the site of a gaze that, although Lacanian in form, carries ideological meanings that have community-wide validity in the painting's original context of production.[6]

THE GAZE

In conversation with Gustav Janouch, Franz Kafka remarked that "Sight does not master the pictures, it is the pictures which master one's sight. They flood the consciousness" (Holland, 65–66). This remark captures in embryonic form Jacques Lacan's conception of the gaze. Looking at pictures, Lacan says, is never simply a matter of receiving externally impressed images and then mastering them by decoding their meanings. Instead, the viewer's eye strains to pick out shapes in a flood of light that always and already threatens to overwhelm it, bursting apart the seams of the visual field. Lacan's name for this flood of light and the field of its effects is "the gaze." The gaze challenges us to make sense of what we see and to form an image, but it also, by a mechanism that I will discuss later, places us under scrutiny.

Lacan discusses the gaze in a story about a boat trip that he took with

FIGURE 7.1. Hans Holbein's *The Ambassadors*. Used courtesy of the National Gallery, Washington, DC.

a group of Breton fishermen when he was in his twenties. It was a sunny day, and a tin can floated on the sea, reflecting sunlight into his eyes. "You see that can?" said one of the fisherman with a laugh, "Do you see it? Well, it doesn't see you!" Lacan recounts his reaction:

> the can did not see me . . . [but] it was looking at me all the same . . . and I am not speaking metaphorically. . . . I, at the moment—as I appeared to those fellows who were earning their livings with great difficulty . . . looked like nothing on earth. In short, I was rather out of place in the picture. And it was because I felt this that I was not terribly amused. . . . (Lacan, *Concepts*, 96)

Thus the light not only unsettled his visual field but also made him feel under scrutiny, challenging his sense of self. He came to feel, as he says, "out of place" in the scene as the indeterminacy characteristic of the glint of light spilled over onto its viewer. Lacan identifies the gaze with this challenging glint of light: "[the] gaze is always a play of light and opacity. It is always that gleam of light—it lay at the heart of my little story. . . . In short, the point of the gaze always participates in the ambiguity of the jewel" (96).

In general terms, then, Lacan restricts the gaze to those points of distortion in the visual field where the appearance of objects threatens to disintegrate into a play of light and shadow—where, by unmasking light as the raw material from which appearances are fashioned, viewers glimpse their own active contribution to what they see. Thus, the gaze is like the moment in a movie when the mechanics of image production come into view, when, by showing the grain of the film or a shadow cast by the projectionist's hand, the movie affords a glimpse of its own nature as a constructed image. In film theoretic terms, the gaze is the point at which the illusion of realism wavers. Or, in cognitive terms, it is a point where the visual field breaks out of the system of percepts in terms of which it is symbolized.[7]

More specifically, Lacan insists that the gaze belongs to the order of the Real, meaning that it is not only a point where the visual field escapes the processes of symbolization but also a site where the subject experiences an unrealistic anxiety such as the young Lacan's evident discomfort at the glint of light.[8] In Freud's view, such anxiety is associated with repetitions (*Wierderholungen*), that is, events connected by chains of unconscious associations with the domain of the repressed (*Verdrängt*). Even from the slim evidence Lacan offers us we can speculate what the relevant train of associations might be that connects the glint of light to the young Lacan's repressed.

Before doing so, however, it is important to remark upon a certain ambiguity that affects the Lacanian conception of the gaze and is endemic to his writings at large. In the story of his youthful adventure at sea Lacan locates the gaze equivocally between the actual upwelling of light that blinded him, its subjective effect as a distortion of his visual field, and its objective cause, specifically the glinting surface of the tin can. This ambiguity takes a more general form in Lacan's writings, as an uncertainty whether the "*objet a,*" of which the gaze is a special case, is a concrete object, such as the cotton reel in the famous *Fort-Da* game described by Freud, or rather a "lost object," such as the absence in the child's life opened up by loss of access to its mother's breast. In the latter case, the *objet a* is a fiction, namely, the idealized cornucopia to which the subject never had access but around which a certain narrative of lack is constructed. Such fictions are connected to concrete objects only by metaphoric relations of substitution, in the way that the cotton reel in the

Fort-Da game substitutes for the missing maternal breast. I make no attempt to resolve this creative ambiguity in Lacan's architectonic except where clarity of exposition requires. In so doing, I follow Lacan's own strategy of refusing to define the *objet a* (282). For the specific purpose of discussing Lacan's story of his day at sea, however, I take the gaze as identical with the physical glint of light rather than the tin can or the distortion created in the young Lacan's visual field.

UNCONSCIOUS ILLUMINATION

The fisherman's sardonic remark "You see that can? . . . Well, it doesn't see you" thrust upon the politically radical young Lacan an unwelcome image of himself as a day-tripper, tourist, and class enemy of those men whom he admired and counted as friends and who were, as he says, "earning their money with great difficulty." Insofar as he recognized himself in this image—recognized the justness of what was not only a self-accusation but also an accusation by one he regarded as friend—he felt himself at a loss or, as he says, "rather out of place in the picture."

This loss of sense of self is structurally similar to a central incident in Freud's account of the formation of human subjects, that traumatic moment when, by experiencing a need for what they lack, for example the mother's breast, infants first recognize themselves as a site of loss. Children subsequently repress the memory of this originary loss, but it continues to structure their subsequent activities at a symptomatic level. In other words, in certain respects children continue to act as if they remembered the primal scene even though they do not.[9]

Because it creates a structure of loss, the joke is able to function as a disguised means of repeating the primal scene; in other words, the young Lacan's perception that he is laughed at functions as an indirect means of recalling the primal scene. Following Freud, Lacan regards perceptual experiences generally as representations or, in Freud's terms, *Sachvorstellungen*, that is, ideas, and in particular images, in terms of which subjects represent or "picture" the things they experience. Thus the perception created in the young Lacan by the joke is a representation substituting for, that is recalling, another representation, namely, the always and already repressed representation of the primal scene. This means that the perceptual experience of the joke takes the classic form of a metaphoric signifier, a representation substituting for another representation on the basis of structural similarity. Such metaphoric connections, which in the terminology of nineneteenth-century psychology Freud calls "associations," constitute the basis of the unconscious.[10]

By focusing upon the glint of light rather than his friend's joke as the cause of his discomfort, the young Lacan concealed from himself, as much as his companions, the shame he felt when looking at himself through their eyes. The glint of light was not only close at hand, indeed the pretext for the joke, but also a source of discomfort in its own right, albeit of a purely physical kind, and thus similar to the joke in respect of its negative affective connotations. In virtue of these relations of contiguity as well as affective similarity, the impressions created by the glint of light functioned as indirect reminders or, in Lacanian terms, metonymies and metaphors for the joke that discomforted the young Lacan.

The chain of multiple associations of both a metaphoric and metonymic kind between the glint of light, the joke, and the primal void at the center of the infant Lacan's being created the possibility of these three events converging at an unconscious level. The discomfort stimulated in the young Lacan by the glint of light as well as its long-lasting psychic effects, in particular the fact of its memorialization more than twenty years later in his writings, are evidence that such unconscious convergence in fact took place. Thus the discomfort created by his experience at sea falls under the category of "unrealistic anxiety": a manifestation of repressed fears associated with the primal scene that continue to circulate at an unconscious level and surface in disguised form by fixing upon the young Lacan's moment of maritime embarrassment.

In sum, the glint of light takes on the dimensions of the gaze. It distorts the visual field but also is a source of "unrealistic anxiety," a fact established by its later effects as much as its contemporaneous affect. Because of its unconscious connections with culturally generated images, the glint of light also functioned as a relay point for ideological effects, a point to which I will return.

My account of the gaze so far leaves unanswered a key question. How do distortions constitutive of the gaze create the feeling of being under scrutiny described by Lacan in his seafaring story: "the can did not see me . . . [but] it was looking at me all the same"? From a position strongly affiliated with the Screen theory tradition, Kaja Silverman suggests an answer to which I now turn.

SCREEN THEORY AND THE GAZE

According to Silverman, as for Screen theory approaches more generally, the gaze is a means of projecting onto individuals images in terms of which they are constituted as subjects. As Silverman puts it:

> . . . the gaze . . . has . . . power to constitute subjectivity . . . by projecting the screen [her term for the image] on to the object. . . . Just as Lacan's infant can see him or herself only through the intervention of an external

image, the gaze can "photograph" the object only through the grid of the screen. (*Male,* 150)

She also insists—and here she draws a contrast between herself and Lacan—that images projected by the gaze are "culturally generated" and in a quite traditional sense "ideological":

> Although *Four Fundamental Concepts* does not do so, it seems to me crucial that we insist upon the ideological nature of the screen by describing it as that culturally generated image or repertoire of images through which subjects are not only constituted, but differentiated in relation to class, race, sexuality, age, and nationality. (150)[11]

For Silverman, the gaze operates as does Foucault's panopticon: It is a disciplinary apparatus by which "subject positions," socially prescribed images of how to be a subject, are transmitted to and enjoined upon individuals. The images transmitted are often multiple and incoherent. Indeed, insofar as they are ideological in something like the original Marxist sense, they must incorporate internal contradictions that it is their function to mask.

In receiving such images individuals recognize themselves as if they were looking in a mirror: "It's me, that's how I really am!", which is to experience oneself as on display. This does not mean that viewers simply identify with a character or viewing position encoded in an image. On the contrary, as Fiske and others have argued, the viewer is engaged in a complex relation of "implication-extrication" with such characters or positions, one which allows a pleasurable variation between empathic identification and critical distancing.[12] Instead, viewers identify with what Fiske refers to as the "play of similarity and difference along the axes of nation, race, class, gender, power, work, etc." (*Television Culture,* 178). In other words, insofar as viewer identification involves specular recognition, it is through recognizing a range of possible identities.

In particular situations a single object may function as an apparent focus or relay point for transmitting ideological images. For example, a television camera mounted on the wall or a policeman's shout "Hey you there" may not only insert us as objects into a field of visibility, that is, make us feel under scrutiny, but also disturb our sense of self. According to Screen theory, such objects take on the role of the gaze.

According to Screen theory, then, the gaze constitutes subjects by leading them to recognize themselves in terms of culturally generated images. Insofar as those images are incoherent they impose upon subjects a degree of indeterminacy that it is the task of ideology to mask. The experience of being scrutinized emerges as an aspect of the specular nature of this process.

Screen theory offers a plausible explanation of the effects of a range of visual phenomena, especially mass-mediated images, but faces major difficulties in accounting for the effects of the glint of light encountered by the young Lacan. Because the glint did not encode an ideologically loaded image with which he could identify, it is difficult to see how Screen theory can explain the presence of a gaze in this case, let alone account for the young Lacan's experience of being under surveillance. It is true, of course, that the glint did have unconscious connections with meanings of an ideological nature. But such connections are not germane to Screen theory, which concerns itself with ideological meanings encoded in predetermined images according to generally accepted conventions, rather than amorphous glints of light that stimulate unconscious associations for particular viewers. In the next section I suggest an alternative to Screen theory that does justice to Lacan's story of his youthful adventures at sea and manages to explain his feeling of being under scrutiny.

THE GAZE AS SITE OF SCRUTINY

The glint of light distorts the young Lacan's visual field. Because of its unconscious resonances, manifested in the anxieties that surround it, he cannot ignore it. On the contrary, it fascinates him. Gripped by the situation into which it precipitates him, he steps back and forward, squinting, refocusing, anxiously changing points of view in order to rework what he sees, in the process transforming his own seeing into an object in his field of vision. In short, the glint of light induces him to revisit and review what he has seen, creating a doubling and interplay of points of view through which he observes his own presence in, and effects upon, his visual field. Thus, the gaze creates not a particular look but rather a differential field of looks, which includes among its effects viewers placing themselves under scrutiny.

The effects of the gaze are analogous to the phenomenon of *s'entendre parler* (listening to oneself talk) produced in an echo chamber, when the formal split between the subject of *enoncé* (the subject who utters) and the subject of *enonciation* (the subject as referred to by his or her own speech) manifests as a temporal lag between an utterance and its echo, a temporal lag that distorts the field of speech. In the context of this analogy, it is, as Jacques-Alain Miller argues, a mistake to take the gaze simply as an analogue of the subject of *enoncé,* (or indeed of *enonciation*):

> It [the gaze] is an object articulated not to the subject but to its division, to a subject which does not represent to itself the objects of the world but

which is itself represented. For this reason we cannot say that the structure of this object is identical to that of the *enoncé*. (Miller, 128)

Instead, the gaze is the analogue of the distortion created by the echo
effects. Lacan's name for this invocatory analogue of the gaze is "the
voice."

In sum, then, the experience of being under surveillance resulting from
the gaze is the result of viewers adjusting their sights in response to a failure to see clearly rather than, as Screen theory claims, the effect of a process of specular (mis)recognition in response to an externally projected
image. Because of the anxiety attending the gaze, such surveillance takes on
an uncanny dimension, exemplified by the mask hanging on the wall that
seems to stare back at its viewers: "The world is all seeing, but . . . it does
not provoke our gaze [look]. When it begins to provoke it, the feeling of
strangeness begins too" (Lacem, *Four Fundamental Concepts*, 75).

My account of the gaze differs from Screen theory's in two key
respects. First, by emphasizing the role of the Real rather than focusing
upon the imaginary and symbolic, it grounds itself in Lacan's own account
of the gaze. Consequently, unlike Screen theory, it manages to explain how
the gaze operates during Lacan's seagoing encounter with the glint of light.
Second, it suggests that a gaze carries ideological meanings via chains of
unconscious associations rather than by encoding them according to publicly instituted conventions. Since unconscious associations vary radically
from person to person, this raises the possibility that different viewers
within a community may construct quite different meanings for the same
gaze. In such a case, since there is no general, community-wide ideological
meaning to function as an object of critique, a politics of the gaze in the
sense envisaged by Screen theory is not possible. In the next section, I
resolve this difficulty by showing how my account of the gaze allows it to
have widespread ideological effects in the case of Holbein's painting *The
Ambassadors*.

THE AMBASSADORS' BODY

Holbein painted *The Ambassadors* during 1532, the year after he settled in
England. The picture portrays two French men: Jean de Dinteville, Seigneur
de Polisy (1504–1965) and Georges de Selve, Bishop of Lavour
(1509–1542). The picture was a private commission by de Dinteville upon
the occasion of a secret visit to England by his friend de Selve, had been
unsuccessfully negotiating on behalf of the French king with England's
Henry VIII concerning the highly sensitive question of relations with Rome.

In the lower foreground of the painting is an anamorphically projected image of a skull, an object that comes into focus only when the viewer steps to the side of the picture and looks at it awry. Lacan claims that this distorted image is "the gaze as such, in its pulsatile, dazzling and spread out function" (Lacan, *Concepts*, 89). He contextualizes this assertion with a few remarks concerning the "furious polemics" to which the production of anamorphic images gave rise in the sixteenth century, when researches into geometric perspective and the invention of Dürer's "window" (the perspectival device pictured in Dürer's famous woodcut—see John Berger *Ways of Seeing*, 62) enabled the development of mechanical techniques for perspectival painting. What justifies the claim that Holbein's anamorphic image of the skull constitutes a gaze in Lacan's sense of the term? More specifically, what links the phenomenon of the glint of light that blinded the young Lacan during his adventure at sea to the formal tensions in Holbein's portrait of the ambassadors?

The art critic and historian John Berger points out that *The Ambassadors* dates from the inception of the tradition of oil painting on canvas, which had its beginnings in Northern Europe in about 1500. It also coincided with the inception of the free market for art, which gradually came to displace the medieval patronage system through which artists had earned their living (*Ways of Seeing*, 84). Gold leaf and expensive pigments became de rigeur for the artist-craftsman as paintings themselves became costly objects, sought after by a new class of connoisseurs and entrepreneurs with an eye for expensive materials rather than a predilection for classical allusions.

The oil painting was valued not only for the intrinsic value of its materials but also for what it represented. Berger cites Claude Lévi-Strauss on this point:

> Rich Italian merchants looked upon painters as agents, who allowed them to confirm their possession of all that was beautiful and desirable in the world. The picture . . . represented a kind of microcosm in which the proprieter recreated within easy reach and in as real form as possible, all . . . to which he was attached. (*Ways of Seeing*, 86)[13]

In order to achieve the end of "recreat[ing] within easy reach and in as real form as possible" those things to which nouveau riche merchants were attached, the oil painting mediated the connection between representation and represented in a new way: that is, not through the classical analogies which only the well-educated could interpret, but rather by direct surface resemblances that anyone with eyes could see. In addition, the new realistic style of painting simulated not only the look but also the tactility of surfaces, "importun[ing] the sense of touch," as Berger remarks in connection with *The Ambassadors*:

Every square inch of the surface of this painting, whilst remaining purely visual, appeals to, importunes the sense of touch. The eye moves from fur to silk to metal to marble to paper to felt, and each time what the eye perceives is already translated, within the painting itself, into the language of tactile sensation. . . . Except for the faces and hands, there is not a surface in this picture which does not make one aware of how it has been elaborately worked over—by weavers, embroiderers, carpet-makers, goldsmiths, leather workers, mosaic-makers, furriers, tailors, jewellers. (90)

The art historian Jurgis Baltrušaitis indicates that the "realism" of this new style of painting verged upon the excessive:

Everything is so realistic as to verge on the unreal. The numbers, the letters, the globes, the texture of the clothes are almost deceptively life-like. Everything is astonishingly present and mysteriously true to life. The exactness of every contour, every reflection, every shadow extends beyond the material it represents. The whole painting is conceived as a *trompe l'oeil*. (Baltrušaitis, 93)

Excess was not a matter of overt distortion, such as is found in the selective magnification of individual details in naif paintings, but rather a subtly overdone richness in detail twinned with an overly sharp visual definition, specifically a dense panorama of folds and surfaces that discriminated between details usually seen only upon close inspection.[14] In Susan Stewart's useful terminology, the result of such excess was "to increase not realism but *the unreal effect of the real*. . . . It does not tell us enough and yet it tells us too much" (Susan Stewart, 26–27, emphasis in original).[15]

The new style of painting provided a vehicle for an abstracted form, that of the "simulacrum," a simulation that acknowledges its own status as the appearance of something else.[16] The paintings managed such acknowledgments through their overdone, hyperrealistic form of representation, which signaled that they were, so to speak, "too good to be true"—mere appearances rather than the real thing. In this respect, as Baltrušaitis indicates above, the new style of painting was continuous with the Renaissance tradition of *trompe l'oeil* that charmed viewers at the moment when they recognized what the painting so generously acknowledged, namely, that it was no more than a masquerade:

What is it that attracts and satisfies us in *trompe l'oeil*? When is it that it captures our attention and delights us? At the moment when, by a mere shift of our gaze, we are able to realize that the representation does not move with the gaze and that it is merely *trompe l'oeil*. (Lacan, *Concepts*, 112)

Commodities, the objects around which the new merchant class built their existence, were also simulacra in this respect. In particular, as Marx pointed out, although a commodity simulates an objective value, consumers know very well that its value is in fact totally subjective, determined by the conventions of the market. As Žižek makes the point, the mystification characteristic of the commodity is not so much ignorance concerning the objectivity of its value as a failure to recognize that consumers act as if that value were objective despite knowing it is not:

> When individuals use money, they know very well that there is nothing magical about it—the money, in its materiality, is simply an expression of social relations. . . . The problem is that in their social activity itself, in what they are *doing*, they are *acting* as if money, in its material reality, is the immediate embodiment of wealth as such. (Žižek, 31)

Thus, in sharing the form of the simulacrum, the new style paintings acquired an ideological dimension. That is, they were ideological insofar as they reproduced the simulacral form of the commodity.

However, not all elements in Holbein's painting conform with the conventions of simulated tactility. The face and hands of the ambassadors are rendered in an almost careless, lackluster fashion. They totally lack tactility, thus constituting an exception, indeed a site of resistance, to the simulacral form of representation:

> Every square inch of the surface of this painting, whilst remaining purely visual, appeals to, importunes, the sense of touch. . . . Except for the faces and hands, there is not a surface in this picture which does not make one aware of how it has been elaborately worked over. (Berger, *Ways of Seeing*, 90)

This lackluster representation of the ambassadors' flesh is highlighted by its contrast with the vivid rendering of other objects in the picture as well earlier works by Holbein, such as his *Christ in the Tomb* (1521), in which the punctured skin of Christ's body vividly displays the physical traces of painful death.

The Ambassadors inhabit their finery as if it were made for them. They are, as Berger says, "confident" and "relaxed" with each other (*Ways of Seeing*, 94). But this impression, determined by their bodily deportment in relation to each other, is in tension with a certain "aloofness" and "wariness" that the figures display in their look toward the viewer (97). Thus, an element of uncertainty is introduced: are their gorgeous clothes a tribute to a preexisting, "natural" eminence or merely an outward show? Is it merely the clothes that maketh the man? This uncertainty about who the ambassadors are reinforces the lack of visual definition of their flesh.

Since the form of the simulacrum coincides with that of the commodity, it follows that the lack of definition in the image of the ambassadors' flesh, its failure to simulate what it represents, provides a concrete model of the failure of a key element in the capitalist relations of exchange central to the lives of the bulk of Holbein's viewers. This failure, in turn, is structurally similar to another, more basic failure in a viewer's social relations to others, namely, to his/her primal failure to secure the presence of caregivers, which, according to Lacan, haunts all human existence from its earliest moments. This chain of connections, as in the story of the sardine can, opens the possibility of an unconscious, metaphoric association between the image of the ambassadors' flesh and the primal scene of lack. For viewers for whom such an association locks into place, the image of the flesh functions as a repetition in the Freudian sense and thus as a site to which unrealistic anxiety attached. For such viewers, the image of the ambassadors' flesh takes on the status of a gaze, that is, a point invested with unrealistic anxiety where the perceptual symbolic order falters. As in the case of the glint of light that blinded the young Lacan, the unconscious association along which anxiety travels in order to invest this element of the painting, as a gaze, is ideologically mediated.

SECOND SIGHT

A second gaze haunts Holbein's painting, unsettling the spectator's attempt to find a proper distance from which to view the canvas. According to Berger, "The surface verisimilitude of the oil painting tends to make the viewer assume that he is close to—within touching distance of—any object in the foreground of the picture" (*Ways of Seeing*, 97). That is, with the exception of the ambassadorial flesh, all the items pictured are goods on display, crying out to be touched.[17] However, the conventions of the genre of public portraiture that Holbein's painting exemplifies insist upon a formal distance between sitter and viewer. To this end, the ambassadors look "aloof and wary. . . . the presence of kings and emperors had once impressed in a similar way. . . . equality must be made inconceivable" (97). Berger argues that "it is this [distance] and not technical inability on the part of the painter—which makes the average portrait of the tradition appear stiff and rigid" (97). The genre, he claims, "never resolved" the contradiction between close and distant relations with the viewer (98).

The unresolved nature of this contradiction is reinforced by the excessive detail of Holbein's painting. Such excess has the effect of unsettling the viewing position. Viewed from a distance, a perceptual contradiction haunts the picture: the figures of the ambassadors imply a distant point of view, while the visibility of the detail on the clothing entails a view from closer in. This difficulty disappears when the picture is viewed from up close and the figures of the ambassadors move out of focus. However, the need to view from afar remains, since it is only from such a perspective that the picture's narrative meaning becomes clear.

A similar unsettling of viewer position is manifested in the grotesque images of faces painted by Arcimboldo in the late sixteenth century. From close in Arcimboldo's paintings appear as juxtapositions of realistically painted images of pieces of fruit, or flowers, or instruments of war, and so on. From a distance a pattern emerges from each of the pictures in the form of a human face. Thus, simply by changing position, viewers cause an incongruous jump from one domain of reality to another, for instance from vegetable to man. No narrative connects these domains of reality. In particular, no narrative connects the faces to the objects constituting them. Instead, the domains of reality represented in the pictures are held together by an aesthetic logic internal to the painting: the face designated "Spring" is made up of the fruits of spring, and so on through the seasons.

As in works of *trompe l'oeil*, where the boundary between objects and their representations is blurred, the coexistence of different levels of reality within Arcimboldo's paintings unsettles the viewer position. So, for example, it is impossible to determine whether the painting *Spring* should be viewed up close, so that individual pieces of fruit spring into view, or from a sufficient distance to permit a "face" to stand out from the images of fruit.

The hyperreal detail on the ambassadors' clothes in Holbein's painting unsettles the viewer's position in a similar way. Does the picture imagine us as looking at the ambassadors from close in as the intricacy of detail visible on their clothes seems to indicate or rather from afar, where the figures of the ambassadors come fully into view?

The difficulty in determining an appropriate distance from which to view Holbein's picture reflects a real contradiction within the social relational field characteristic of capitalism emerging in sixteenth-century Europe. By dint of their occupation, merchants counted as commoners. However, by establishing a communality of interests and way of life with their quality customers, they created a superior status for themselves. This contradiction was an aspect of a more general set of tensions created within the traditional class structure by a radical expansion of the activities of the market. In principle at least, everyone was free to buy what they liked from whomever they liked, and, as money and goods changed hands, different social strata interacted, approaching one another in unaccustomed ways.

Thus the formal difficulties in settling upon a distance from which to view Holbein's painting echoed or, as Marx would say, "reflected" viewers' difficulties in establishing a position for themselves in the new social space created by the expansion of the market. At a structural level, these difficulties resembled the primal difficulty individuals experienced in finding a place for themselves in the world of others. Insofar as, for some viewers, this resemblance became the basis for an unconscious connection, unrealistic anxiety attached to their difficulties in settling upon a viewing position, which thus took on the dimensions of a gaze. Like the gaze associated with the image of the ambassadors' flesh, this gaze was constituted through an ideologically mediated connection.

It may be objected that the dimension of excess in the Holbein painting to which I have drawn attention is more a matter of a violation of an aesthetic preference for simplicity than a case of "objective distortion" of the sort displayed by the Arcimboldo paintings or caused by the glint of light in the story of the young Lacan's fishing trip. The key issue for our purposes, however, is not the origin of the distortion but rather that it unsettles the observer's visual field and thus creates the conditions for a gaze. That may happen as readily in response to violations of aesthetic preferences as to more "objective" forms of distortion. An overly jeweled hand, for example, may be no less violent an assault on the senses, something from which one visually retreats in discomfort, as the "objective" distortions of an Escher diagram.[18] In either case, an instability in viewer position (and thus a gaze) may result. In other words, the aesthetic revulsion I feel in response to the overly decorated hand may indicate a faltering of my visual field that is no less significant from the point of view of creating a gaze than the young Lacan's response to the glint of light.

THE THIRD EYE

The bulk of the imagery in *The Ambassadors*—navigational instruments, a book of arithmetic, a lute, and so on, all symbolic of the sciences and arts—is drawn in linear, single-point perspective and can be properly seen only from the front of the picture. The image of the skull, by contrast, is brought into focus only through surrendering a frontal view and moving laterally to the edge of the picture, by putting the ambassadors to one side, so to speak. Thus the frontal viewpoint brings into focus the mundane ambitions of man—commercial, cultural, scientific, and religious—while the lateral view brings into focus death, the end to all such earthly vanities. In moral terms, then, the lesson seems to be that we are able to bring into focus, or apprehend, either life or death but not both.

The choice Holbein's picture seems to present between life or death is illusory, however. As Lacan points out in his discussion of the forced choice "Your money or your life," no real choice exists, since to die means giving up your money in any case (*Concepts*, 212). Holbein's apparent choice presents a similar deadlock: death cannot be understood since to do so implies dying, thus leaving behind not only the world but also all possibility of understanding. In the end, it seems, the death's head escapes comprehension. Perhaps that is why the ambassadors look so wary. If they get to the point of seeing death, then, like the viewers who move sideways in order to look awry at the image of the skull, they too will have fallen off the edge of the picture.

Man's inability to apprehend death, an interpretation that I have placed upon the painting's symbolism, contradicts an ideology in terms of which a segment of Holbein's audience was constituted. The field of social practices integral to the new form of merchant capitalism involved a radical expansion of man's access to and domestication of the world around him. The ambassadors represented in Holbein's picture typified the new class of men who lived by and promoted these new possibilities. As Berger puts it so eloquently, they "were convinced that the world was there to furnish their residence in it" (*Ways of Seeing*, 96). The objects pictured surrounding them, which include instruments for navigation and tools of the arts and sciences, signify these enhanced capacities for knowledge and control. By entailing that all visible things are to be comprehended in human terms, the humanist catchphrase "man as the measure of all things" captured the spirit of this ideology. Nothing, however different or alien it appeared from the their point of view, was to be allowed to escape the symbolic net constituted by scientific, religious, and cultural knowledge. However, this bold, expansionist, and, on occasion, crudely reductionist philosophy could not accommodate the phenomenon of death, which although visibly existent fell outside human understanding, belonging instead to that world of semi-waking (or nightmare) which, in his reworking of Freud's analysis of the dream of the burning child, Lacan describes as a "rupture between perception and consciousness" (*Concepts*, 56).

As Baltrušaitis argues, the existence of such limits to human understanding constituted a contradiction within humanist writings, which often paired a commitment to man's ability to acquire knowledge with a religiously inspired skepticism associated with the doctrine of the Fall. Such skepticism is apparent in the Renaissance theme of the Vanities, which ran through the work of various of Holbein's humanist contemporaries, such as Cornelius Agrippa, Sir Thomas More, and Erasmus of Rotterdam, the last two of whom were patrons as well as important intellectual sources for Holbein.[19]

Holbein's painting registers the contradiction between death and philosophical pretensions to knowledge by situating the image of the skull, a traditional *memento mori*, in formal opposition to images of other objects symbolizing man's capacities for gaining knowledge. The skull image thus functions doubly as a source of anxiety. First, as a direct reminder of death, it was a source of anxiety in its own right. Second, for those of Holbein's viewers for whom the humanist ideology was constitutive, it focused attention upon a contradiction within the practices by which they lived, a point of failure in their mode of being. As such, it contributed to a disclosure of the Real—the terrifying void at the center of human existence—which, according to Lacan, all human practices are meant to conceal. The image of the skull thus took on the dimensions of the gaze: a distortion of the visual field that, by providing an encounter with the Real, provoked anxiety.

Lacan fails to provide an ideological critique of the visual materials he considers, but this does not mean, as Silverman and others claim, that his conceptual framework precludes the possibility of such critique. On the contrary, in the case of Holbein's *The Ambassadors,* the gaze in its Lacanian formulation functioned as a site where ideological traces gathered. In particular, various aspects of the gaze associated with *The Ambassadors* (I discussed three of them) were constituted not as a vehicles for pre-encoded images (as Screen theory claims) but rather as sites of visual distortions connected by chains of symbolic and metaphoric associations to ideological contradictions within the social milieu where the painting was originally produced. The associations in question were valid for a whole community of viewers, namely, the sixteenth-century middle class and their princes who were making a living in the sphere of economic practices opened up by the new forms of merchant capitalism. By carrying the same ideological meaning for each member of that community, the gaze of *The Ambassadors* raises for us here and now the possibility of a traditional politics of the image which critiques community-wide ideological meanings.

My argument does more than develop a Lacanian perspective sensitive to the role of ideological factors. It also provides a response to the challenge set by the title of this book. In particular, by employing the techniques of semiotics as well as ideology critique, my approach shows that the interests of both cultural studies and rhetoric may be served without falling into the oversimplfying assumptions made by the Screen theory approach.

ACKNOWLEDGMENTS

I am indebted to many friends for help and discussion on this essay, especially Marie-Luise Angerer, Valerie Krips, Moya Luckett, Tom Rosteck, Susan Schwartz, and Daniela Tugendhat.

NOTES

1. Jaqueline Rose offers an interesting participant's history of the Screen theory movement (*Sexuality,* ch. 9). For a more critical backward glance at Screen theory, see Silverman (*Threshold,* 83–90).

2. Barthes's *Mythologies* was first published in English in 1973; Althusser's "Ideological State Apparatuses" essay was published in the English edition of *Lenin and Philosophy* in 1971; and Lacan's 1949 essay on the "The Mirror Stage" was reprinted in the 1977 English translation of *Écrits*.
3. First published in Britain in 1978, and in the U.S. in 1979.
4. Lacan emphasized the subject's role in constructing such images. Thus, specular recognition always involves more than simply identifying with an externally projected self-image.
5. First published in France in 1973, and in America in 1978.
6. Lacan returns to this picture in an almost obsessive fashion. Following this line of thought, and in light of my later arguments, one could argue that the kernel of the Real to which Lacan returns in his analysis of this particular painting is the patently ideological nature of its gaze. The fantasy that conceals this kernel is, then, a certain "scientism" with which Lacan seeks to invest his theoretical discourses, a scientism that cannot easily accommodate the fact of the ideological nature of the objects it studies.
7. Lacan's account of the gaze is complicated by a certain obeissance to Merleau-Ponty. Specifically, Lacan refers to the gaze as a certain "given to be seen" (74), or quality of visibility, which preexists vision:

   . . . the ways through which he [Merleau-Ponty] will lead you . . . set out to redis-
   cover . . . the dependence of the visible on that which places us under the eye of the
   seer. But this is going too far, for that eye is only the metaphor of something that I
   would prefer to call the seer's "shoot" (*pousse*) something prior to his eye. What we
   have to circumscribe, by means of the path he [Merleau-Ponty] indicates for us, is the
   preexistence of the gaze—I see only from one point, but in my existence I am looked
   at from all sides. (72)

   Unfortunately this path to understanding the gaze heads off in a potentially misleading direction. In particular, by associating the gaze with a certain given to be seen, and correspondingly the eye with seeing, Lacan seems to locate the functions of the eye and the gaze in opposite ends of the scopic drive, the gaze being associated with exhibitionism and the eye with voyeurism. Instead, the gaze is the object at the center of the scopic drive, the *objet a* around which the scopic drive as a whole turns (*fait le tour*), and as such involves the outward (voyeuristic) as much as the inward returning (exhibitionistic) arm of the drive. Here we see the *objet a* in its other role as object of the drive rather than object-cause of desire.
8. The Real may take either of two forms: either an unsymbolizable point of excess, that which Freud associates with *das Ding*, or as a residue, a leftover from the process of symbolization, a piece of white noise from which all categorizable images have been sifted.
9. Freud also makes the point that the traumatic nature of the originary experience of loss may be a fiction, retrospectively constructed through the child's actions. Indeed, the experience may be a fiction in its entirety, carried by the child's actions rather than corresponding to some real event.
10. The Freudian concept of "association" is rooted in nineteenth- (indeed eighteenth-) century associationist psychology. Lacan, under the influence of

Jakobson's structural linguistics, rethinks the concept of association in terms of the linguistic notion of metaphoric connection. Such rethinking stays within the Freudian architectonic insofar as it presupposes Freud's conception of perceptual experience as *Sachvorstellung*, that is, a form of representation. By preserving this outdated notion of perception as the projection of an image onto an internal mental screen, Lacan may be accused of incompletely divorcing himself from Freud's nineteenth-century roots. Alternatively, however, he may be seen as (metaphorically) extending both the notion of representation and that of metaphor. Note too that, as Gilbert Chaitin argues, the connection between signifiers and the primal scene may be seen as catachrestic rather than metaphoric, since technically the primal scene is unrepresentable, that is, the site of a lack of representation (Chaitin, 86–92).

11. The distinction she draws here between her position and Lacan's is an aspect of exactly the criticism of Lacan that I am questioning here, namely, a criticism for omitting ideological factors from the process of constituting subjects.

12. Fiske, *Television Culture,* 169–178.

13. The painting itself, as a commodified object, thus became an apt subject of representation. The many paintings of paintings from this period indicate this dual role of the painting as both representation and represented (Berger, *Ways of Seeing,* 85–87).

14. I have in mind here the naif paintings of trees that show a whole tree while impossibly distinguishing between individual leaves.

15. Stewart's usage of "realism" here is at odds with Jameson's. That is, for Jameson, "realism" is on the side of incorporating the Real rather than presenting reality effects (see Jameson, *Signatures of the Visible,* 156–158). Note that the excess I am alluding to here is not merely a matter of more detail coming to light as the viewer moves closer to the painting. On the contrary, by including detail that is invisible until one moves in close, a painting may merely simulate reality to the point where approaching it, like getting closer to objects in real life, reveals more to the eye. Rather, the excess I have in mind involves the painting's hyperreal quality, which works against any "reality effect."

16. Thus the simulacrum differs from other types of simulation, such as the fake, that conceal their status as appearances.

17. This cry is more in the way of a hysterical seduction than an open invitation, since a prohibition to touch ("Don't touch the merchandise") often extends up to the moment of purchase, which thus takes on the heightened, magical quality of a honeymoon. The function of the prohibition is not only to heighten the emotional investment in the act of purchase but also, and not unrelatedly, to defer the always disappointing moment when the purchase is complete and the goods are transformed into possessions.

18. For this reason, there is a certain difficulty in distinguishing "objective" from "subjective" distortions in the field of art.

19. On these points see Chapter 7 of Baltrušaitis, who also appears to be Lacan's source in these matters.

PART TWO

ENVISIONING ALTERNATIVES
Beyond the Intersection

Part Two of this volume investigates the academic practice of cultural and rhetorical studies with an eye to envisioning a more transdisciplinary cultural rhetorical studies. These essays meet head-on questions of what might be the impact of cultural studies on the place of rhetorical studies in the academy and the relationship of rhetorical studies to cultural studies. Also of interest is how cultural studies might suggest an alternative approach to the study of public address. In considering the intersection of cultural and rhetorical studies, these essays contribute to a rethinking of how a "new" perspective on public discourse might complicate the traditional canon by considering the economic, social, political, and linguistic "contexts" as well as the historical. Addressing the relationship between text and context, the essays question what constitutes the appropriate "context" for critical study. Further, the essays in this part are animated by questions of how the intersection of rhetorical criticism and cultural studies might address critical questions about the relationship between theory and practice. They ultimately speak to whether we can now, or can ever, speak of a rhetorical cultural studies or a cultural rhetorical studies.

Cary Nelson (Chapter 8) considers the clear but often forgotten connections between traditional rhetorical studies and cultural studies. Providing the "warranted reminder" that from its first inception—in work by Raymond Williams and Richard Hoggart—British cultural studies depended centrally on rhetorical analysis and discursive evidence, Nelson uses this fact to question whether and how bases for alliance might exist between rhetoric, literary studies, and cultural studies. He argues that cultural studies must continue its tradition of close readings of texts and that to do so swings it into the orbit of literary studies. A comparative reading of the now classic text *Policing the Crisis: Mugging, the State, and Law and Order* (Stuart Hall, Critcher, Jefferson, Clarke, and Roberts) with the recent volume *Representation: Cultural Representations and Signifying Practices* (Stuart Hall, ed.) suggests how literary studies and cultural studies might "make one another more thoroughly and deeply historical." Nelson proposes that literary studies and cultural studies might learn from each other by embracing a "cultural studies mission" in and through a "return to rhetoric of a special historicized and politicized sort"—what he calls an "historicized linguisticality." Thus, for Nelson rhetoric has the capacity to function as a kind of rapprochement between literary studies and cultural studies. In this proposal, Nelson's argument necessarily engages questions of pedagogy and disciplinarity.

Arguing that there is a "lost" tradition of cultural approaches in rhetorical studies, my essay (Chapter 9) derives a prospectus for a cultural rhetorical studies from the little read, and the often misread, work of Ernest Wrage. I survey a selection of noteworthy essays of rhetorical criticism that seem to share enough commonalities to extract a theoretical position—a position that captures what a cultural rhetorical study might ultimately be, and how it might be different from the contemporary practice of rhetorical criticism. I conclude by noting how the recovery of this "lost" cultural tradition, overlooked in the literature of rhetorical criticism, prepares the way to move beyond contemporary debates and reframe questions of context, text, and function of public discourse.

John M. Sloop and Mark Olson begin their provocative essay (Chapter 10) with the simple observation that increasing numbers of scholars in rhetorical studies are redefining their work as "cultural studies." Taking such scholars "at their word," Sloop and Olson investigate the uses of the concept "culture" in the literature of rhetorical studies over the past decade. They conclude that the meaning of the term is highly contested, and that this contest creates the conditions for the interchangeability between rhetorical studies and cultural studies. But Sloop and Olson are primarily concerned with "what's really at stake in the joint articulation of cultural studies and rhetorical studies," and they warn against easy use of the "popular" term *cultural studies* as a descriptor of rhetorical work. The great harm that they see as a result of the conflating of the two projects is the damage done to both, what they describe as the "apoliticizing" of cultural studies and the blunting of the "analytics" of rhetoric. In the end, Sloop and Olson provide an alternative sense of "culture" as a way to outline productive differences between rhetorical studies and cultural studies. They conclude with a vision of rhetorical studies serving the more general project of cultural critique.

Next, Bruce E. Gronbeck (Chapter 11) presents a compelling account of the development of a purely American cultural studies. Gronbeck's is a study in cultural rhetorical history that relates the narrative of the replacement of a "critical cultural" intellectual tradition (epitomized for Gronbeck in the New York intellectual scene around the *Partisan Review*) with a "new" technical, scientistic, and linguistically grounded approach to "analyzing and understanding culture" (found in Edward Hall's *The Silent Language*). Gronbeck calls this the "scientistic turn" in studies of American culture, where even today the "conceptual ghost of Hall haunts" the domain. Thus, *The Silent Language* is best seen, Gronbeck argues, as arising out of particular historical and material circumstances, but transcending those circumstances to govern the thinking of later periods. The essay speculates that the shift from an intellectual tradition seeking political and social change to an academic tradition (the purely "theoretical") may account for the pervasiveness of this depoliticized and social scientific American tradition. Gronbeck wonders if this uniquely American perspective might not help to account for the rather enthusiastic embrace in the 1980s and 1990s in this country of continental and especially British cultural studies and its critical oppositional approach.

Patrick Brantlinger's essay "Anti-Theory and Its Antithesis" (Chapter 12) takes up the ramifications of contemporary critical theory, which has shifted its attention away from the study of literature and toward "discourse, culture, or rhetoric." In it he finds answers to questions about the irrelevance of theory—the argument that theory has "no practical consequences" or what Brantlinger calls "antitheory." As corrective, his essay proposes an "emancipatory theory"—a pragmatics—that is the antithesis of such "antitheory." To make clear what this means, Brantlinger juxtaposes the work of Paul de Man and that of Terry Eagleton as exemplars of each of these alternatives. In a synthesizing of de Man and Eagleton, Brantlinger argues that "literature already implies, albeit in rhetorical or ideological forms, the social criticism that literary theory aspires to become." This metamorphosis of literary theory into social critique by way of rhetoric and ideology forces a reconsideration of literary studies, rhetorical studies, *and* cultural studies. In the end, true "emancipatory theory" seeks to "understand and bring to practical realization the concrete utopias and emancipatory aspirations expressed in the aesthetic forms of all cultures and societies."

In "Courting Community in Contemporary Culture," Thomas S. Frentz and Janice Hocker Rushing (Chapter 13) recall the "considerable misunderstandings" that exist between rhetorical studies and cultural studies and seek then to draw out the largely antithetical commitments that lead the two fields to value disparate forms and realms of culture and communication. But they also note how both share a central domain of study—how communication constructs and functions within a culture. Arguing that neither field alone can suffice, Frentz and Rushing invite us to think about how the two fields might work together, to unite against a common enemy, namely, the disconnection between structure and *communitas*, with the result of locating a common ground, thereby changing society for the better. In the end, Frentz and Rushing's essay is scholarly work that is political in a most direct sense. In drawing our attention back to one of the central founding interests of British Cultural Studies namely, the preserving and sustaining of local culture, Frentz and Rushing urge our attention to the crucial work of reestablishing community and of understanding the relationships among aesthetic, political, social, and economic practices that determine such "community."

EIGHT

THE LINGUISTICALITY
OF CULTURAL STUDIES
*Rhetoric, Close Reading,
and Contextualization*

Cary Nelson

I. THE CULTURAL STUDIES LEGACY

It would not be much of a revelation, though it might be a well warranted reminder, to recall how heavily British cultural studies depended in its founding moments on the close analysis of traditional sorts of texts. One thinks of Raymond Williams's journey through social, cultural, and intellectual history in *The Long Revolution* (1961) near the outset of his career and, later, when his reputation was well established, of his magisterial rereading of English literary history in *The Country and the City* (1973). E. P. Thompson, of course, could not have written *The Making of the English Working Class* (1963) without making use of standard historical textual evidence. Both these men, to be sure, did very different things with texts than most of their disciplinary colleagues in literature and history had done beforehand, but they issued no call for abandoning the careful interrogation of texts; rather, they sought in some ways to interrogate texts more forcefully than their predecessors had.

Williams in *The Long Revolution* sought to draw out of texts their sometimes unintended contributions to a progressive, democratizing cultural tradition. Later in *The Country and the City* he questioned what authors had willfully or unconsciously failed to depict about their cultures and what that said about the audiences and interests they served. *The*

Country and the City thus places absence and avoidance—what is *unsaid* in a given text—at the forefront of the interrogations appropriate to cultural studies. That practice remains controversial in both literary studies and philosophy, and it points to one of the more disruptive ways that cultural studies contextualizes what it analyzes. Contextualization, through tracking historically pertinent blindness and repression, readily highlights texts' class interests and positioning. It appears, therefore, to politicize what seemed happily innocent and transcendent as long as awkward absences and evasions were not noted. Thus, Williams demonstrates that Ben Jonson's poem "To Penshurst" celebrates the bountiful, Edenic harvests of a seventeenth-century country estate without giving us even a glimpse of the peasant labor that actually made such agricultural wealth possible.

At the same time cultural studies, notably in Hoggart's *The Uses of Literacy* (1958), was already seeking out new kinds of evidence, including nontraditional texts and discourses, as appropriate objects of analysis. Despite Hoggart's antagonism toward American popular culture, his interest in British working-class practices gave popular culture part of its early warrant in cultural studies. It would open up possibilities for subcultures and the texts of conversation to be worthy objects of study. Although the field as a whole was thus at its moment of inception already pointed toward analyzing all sorts of linguistic practices—and even nonlinguistic signs, behaviors, and rituals—discourse was always a prime focus. Links with rhetorical analysis and with close reading traditions, however ambivalent and transformative, were thus established at the outset. The links are still there, I will argue, but the ambivalence is if anything more intense.

II. CULTURAL STUDIES AND CLOSE READING

In the introduction to the widely read collection *Cultural Studies* (1992), it was such ambivalence, along with differences of opinion among myself and the other editors, that marked our reference to close reading. There we noted in a rather gingerly fashion that close reading was acceptable in cultural studies but not required. In fact, two of the editors, myself and Paula A. Treichler, had published numerous close readings of literary and other cultural texts and phenomena and continue to do so. On the other hand, the third editor, Lawrence Grossberg, had never done close readings and saw certain types of close readings as the leading edge of literary studies imperialist ambitions. Our positions on the relative centrality of linguistic evidence in cultural studies were similarly conflicted. So we compromised as best we could, perhaps unwisely papering over our differences.

Only a few years later, however, in the introduction to *Disciplinarity and Dissent in Cultural Studies* (1996), edited by myself and Dilip Parameshwar Gaonkar, I could argue that

> discourses have not been cultural studies's only objects of inquiry, but they have been central evidence; and neither a structure of feeling nor a subculture is critically available except as a linguistic simulacrum. Even Lawrence Grossberg, who among our contributors has perhaps the most wary attitude toward discourse-oriented cultural studies analysis, insists that discourse is the primary form in which culture survives and that discourse analysis is a necessary moment in any cultural studies project. One need only read through the present volume to see how many kinds of linguistic evidence cultural studies uses—here it includes congressional testimony, news stories, headlines, song lyrics, television and film scripts, radio broadcasts, literary texts, scientific papers, interpretive theory, interview transcripts, popular nonfiction, personal letters, speeches, captions, banners, jokes, and rumors. These essays also make it clear how crucial various kinds of discourse analysis are to various cultural studies projects and thus make it possible to estimate the potential of a working relationship between rhetoric and cultural studies. (9)

There was much at stake at both these moments, and there continues to be now, at least for the territories policed by the academy, in the struggle over how cultural studies will negotiate its relationship with textual and linguistic evidence and with the close reading of texts. At stake first of all is how persuasive cultural studies readings are to be and what appeal they can have for readers accustomed to the close scrutiny of historical and cultural discourses and documents, especially to readers outside the cultural studies community. In fields like English or speech communication, close reading is all that provides for anything resembling persuasive evidence. Concomitantly, as cultural studies does or does not embrace these analytic techniques and traditions, openings for people trained in them to participate in cultural studies will either become available or be closed down. At the most crude level, as I point out in *Manifesto of a Tenured Radical* (1997), simply renaming or repackaging close readings of individual texts as "cultural studies" opens a cultural studies identity to thousands of scholars who need learn nothing about the field's traditions and take on none of its political commitments. On the other hand, castigating close reading that is done under the cultural studies banner may be a defensive manner for those who either prefer free-wheeling and ungrounded speculation as their cultural studies style or who have no patience or talent for detailed observation and analysis.

In literary studies, for example, either authors or texts have long been granted a kind of miraculous intentionality; they somehow manage to shape and limit their meaning internally. This is a power cultural studies is deeply committed to denying. Cultural studies typically maintains that meaning is the product of social, cultural, and political interaction. Neither texts nor authors, nor even their readers, can simply *mean* on their own. Declaring immanent, English-style close readings to be "cultural studies" can thus be quite misleading. On the other hand, English offers cultural studies a rich tradition of close reading techniques and an exemplary model of rhetorical attentiveness and analytic care. An alliance between literary studies and cultural studies properly entails English moving radically outward from texts to contexts and partly desacralizing the field's traditional objects of study. Cultural studies, on the other hand, is thereby required to take up close reading in ways some of its American proponents have resisted.

As analytic practices and objects of study fall in and out of favor, the entire relationship between cultural studies and various academic disciplines waxes and wanes. Thus, for example, those who want to create alliances between cultural studies and traditional rhetorical studies might try to exploit and develop the points of correspondence between the two; those who dislike the idea of merging them might work to deny or belittle the existence of any points of correspondence. Underwriting the close reading of texts as central to cultural studies, on the other hand, potentially grants English, rhetoric, and speech communication departments considerable power and political mobility in the cultural studies wars; belittling close reading, conversely, tends to disempower these fields. The risk is particularly great for English, which has fetishized close reading and trained students in it for decades. For departments of speech communication, on the other hand, adjudicating the centrality of rhetorical analysis now involves a potential cultural studies taint; for some scholars "rhetoric" is now a Trojan horse filled with unwanted cultural studies warriors. The disciplinary battles over cultural studies, then, are not just about which objects of study are appropriate but also about discursive practices, about which methods and analytic techniques are validated and privileged.

These battles over disciplinary identity and turf take place both nationally and locally, both across disciplines as a whole and within individual departments. A given speech communication department can thus try to build programmatic and pedagogical bridges between cultural studies and rhetoric, or it can do everything in its power to block their realization. That means encouraging or discouraging appropriate faculty appointments, opening the curriculum to new courses or barring their introduction, supporting or discouraging doctoral dissertations that make connections between cultural studies and rhetoric, and funding or defunding research and conference travel that works the cultural studies terrain. A "field" and a "department" can sometimes be widely divergent, offering very different disciplinary maps. That numerous scholars in a field are hospitable to cultural studies does not mean that a given department will be hospitable in the least. It depends on the department's traditions, on the power that various people wield, on the sympathies of relevant administrators, and on the distinctive competition or collaboration between departments that characterizes each campus.

Sometimes, therefore, arguments for or against rhetorical analysis or close reading of texts in cultural studies are mounted on deceptively abstract grounds when what is actually at issue is disciplinary or departmental and personal power and influence. Especially in the volatile and contentious American scene, a certain amount of high-minded cultural studies theorizing—like all theorizing—can be read as maneuvering for personal advantage and influence. If these wars of position are immensely interested and compromised, we might be better off admitting that and seeking to identify those interests when they are put in play.

III. CULTURAL STUDIES AND LANGUAGE

Given this argument, it would be foolish for me to suggest that I could settle these debates in a grand gesture of objectivity. It is possible, however, to give them some useful contextualization and clarification. To some extent, two of the problems I have raised—the relative importance of textual analysis and close reading in cultural studies and the relationship between cultural studies and rhetoric—are subsumed under a third issue, the actual or potential linguisticality of all evidence in cultural studies. Cultural studies and language, then, is the broad umbrella of concept and practice that covers all these topics.

Like so many bodies of theory in the 1960s and 1970s, cultural studies underwent a period of engagement with structuralism and for a time toyed with the notion that a rationalized linguisticality could provide a model for all systems of meaning. Every relatively autonomous cultural domain, we were urged by various writers to believe, "operated like a language." Indeed, orderly and surprisingly regimented charts of signification could be teased out of any seemingly regularized cultural practice. Conceived as a system of relational but specifiable meanings, language could give us the template for understanding even nonlinguistic gestural and iconic practices. In some extensions of this linguistic imperialism, even nonhuman behavior was said to "operate like a language."

There were, briefly, two serious problems with this claim. First, as poststructuralism began to show us by the late 1960s or early 1970s—dates that have to encompass both original publications in French and eventual translation into English—language as a system of meanings was simply much less orderly or predictable than structuralists supposed. A rearguard attempt to differentiate between a relatively stable set of *denotative* meanings and a fluid, unstable set of *connotative* meanings proved equally unsatisfactory. Denotative meanings were said to be primary and consensual, connotative meanings secondary and potentially idiosyncratic. But, as Roland Barthes pointed out in *S/Z* as early as 1970, denotation was little more than a cultural and political effort to fix and control the unchecked spread of connotation. "Denotation," he wrote, "is not the first meaning, but pretends to be so; under this illusion, it is ultimately no more than the *last* of the connotations (the one which seems both to establish and to close the reading), the superior myth" (9; emphasis in original). Connotation "corrupts the purity of communication." "Each connotation," he argues, "is the starting point of a code (which will never be reconstituted)." These were not two different kinds of meaning but rather different social activities. Denotation was an effort to install certain connotations within popular common sense as privileged and as having certifiable meanings.

Studying that sort of process was exactly the job of cultural studies; being taken in by it, assuming that a given hierarchy of meanings was a fact of nature, was not the mission of cultural studies at all. As Stuart Hall and his Birmingham colleagues would show in the ground-breaking *Policing the Crisis: Mugging, the State, and Law and Order* (1978), and Hall would later confirm in *The Hard Road to Renewal: Thatcherism and the Crisis of the Left* (1988), the struggle to install meanings within popular common sense, to establish and naturalize certain connotations, was central to culture and politics.

The second problem with the claim that everything operates like a language is equally fundamental. The fact that all knowable systematicity translates into linguistic simulacra says less about the supposed systems of signification than it does about the folks doing the translating. It is entirely possible that everything operates like a language because we see it that way, because we organize our world and make sense of it through language. If bees have a language it is, in effect, because we've taught them how to talk. Our linguistic constructions will inevitably represent and misrepresent, omit and include, organize and reorganize, idealize and demonize everything they encounter. Everything we can know passes through the fire of our languages to be remade therein; that is a fundamental part of human culture. For our perceptions to become known to us, for us to be able to represent them to ourselves and others, they must be given linguistic form or its equivalent. Once again, it is altogether to the point for cultural studies to examine that process, despite the fact that it is inherently impossible to do so, because that any such examination will itself be conducted within language and saturation by any culture naturalizes its languages. At the very least, however, cultural studies can take such linguistic representations *as* cultural artifacts rather than as reflections of the real.

In its own moment of structuralist infatuation, notably in Stuart Hall's essay "Encoding/Decoding" (1980), cultural studies took up the structuralist banner because the "like a language" motto offered an irresistible coherence to an enterprise determined to study so many different kinds of cultural phenomena. It created a kind of level playing field, a uniform space and style of apprehension, where any cultural practice could earn our attention. At least for cultural studies, the "like a language" refrain was notably democratizing, making everything theoretically and methodologically interchangeable. In juxtaposing high and popular culture it thus had some real political effectivity. Meanwhile, it lent an air of rigor and systematicity to critical practice itself, an effect at least as appealing as any impact it had on any objects studied.

The motto has now surfaced again in the Open University's 1997 series of textbooks, including Hall's own contributions to *Representation: Cultural Representations and Signifying Practices,* where it takes center stage in justifying both the overall cultural studies enterprise and its various methodologies. Here it sometimes comes off as a convenience and other times seems an article of faith. It brings with it both of the difficulties briefly outlined above, despite all efforts at complication and clarification.

After warning us that "the term 'language' is being used here in a very broad and inclusive way," Hall invokes

> the "language" of facial expressions or of gesture, for example, or the "language" of fashion, of clothes, or of traffic lights. Even music is a "language," with complex relations between different sounds and chords. . . . Any sound, word, image, or object which functions as a sign, and is organized with other signs into a system which is capable of carrying and expressing meaning is, from this point of view, "a language." (18–19)

This is, of course, classic semiotics, as yet unproblematized by poststructuralism's more radical take on signification. Hall brings the poststructuralist critique into play when he points out in detail that the whole range of meanings circulating in a culture are necessarily both indeterminate and in flux, but he cannot resist holding on to a more rationalized model of communication to undergird language's more unpredictable signifying powers. In order to nail down a rationalized base for cultural criticism, he evokes a first order set of codes that functions like a set of temporarily fixed denotations. A given culture's codes, Hall argues, enable us to translate a "conceptual map" roughly shared by all its members into language that can be shared and communicated. The code "sets up the correlation between our conceptual system and our language system" (21).

This universal "conceptual map" or "system of concepts" is a particularly weak notion, in part because it cannot exist in any individual apart from the influence of psychic process of every sort and from the messy connotative field of associations and illusions that make up our actual experience of the world. It is a largely heuristic and hypothetical notion, but one whose comforts are misleading, because the "conceptual map," if it exists, is already linguistic, contaminated with mobile and contradictory meanings. The code too, then—if it exists, and there is no reason to believe it exists in anything like the orderly form Hall imagines—is implicated in all the complications of real discursive practices. Hall himself will later argue that the catchphrase "like a language" is largely an intellectual convenience, but by then he has effectively bought into a structuralist model of how these hypothetical languages function.

This structuralist bias also leads Hall in his contribution to *Representation* to invoke only the two first-order forms of relationality in language. Language is relational, Hall recalls, because it depends on relations between signifier and signified and on differences between signifiers. But we can actually isolate several different levels of pervasive relationality:

1. The relation between signs and what they signify.
2. The differences among signs that enable us to distinguish between them.
3. The differential (and mobile) relations among meanings that traverse the whole field of signification and that potentially put all meanings in relationship to one another.
4. The differential relations both within and between relatively autonomous texts, discourses, and cultural domains.

The third and fourth forms of relationality are of course not only structural and associational but also competitive and conflictual. The complex associational component was acknowledged within semiotics, notably in the Q-model of communication that Umberto Eco described in *A Theory of Semiotics* (1976), but it took cultural studies, drawing on Gramsci and others, to develop a full model of how meaning is produced through cultural struggle.

Representation is admittedly a student text and thus somewhat simplified, but it is usefully indicative of how a certain misleading positivism can enter cultural studies to underwrite the field's will to certify its own knowledge. Left without an alternative way of explaining why the linguistic codes should be so universal and dependable in a given historical moment, Hall employs the denotation/connotation distinction as warrant for the apparent regularity of the connections the codes guarantee. Thus, he invokes the denotation/connotation model without politicizing it and treating it as an unstable field of struggle rather than a given set of culturally fixed distinctions.

Representation thus reenacts the traditional semiotic engagement with metaphors of linguisticality, adopting the "like a language" motto to ground a rationalized system of signification and borrowing an unwarranted air of scientificity in the process. Of course, it does not have to be that way; cultural studies itself has a long history of deploying more complex notions of linguisticality and placing them at the very center of its enterprise.

IV. THE CASE OF MUGGING

Actually Hall's other work offers a far more powerful model of how language operates in culture and what cultural studies can gain from a deep investment in a contestatory model of linguisticality. *Policing the Crisis,* perhaps the most fully realized of the collaborative books from the University of Birmingham's Centre for Contemporary Cultural Studies, is the key text. There Hall and the other authors demonstrate that the term "mugging" as it was deployed in Britain in the 1970s never really had a single, clear denotative meaning. To the extent that "mugging" in Britain eventually came to refer to a specific sort of street crime, a violent robbery and assault on an individual, it only did so *after* acquiring a whole host of other social meanings and uses, such as:

a catchall label for mindless hooliganism rather than anything concretely recognizable as "muggings"; (328)
a sort of incipient breakdown in "law and order" and general rise in violent crime and lawlessness in Britain; (23)
and a whole historical construction about the nature and dilemmas of American society (27)

Articulated as applying to a host of public anxieties in the United States, the term "mugging" came to Britain first as a symbol of those themes:

mugging . . . had become a central *symbol* for the many tensions and problems besetting American social and political life in general. "Mugging" achieved this status because of its ability to *connote* a whole complex of themes in which the "crisis of American society" was reflected. These themes included: the involvement of blacks and drug addicts in crime; the expansion of the black ghettoes, coupled with the growth of black social and political militancy; the threatened crisis and collapse of the cities, the crime panic and the appeal to "law and order"; the sharpening political tensions and protest movements of the 1960s leading into and out from the Nixon-Agnew mobilization of "the silent majority." . . . The image of "mugging" came ultimately to contain and express them all. (19–20; emphases in original)

Hall and his coauthors argue that "the use of the label is likely to mobilise *this whole referential context*, with all its associated meanings and connotations" (19). Indeed, given their demonstration that mugging historically *"meant* 'general social crisis and rising crime' *first,* a particular kind of robbery occurring on British streets second" (23; emphases in original), any later claim that it had a restricted referential and denotative meaning—a dominant meaning that in some way would precede any wider connotations—would seem not only improbable but disproven. The textual analysis put forward in *Policing the Crisis* is in fact our best evidence of what our mental response to concepts like mugging might be.

Of course one could argue that "mugging" had become a complex, overdetermined concept, like truth, freedom, evil, religion, beauty, sex, death, darkness, and so forth; thus it was not a good general guide to how language operates. But we obviously do not lack for such words; language is permeated with them and they gain their meaning from their connotations and interrelationships. Are we really confident that apparently more comfortably referential words like "pencil" or "table" function differently? What poststructuralism has shown us is that there is no practical or theoretical moment when discourse is free of such associational complication.

What cultural studies can do, as Hall has shown in the analysis of mugging and Thatcherism, is to take on such socially constructed networks of meaning in their historical and political contexts and show how they are constituted and what interests they serve. Even with the use of clear textual evidence, however, social life cannot be disassembled and reassembled scientifically. The analytic process creates its own simulacra of preexisting connotations. It adds to them, selectively amplifying and interpreting them anew.

Representation attempts to ground that larger project in a more positivistic moment, a move that has tempted critics for decades. As the basis of an infinitely transferable analogy, the linguistic metaphor is haunted by historically recurrent dreams of positivistic knowledge, of a system of signs that can be decisively established and known. Making these systems changeable in time, as even Saussure did, does not abrogate the scientistic fantasy pervading their construction. For cultural studies, of course, it is not only the proto-science of semiotics that haunts this model but also the scientific pretensions of traditional Marxism. A more fully reflexive cultural studies cannot stand on this ground, despite its temptations in a pedagogical context like that of the Open University's "Culture, Media, and Identities" course. That does not make cultural studies less invested in linguisticality; it just makes the investment a somewhat different one.

There is really no reason why cultural studies needs to assert a common, intrinsic basis for the systematic communication patterns it finds in various cultural contexts, let alone in nature itself. If these systems are in some ways analogous to one another, that is perhaps most notably because they are products of our analytic procedures. We make bees and fashion designers communicate like users of a coherent language because it is instructive and informative to do so. Describing their "languages" enables us to know what we most need to know about these practices, to communicate that knowledge to one another, and if necessary to intervene in or act on the practice being described. In all cases there will be meaning production we have missed, dismissed, misrepresented, or repressed. The critical "language" we construct will be incomplete and partly erroneous, and its linguisticality belongs to the analytic process, not to the objects, practices, behaviors, or texts being analyzed.

As Hall himself writes clearly, "language is the privileged medium in which we 'make sense' of things, in which meaning is produced and exchanged," and "representation through language is therefore central to the processes through which meaning is produced" (1). Representation through artifacts of more organized and systematic linguisticality may, furthermore, be central to the process by which cultural studies produces meaning. There's no need to insist that these systems are inherent in the cultures being described. A more reflexive cultural studies practice can try to recognize its own interventions for what they are.

We know, for example, that the "language" of fashion would signify differently for fashion designers than for the ordinary run of buyers and wearers of fashions. We know that the "language" of literature signifies differently for writers or literary critics than it does even for college-educated readers, let alone members of the public without specialized training. Even language systems, therefore, signify differently to different groups. Of course, some semioticians get around that problem by aiming for a more primary, base-level, schematic "language" to ascribe to practices or groups of texts. But that would be untenably impoverished and politically incapacitating for cultural studies. The cultural studies equivalent of a schematic model of narrativity, like those devised for fiction, would eliminate the historical and contextual specificity that is cultural studies' lifeblood.

V. CULTURAL STUDIES AND THE DISCIPLINES: THE EXAMPLE OF ENGLISH

Given all the risks and warnings detailed above, how might linguisticality be productively placed at the center of a discipline like English as it embraces a cultural studies mission? It is certainly in this context worth recalling how English has dealt with other bodies of theory over the last several decades. For much of this century, in fact, literary studies has been successful at absorbing, even co-opting, all the theoretical initiatives that might have challenged the fundamental assumptions sustaining its disciplinarity. From Marxism and psychoanalysis through feminism, poststructuralism, and deconstruction, every body of theory that might have desacralized the literary text has made its peace with the discipline and ended by finding a way to install literary idealization at the center of its enterprise.

Cultural studies, however, presents challenges to literary studies that both are and are not structurally similar to those put forward by other theoretical traditions. Its most significant challenge, the pressure toward radical linguistic and political contextualization, has been either explicit or implicit in many of the methods literary studies has taken up and adopted, from traditional historiography through Marxism, structuralism, and semiotics. All these traditions have had the potential to dissolve the individual literary text into its determining forces and discourses, but none has succeeded in doing so. Cultural studies now voices the call to historicize and contextualize yet again, invoking a still wider field of influences, but I doubt the call will be heeded very fully at first.

Yet, cultural studies also proposes a different sort of threat to the status quo in literary studies—a radical multiplication of alternative object choices. Until now, English has been very cautious in importing new primary objects of study. When films first entered the literature curriculum, they were consistently aestheticized and their literary origins or components foregrounded. But no progressive cultural studies scholar is likely to idealize the political speeches of Margaret Thatcher or Pat Buchanan. Some cultural studies work idealizes the resistance potential in subcultural practice and production, but that is really political rather than aesthetic idealization. Moreover, the sheer number of potential objects and practices available to cultural studies makes the field inherently uncontainable and only temporarily representable. A literature department that tried to represent the whole range of cultural studies interests and objects in its curriculum or in its faculty would soon be overwhelmed. New interpretive theories have, of course, been steadily integrated into the discipline, but the assumption remains that these theories are secondary, to be used in analyzing other phenomena.

How many national or regional traditions should a cultural studies program have represented on its faculty? What North American subcultural and ethnic constituencies should U.S. cultural studies programs treat as priorities for faculty hiring? Which of the many interpretive traditions that feed into cultural studies needs to be represented with faculty expertise? Should an

English department making the turn to cultural studies include faculty members and courses representing each of the different methods and categories of objects that cultural studies scholars study? Should an English department make hiring an expert in John Keats or Tokyo architecture its main goal for next year? The questions multiply rapidly.

If other bodies of theory have risked altering the status of literature—psychoanalysis, Marxism, and feminism, for example, all in various ways tending to see it as symptomatic rather than transcendent—cultural studies proposes to deny its centrality altogether. Literature would merely be one of the discursive traditions English departments studied; indeed, English departments might also study some cultural practices that are entirely nondiscursive. Already, literature professors and doctoral students are publishing books and writing dissertations where traditional literary texts make no appearance. What would it mean for the discipline to make such interests central and serve them fully?

One thing it might mean is that literature would no longer be the central preoccupation of departments of English and American literature. Here and there across the country some administrators concerned about truth in advertising might think such a department should be renamed. Yet the shift in people's research interests is already under way and cannot be successfully resisted, so the real crisis will come as pressure increases to replace literature faculty and courses with cultural studies alternatives. The resentment that accompanied the turn to theory in the 1970s and 1980s may look mild by comparison, as some faculty members find themselves left behind by a curriculum they no longer recognize.

So what should be done? As several of us argue in *Disciplinarity and Dissent in Cultural Studies,* the ideal relationship between traditional disciplines and cultural studies is one of mutual critique and transformation. Although cultural studies presents English with the possibility of making the discipline unrecognizable, cultural studies in its present form also offers productive challenges. These include an indirect result of bringing many different kinds of discourses and objects of analysis into the discipline: the possibility of giving history its full due.

For decades literary historiography has been the refuge of choice for those resistant to the theory revolution, but literary history has often been little more than a genteel background for the objects of real veneration. Despite its associations with contemporary popular culture, cultural studies in its more historical incarnations has the potential to help put literary texts in their proper determining context of similar and dissimilar discourses and practices. Thus, literary studies and cultural studies can make each other more thoroughly and deeply historical. Increasingly international in its reach, cultural studies can also help literary studies reach beyond the nation state, a transformation comparative literature has not successfully forced on literary studies as a whole. Literary studies and cultural studies are also implicit allies in the effort to open up the canon. On the other hand, literary studies can encourage cultural studies to give more detailed attention to individual texts and practices and to recognize the value of traditional areas of study, things some cultural studies scholars seem not to have the patience or training to do.

Yet, the study of literature as a *relatively* autonomous tradition should be sustained and preserved. Literature has had an important history and retains unique powers in a variety of contemporary cultures. It is not in the discipline's best interest to replace Shakespeare with music videos, or even with the more important topics cultural studies has recently addressed, from the rise of the New Right to the psychology and politics of postcolonialism. A serious dialogue between literary studies and cultural studies can avoid such damaging confrontations and focus instead on what these traditions can offer each other.

The dialogue, I believe, has to be conducted in the context of a shared commitment to a *historicized* linguisticality. The catchphrases "like a language" and "like a text" need to be combined and historicized. I am calling, then, for a return to rhetoric of a special historicized and politicized sort, rhetorical analysis that focuses on historically delineated struggles over meaning and form. Various sorts of texts and discourses would be studied in relation to one another within temporal frames.

No literature department could thoroughly institutionalize a historicized linguisticality across all the periods it studies. But a department could, depending on its size and resources, choose one to several periods in which to specialize. In other words, a department might do thorough cultural studies hiring and curriculum development in, say, eighteenth-century Britain and twentieth-century America. Questions could then be raised and debated about how best to teach and research the diverse textual and linguistic heritage of a limited number of historical periods. This would also revive periodization and give it a productive rather than reactionary form of institutionalization. Representing key object domains across all periods in the curriculum or the faculty is a practical impossibility. Nor does the alternative of representing methods or bodies of theory suffice, for it gives no guidance in a cultural studies driven model of historiography. But students and faculty could learn a linguistically contextualized cultural studies method from studying one or two periods. What they learn could then be applied to other periods that have less full representation in a given department. Rational discussions about priorities could take place in this context in a way that they really cannot take place now, especially if the cultural studies challenge is applied to the entire existing curriculum. That simply produces brutal competition and random, irrational hiring and curriculum development.

In a way there is no viable alternative. Fetishizing periodicity and comprehensive coverage has served little purpose except to regulate and bureaucratize humanities disciplines. It has increasingly seemed an empty structure. But cultural studies now makes it possible for periodization to offer a more intense, rigorous, and deeply relational historiography than we have had before. History in this widely comparative and relational form is the most radical challenge to the dominant norms of disciplinarity, the divisions that now segment intellectual life in higher education. At the same time selective periodization can put some limits on cultural studies' voracious appetite for diverse discourses, objects, and cultural domains.

Language, rhetoric, and discourse in this context will be a good deal more than necessary "moments" through which cultural studies must pass. Language is the preeminent form of culture, at once the record of the past and the mode of its present reconstitution. It is the medium of consciousness and the means by which cultural studies forms and transmits its insights. It is cultural studies, however, that may be able to track for the first time the struggles over meaning that constitute the true historical life of linguistic practice.

NINE

A CULTURAL TRADITION IN RHETORICAL STUDIES

Thomas Rosteck

"Culture" is not a term that appears with any great regularity in the literature of rhetorical criticism. When it does, its application is rather predictable, and its meaning often submerged beneath narrow definitions of "situation" or "setting," or rendered synonymous with "art," or sometimes with "shared value" or with "belief." In all such expressions, its usage is orthodox and unexamined, the result of preexisting assumptions about public discourse, the role of agency, and the classical humanist heritage of rhetoric's institutionalized study. A part of the difficulty, of course, is that the term "culture" *itself* is highly contested, and is, as Raymond Williams has lamented, "one of the two or three most complicated words in the English language" (*Keywords,* 78).

This complexity surfaces directly before us when we consider more precisely the ways "culture" has been conventionally positioned in rhetorical studies, for there we find a determining pattern of distinct usage.[1] First, "culture" has been utilized quite generally to refer to a particular social setting, whether of a people, a period, or a group. When used this way, it is in such terms as "American culture" or "antebellum culture" or even "counterculture." But scarcely ever is this use of "culture" analyzed critically, and instead more often signifies either, quite broadly, "situation," or, again broadly, a backdrop of shared values and beliefs—a sort of vaguely held *sensus communis*—which is usually assumed to provide a store of inventive possibilities for persuasion. Culture, in this sense, is static, often operating as the broad ideational component of "context."

This gloss of culture as part and parcel of a rather simplified notion of situation lies at the base of some increasingly pointed critical problems. Primarily, it is symptomatic of an attenuated view of the context of rhetorical acts—what James Jasinski has described as the "hypervalorization of the particular" (198). By this, Jasinski means that rhetorical critics seem prone to focusing analysis around the immediacies of rhetorical performance without an active sense of the social forces involved in the production of discourse. Such concentration upon the immediate severs the text and the context from the flow of history (201). Dilip Gaonkar reaches the same conclusion, charging that "the rhetorical critic is so preoccupied with the immediate pragmatics of the text that s/he has not devised an adequate strategy for signaling the constitutive presence of the larger historical/discursive formations within which a text is embedded" ("Very Idea," 336).

Edwin Black suggests that this view of context as local, immediate, and particular is inevitable, given rhetorical studies' early development within a classical model. In *Rhetorical Criticism: A Study in Method,* Black notes that the "work of rhetoric is fragmentary outside its environment; it functions only in a particular world" (39). But, Black continues, "neo-Aristotelian critics tend to take a restricted view of context, their tendency being to comprehend the rhetorical discourse as tactically designed to achieve certain results with a specific audience on a specific occasion" (39). Such narrow assumptions, however much their residues may currently influence rhetorical analysis, clearly cut the ground from under any notion of culture as much beyond the imaginary dimensions of any discrete situation.

"Culture" appears in rhetorical studies with a second meaning also, one more centered on its aesthetic dimensions. This usage directs attention to the artistry of public address—the preservation and interpretation of the "best" of public performance. Here the guiding assumption is that "a well constructed oration possesses a high degree of artistic integrity and density" (Leff, "Textual Criticism," 381). In this sense, "artistic" refers to the formal or aesthetic properties in a text, culminating in the identification of "touchstones"—exemplars of the "rhetorical art" that are then used to define an oratorical ideal and to serve the pedagogical function of demonstrating the "art of rhetoric."

Yet, such valorizing of "oratorical masterpieces" as examples of the "rhetorical art" comes with its own set of potentially debilitating assumptions (e.g., Gaonkar, "Object," 310–312). First, this method usually seems to concentrate on platform oratory as the paradigm case, and even more typically on the classical deliberative genre. Other practices, including mediated texts, are seldom considered. Also, though usually associated with the so-called textual turn in rhetorical criticism, the analysis of rhetorical masterpieces typically is undertaken in what Gaonkar has described as "radically situated" contexts ("Oratorical," 273; see also Warnick, "Leff in

Context"). Thus, one of the oft cited primary difficulties with the textual turn has been the temptation to neglect context in favor of the "artful text" and to lose sight of the larger ideological horizon (Hariman, "Time," 213). There is also another troublesome result of this usage of culture as implying "oratorical art." Tied to such meaning is a necessarily circumscribed conception of the producer of these masterpieces. Some have pointed out that currently dominant critical topics include "a particular ideology of human agency" that functions to support a "model of intentional persuasion" (Gaonkar, "Idea," 33, 48). This model situates the "artful" text as a manifestation of the single master rhetorician's conscious design and thus embodies a "functionalist" or instrumental view of rhetorical practice (57). In all these ways, culture as "art" patrols what artifacts may be studied in rhetorical analyses and directs the way in which those artifacts may be read.

Finally, there is another typical sense of "culture" that also finds its way in to rhetorical studies, this one referring to a general process of intellectual, spiritual, and aesthetic development. Bound up with this now largely archaic meaning is the notion of the superiority of Western (European) culture. In this usage, culture suggests a civil and social refinement that is the property of certain (e.g., Western) groups and that then may be delivered to those who lack it (e.g., "the white man's burden"), with the result a generally ameliorative social process of "improvement" for the subaltern. In rhetorical studies, this often silent assumption has been manifest in a curriculum that until very recently was notable for its lack of diversity and its concomitant overattention to the platform oratory of white males. The rhetoric of those "in need of civilizing"—whether they were groups marginalized due to race, gender, class, or social activism—was rarely considered (Karlyn Kohrs Campbell, "Silence," 137).

Thus, working in tandem with the view of oratory as "art form," this usage tends to valorize particular rhetoricians as exemplary and thus to establish a canon of oratorical masterworks. Both what representative discourses are studied, and in what context they are studied, ultimately result from this tacit critical hegemony. What is slighted is a conception of public discourse as a form of power that seeks to maintain the interests of certain groups at the expense of others.

Each of these three senses of "culture" within rhetorical studies is the product of its own particular history and comes with its own entailments. And, as J. Hillis Miller reminds us, ultimately every way of articulating the relationship of discourse to culture is but a figure of speech arbitrarily asserted over possible other figures of speech (6). However, I suggest we use these applications of the term "culture" in rhetorical studies not as problems themselves but rather as signifiers of a set of critical problematics within our thinking about rhetorical analysis more generally. We do not have to search very far to find evidence of these discouraging problems in our contemporary debates.

While many have announced a "renaissance of public address" (e.g., Lucas; Zarefsky, "State"; and Medhurst, "Public Address"), there is little unanimity as to how this revitalized area ought to take up the social or cultural context or what its ultimate purpose ought to be. For instance, in a recent essay (part of a National Communication Association Presidential Task Force report on "The Future of the Field") one of our most respected critics, Karlyn Kohrs Campbell, after reviewing the spate of recent anthologies of public address, concludes that "courses or anthologies devoted to teaching the history of U.S. public address make no sense at all." The particulars in Campbell's list of charges seem by now familiar: no sense of the movement of rhetorical discourses through historical time, no consideration of the material situation, no diversity in the selection of "masterpieces" for study.

Instead, as a remedy, Campbell offers a wholly different prescription:

> Perhaps it is time to develop courses designed to teach people how to study discourse in ways that focus on assessing the role of rhetoric in shaping the course of economic, political, social, and intellectual history. ("Silence," 143)

It is time, that is, for a mode of analysis and interpretation that might complicate and enrich our capacity to understand the interaction between texts and the wider context within which they function (Gaonkar, "Oratorical Text," 268) without merely noting or valorizing the "intellectual influences" of particular individual public leaders (Jasinski, 216). Or, put another way, what is needed in our practice is a perspective that would understand both that rhetorical discourse represents the shared meanings of a particular society *in history* and that such discourse is itself a cultural practice that *shapes history*. In short, a revitalized sense of culture might bridge the apparent gap between text and context and satisfy Campbell's prescription for a textual public address studies that is also a study of contexts.

I believe we can find just this condition of culture *already* inscribed within rhetorical studies, and, further, that there is what we might eventually recognize as a distinct "cultural tradition" there. But it is not a tradition that these days appears in the mainstream; rather, it is allusive and in the background, if not altogether neglected. I propose to excavate this latent cultural tradition by selectively reading some noteworthy essays in rhetorical criticism and asking whether there seem to be points of shared assumption and discovery that may be summed up in theoretical insight. This rather inductive construction of the "genre" of cultural rhetorical studies thus concentrates upon the *practice* of rhetorical analysis, noting similarities concerning the relationship between text and culture.

ORIGINS OF CULTURAL RHETORIC

While it has become conventional to mark the origins of "modern" rhetorical criticism in Herbert Wichelns's 1925 essay "The Literary Criticism of Oratory," to find the obscured currents of a cultural tradition in rhetorical studies, we begin at a quite different source.[2] We must move forward some twenty years to the publication of Ernest J. Wrage's "Public Address: A Study in Social and Intellectual History," which calls for a "new" paradigm of public address studies to shift attention away from individual orators and toward a "point of view [that] analyz[es] and interpret[s] speeches as documents in social history" (454–455).[3] At its most general, Wrage outlines a curriculum that concentrates on the "function" of ideas in the history of society and argues that this function is to be identified by reading individual texts, what Wrage calls "the records of responses to the social and physical world as expressed in formulations of thought" (451).[4]

Wrage is quite specific about what rhetorical analysis should engage, and he urges consideration of the whole ensemble of a culture, its "mosaic of documents" (452), including "constitutions and laws, . . . scientific treatises, . . . lectures, [and] sermons." But, more than that, also its "literature and song, . . . folklore, . . . speeches"—in short, all the artifacts of popular culture. Wrage argues that an "adequate social and intellectual history cannot be written without accounting for popular opinions, beliefs, [and] constellations of attitudes" (452). Considered, then, as a "whole way of life," culture is more than the exhibition of "grand or high ideas." Instead, a society's "fugitive literature" has the potential to yield "knowledge of . . . cultural strivings and heritage" (457).

In a stroke, Wrage's program multiplies the objects open to critical inquiry to include the popular (and not only the "official" or "artistic") culture. This "ordinariness" of culture is an idea that has become more influential in recent years in part due to the influence of cultural studies; here, its implications spin out beyond just a change in the object(s) of study. To read the "rhetoric of popular culture" is, at once, to extend the artifacts open to reading and the approaches to their reading beyond the traditional oratorical paradigm.

But Wrage's idea also pivots on the implied assumption that the cultural object is a self-conscious commentary on social life. Addressing why rhetoricians should study this "mosaic," Wrage is seemingly convinced that the "study of ideas provides an index to the history" of values and goals, hopes and fears, aspirations and negations in society (451). The discourses in the cultural mosaic function as "agents of their time," providing a "repository of themes" and "elaborations from which we may gain insight into the life of an era." From a study such as this, "it is possible to observe the reflections of prevailing social ideas and attitudes" (455–456). In short, ideas find expression within discourses, and, if we follow Wrage on this point, it seems possible to investigate the influences and residues of ideas within society in and through the artifacts of society.

There are two implications to this seemingly straightforward position, of course: the one, an injunction that analysts ought to work with case studies that express culture rather than to talk in the abstract about cultural ideas—that is, to privilege the *practice* of public culture above all else; the second and, I think, more significant implication is the emphasis upon the textualization of ideas within culture.

The orthodox gloss on Wrage's use of the key term "ideas" renders it equivalent in meaning to "content" or subject matter or *res.*[5] However, from the opening paragraphs of his essay, Wrage is consistent in treating "ideas" not as abstractions, but rather always in terms of their expression in discourses, as shaped by and shaping form or structure or style. For instance, he repeatedly emphasizes that "idea . . . is dependent upon language" (454). He notes, for example, that "thought is [always] expressed in formulations" (451) and that any ideational content, once it is presented in a text, is, as he puts it, dependent on configurations of language (454). Indeed, Wrage says, rhetoricians must study "what happens to ideas under the impact of the interaction" of rhetor, text, and audience (453). For he seems aware (in a phrase eerily contemporary) that texts can be understood best by studying "not only the conditions of the creation of ideas but also the conditions of their reception" (454). "Ideas," as he uses it here, is clearly not the taken-for-granted notion of more-or-less "transcendent" "great and noble thoughts"; rather, Wrage entertains a more complex conception that ideas are the product of a "social environment" and do not "enjoy an independent existence" (451).

Contrary to the received vernacular, Wrage is, then, rather more complicated; he seems committed to the position that ideas take on substance within concrete acts of performance, and that this practice, which itself relays and shapes ideas, is part and parcel of the history of culture. "Idea" in this way resists reduction to "content"; instead, its material manifestation in textuality warrants attention to the "structure, idiom, tone and imagery" of rhetorical texts. That is, culture is not mere idealism; rather, ideas are realized—materialized—in practice, and these specific cases are the right objects of rhetorical analysis.

These passages suggest several points of significance concerning questions of idea, form, context, and criticism. First, Wrage's essay may be read against the traditional emphasis on the production of discourse and on the inventive, self-contained subject-center. Instead, it is clear that this must be balanced against the totality of social and cultural factors that shape ideas and their presentation.

Second, it is too simple to read Wrage as saying that texts are repositories of the history of cultural ideas merely or only because they contain within them the traces of ideas. Rather, there is considerable evidence that Wrage uses the insight that the "mosaic" of texts available to the critic are culture in practice, ideas in action, materialized in texts, aimed at an audience, received in specific conditions by specific people. Far from being objects of aesthetic contemplation, texts are "pitched to levels of information, to take account of prevalent beliefs, and to mirror tone and temper of audiences" (453), and so they are the best means to disclose the prerogatives of a culture set in specific conditions of reception—conditions that necessarily entangle the critic in cultural, economic, and political intertexts.

Finally, it also seems clear that the metaphor structuring Wrage's discussion of the relationship between "ideas" and rhetorical form is hardly the conventional one of "container versus thing contained" or matter versus manner or *product* versus *process*. Rather, in his project, ideas do not just "sit" passively on the surface content of the text, nor are they "poured" into preexisting forms. Instead, the term "ideas" represents a richer, fuller conception than mere abstract impression or sentiment: "ideas" are embodied in rhetorical forms and structures, and this embodying is itself cultural practice. Once framed as public *practice,* and within the contexts of reception, the critic cannot separate "idea" from its materialization in the texts of culture. What is available to the astute reader is a kind of sedimented content to be found in the structure and forms of texts.[6] The formal processes of the discourse may carry ideological messages quite apart from the manifest content. This "content of the form" is an index of a prevailing larger ideological unity of the social system, and serves as a way better to read these larger structures (Jameson, *Political Unconscious,* 88).[7]

There is, then, nascent within Wrage's "Public Address: A Study in Social and Intellectual History," an invigorated sense of culture in rhetoric. Precisely because ideas must be manifested in the form of discourse, as cultural practice, Wrage's ideal critic must hold open the view that the structure of discourse may represent ideas or ideology.

But, just as texts are manifestations of ideas, they are also, as Wrage reminds us, the record of cultural practice, residues whose practice is an action upon an audience and "artifacts" that should be studied as specific cases. Paradoxically, such localized critique expands the rhetorical situation beyond the immediate, taking in the wider range of social, economic, political, institutional, economic, and belief systems.

For all its provocative implications, within the orthodox history of rhetorical studies, Wrage's program is without great contemporary influence.[8] But sometimes influence may hover below the obvious. In the work of some of our most respected critics, similarities begin to emerge, not from the nature of the messages examined, nor from the categories of data analyzed, but rather from the critic's interpretation of the relationship between a text, its content, and its cultural context. I believe we can identify vestiges of Wrage's program—a more sophisticated formation of culture—in the rhetorical tradition.

CULTURE IN THE RHETORICAL TRADITION

Let us turn first to a sensitive piece of rhetorical criticism, Edwin Black's "The Sentimental Style." Black sets out to demonstrate the proposition that there is a relationship between a rhetorical form and a form of consciousness, neither of which can be fully understood without the other, because such "form[s] of consciousness [are] affected by and manifested in the symbolic currency of rhetorical transactions" (85).

Black's argument begins by remarking on the popularity of what he calls the "sentimental style" in the nineteenth century: a form of rhetoric that is obsessed with "detail" and "notable for its stately movement, . . . its piling on of adjectives, . . . its tendency to tear passions to tatters" (78). Drawing his specimen from Daniel Webster's "Bunker Hill Monument Address," Black notes there the "shuttling back and forth between images and descriptions of internal states and emotional seizures" (78) and hypothesizes an association between such didactic rhetorical style and its potential response—an instruction to "the audience how they are to respond and what sensations to experience" (78).

Black is constantly aware of two crucial variables as he reads Webster. First, the cultural milieu of the time: here Black widens the context from the immediate (that of Webster on a ceremonial occasion) to the cultural setting of the 1830s, its attitudes and practices, especially its dominant institutions, most especially, slavery (80). Second, Black focuses on Webster's rhetorical *performance*: the "function" of the rhetoric and "what it do[es] to people" (78). This function, textualized in the formal control over depiction represented in Webster's discourse, ought be taken, Black says, as "a symptom of disquiet and unease, . . . a tacit agreement to repress" moral ambiguities (80)—an "instrument of distraction" (77).

But a distraction from what? Black argues that the sentimental style is a "manifestation of a disposition to subordinate all values to aesthetic values in order to escape a burden of moral responsibility" for the toleration and expansion of slavery (83). Thus, the discourse manifests a "set of perceptual filters" (83) (what we might call an ideology) to give meaning to experience.

Black concludes that Webster's rhetorical form is the embodiment of his ideology or ideas:

> Groups become distinctive . . . not by the beliefs they hold, but by the manner in which they hold them and give them expression. Such people do not necessarily share ideas; they share rather stylistic proclivities and the qualities of mental life of which these proclivities are tokens. (85)

And so, in a way quite consistent with Wrage's, Black recognizes that the consciousness of a particular historical moment may be mirrored in the form of discourse that characterizes such a moment, and the rhetorical style functions both as source of group identification and a distraction from the evils of an immoral social system.

What is very interesting for our investigation is the way in which Black works both ways—from the style to the attitude and from the attitude to the example of it instantiated in a particularly noteworthy example. Black presents a critical argument that moves from cultural context to form of discourse and back to history, and thus models an analysis that appreciates that idea is of necessity materialized in rhetorical form, and that this form is itself a kind of "content" that reveals shared and common cultural "ideas."

Consider next a study of the archetypal symbol of the "sea" conducted by Michael Osborn. Osborn's purpose is clear from the beginning: his is a study in intellectual history, launched to reveal how the archetype of the symbolic sea is "transformed by dramatic changes in human circumstance," to "trace the process of change," and to speculate about what such changes might reveal about changes in culture ("Evolution," 347). In short, the burden of the study is to chart the changing use of the symbol and to explicate homologous changes in social history (349).

Osborn begins with a series of contrasts: the first, a romantic versus classical use of the sea archetype; finding changing and ambivalent senses (349–350), Osborn argues that changes in sea imagery are related to "larger cultural forces at work" (350). Such forces Osborn defines as the stirrings of colonialism and exploration in the late seventeenth century ("the riches of the orient available from the sea"). In this material context, Osborn says, "the excitement of exploration was in the air, and with the development of navigation, ships became more adequate to the challenge of the sea. . . . The tall sailing ships return[ed] from Mediterranean harbors laden with silks, fruit, wine" (350–351). So, changes in the sea symbol from one of danger and unease to one of calm and surplus, found in the discourses of a specific historical setting, are explained in part by changes in the material (in this case, economic) situation.

Likewise, when he takes up the sea archetype in the "romantic vision," Osborn identifies a contrast in usage between the "horrors" of new industrial cities and the naturalness and freedom configured in the wild "romantic" sea (353). Thus, "technology dawned and workers swarmed into the cities to provide the human grist for its machines, [and] the urban experience . . . quite soon became intolerable" (352). In such context, the sea as "a place of wildness beyond control and as a reaction to stifling orthodoxy" provides an escape from the intolerable (352).

It is quite striking that Osborn centers his explanations of the evolution of the symbol not on literary or idealist explanations but rather on the tangible, the material, the economic, and the historical. The result is a form of history dealing with attitudes and with "mind sets" expressed in style and symbol. These symbolics are, for the author, representative of the changing ideologies of these periods.

In the second part of the essay, as he turns to analyzing the way in which the genres of poetry and rhetoric use the figure of the sea quite differently, Osborn implicitly shifts from how the social condition shapes symbols to how symbols influence social practice. He suggests that differences in the symbolic mobilization of the archetype are reflective of pathological and psychological separation (357)—a cultural clash between the demands of society (the "social hierarchy") and the idea of the freedom of the individual, both conceptions regnant in the eighteenth century. In short, the difference in metaphoric entailments is *itself* read as a symptom of social unrest and disharmony (356). Osborn maintains that these different uses of the archetype are vehicles of arguments that have shaped society. Citing cases where the metaphor, as he puts it, "takes over" the situation, Osborn points out how the archetype defines and determines the meaning of situations and provides cases where changing symbol use both "shapes" as well as "reflects" experience.

Osborn's is a sophisticated semiotic analysis, moving diachronically, reconstructing the discourse of the sea symbol in and through a cross section of texts. Further, the essay erases the distinctions of "high" versus popular/everyday culture, and Osborn tacitly assumes that aesthetic standards in the societies he examines are also social/political standards. This assumption lets him shuttle between art and politics, and throughout Osborn binds his readings of the texts to local and immediate material situations; at the same time he moves across history so as to provide insight into the guiding ideas of these societies.

Next, consider a critical study that deals even more explicitly with discourse not only as a symptom of acute cultural strain but also as constitutive of experience. Thomas Farrell and G. Thomas Goodnight begin their analysis of the discourse surrounding the 1979 accident at the Three Mile Island Nuclear Facility, "Accidental Rhetoric: The Root Metaphors of Three Mile Island," with the assumption that everyday, ordinary communication practices typically constitute "patterns of life within a culture" (272).

Arguing that the Three Mile Island accident (TMI) cannot be understood apart from the social processes that produce it, classify it, perceive it, and explain it, Farrell and Goodnight's study is less "about" the incident than it is an attempt to go behind the discourse of the incident to the social content that is reflected in it and to what this indicates about the process of giving meaning to experience in the era of mediated mass communication. Farrell and Goodnight frame the accident as an index of a crisis in contemporary society—a crisis they characterize as a split between two "cultures"—what they call the technical sphere and the public sphere. Here Farrell and Goodnight dramatically amplify the situation beyond the commonplaces of immediacy and the particular, placing the TMI discourse within the intersection of three contingent world views that may be traced back in history "at least one hundred years" (274). Maintaining that these constitute differing "visions of nature and man," Farrell and Goodnight capture these worldviews within the three root metaphors of "industry," "ecology," and "energy" (274)—and define them through a wide range of discursive practices. So, for instance, in explicating "industry," they begin with Frederick Taylor and Henry Ford, and include Teddy Roosevelt, the Boy Scouts, and Franklin D. Roosevelt (275). Likewise, "ecology" begins with Rachel Carson's naming of the "silent spring" and is identified and explained by a reading of exemplary discourses of the ecology movement.

Ultimately these three worldviews are materialized in the current debate over nuclear power, a debate Farrell and Goodnight contextualize and from within the "peaceful uses of the atom" controversy in the early 1950s, the cold war, the Price-Anderson Act (which limited the liability of the nuclear industry), the creation of the Atomic Energy Commission, the passage of the National Environmental Policy Act of 1969, decisions of the Supreme Court, a series of "incidents" in the nuclear industry in the late 1970s, the Karen Silkwood case, and even the film *The China Syndrome*.

In other words, these critics work to develop the sense of a wider and more "material context," and, in doing this, the incident that is the TMI becomes more fully contextualized and embedded in this linked frame. Moreover, what Farrell and Goodnight identify is but a set of American ideologies of progress, and for them the TMI becomes a site not just of a nuclear accident, but a site for studying the intersection of ideologies whose forms of argument characterize contemporary American culture.

But, even as they expand the situation beyond the immediate, Farrell and Goodnight also focus quite closely upon the local situation with the intention to "reconstruct" the "crisis discourse" of Three Mile Island (281–292). Tracing the "narrative" of the incident and its "failure" to reassure and calm fear (285), they concentrate on the news media. Reading the semiotics of newspaper headlines, photographs, and published feature articles of people coping with the accident, they arrive at a story "constructed" through folk ideologies of "apocalypse and disaster" (290). Farrell and Goodnight suggest that, when technical discourse falls short (as it apparently does with the TMI), the media resort to the alternatives of more "animistic" themes or "ecological" frames as the base for explanatory discourses and construct explanations within those ecological and populist frames (287). This crossing of themes is a contest or struggle over which worldview will eventually succeed in organizing the conflicted and complex events of the TMI.

As with the Osborn study, Farrell and Goodnight make no critical distinction between politics, the popular, or high/low culture artifacts. They variously consider congressional legislation, Supreme Court decisions, public statements, press conferences, newspaper coverage, television news reports, movies, popular books, and real-life events as texts they read to define the social formation within which the TMI incident is framed and its discourse made intelligible. Farrell and Goodnight, through their case study of the communication practices around the TMI, move their reading to the structural level. And when seen this way, it is not merely the "ideas" that are the material through which cultural history is written, but rather the conflict or intersection of these ideologies itself serves as a symptom of social crisis.

Clearly, while there are significant differences in these essays regarding what they study or even what their conclusions are, there are also obvious similarities between Farrell and Goodnight's interpretation of the discourse of Three Mile Island, Black's reading of the sentimental style, and Osborn's view of the relationship between symbolic form and culture. These are studies that consider textuality as a manifestation or a reflection of culture (Black), that locate changes in culture by explicating changes in the symbolics of discourse (Osborn), and that take discursive strategies as not only mirroring but also shaping understanding of experience (Farrell and Goodnight).

Further, each of these studies seems to share a sense of culture that is at once more broad and more anthropological than the more orthodox rhetorical usages I noted at the outset. Each of them shares the sense of culture as both the meanings and the practices in a particular social formation. In other words, they share a view of culture that, as Stuart Hall has put it, encompasses

> *both* the meanings and values which arise amongst distinctive social groups and classes, on the basis of their given historical conditions and relationships, through which they "handle" and respond to the condi-

tions of existence; *and* the lived traditions and practices through which those "understandings" are expressed and in which they are embodied. ("Two Paradigms," 63; emphasis in original)

Moreover, and much more to the point of this reclamation project, I think assumptions about culture, context, history, and textuality that shape these three critical studies are refined from Wrage's argument in his "Public Address" essay. There are implications here that I will turn to shortly. But first, let me briefly refer to other noteworthy critical interpretations, interpretations that seem also to operate with similar assumptions.

In their "Sweet Talk: The Moral Rhetoric against Sugar," Elizabeth Walker Mechling and Jay Mechling "go beneath the surface text[s]" (19) and investigate the residues of how entire American belief systems are displayed and contested in "popular science" discourses and "self-help books" that deal with sugar (19). What they find is that the "addiction to sugar" is figured metaphorically via associations to other kinds of addiction, with the result that dietary or nutrition matters come to be understood as emblematic of other more general "human weaknesses."

Taking this analogy as paradigm and drawing from religious, scientific, and political texts, Mechling and Mechling find that this dietary analogy has its own homologue in the social context. It is significant, they note, that the antisugar literature is historically "exclusively a phenomenon of the 1970s." This insight implies a central and controlling analogy—pollution of the body by sugar is homologous to pollution of society by disorder (22), and becomes, for Mechling and Mechling, a "powerful comment from the 1970s upon the 1960s." Ultimately, even proposed solutions are identically figured: the return of the body to normalcy through the purging of the pollutant sugar is matched by the return of the society to controlled order through the purging of the excesses represented in the 1960s (29–30). Thus, their insight is that this popular and seemingly inconsequential "self-help" literature on nutrition encodes the basic agon of control versus desire that animates the social and cultural spheres in the 1970s, and the discourse of sugar serves to reveal a basic conflict in American society in a specific historical context.

It is just this sort of encoding that Janice Hocker Rushing has in mind in her analysis of the "American Western myth." Beginning with an assumption about how dramatic media both reflect and create societal events, Rushing is convinced that "media and societal values reciprocally influence one another; by projecting collective images of a culture, by serving as symptoms of cultural needs, and by symbolizing trends" (Rushing and Frentz, "Rocky," 64). To demonstrate one way this might happen, she studies a "history of the Western myth" to expose "the fragile balance between the values of individualism and community" (17). Rushing's is a study of ideology that simultaneously moves paradigmatically across communicative forms and synchronically across history, ranging from motion pictures and 1950s television, presidential campaign discourse, interactions in contemporary political and popular culture (31), and from "early 1920s–40s Westerns" to more contemporary ones (18–19). But, beyond merely summarizing content, Rushing reads cultural texts that widen the historical context, among them: the New Deal, the rise of television and its influence on the film industry, a 1950s religious revivalism "championed by Billy Graham and Norman Vincent Peale" (20), the image of the "organization man" in the 1950s, changes in the economy, women entering the job market, and the women's liberation movement, each of which is a significant "change to community and the . . . geographical and psychic landscape of the urban America" (23).

Searching for the "larger meaning" of the "urban cowboy phenomenon," Rushing argues that it represents in symbolic form the choice of "appearance versus reality," which she suggests is likewise manifest in the discourse surrounding the election of a retired motion picture actor as president in 1980. By explicating a homology between text and context, the formal links and similarities between changes in the form and changes in culture, Rushing looks at "discourses" less as self-contained entities and more as forms that move in and through a variety of everyday texts.

Thomas Benson's essay on the 1974 documentary *Primate* is another example grounded in similar perspectives on culture. Because he is interested in the way that "facts" are transformed in mediated texts, Benson positions Frederick Wiseman's documentary as part of a cultural dialogue over the uses or judgments of "fact." Placing Wiseman as "part of a tradition"—part of a "continually evolving dialogue in the arts and social sciences of the past century" (204), Benson's critique is a search for the proper context for reading the film. This context is ultimately fixed as what Benson calls a "culture" of the American obsession with "facts," a long line of succession running from Anthony Trollope through James Agee. "Our literature," Benson writes, "our journalism, and popular arts have been dominated in this century by various forms of flight to and from facts" (206). In this regard, Benson cites Charles Dickens, John Fowles, Upton Sinclair, and Norman Mailer—not only these but also documentary filmmaker Robert Flaherty and the CBS television program *60 Minutes*. Thus, Benson sets the controversial film documentary in the context of a much wider social and cultural dialogue that stimulates an increased understanding both of the single film text and of the social formation (206).

An essay that ventures even further in its questioning of textual ontology and the traditional strategic character of rhetoric is Robert Scott's analysis of the work of Mexican mural and fresco painter Diego Rivera. Initially, Scott takes Rivera's frescoes to be self-contained "texts," reads their surfaces, and notes their emphasis on color (79) and consistent representation of workers (80). But professing an abiding interest in the "ideological and cultural components" (71) of Rivera's work, Scott expands what is traditionally meant by "text" and argues that what is most interesting in the case of Rivera is the cultural debate over values that is played out in the *controversy* in the United States surrounding Rivera and his work and the socialist politics they seemed to celebrate (76). For Scott, this controversy includes questions of power, economics, the value of art, the propriety of ownership (79), and thus Rivera's murals provide the occasion for the investigation of these societal conflicts. Quite simply, the "frescoes" of Diego Rivera and the furor they created reveal "the conflicting value structures in our country" (82). In the end, expanding what counts as a rhetorical text and how it might be studied, Scott examines historical incident and argues the "cultural" force of the event as homologous of who and what we are (81).

A CULTURAL RHETORICAL STUDIES

At the outset, I questioned whether a suspended tradition of culture in rhetorical studies might not be restored, or at least recognized and appreciated, by way of a rereading of certain significant essays in rhetorical criticism. As we have seen, these essays differ significantly in the nature of the communication messages they examine and in the conclusions they draw from their study. Yet, each takes up culture as a key hermeneutic category, each offers a model of how rhetorical criticism might conceptualize the relations between texts and their cultural contexts. A grounding for this sort of cultural approach becomes clearer if we look at methodological correspondences and theoretical connections that emerge from the critical essays we examined.

The "Mosaic of [Popular] Culture"

One aspect of these studies is the variety in the kinds of discourses taken up. Included were ceremonial orations, public statements, acts of Congress, Supreme Court decisions, newspaper coverage, visual art, television news reports, motion pictures, best-selling books, social movements, and "real-life" events. There is a convergence here around the idea of *what* should be studied, a common focal point: by implicitly urging attention to the "mosaic" of culture, of popular as well as official and authorized texts, these studies broaden the idea of what counts as culture and so of what is open to study. Several implications follow. First, these critics have each taken for granted that creating and managing meanings happens in a variety of texts across a wide field of communicative forms and that texts not marked traditionally as political are often those that are most political. Also, while certain of them do take up speeches, none of these studies is bound to the traditional paradigm of the platform oration as the preeminent object of critical attention. And so, not only is popular culture often the object of critical attention, but the artifacts represented are sometimes oppositional and often outside the established order. In short, these essays embody the shared assumption that "culture" encompasses the whole way of life of a society rather than the "officially" sanctioned culture of the "artistic" or the "powerful."

Discourse and History

A second common element of the studies described is notions of the relationship between discourse and history—a relationship seen in two different polarities. Expressions used in these essays such as "tokens," "mirror," "homologue," "symptom," "instrument," or "manifestations," and phrases such as, "form[s] of consciousness affected by and manifested in the symbolic currency of rhetorical transactions," all indicate a shared sense of how history is *represented* in rhetorical discourse. Thus, as culture in practice, the forms and styles of the discourses under investigation are not seen as mere supplement to ideas; rather, they are themselves "ideas" that index the way a culture appropriately encodes ideas and what that assumes about the nature of the receivers who decode them.

But in these essays influence seems to flow in the other direction as well. Such phraseology as "ordinary communication practices typically constitute patterns of life within a culture" and the common professed interest in "how symbols influence social practice" reverses the valence and helps to ground common assumptions about the way rhetorical discourses *shape* history. These analyses seem to share the sense that structures of representation are also structures of consciousness; in other words, they are ways of construing "the real," or constructing reality, or of "giving meaning to experience."

It seems clear enough that each of the critics in our brief survey operates with the rather modern idea that experience must be made to mean—that it is culture manifested through discourse that gives "meaning" and significance to history for members of a particular society. For each of the critics we reviewed, how experience "gets defined" is pivotal; if reality is not a given set of facts but is the result of a particular way of constructing reality, then rhetorical discourse does not merely reproduce "reality" through the transmission of an already existing meaning but instead constitutes an active process of "making things mean."

Materializing Ideology

A third aspect the studies share seems to converge around notions of the purpose of cultural rhetorical study. When they express the goal to reveal the ideas embedded in everyday discourse or the idea that "media and societal values reciprocally influence one another," we may note that these studies manifest a compulsion to explain discourse functioning within society. As such, this compulsion results in an alternative way of considering textuality and ideology.

Using such terms as "perceptual filters," "forms of consciousness," and "cultural worldviews," these studies assume that cultural artifacts are produced by specific individuals under specific legal, economic, political, cultural, and organizational constraints. Thus, some formal features and thematic content can be traced not just to individual minds but also to organizational interactions and constraints. And, what is more, the texts that these scholars bring to our attention are less unproblematic reflections of culture, or "mirrors of the real," than they are particular bids at constructing what is "real" and giving it specific meanings. Because the shaping and structuring of discourse is also a way of giving meaning to the world, each of our sampled critics implicitly recognizes that texts are never entirely benign or "neutral" but rather always serve some interest.

In this sense, discourse reveals the shaping force of ideology materialized in the "transmission" of discourse and shaped and framed in this transmission. For this reason, most of the essays we surveyed propose to "go behind the discourse of the incident to the social content"; or to try to locate the "larger cultural forces at work"; or to "go beneath the surface"; or to locate the "residues" "coded" into the rhetorical discourse. What seems implicit in such idioms is the argument that texts are concrete material instances of culture/ideology and that culture itself is this rhetorical mosaic writ large. The critical studies we held up assume that if this "cultural text" somehow writes or produces all of the smaller versions of itself, then analysis may articulate the one to the other.

Conditions of Reception

A fourth convergence is in the way these critics expand their conception of the situation beyond the immediate. For instance, critics interested in nuclear power invoke Frederick Taylor, Henry Ford, Teddy Roosevelt, the Boy Scouts, Franklin Roosevelt, "Atoms for Peace," the cold war, the debate over the creation of the Atomic Energy Commission, passage of the National Environmental Policy Act, decisions of the Supreme Court, a series of "incidents" in the nuclear industry in the late 1970s, the Silkwood case, and so on. Similarly, a study of the "Western myth" ends up referencing the urban experience, the New Deal, the rise of television and its influence on the film industry, a 1950s religious revivalism, the "organization man," economic conditions, and gains by women in the workplace, among other phenomena.

But, besides merely broadening the notion of the rhetorical situation beyond the immediate, these studies situate the discursive practices they examine within a more comprehensive "material context." As is clear in terminology such as "tracing the process of change" and the commonplace consideration of extradiscursive elements, these analyses assume a more material sense of history. But "thinking historically" in this way means much more than merely adding context or genre onto the same old study of the text, or even of just seeing the text in a new way. On the contrary, it entails seeing a "new" text. These studies seem to operate under the principle that a text exists only in relationship to some particular discursive or historical conditions under which it is read. This does not deny the objective marginal existence of texts, but rather emphasizes that texts differ in the way their external relations to other texts and practices are ordered. It follows that every text is "intertextual" not only in the traditional sense that it is related to others generically or historically but also in the sense that the discourses of history, of economics, of production, or (even) of readers interact with texts, shaping them and influencing readings of them.

The end result is that these studies are neither historicist, radically particular, nor nominalistic. They consider the text as a kind of miniature for larger forces and ideologies. But neither are they universal, totalizing, or essentializing. They recognize the particularity of rhetorical performance and understand that this particularity must be read within a local context.

Agency and Intentionality

Finally, there is a convergence around the problematic question of agency in these rhetorical studies. From its inception, the study of rhetoric has assumed that any discourse is the product of a specific historical person whose design is enacted in discourse in order to achieve a specific particular objective with "his" audience. This is part and parcel of the Aristotelian "art of persuasion." Yet, the studies we read do not address specific local effects in any telling detail. Instead, along with a widening of the rhetorical situation and the rethinking of the text as being penetrated by ideology, authorship becomes of less significance: either it seems not discussed at all (sometimes because it is difficult to determine precisely who is the author in media texts) or because the author actually might better be described as the "culture" itself. Even Black's essay on Webster and his "sentimental style" (which might seem at first to come closest to the traditional subject-centered persuasive model) does not engage the standardized assumptions about agency. Black treats Webster less as an individual force and more as a type or model: "such examples of the sentimental style," Black writes, "could be multiplied from discourses of the time; Webster is only an acutely sonorous representative of the type" (78).

PROBLEMATICS OF TEXT AND CONTEXT, OF RHETORIC AND CULTURE

From our reading of a set of noteworthy critical analyses and the identifying of clusters of methodological or theoretical correspondences, we have inductively distilled what we might well call a cultural rhetorical perspective. In bringing to the surface this submerged tradition of culture in rhetorical studies, we are in a position to reconsider texts in relation to their cultural context and to understand how these representations of culture are themselves social documents that both treat and mediate questions of power and interest. Moreover, the correspondences implicit in the studies suggest alternative modes of dealing with currently perceived problematics in rhetorical and cultural analysis.

It can be argued that presently our received approaches conduce toward either of two unsatisfactory extremes: either the neglect of context or the rendering of the text as "transparent." We find these emphases in their most concise expression in two of our most eminent scholars.

For instance, Lawrence Grossberg has faulted "communicational cultural studies" for idealizing issues of power and context. Grossberg characterizes such studies as concentrating too much on textuality, with the result that structures of meaning are analyzed independent of real material and economic conditions of the world and of people's lives ("Can Cultural Studies," 94). What Grossberg calls textual studies "reduce culture to a symbolic representation of power and grant it a certain apparent autonomy" (95). Thus, Grossberg charges, such studies never come into contact with "real" material practices and social relations.[9]

The studies we have seen here, however, disclose a different protocol. Each example looked at centered on the case study method. Each of these critics implicitly acknowledges that the relationship between history and text cannot be theorized in general terms but must be painstakingly worked out, based on the particular context and the material social setting. And each engages the difficult business of actually reading a text and showing how the historical context inheres in it. These critical studies attempt to go beyond the rather vague claim that the context "explains" the text, and the analytic burden taken up in each of these studies is to explicate social influence in the action of these cultural texts. Dominick LaCapra puts it this way: "The question becomes how precisely the discursive practice, deep structure or ideology . . . is situated in the text other than in terms of instantiation or simple reflection. . . . One must elucidate in a more detailed way how the borrowed or common ideas actually function in the texts in question" (42, 51). In the most satisfying of these cultural rhetorical studies, each critic, I suggest, is trying to find a language of cultural critique to specify this practice.

Likewise, another influential critic, Michael Leff, has warned about a complementary problem. In any critical practice that goes beyond the explication of the single case, Leff notes, such criticism tends to lose sight of the actual message ("Interpretation," 338) and ends up neglecting the textuality of situated rhetorical performance in favor of more broadly brushed summation of symbol use. But such a charge is not valid with regard to the analyses we have examined in our survey of cultural rhetorical studies. Instead, each of these analyses examines a discrete case of rhetorical practice and seeks to explain the functions of the particular case within the local conditions of its production and reception. And, while it is the cultural aspects that are the center of focus, the critical account pays quite close attention to the actual texts—indeed, the form and the structures of such texts serve as the primary data for the cultural critique, as the critics read the structures of texts as manifestations of cultural "ideas." In every case, it seems unpersuasive to discuss ideology apart from its textualization and the formal processes involved.

In undertaking to identify subtle currents of a submerged tradition of cultural examination in rhetorical studies, we may take some consolation in the perception that, instead of having to "invent" a kind of rhetorical analysis that, in Karlyn Campbell's words, would "focus on assessing the role of rhetoric in . . . history," we already have a legacy of studies of discourse set in cultural context—though a legacy in need of refurbishing. Each of the critical studies outlined above in its own way holds a double sense of the relationship of text to context. In short, the exemplary critics we have looked at neither eliminate the text as a critical category by dissolving it into history-economics-politics nor reify it as a formal self-contained abstraction. Consequently, I believe, this "lost" tradition sustains a critical perspective that transcends the heuristic bifurcation between hermeneutics and materialism, that is, about whether one should study the product of rhetoric or the process, study the iconic text or the textual fragment, study the text or the context, the intrinsic or the extrinsic, the discrete or the diffused. Instead, these studies, focusing upon specific cases and upon their material context and seeking to explain the functions of discourse in culture, provide a model of what a cultural rhetorical studies should look like. There is, indeed, a "cultural" tradition from which to draw, one that takes account of how history and popular culture together function as the "canvas to build up together a picture of institutions, ideologies, rhetors, media and audiences"[10] and that does not reduce culture to the symbolic representation of power nor grant textuality a totalizing autonomy.

All in all, the tradition of cultural rhetorical studies that we have reconstructed here is a tradition implicitly aware that discourse is performance that materializes ideology; that seemingly knows that this ideology must be explained in terms of whose interest it serves; it understands that this manner of materializing is itself part and parcel of the ideological "content"; and the tradition prescribes that the best means of such study is via specific cases set in their historical context of institutions, economics, and ideologies. Not only do the authors of the studies each believe that the texts they study are symptoms or superstructures of something else more real and more important, but also that the text shapes this something else. The texts they study are by-products of a particular historical cultural moment, but are also always making history.

We are, I think, as Ernest J. Wrage lamented fifty years ago, still in need of a body of interpretive work that places "fugitive literature" or "the popular" in its right relationship to "culture" and "history." But what has been less obvious in our tradition is that in rhetorical studies forms of cultural analysis are routinely evolving in ways that are little noticed but that would have been unimaginable as recently as two decades ago.

ACKNOWLEDGMENT

Portions of this essay first appeared in "Rhetorical Criticism and the Context of Culture: Rereading Ernest Wrage," a paper presented at the 1996 annual meeting of the Southern States Communication Association, Memphis, TN, March 1996.

NOTES

1. For a thorough review of the terms "culture" and "rhetorical studies" as they have appeared in communication studies, see John M. Sloop and Mark Olson's essay in this volume (Chapter 10).
2. Others have noted the contrasts between Wrage's position in rhetorical studies and that of Wichelns; as William R. Brown describes it, Wrage is more interested in society's influence on oratory, while Wichelns focuses on oratory's influence on society (see Brown, "Mass Media and Society," 203).
3. Charles J. Stewart, writing his "Historical Survey" on rhetorical criticism, assesses movement studies as similar to Wrage's program in that both are reactions to the then dominant program of neo-Aristotelianism. Both represent an early sign of discontent with figure studies and discontent with effects studies.
4. Wrage's argument has been traditionally understood in either of two orthodox readings. One such interpretation we may call the "history of ideas" reading. This reading emphasizes Wrage's arguments defining public address as "instrumental" for the "transmission of ideas." A more recent interpretation of "Public Address: A Study in Social and Intellectual History" we might label the "textual criticism reading." It inflects Wrage's argument as uninterested in mat-

ters of textuality or form, concerned exclusively with content in public address. Typical of this textual criticism interpretation, Wrage is said to continually "defer" attention to textual dynamics, and as a consequence to see texts as "passive receptacle[s], something transparent," where the true point of analysis is found in the "ideas" (Gaonkar, "Oratorical Text," 261). I have argued that neither of these conventional understandings of Wrage's project is complete or satisfactory, and to cling to received interpretations of the essay no longer seems especially profitable. In particular, the "history of ideas" version holds that Wrage maintains ideas may be studied quite apart from the discursive forms within which they are enscribed; while the "textual criticism" reading must simplistically position Wrage as forever separating form and content and, worse, as privileging the latter over the former. What I am attempting, then, is a very different reading of Wrage's essay, one that goes against traditional and unexamined interpretations (see Rosteck, "Rhetorical Criticism and the Context of Culture").

5. See Gaonkar, "Oratorical Text" and "Object and Method"; for another reading, see Rosteck, "Rhetorical Criticism and the Context of Culture."

6. The phrase, of course, is Fredric Jameson's, in *The Political Unconscious*, 39–99.

7. These concepts—the materializing of culture, the sense of rhetorical form as idea—have been briefly noted in Wrage's program before. In a rarely cited essay (yet, one that presages our contemporary critical debates), Malcolm Sillars argued that rhetorical events are best understood as "acts" (278). Sillars concludes (as we have) that Wrage cannot mean that "idea" is an entity apart from its mode of communication. Thus, Sillars contends that "critics must study language, organization, delivery as integral parts of the 'idea.' " For only, Sillars concludes, "when 'idea' is understood in its full rhetorical ramifications can the term *idea* be really useful" (see Sillars, 283–284; emphasis in original).

8. The disciplinary status of Wrage's "Public Address" is peculiar; while the essay has come to be read as a "landmark" and has been reprinted many times (see Medhurst, ed. *Landmark Essays*; the first and second editions of Brock and Scott, eds.; and most recently, Burgchardt), there is no gainsaying that Wrage's program has been forgotten and overlooked. In our disciplinary histories, Wrage and his essay are seemingly without influence; there is no mention of Wrage or his revisionist program of public address in Rogers (*A History of Communication Study*) or in Herman Cohen's (*History of Speech Communication*), and Wrage gets only two brief mentions in Benson's (*Speech Communication in the 20th Century*).

9. The phrase "communicational cultural studies" is Grossberg's and would seem to include what I am calling here "rhetorical studies" as that part of the field that Grossberg defines as interested in only the "encoded meaning" of the text ("Can Cultural Studies," 93). Grossberg expands this discussion of communicational cultural studies in a later essay (see "Toward a Genealogy").

10. This phrase is Sproul's (477); as he argues, this aspect of Wrage's project is the most "controversial."

TEN

CULTURAL STRUGGLE
A Politics of Meaning
in Rhetorical Studies

John M. Sloop
Mark Olson

In a twist on Barnet Baskerville's question "Must we all be rhetorical critics?" it may be more appropriate today to ask, "*Are* we all cultural critics?" At many conference presentations and in seminar rooms across the country, the implied response to this question is, "Yes. Well, at least I am. Always have been." As the broad interdisciplinary area of "cultural studies" has witnessed a rise in currency across the academy, the number of people claiming to "do" cultural studies, regardless of what they called their work in the past (e.g., public address, popular culture, the rhetoric of science), has followed suit. Moreover, even a cursory scanning of academic job descriptions would indicate that "cultural studies" has become a catchall requirement for numerous positions.[1] It is the story of a utopic small town that everyone suddenly discovers. While the influx of a new population brings new energy and attention to the town and its more prominent citizens, it also brings some of the dangers of urban sprawl: the original settlers rally to protect their landscape; people from towns with relatively depressed economies rush to the new market, trading past allegiances for their new home; the very personality of the town and its citizens is up for grabs. Before the settlers know it, they live in just another big city—diverse in person and population. And, while it may still be known for its original flavor, one has to search far and wide for the nontouristy, "authentic" sections of town and, for that matter, for the towns that previously surrounded it.

To a large degree, I have been sympathetic to the growth of the city.[2] When I would hear Larry Grossberg speak at National Communication Association (NCA) conference meetings and posit seemingly hard definitions of what cultural studies *is* (or what cultural studies *are*), I would grumble in my seat, thinking under my breath: "Just do your work. . . . Who cares what it's called? If people want to migrate, let them. Just mind your own business. Sure, the rush hours will be a little rough, but when you're alone in your home, it's just like old times. You do your work; you let your neighbors do their work—there's no need to complain about who is living next door or to be concerned about what they're doing."

However, I have found it impossible to ignore a seemingly geometric increase in the number of colleagues at conferences who have learned to answer, "Rhetoric and cultural studies" when asked, "And what do you do?" Moreover, in the past year, three different friends remarked to me that they were advised by separate publishers to add some allusion to "culture" to the titles of forthcoming books because, each was told, a "cultural study" will outsell a rhetorical one. With each instance, I began to wonder more about the stakes of this joint articulation of rhetorical and cultural studies or, in some cases, of the replacement of "rhetorical criticism" by "cultural studies" as a description of one's critical activities. When rhetoric is articulated with, or replaced by, culture (even partially), there is an obvious danger that both rhetorical studies and cultural studies will lose something important—rhetorical studies risks its focused inquiry into the available means of persuasion, and cultural studies, as an interdisciplinary project, risks the fruits of rhetorical studies' focus.

In short, I want to argue that there is indeed something at stake in the increasing universalization of the terms *culture* and *cultural studies,* and that there is reason to delineate a more specific meaning, or at least a broad parameter, for what it is that "doing cultural studies" implies and how it is distinguishable from *rhetorical studies.* In brief, my concern is this: if cultural studies implies as one of its characteristics an active and public form of politics by those placing themselves under its banner, the universalization of "cultural studies" to include traditional genres of rhetorical research (e.g., historical public address studies, contemporary public discourse studies) has the potential (albeit unintended) effect of curtailing these proactive aspects of cultural studies. That is, if what we were always already doing was cultural studies, then we need do nothing different; the role of criticism need not be rethought or reworked as we take on a new label. Moreover, if rhetorical studies itself partially drifts into a vague notion of the study of popular culture, then rhetorical studies' own unique offering (i.e., understandings of the power of symbolic action and its deployment) to broader interdisciplinary conversations will also be weakened. In short, a partial conflation of cultural studies and rhetorical studies threatens to loosely undermine the politics implied by the former and the latter's insights into the process of carrying out those politics.[3]

In the broader terms of *communication* studies (rather than rhetorical studies) and cultural studies, this conflation has recently been commented on by Grossberg under the heading of "communicational cultural studies" ("Toward," 131).[4] The problem with this term for Grossberg, and this is worth quoting at length, is that it

> reduces culture to the symbolic representations of power and grants it a certain apparent autonomy. As a result, communicational cultural studies finds itself constantly rediscovering what it already knew: regarding domination, that particular cultural practices reproduce the structures of domination and subordination, and that they reinscribe relations of identity, difference and inequality; regarding subordination, communicational cultural studies seems satisfied with finding cracks in the processes of reproduction and reinscription. . . . But real questions remain unasked and unanswered: Questions about the specific forms in which domination and subordination are organized, about the ways they operate, about how they are lived, mobilized and empowered. ("Toward," 141–142)

In the end, "communicational cultural studies" is defined by its focus on a particular type of text (popular cultural texts) and is limited by its employment of traditional assumptions about dominance and subordination. In effect, Grossberg argues that, by conflating communication and culture, communication scholars abandon overt politics in pursuit of observations about representation and identity.

It is the partial conflation between rhetorical studies more specifically and cultural studies, however, that is the concern of this essay. Fittingly and ironically, the very essay that acted as something of an impetus for the book you are now reading reveals evidence of this tendency. In Thomas Rosteck's provocative review of a number of "introduction to cultural studies"-themed books, he articulates a relationship between rhetoric and cultural studies and argues explicitly for a critical practice that is alternatively posited as "rhetorical cultural studies" or "cultural rhetorical studies." Rosteck's discussion of this "rhetorical cultural studies" is scripted in words that read almost as if Grossberg had penned them himself as an imagined example of communication cultural studies:

> Perhaps we ought to frame this question thusly: *are cultural studies rhetorical studies in embryo?* After all, rhetoric has known all along what cultural studies is seeming just to discover: all discourse is constructed with a purpose to serve an interest, and it then offers itself as an "imagi-

nary" frame that historical women and men might use to understand the conditions of their lives. ("Cultural Studies and Rhetorical Studies," 400, emphasis added)

And while Rosteck earlier in the essay notes the more overtly "political" character of cultural studies, later admitting that cultural studies and rhetorical studies might be used to reread one another, the impulse in the above passage conflates the two, places cultural studies under the rubric of rhetorical studies, and positions "rhetorical cultural studies" both as the study of discourse (ideology) and as an autonomous zone separate from issues of production and the economy, the material conditions of possibility and effectivity. As a result, in attempting to understand the relationships between rhetoric and cultural studies, Rosteck problematically highlights links and similarities that, in my mind, dissolve the more proactive potentialities of cultural studies, constructing cultural studies as rhetorical studies doing its business as usual.

As a way to explain the ease with which the study of rhetorical versus cultural studies has been made interchangeable, in the following essay I will discuss some of the primary uses of the term "culture" as it has been employed in rhetorical studies essays over the past decade. My understanding of the use of "culture" in rhetorical studies comes from a larger study of its use in National Communication Association journals.[5] In the broadest sense, I would argue that "culture" and "cultural studies" have been configured within communication studies in five different senses, each drawing on traditions as diverse as organizational communication and intercultural communication. In this essay, given that my interest lies primarily with how rhetorical critics/theorists and cultural critics have employed "culture" in recent studies, I will limit my discussion to only three of those categories.[6] After discussing the way that some uses of "culture" in these various categories create the conditions for an interchangeability between rhetoric and culture as terms, I will draw upon other essays published within communication studies that are less rhetorical in a traditional sense and more "mass media/cultural studies" in order to provide a contrasting and, to my mind, more productive use of "culture."

In short, then, I suggest that, within the period of time covered in this study, rhetorical critics have employed "culture" in such a way that, when employed to make a "rhetorical cultural studies," allows for a nonovertly (perhaps unacknowledged) political study of various locations and logics of meaning rather than a focus on the political circulation of meaning and its transformation in the activities of daily life. This, coupled with the academic market's current demand for cultural studies, has led to a situation in which cultural studies is threatened with an abandonment, or at least a lessening, of its political force. I am not suggesting that there is anything intentionally sinister afoot here; no one has purposely attempted to tame cultural studies. It is more that the variety of uses to which rhetorical scholars have always put the term "culture," coupled with the growth of interdisciplinary cultural studies, has encouraged a conflation of meanings. While on the surface valuable to each individual area, this conflation worked as a whole to generalize the meaning of culture and cultural studies such that it could be claimed as a descriptor for work traditionally being performed under the rhetorical studies banner.

Specifically, culture has been defined within rhetorical studies (and mass communication studies) as: (1) a grammar or logic of communication on a disciplinary (e.g., various sciences) or mediated basis (e.g., oral vs. print); (2) a space or context for analysis (i.e. popular culture); and (3) the circulation of meanings and pleasures that provides the materials out of which identity and knowledge can be (temporarily) fixed.[7] I will use the third use of culture as a way to outline productive differences between rhetorical studies and cultural studies.[8]

CULTURE AS LOGIC

One primary use of "culture" in rhetorical criticism is its signification of a set of general epistemological assumptions and procedures based within a particular formal and disciplinary structure (e.g., science culture, political culture) or of various cultural assumptions based on changes in dominant media (i.e., in McLuhan/Ong fashion, this is an articulation of oral culture, literate culture, print culture, etc.). While the distinctions being made between various meanings of culture would have some resonance with contemporary senses of culture in "cultural studies," they are used here more to *describe* (rather than to change) a general area of study or to indicate changes in overall ways of thinking and understanding. Moreover, while some work in this area is focusing on politics, it posits politics as primarily taking place within "political culture" rather than viewing the activities of everyday life as all having political dimensions.

For an example of a study of epistemological "disciplines," John Angus Campbell argues that Darwin's *Origin of Species* was an acceptable document within his contemporary scientific community primarily because it was written in the cultural grammar of "prior tradition": "The rhetorics of the various sciences, like the rhetorics of public deliberation and debate, were dependent on a cultural grammar" (351–352). In this case, "culture" indicates the accepted vocabulary and logic of a loosely constituted scientific community. Similarly, in John Lyne's review essay of the works and thought of Richard Rorty, culture is used somewhat interchangeably with "community" in order to explain the ways in which theories are tested. That is, theories are not tested against experience alone, but against culture, "procedures that are credible and meaningful to a community of inquiry" (199).

A similar employment of culture is found in public address discourse concerning assumptions made within arenas of political activity. That is, culture here signifies particular spheres of public life that have their own unique rules of behavior and conduct. For instance, while never providing a specific definition for culture, Stephen Browne borrows from James Boyd White and employs culture in reference to the rhetorical expectations faced by Edmund Burke in fashioning his *Present Discontents*. In attempting to understand the "real or imagined world" of which Burke was a part, Browne attempts to reconstruct the political culture that placed limits on how Burke could persuade his audience, both topically and logically (53). The same, or at least a very similar, use of the term is employed by Kenneth Zagacki and Andrew King in their reading of the discourse of Ronald Reagan and the discourse surrounding the Star Wars project.

These uses of culture reflect its definition (perhaps its unacknowledged grounding) in Michael Osborn's notion of the "culturetype" (*Orientations*, 16; "Rhetorical," 82). Closely paralleling Richard Weaver's discussion of "God and Devil terms," Osborn notes that culturetypes are those words within a given social order and moment that "express the key values of the day" and "wear a kind of halo" (*Orientations*, 16). Again, as with similar uses of "culture," its specificity is a specificity of meaning primarily within time ("Rhetorical," 82). It is only specific to place when one considers "cultural space" in a broad "nation state" sense rather than positing a radically specific (in time and space) meaning.

In addition to referring to political logics, culture is employed similarly to signify the logic of communication within particular physical, economic, and/or organizational spheres. For example, Dean Scheibel notes that film schools have a culture of communication that implies particular uses of graffiti as a form of communication expectations between students, a communication form that involves its own peculiar rules of conversation ("Graffiti"). Similarly, Farrel Corcoran ("Pedagogy") uses the term culture to signify the subspace of discourse that is created within prisons, again a subspace defined by audience logic and expectations.[9]

In the area of media theory, studies have attempted to illustrate the ways in which differences between the sensibilities of "media culture" (e.g., oral culture, literate culture) work to provide different rhetorical constraints on communication possibilities. For example, Ellen Gold focused on the "oral sensibilities" of Ronald Reagan in a changing media (and therefore epistemological) environment, labeling the change in media epistemology a cultural change. Using a fairly similar understanding of culture, Richard Johannesen employed "cultures" in his attempt to explain the way in which the "oral" epistemology understood by Martin Luther King, Jr., worked to encourage a logic of a "sharing of ideas" that, translated into the codes of the ownership of ideas of "literate" culture, caused his written and spoken body of work to be seen by some as plagiaristic. Here, again, culture refers to the logic of the audience, a logic based on the changes wrought by a changing media environment.

I'm obviously being criminally brief in pointing to such a wide array of examples, and I do understand that each employment of culture in my examples has its own subtleties. However, because my interest lies in the way in which the use of culture in rhetorical studies allows for a conflation of rhetorical and cultural studies, my main interest is in the general idea of "culture" that emerges from each of these arguments. In brief, then, this general usage of culture conceptually allows critics to see the "real or imagined" rhetorical world of the subjects under study. Culture is certainly not a fixed, objective, or determined environment in any of these arguments; it is indeed fluid and rhetorical. In each instance, we learn about the workings of a particular "cultural logic" and/or about the rhetorical mastery of a particular speaker in meeting the demands and constraints of that particular rhetorical culture. At their best, essays of this nature teach the reader about the "art of persuasion" in its highest moments and help the general critical and pedagogical community understand how symbols can be used in meeting or challenging the needs of particular communities. Culture here, then, is employed in attempts to explain and heighten the art of persuasion, certainly a noble project, and one to be encouraged if an interdisciplinary focus such as cultural studies is to meet with political success.

I want to be clear that I am not outlining this use of culture to find problems with this dimension of rhetorical criticism. Rather, I'm trying to mark out one of the dominant uses of culture that is part of a general climate that has made it relatively easy to construct a rhetorical cultural studies that sees one as embryonic of the other rather than each as distinct projects that can support a larger project.

CULTURE AS CRITICAL CONTEXT

In a second sense of its meaning in rhetorical studies, culture signifies a location or context a rhetorical critic uses for the archaeology/description of the logic of dominant society, rather than using that logic itself (as in the first meaning of culture), or rather than as a medium for the construction of sentiments or identity (i.e., the circulation of meanings drawn upon by individuals in the construction of identity). If the first category pointed to culture as a logic of communication and how that logic could be mastered, here culture refers to a metalocation, contextualized in time, where meaning "happens." This use of culture in rhetorical studies could be said to provide general studies of popular culture rather than cultural studies of the popular.

One form of this use of culture is found in critical work that focuses on discourses of "popular culture" and understands such discourses to be manifestations of structuring principles or foundations. A great number of examples could be drawn from the body of work of Janice Rushing and Thomas Frentz (Rushing alone, Rushing and Frentz, and Frentz and Rushing). While the degree to which they see structures as determinate varies (between essays and over time), their investigations in general look at culture as the location in which archetypal myths manifest themselves, in film, literature, and other popular texts. Lynn Stearney's exploration of ecofeminism and the maternal archetype can also serve as an example of this orientation. In each case, "culture" is the location in which the manifestation of myths, and their function in cultural life, can be examined.

A second division is made up of those rhetorical projects that attempt to understand the dominant (or consensus) meaning of an event/subject without focusing on resistances to these dominant meanings and without interrogating the overall struggles (and struggles at the level of everyday life) that take place for the grounds of meaning. Moreover, such studies do not position the study itself (and do not suggest a space for such positioning) as critical interventions in the overall battle for meaning. In a sense, such a perspective limits cultural "space" to a particular national or spatial boundary, be it the popular culture of the United States or of any other nation. Here, then, culture is the location where one can find the dominant meaning of a rhetorically defined collectivity of people. While individual essays include acknowledgments that the meanings of a culture are struggled over and change over time, the implied assumption is that the meaning is shared across culture at any given time (i.e., there is an "implied consensus" of meaning). In effect, the critical focus implied by this definition assumes a diachronic struggle rather than one that is both diachronic and synchronic—while providing a context of meaning in time, meaning is not radically contextualized by space or consumption. For example, George Dionisopoulos and Steven Goldzwig's analysis of George Shultz's revisionist history of Vietnam acknowledges how the meaning of an event is struggled over and, in such a way, represents an acknowledgment of the potential for resistances within popular culture and for the politics of the critical act. However, in investigating the meaning of Vietnam through its articulation on a dominant level, they do not investigate the way in which its meaning is dispersed and fragmented in any given synchronic moment (i.e., focus is placed on the general as opposed to the local), placing politics on the level of the general or dominant as opposed to specific subgroup uses and acts of consumption. Other examples of this type of study include: Kathryn Olson and Thomas Goodnight's focus on the meaning of the controversy over "fur" in consumer culture; Goodnight's textual analyses of popular films as a way of understanding cultural impulses; Tamar Katriel's ("Rhetoric") investigation of the meaning of fire inscriptions in Israeli youth movement ceremonials as semiotic deployment; Helen Sterk's ("Praise," "Metamorphosis") analyses of the changing meaning of Marilyn Monroe; Michael Calvin McGee's ("Text") discussion of culture as a site of practice for rhetorical critics (see also Cloud, "Materiality");[10] Ann Makus's discussion of the usefulness of the work of Stuart Hall in communication studies;[11] and Sloop's analysis of the meanings of alternative forms of punishment.[12] The list of examples need not end here; indeed, a seemingly endless number of articles could provide reinforcement of this employment of the term "culture" as a replacement for dominant meaning.[13]

Again, it is not that these studies do not serve a powerful function and exert a useful force in moving rhetoric toward the political investigation of changes in meanings on a dominant level. Rather, they indeed do provide powerful readings of struggles over dominant meaning at the level of popular culture—and this is no small task. It is more that in circumscribing the meaning of culture to that of struggles and debates in various public forums (e.g., the legislature), they curtail the politics of everyday life, the meanings and use in subgroups, transforming culture into a location for the struggle over meanings and pleasures across time rather than the specific uses/production of these meanings and pleasures across both time and cultural subgroupings. By focusing on specific institutional locations for meaning production rather than on their circulation among individuals in time and space (identity space), one comes to understand institutional meanings without focusing on their consumption and without necessarily seeing oneself involved in the process of changing this circulation. What this allows in the larger picture of the relationship between rhetorical and cultural studies is their conflation into a rhetorical cultural studies that can allow "cultural studies" to refer to any study of popular culture rather than to cultural studies of the popular.

CULTURE AS THE CIRCULATION AND PRODUCTION OF MEANING IN USE

In a 1993 special issue of the *Western Journal of Communication* on ideology, edited by Philip Wander, Richard Morris notes with some sense of frustration the vague uses to which the term "culture" has been put in rhetorical (and communication) studies and goes on to argue that the term has been used as a top-down category that serves the purposes of critics and theorists to indicate the characteristics of a critic-identified group rather than one emerging from the practices and politics of everyday life: "What is the logic at work here? That individuals belong to a collectively termed 'culture' whenever and for whatever purposes priest/priestess interpreters insist they do" (143). In this same issue of the journal, James West argues for a relativistic, discursive practice of ethnography based on the idea of culture as the interplay of identity, power, and knowledge, and he simultaneously posits cultural studies as indicating overtly and thoroughgoing political acts engaged in by critics on micro and macro levels. It is the concern raised by these two essays, and the emphasis on a meaning of culture that focuses on a dynamic of power, meaning, and identity and on cultural studies as political activities, that I am most interested in here.

The ground I'm getting into here is a bit messy in that, up to this point, I have tried to focus primarily on essays that I see as emerging from what would commonly (in loosely defined NCA circles) be seen as "rhetorical studies." However, in this section, in wanting to make a distinction between definitions of culture that incidentally lead to a conflation of rhetorical and cultural studies, I'm interested in searching for, and positing, a definition of "culture" and cultural studies that is different from, but complementary to, "rhetoric" and rhetorical studies. This desire, coupled with my desire to understand how some rhetorical critics have come to think of their own work as a branch of cultural studies, leads me to continue drawing examples from NCA journals. As a result, while I'm focusing now on "nonrhetorical" meanings of culture, a great number of my examples (although not all) in this section are drawn from essays published in *Critical Studies in Mass Communication* (*CSMC*). This section, then, involves a shift from an explanation of how rhetorical and cultural studies could be so easily conflated to an investigation of possible meanings of culture that emerge from "cultural studies" and that might serve well to complement and work with rhetorical studies. I am not attempting to suggest that all rhetorical critics were introduced to "cultural studies" through reading *CSMC* (indeed, some of my examples come from authors who might more commonly be considered rhetoricians publishing in more traditional rhetorical studies journals); more simply, I am suggesting that the introduction of cultural studies through *CSMC* provides some residual idea of how cultural studies might have come to the attention of rhetorical studies and provides some idea of how its project might productively differ from that of rhetorical studies.

As I pointed out earlier, drawing on Grossberg ("Toward"), as cultural studies emerged in the American field of communication studies in general, the dominant methodologies and problematics of cultural studies were mapped onto already ongoing debates within communication studies at large, debates familiar within rhetorical studies as well. The debates into which cultural studies entered were occurring on two distinct but mutually entangled terrains that eventually ran together as cultural studies emerged within their parameters: (1) one in which Frankfurt School and Marxist functionalist pessimism about mass culture (e.g., Adorno and Horkheimer) clashed with humanist assertions about human agency in the face of power; and (2) another that pitted the behavioral/functionalist paradigms of communication research against meaning-centered models of communication as culture formation advocated by such scholars as James Carey.

Consequently, when Grossberg and Jennifer Daryl Slack authored a brief introduction for a Stuart Hall essay for *CSMC* and, by extension, provided an introduction to cultural studies' "take" on ideology, it was Hall's assertion about the relative autonomy of ideology that mediated between the Frankfurt School denigration of mass culture and the humanistic celebration of it. And, to a much greater degree, Hall's model of encoding/decoding (again stressing the relative autonomy of each moment in the circuit of production) was positioned as a response to the second debate insofar as it seemed to overcome critiques leveled at Carey's model that insist it ignores questions of power, domination, and cultural struggle. In order words, cultural studies entered NCA journals with an already formulated model of overdetermination in the relationship between culture and power: not as merely economically determined and determinate ideological injection but also not as an uncontested site for articulating common meanings. Instead, cultural studies entered as an argument that situated culture as a site of struggle and contestation, a struggle contextualized in time, space, and identity.

In a general sense, then, culture is here viewed as the struggle over meaning and ideology, configured by both experiential and structural factors and implying, in its study, a proactive political activity by the scholar. This notion of culture is largely positioned over and against monolithic definitions of culture as a reflection only of the "dominant" interests and ideology and is enabled by the encoding/decoding model introduced by Stuart Hall, as well as encounters with semiotics. Fiske ("Television and"), for example, writes: "And this is what I understand the study of culture to consist of, the study of that incessant play of meanings that relate the subject with the social system and that underpin and maintain that system. These meanings and relationships are determined by and made manifest in discourses, which are then circulated by a variety of media" (200). Or, in a later essay, Fiske ("Critical") writes: "The cultural process is the generation and circulation of meanings and pleasures" (247). While politics always occurs in the very process of encoding of cultural texts or in the "active" oppositional or negotiated decoding practices of people in their everyday lives, it is also a function to be taken on with purpose by the cultural critic.

Studies that either implicitly or explicitly define culture as the production of, and struggle over, meanings include David Barker's study on encoding ideology in *M*A*S*H* ("Television Production"), Linda Steiner's analysis of oppositional decoding in the "No Comment" section of *Ms.* magazine, Fiske's general analysis of television criticism ("Television and Popular Culture"), Barker's discussion of "active reading" of a *Hill Street Blues* episode (" 'It's Been' "), Marian Meyers's discovery of oppositional "encoding" in the news, Alfred Kielwasser and Michelle Wolf's investigation of the oppositional, yet constrained, decoding of television by homosexual youth, Jodi Cohen's reading of the reception of Harvey Fierstein's *Tidy Endings,* Gordan Nakagawa's critical analysis of the reception of Japanese American internment stories ("What Are We Doing"), and Deborah Borisoff and Dan Hann's analysis of how sexual metaphors are used in sexual identity construction. All of these studies, in one way or another, define culture as the terrain in which people make meaning, but not in conditions of their own making.[14]

Given that culture is itself posited as inherently political, authors working with this general meaning overtly see their own work as, if not political intervention itself, at least as pointing to more politically effective practices of resistance and social change. It is here that we see a major difference with the definition of culture provided in the "Culture as Logic" section. While, at its worst, this perspective conflates active reading with political activism, for the most part, cultural criticism is posited as one element of larger political projects and generally taking place within specific domains (e.g., institutional politics). And while this general notion of an overtly political criticism is fairly widespread, the particular ways in which cultural criticism is posited as political are varied. For instance, many authors call for critical practices that seek to explain the relationship between the production and consumption of mass-mediated texts and work to enable consumers to consume in ways that allow for greater political empowerment (e.g., Fiske, "Television: Polysemy"; Schudson; Steiner; Condit, "Rhetorical Limits"). Others see more work to be done in connecting critical practice (especially academic criticism) to questions of public policy and polity (Meehan). For example, John Hartley reflects on the task laid out for individuals in cultural studies to encourage the implementation of their "preferred positions" when he asks, "How can we 'persuade' audiences to take up, unproblematically or otherwise, those positions that our critical analysis suggests are 'better' than others? If we do not start asking this question in relation to the popular media, the third world is undoubtedly where, as a discipline, we shall stay" ("Critical Response," 238). Finally, Fiske ("For Cultural Interpretation") acknowledges the role of the critic in and alongside of—not above—the quotidian struggles over meaning. He writes: "Any cultural interpretation acts upon the sociocultural order that it interprets, and such action will finally be evaluated by assessing which aspects of that order it works to endorse and which to criticize, and therefore, which sets of social interests it aligns itself with and which against" (472). Hence, in the most general sense, "cultural studies" sees one of its primary tasks to be the encouragement of particular ways of seeing and ordering the world.

Examples of calls for engagement in more specific studies of texts from popular culture can be found throughout the era. Hence, in a study of the way heavyweight boxer George Foreman came to have a successful and economically profitable persona, David Engen not only defines culture as a location for the struggle over the meanings connected to racial characteristics, but he also makes an explicit call for cultural critics to become involved in understanding why racist depictions are popular ones and, further, to place themselves in public forums when given the opportunity to engage in popular struggles to deconstruct these articulations and create other meanings (149).[15] Similarly, in his analysis of supermarket tabloids as "Menippean satires," Kevin Glynn investigates the class struggles that are part of the makeup of political culture through the struggles over cultural capital and encourages critics to seek out ways to refigure political struggles and representations of tabloids and tabloid readers (see also Buxton; and Shaw). As a final example, one emerging from social movement studies, Michael Salvador has recently called for a focus on the "culture" of social movements as a site for the meanings of the social order and their use and consumption; Salvador explicitly calls upon the term culture to imply both the location of meaning and the struggle for it (and calls upon critical acts that explicitly and "publicly" work to change or rearticulate meanings). Here again, culture describes a circulation of meanings rife with incommensurability and cultural studies includes as one of its dimensions acts that work within sites of incommensurability to provide new articulations of meaning and possibilities.

Of course, the relative autonomy of oppositional readings by individual consumers is a matter of some debate within this general definitional zone of "culture." There are those who assert that oppositional decoding has been seen as either too autonomous or too determined, instead of held in tension as only "relatively" either one. Those who would assert that cultural studies posits culture and meaning in a too autonomous manner include those who suggest that "cultural meanings" are more economically determined than is currently being posited (see, for example, Meehan; Murdock, "Cultural"; and Murdock, "Across"), and those who suggest that the range of resistive consumptive practices are limited either by more explicit state/political definitions (Leong) or by more rhetorical/linguistic dimensions (Condit, "Rhetorical Limits"; and Cloud, "Limits") that had been posited by the more optimistic cultural critics.

In his recent *Elvis After Elvis,* Gilbert Rodman delineates a set of three characteristics that he sees as setting the wide parameters of what should be considered cultural studies. While any one of these characteristics might be claimed by a wide variety of academic disciplines, these three characteristics combined can act as a summary of the definition of cultural studies that is found in this third meaning of culture. Rodman notes that cultural studies first "entails a radically contextual approach to scholarship" (i.e., there is no fixed theoretical or methodological paradigm); second, it has a commitment to theory to the degree that theory must be traveled through in order to deal with "real-life" problems; and third, it assumes that any serious discussion of popular culture must include questions of politics and attempts to carry out political projects through critical activity (19–22).

If one takes these three criteria back to those studies that work with other meanings of "culture" in rhetorical studies, one could note varying degrees to which each of these aspects are employed in particular studies. However, because in general the first definition relied on a definition of culture as provisional "logics" (e.g., science culture, political culture) and the second as a space for the study of meaning (i.e., popular culture), neither specifically entailed a project that was contextualized in time and space (subgroup usage) nor explicitly pursued a political agenda. As I noted above, the danger here lies in the fact that in each case one can in some way lay legitimate claim to the study of culture. Hence, as cultural studies gains cultural capital, its meaning is easily generalized and its potential for politics automatically dispersed. By virtue of the fact that the "study of culture" is a relatively open phrase, rhetorical studies and cultural studies partially merge into each other rather than having separate projects that support each other.

CONCLUSION: CULTURAL AND RHETORICAL STUDIES

Michael Calvin McGee ("Social") once noted that social movements should not be studied from the top down but from the bottom up, that we should not study social movements as phenomena but as meaning, as clearly rhetorical and terministic activities. In this essay, starting with a perceived concern about the dangers of conflating cultural and rhetorical studies, I have taken the assumption that the meaning of culture and the practice of cultural studies within and beside rhetorical studies can best be understood by investigating the contemporary use of the term "culture" in essays focusing on rhetorical studies and cultural studies within communication journals. What I have suggested is that "culture" has been used to signify a number of different primary meanings and that this variation of meanings allows for a situation in which cultural studies and rhetorical studies are in danger of losing separate and productive identities as critics are encouraged by the dictates of the job market, the book market, and academic cultural capital in general to claim the study of culture and cultural studies as their own domain. Again, this partial conflation of rhetorical studies and cultural studies (or perhaps, this softening of cultural studies within rhetorical studies) does not occur as the result of a conspiracy to tame cultural studies, but instead is in large part an unintended and often unnoticed side effect of the growth and popularity of cultural studies within a field in which the term culture was already commonly and generally employed.

My purpose is not to police terms simply for the sake of purity. Rather, I am concerned first that this partial conflation endangers the potential of a critical practice that might encourage critics, especially a younger generation of critics who are currently being trained in graduate programs, to focus on meanings in specific acts of consumption and to take on proactive political projects. However, the problem is not just on the side of limiting the potential of cultural studies—the degree to which cultural studies and rhetorical studies are conflated is the degree to which both are harmed. Secondly, if we take the project of rhetoricians, as Michael Calvin McGee does ("Text," 280–281), to be understanding the ways in which "*doxa* can be used to authorize a redress of human grievances," we certainly would want to preserve that practice on its own grounds. If we do so, rhetorical studies provides a space in which the political employment of the available means of persuasion is studied, with focus being placed on how "rhetoric" works in any given situation, how change and exploration can be encouraged. For its part, cultural studies can then draw upon the findings and discoveries of rhetorical studies as a way to empower its political project. I am not interested in claiming, then, that rhetoricians can "only do this" or that cultural studies can "only do that." After all, critics will do as critics do. But if we are interested in seeing cultural studies as a productive *interdisciplinary* space rather than a generalizable phrase employed in the study of culture, it must have productive disciplines, such as the study of rhetoric, from which to draw upon in the implementation of its project.[16] Perhaps this volume bespeaks an ideal time for cautious reflection on what "we" study and how we label it.

ACKNOWLEDGMENTS

We would like to thank Thomas Rosteck, Lawrence Grossberg, Celeste M. Condit, and Kent Ono for their encouragement and comments on this essay. Researching and writing on the struggles over the meanings and uses of culture and cultural studies has itself spawned debates and disagreements between the two authors over the position argued in this chapter. We make note of some of these differences in end notes.

NOTES

1. Two brief personal anecdotes serve to make this point. First, when one of the authors (Sloop) was involved in his first post-PhD job search several years ago, he noted that many job ads indicated that the applicant should be well versed in cultural studies. Not quite sure whether he was (not having taken course work in "cultural studies" proper), he asked members of his dissertation committee if he should apply for jobs in cultural studies. The general response was affirmative, as "rhetoricians have always (already) been involved in cultural studies." Second, when interviewing for a position in a department of communications that was attempting to configure itself as a center for "cultural studies," Sloop received a description of the department and its faculty before his campus visit. In the descriptions of the areas of emphasis of most members of the department were included the words "cultural studies," indicating an extremely broad definition of the area.

2. Throughout the essay, we will use "I" when we write in the first person for two reasons: first, because we move back and forth from general claims to stories that indicate only the experience of one of the authors, the transition from "I" to "we" would become awkward; second, we use "I" to indicate that the authors struggled over some of the positions being argued here. While "we" sometimes agree on an argument, often only "I" endorse it fully.

3. I should be clear on two points here: first, I am not arguing that "rhetorical studies" does not have examples of overt or implied political work. This is clearly not the case historically, with a good deal of critical research, especially ideological and feminist critical work, being significantly influenced by specific political orientations. Secondly, I also do not wish to suggest that critical work should not draw on both cultural studies and rhetorical studies. Works like Celeste Condit and John Lucaites's *Crafting Equality* serve as examples of work that, in my mind, productively draw from both rhetoric and cultural studies. I am more concerned about work that claims both areas without consideration of what either is or how one tradition can aid the other. That is, I don't mind a "rhetorical and cultural study" so much as I find "rhetorical cultural studies" problematic.

4. To be clear, Grossberg is not claiming that all work going by the name "cultural studies" within communication studies has this focus. Rather, he is implying that this is the dominant form of cultural studies within communication studies.

5. Here, we are limiting communication studies to an array of journals published by the National Communication Association (NCA; formerly Speech Communication Association) and its regional affiliates. Specifically, we read through issues of *Critical Studies in Mass Communication, Communication Monographs, Quarterly Journal of Speech, Communication Education, Western Journal of Communication, Southern Journal of Communication Studies, Communication Studies,* and *Communication Quarterly.* We read through the titles and abstracts of each article, as well as leafing through the article for any discussion or use of the term "culture" or its derivatives. When the term "culture" or variants of "culture" (e.g., cultural, intercultural) were used, we made extensive

notes on its usage and purpose. For this essay, we have tried to include only those articles that we considered to be rhetorical studies or cultural studies. There is no precise "methodology" for these choices, but the choices we've made are ones that we think would match those of the general body of rhetorical theorists and critics aligned with NCA.

6. I would be more than happy, however, to send the remainder of my analysis via e-mail attachment to anyone who is interested in uses of culture in intercultural and organizational communication research. My first suggestion for those interested in the use of the term "culture" in intercultural research is to read Dreama Moon's 1996 treatment.

7. As with all constructed typologies, no given article fits perfectly within any single category, and I would assume that particular authors might be critical of my placement of their argument and, perhaps, my construction of "rhetorical studies." What I am attempting to do is to describe general tendencies within rhetorical studies, and I apologize beforehand for perceived "miscategorizations" on my part.

8. Here is one of the points of debate between the authors that makes the use of "I" necessary rather than "we." The valorization of the more Gramscian perspective has been a point of some healthy debate between the authors. Olson embraces to a greater degree a Foucaultian/Deleuzian position, a position that sees culture, identity, and criticism as sites of governmentality structured by modern forms of power. Of course, this latter position is more inimical to the project of what might constitute a critical practice for critical rhetoric's version of cultural studies.

9. See, for example, Peterson; Mayer; Lange; Ball; and Scheibel, "Making."

10. Indeed, there is a sense in which the entire critical rhetoric project found its origins in the study of dominant culture rather than in the study of the politics of the synchronic struggles over dominant culture, including resistant practices, pleasures, and meanings.

11. This article demands special notice if only because its focus on Stuart Hall would lead one to expect a focus on a complex and indeterminate meaning of culture. Instead, we get a rather more subdued focus on ideology that places the emphasis on dominant ideology and thereby employs culture to signify dominant culture.

12. Here, we are "indicting" one of the two coauthors for taking on a meaning of culture that was a diachronic dominant cultural meaning. Quoting Sloop, "Rather than attempting to follow individual speakers who are predetermined to be important, a critical rhetoric perspective encourages an examination of changes that occur in discourse over time and that emerge culturally rather than through individual speakers" (11). So, despite articulating the meaning of the term as a struggle "over time," it is only a struggle over time in dominant discourses (i.e., it ignores the way in which meaning is reworked in consumption).

13. For further examples, see Cleary's analysis of articulations of revolution in the prerepublic United States; Makay and Gonzalez's work on the discourse of Bob Dylan's songs in general American culture. Gaonkar's analysis of the meaning of rhetoric on a mass cultural level ("The Idea of Rhetoric"); Mechling and

Mechling's ("Jung and Restless") analysis of the men's movement; Jeffrey Nelson's work with the representation of homosexuality in American film; Richard Campbell's discussion of the role of *60 Minutes* in constructing American values; Aden's analysis of the therapeutic value of sports metaphors in American culture and American cultural history; Fjelstad's discussion of legal motivation in dominant culture; Brinson's criticism of the myth of white supremacy in American culture; Warnick's analysis of metaphors in dominant speeches ("A Ricoeurean Approach"); Foss and Edson's delineation of the meanings of married women's names in dominant culture; Mechling and Mechling's analysis of national campaigns concerning the atom bomb ("The Campaign"); Taylor's work with women's voices within mass culture; Carlson's notation of changes in the meaning of femininity; and Brennen's media history.

14. In a very interesting and very telling forum/debate between John Fiske and Donal Carbaugh over the impact and meaning of Carbaugh's *Talking American*, there is a clear distinction between two meanings of the term culture. In Carbaugh's argument, culture is a medium where meanings and identity are inherently unstable, always changing: "a system of expressive practices fraught with feeling, a system of symbols, premises, rules, forms, and the domains and dimensions of mutual meanings associated with them" ("Soul," 182). However, it is not the meaning of culture that proves problematic in Carbaugh's project but instead his description of the critical act. Carbaugh describes the role of the critic in the task of cultural interpretation to be the rendering of "participants' communication practices coherent and intelligible, through an explication of a system of symbols, symbolic forms, and meanings which is creatively evoked in those practices" ("Communication," 336; see also Carbaugh, "Cultural"). That is, the critical task is to come up with a shared meaning of a text, rendering various communications as intelligible under one system of meaning. However, and much more along the lines of a politics of struggle, John Fiske notes in his response to Carbaugh that Carbaugh's desire is for "culture as consensus" (one meaning) rather than culture as "conflict" (a continual upheaval of meanings, a displacement of the centering ("Writing," 330). Hence, Fiske wants to make culture not only a location of potential struggle but, borrowing from Lyotard, to see cultural discourses as at times incommensurable, providing a location for critics to promote and understand the incommensurability of conflict itself.

Similarly, and aligning explicitly with Fiske's response to Carbaugh, Tamar Katriel, in a study of the location of memory in Israeli settlement museums, notes that, while culture should be seen as the discursive production of "community," the critic must also be "attuned to the exclusions that are inevitably involved" and be "interested in the way in which they become negotiated," battled for, struggled over ("Sites," 18).

15. For examples, see Budd, Entman, and Steinman's critique of Fiske; and Barker (" 'It's Been' ").

16. Ron Greene has made an interesting argument on this relationship and the shape it could take in rhetoric and policy studies.

ELEVEN

THE TRIUMPH OF SOCIAL SCIENCE
The Silent Language *as Master Text in American Cultural Studies*

Bruce E. Gronbeck

The period before and after World War II was a difficult one for American intellectual liberals. Even as they joined with most of the rest of the world in resisting fascism and its association with industrialization and capitalism, they were betrayed from within their own ranks by Stalinist Russia. As word of the Russian gulags, kangaroo courts, and mass executions leaked out, it became clear, as Dwight Macdonald noted in 1947, that "the Russian Revolution has not only failed to realize the hopes invested in it, but has actually produced a totalitarian system with a dynamism of its own that throttles the development of socialist thought and democratic social movements" (Hook, 23). He was saddened that American workers "have not been able to distinguish between true socialism and its Stalinist perversion" and that, consequently, "the Left has fallen into a state of intellectual disorientation and political impotence" (23).

Macdonald's comments appear in his introduction to a series of five essays on "The Future of Socialism," published in the little magazine of liberal New York intellectuals, the *Partisan Review,* between January and October of 1947. Political philosopher Sidney Hook led them off, declaring his allegiance to social-democratic principles but his utter hatred for communism. Novelist-critic Granville Hicks followed, eschewing even political liberalism in his defense of what he called "critical liberalism" (127–129). Harvard historian Arthur Schlesinger, Jr., was next, with a pragmatic essay urging a political gradualism that would allow social democracy to spread across the United States (231 ff.) at the expense of the capitalists who seemed in the ascendancy following the war. Much darker was the statement of novelist George Orwell in the late-summer issue of the *Partisan Review*; he saw socialists as doctors trying to keep alive a hopelessly ill patient (346), and thus he held little hope for a socialist revolution in the United States. But Frenchman Victor Serge concluded the series of essays with a piece predicting the triumph of socialism in the inevitable fall of both capitalism and communism (especially 516–517).

The struggle to reformulate a leftist, intellectually examined, yet viable politics following World War II is a happening important to the student of cultural studies. Out of that struggle, perhaps oddly, was born what can be termed American cultural studies, a set of strongly descriptive-analytical practices for studying societies through an essentially linguistic model of scholarly practice. In this chapter I will argue that the Old Left intellectuals and their critical approach to politics, culture, and literature gave way to a new breed of scholars with scientistic outlooks on social and diplomatic interaction. More particularly, Edward Hall's 1957 book *The Silent Language* is the master text for American cultural studies as it developed and spread through the academic world of the 1960s and 1970s. The critical-cultural tradition of social theory was largely moribund until British and Continental versions of cultural studies reinvigorated it in the American academy in the 1980s and 1990s.

A book chapter is not enough space to fully develop these interpretive arguments, although a new generation of cultural and intellectual historians presently is helping, reworking the postwar history of the Left (e.g., Kutulas; Gorman; Shannon). A sketch of the battle between normatively nuanced and descriptively grounded approaches to cultural studies, however, can be provided, as can some evidence of the robust normative-critical tradition of cultural analysis offered by the Old Left. That should provide enough context, then, for a more careful look at Hall's little book of 1957. We'll examine its cultural assumptions, operative vocabulary and principles, and its conceptual impact before positioning the European invasion of the 1980s and 1990s within American social thought.

THE COMING OF CULTURAL STUDIES
IN ANGLO-AMERICAN THOUGHT

In 1869, British poet and essayist Matthew Arnold wrote in *Culture and Anarchy* that

> Culture [is] a pursuit of our total perfection by means of getting to know, on all the matters which most concern us, the best which has been thought and said in the world; and through this knowledge, turning a stream of fresh and free thought upon our stock notions and habits, which we now follow staunchly but mechanically. . . . The culture we recommend is, above all, an inward operation. (x)

With this statement he launched the English-speaking world's first fully developed theory of culture. It was strongly normative, politically conservative, oriented to a proper critique of "our stock notions and habits, which we now followed staunchly but mechanically," with cultural theory to be focused on the spirituality—at least transcendence—of the best theology and the best art. Those capable of such study had to pursue, in Arnold's mind, "the harmonious perfection of our whole being, and what we call totality" (xxvii). "Culture" thus was to be nurtured and pursued by a class-based group of elites in a society.

Soon after Arnold circulated *Culture and Anarchy,* another conception of culture and cultural studies was penned by the American sociologist William Graham Sumner. In 1906 he published *Folkways: A Study of the Sociological Importance of Usages, Manners, Customs, Mores, and Morals.* The proper study of individual and social character, he argued, flows from an examination of the everyday beliefs and actions of a people, the folk of a society:

> Folkways are habits of the individual and customs of the society which arise from efforts to satisfy needs; they are intertwined with goblinism and demonism and primitive notions of luck . . . , and so they win traditional authority. Then they become regulative for succeeding generations and take on the character of a social force. . . . They can be modified, but only to a limited extent, by the purposeful efforts of men. In time they lose power, decline, and die, or are transformed. While they are in vigor they very largely control individual and social undertakings, and they produce and nourish ideas of world philosophy and life policy. (iv)

Here is a more descriptive and observationally based understanding of culture, tapping into conceptions of social life that were emerging in the new science of anthropology. In this tradition, culture is what holds a society together—the beliefs, habits, values, and customary ways of acting collectively that distinguish one people from another. And thus, coming into the intellectual world of the twentieth century were two Western concepts of "culture," the one normative and reformative, and the other, descriptive and preservational; one born in the aesthetic consciousness of an elite literary-social critic, the other, in the pragmatic spirit of a Yale social scientist.

As early as 1915, Van Wyck Brooks sought a relationship between the two conceptions, in the process inventing the terms "highbrow" and "low-brow." He saw men of highbrow and lowbrow tastes—epitomized for him in Jonathan Edwards the intellectual and Benjamin Franklin the practical man of common virtue—as compensatory for each other's weaknesses. Hence, both were necessary for a fully functional society (3–39 passim). Brooks's implicit attempt to break the power of class, however, did not work. Much more popular was Dwight Macdonald's conception of "mass cult" and "mid cult," which first appeared in his magazine *Politics* in 1944, in its final form in *Against the American Grain* (1963). It was a position on the matter of culture that depended upon an explicitly class-centered theory of both social organization and individual development.

Before we examine Macdonald's take on culture and politics, however, we should look briefly at the American social-intellectual milieu within which he was operating. That takes us into the world of the Old Left in the United States of the 1930s.

THE NEW YORK INTELLECTUAL SCENE: THE OLD LEFT

Variously termed the "Old Left" (vis-à-vis the "New Left" of the 1960s), "anticommunist liberalism" (Gilbert, 108), even "the narrow class of New York intellectuals" (Trilling, *Beyond*, ix), a group of social and (especially later) literary commentators were at the center of discussions about culture—more particularly, culture, politics, and literature—in the United States from the late 1930s until the mid-1950s. Christopher Brookeman has overviewed their social and cultural thinking, Paul Gorman has probed their disdain for popular culture, and Judy Kutulas has offered the latest in a series of works on their international and domestic politics. These were the writers in the little magazines and other organs of intellectual commentary against whose positions conceptualizations of political liberalism and cultural processes were defined for a quarter of a century. To comprehend the force of Edward Hall's *The Silent Language*, we need to understand the rudiments of their politics and their cultural wars.

The Old Left's Culture of Politics

Many in the New York crowd tried out varieties of leftist politics in the 1930s—the American Communist Party, the Social Workers Party (Trotsky's organization), the Workers Party (Max Schachtman's splinter group). However, Stalin's purges and trials of dissidents, the Nazi-Soviet nonaggression pact of 1939, the avant-garde's suppression by the organs of socialist realism in art, and then, later, Hiroshima-Nagasaki, the assassination of Gandhi, the Berlin blockade, and such events one by one drove the intellectuals toward the center and the right. Some, such as Sidney Hook, moved more quickly and resolutely; others, such as Macdonald, took longer. As a result, within the New York coterie were rival factions trying to convince the others to adopt a vision of politics and political action consonant with humane principles yet effective in democratizing countries around the (especially Western) world.

So, for example, Sidney Hook and John Dewey founded the Committee for Cultural Freedom before the start of World War II as part of an effort to counter possible Communist and Nazi influence among American artists and intellectuals even while urging prodemocratic reform. Following the war, Russia accelerated its efforts to capture international support, using such forums as the 1949 Waldorf-Astoria Hotel peace conference to further its interests. In that conference, Lillian Hellman, Aaron Copland, Arthur Miller, and Norman Mailer lined up with European and Soviet delegates to attack American warmongering and capitalistic fascism. Also present was Sidney Hook, having formed a new anticommunist group, the Americans for Intellectual Freedom, that included such leftists as Dwight Macdonald, Mary McCarthy, Max Eastman, and a reporter named Arnold Beichman, whose labor connections got the group good publicity and a patch of phone lines in the Waldorf-Astoria to make a public splash in the enemy's forum (United States, Central Intelligence Agency [CIA], 2).

The success of the Americans for Intellectual Freedom at that conference piqued the interest of Frank Wisner of the Office of Policy Coordination (OPC). Wisner figured out how to use such groups to forward the work of the OPC and the CIA, and ultimately sponsored another conference in response to the New York adventure, a gathering in Paris. Its tone was not totally anticommunist, so an even larger gathering was planned with a $50,000 budget; this became the 1950 Berlin conference, the Congress for Cultural Freedom. John Dewey, Bertrand Russell, Benedetto Croce, Karl Jaspers, and Jacques Maritain were named the honorary chairs. Hook, another NYU philosopher James Burnham, novelist James T. Farrell, playwright Tennessee Williams, historian Arthur Schlesinger, Jr., actor Robert Montgomery, and Atomic Energy Commission chair David Lilienthal led the American delegation. The day before the conference began, news of North Korea's massive invasion of South Korea reached Europe. The 4,000-plus delegates condemned the action, radical Arthur Koestler shouted, "Friends, freedom has seized the offensive!" while reading the Congress's Freedom Manifesto at a Berlin rally of 15,000 people, and even President Truman was "very well pleased" with the Left's support (CIA, 7–9).

An editorial in a 1952 issue of the *Partisan Review* noted, "The American artist and intellectual no longer feels 'disinherited' as Henry James did, or 'astray' as Ezra Pound did in 1913" (quoted in Aronowitz, 32); yet, Dwight Macdonald would write that "politics is a desert without hope" (quoted in Gewen, 14), as he came to the conclusion that no particular form of government could guarantee the protection and development of the individual. As he noted in *Against the American Grain,* "The tendency of modern industrial society whether in the U.S.A. or the U.S.S.R. is to transform the individual into the mass man" (8). More than that, Macdonald argued, the modernist, especially American, society flattened and even eliminated social distinctions among ethnic subgroups, as the melting pot did its work too well: "New England culture dwindled to provincial gentility. . . . The tragedy was that it melted so thoroughly. A pluralistic culture might have developed enriched by the contributions of Poles, Italians, Serbs, Greeks, Jews, Finns, Croats, Germans, Swedes, Hungarians and all the other peoples that came here from 1870 to 1910" (34–35).

The culture of politics was such to Macdonald and many of the others that about all they could do was rail against its abuses and seek to save individuals. Political revolution running on a war of words seemed impossible.[1] The mechanisms of change might well depend more on social than political forces.[2]

The Old Left: The Politics of Culture

Perhaps the best path to revolution lay through the undergrowth of social life, in particular, in the attempt to produce an elevated sensibility of the sort Matthew Arnold had called for even in the face of the economics of democracy, which had produced the dreaded consumer and mass-mediated cultures so evident in the postwar West. Already in the mid-1940s,[3] two German émigrés from the Frankfurt School for Social Research, Theodor Adorno and Max Horkheimer, had blasted the "culture industry." The culture industry, to Adorno and Horkheimer, was pure capitalism at work in controlling individual consciousness through mass communication technologies that eliminated style, complexity, seriousness of critique, and art itself, replacing them with "surrogate identity," "aesthetic barbarity," and "a cathedral dedicated to elevated pleasure" (37–41; for their move into modes of critique, see Dubiel).

And so, many of the East Coast leftist intellectuals turned inward on American society, critiquing the leveling of culture that seemed to characterize the postwar rise of consumerism even while holding out hope that reformation of the United States and its citizens could foster democratic movements in foreign lands. Lionel Trilling was especially eloquent on this subject. For a 1952 symposium on "Our Country and Our Culture" in the *Partisan Review,* its editors set for Trilling and others an agenda to follow in their inquiries:

1. To what extent have American intellectuals actually changed their attitudes toward America and its institutions?

2. Must the American intellectual and writer adapt himself to mass culture? If he must, what forms can his adaptation take? Or, do you believe that a democratic society necessarily leads to a leveling of culture, to a mass culture which will overrun intellectual and aesthetic values traditional to Western civilization?

3. Where in American life can artists and intellectuals find the basis of strength, renewal, and recognition, now that they can no longer depend fully on Europe as a cultural example and a source of vitality?

4. If a reaffirmation and rediscovery of America is under way, can the tradition of critical nonconformism (going back to Thoreau and Melville and embracing some of the major expressions of American intellectual history) be maintained as strongly as ever? (Trilling, *Gathering*, 63)

Trilling's own answer to these questions in "The Situation of the American Intellectual at the Present Time" (*Gathering*, 60–78) was that new intellectual classes, growing up around money, power, and the American college and university, had to be taken seriously in their restructuring of knowledge and, given their diverse backgrounds and life experiences, their development of pluralist models of thought and learning.

A more popular pursuit, however, was to rail against the destruction of traditional (elite) culture. Cultural critique became the rage to a group of neo-Arnoldians. Certainly some of the more conservative among them—the former liberals-now-turncoats such as Sidney Hook, John Dos Passos, and Max Eastman—were castigated for what was seen as a tendency to strictly subordinate cultural analysis to institutionalized politics. Macdonald was especially hard on them and on Van Wyck Brooks in a famous essay in 1941, "Mr. Van Wyck Brooks and Kulturbolschewismus," where he feared the coming of an "official aesthetic" that would "impose on the writer *from outside* certain socio-political values, and . . . provide a rationalization for damning his work *aesthetically* if it fails to conform to these *social values*" (*Responsibility*, 139, 138). By 1945, he called this view "totalitarian liberalism" (187–191).

Most of the cultural wars of the 1950s, however, were focused on what was percolating from the bottom up, and it was on this topic that Macdonald had what was probably his greatest influence on American social thought. In identifying the enemies of "the best which has been thought and said" as *both* mass culture (materials and ideas marketed to everyone without any differentiation as to need or use) and middle culture (materials and ideas focused on serious questions or needs but formulary in their responses to them), Macdonald ripped at the economic, social, and aesthetic foundations of American society. Perhaps his most memorable example of "mid cult" was Thornton Wilder's *Our Town*, where the stage manager in a folksy way would articulate some verity such as, "There's something way down deep that's eternal about every human being." Such sentimental aphorisms drove Macdonald to reply that "The last sentence is an eleven-word summary in form and content of Mid cult. I agree with everything Mr Wilder says but I will fight to the death against his right to say it in this way" (quoted in Brookeman, 51–52). There was, as well, a lack of distinction between the significant and the insignificant in middle culture to Macdonald, noting that the same issue of *Life* "will present a serious exposition of atomic energy, followed by a disquisition on Rita Hayworth's love life" (52).[4]

Macdonald and the other elitists hammered away at mass- and middle-culture excesses. Their debates raged in the little magazines and, soon, in larger books. The journal *Daedalus* sponsored a mass culture symposium in the Poconos, assembling such 1950s giants as sociologists Daniel Bell, Edward Shils, and Nathan Glazer, historians Oscar Handlin, H. Stuart Hughes, and Arthur Schlesinger, Jr., philosophers Hook and Charles Frankel, poet Randall Jarrell, novelist-playwright James Baldwin, critics William Phillips, Macdonald, and Ernest Van den Haag (see Ricco for a summary). The Tamiment Institute conference was edited by Norman Jacobs and published as *Culture for the Millions?* (1961). The debate was institutionalized when Bernard Rosenberg and David Manning White published *Mass Culture: The Popular Arts in America* in 1957, which stayed in print until the 1990s. Rosenberg and White framed the negative and positive positions of the players in the mass culture debate and then systematically arrayed essays under seven headings: (1) perspectives on mass culture, (2) mass literature (books, detective fiction, comic books and cartoon strips, magazines), (3) motion pictures, (4) television and radio, (5) divertissement (music, card-playing, Broadway), (6) advertising, and (7) the overview (larger visions of American society in general).

Worthy of note here were the ways in which the politics of culture came to be organized into American social thought. While Jarrell at the Tamiment Institute conference thought that the genuine artist "ought to be violently ill-adjusted or maladjusted" (quoted in Ricco, 13), many of the critics assented to the admonition of Hughes "to make our peace with mass culture" (Jacobs, 143). Those on Jerrell's (and Macdonald's) end of the social adjustment continuum tended to be celebrants of the hearty individual, even the avant-gardist, whose very solitude and disconnection became the source of creativity. Trilling's 1955 collection of essays *Beyond Culture* was given that title in the belief that "it is possible to stand beyond the culture in some decisive way" (xii) as both artist and thinker. Those on Hughes's end generally decided to ignore the matter of metaculture and make their peace with popular and mass culture by studying it.

"Studying" generally signaled work from inside the ivy walls of academe. Here, too, was a question designed to fragment the Old Left. Most of them probably accepted J. F. Wolpert's arguments in "Notes on the American Intelligentsia" (1947), which cast "the university man" in an unfavorable light: someone living in a place "resembling the assembly line" and a bureaucratic structure whose "divorce of administration and scholarship . . . results in the dependence of the scholar upon the administration"; where "the authority of the boards of trustees gives them the power to withhold economic rewards in case of deviation from accepted norms. . . . They are businessmen of repute or their satraps in the state universities, the politicians who live off politics";[5] where the move from instructor to full professor depended upon "the inculcation of proper occupational norms"; where writing "pulverized [a] particle of knowledge without relevance to general problems"; where professional conventions were "a version of the businessman's club, in which the mores of American culture operate in a more subdued way"; and where the creation of an artificial environment requiring a standardized way of acting and even dressing produces "the contradiction between his style of life and his critical attitude toward the prevailing norms" that takes "a heavy psychological toll" (241, 242, 243). For Wolpert, the true "avant-garde bohemian intellectual" who required "estrangement from the population at large" (245) to do creative work, who must suffer anomie to find new levels of spiritual development, could not survive in a university. Such a view, though, was not universal among the independent intellectuals. Indeed, Alvin Toffler's first book, *The Culture Consumers: Art and Affluence in America* (1965), was written to contradict Wolpert's views emphatically by praising the productivity of university scholars, and of course there was such momentum behind the growth of colleges and universities following the war that it would have been impossible to stem their influence upon American intellectual life. Yet, they were conceded to be one more manifestation of the power of popular and mass culture in the postwar United States.

Overall, the Old Left valiantly fought demons from the far Left and the far Right, from capitalism and Christianity, from mass culture and mass education. Yet, as they aged and as their causes seemed to fall before new money, bureaucracy in the place of intellectual complexity, and a lazy citizenry, they gradually lost influence and visibility. They hunkered down, taking jobs in universities themselves or, as in the case of Macdonald, in the employ of larger magazines (as a film critic, especially in *Esquire* and the *New Yorker*). Their socialism had metamorphosed into a kind of critical liberalism or even strident individualism (see Aronowitz, 32–37; the role of the witch-hunts in all of this is suggested by Halberstam).[6]

The federal government played a role here, as it sought cultural training for the technical advisers and Foreign Service employees it was sending abroad. In 1951, a young anthropologist joined the State Department as

Director of its Point IV program to train those technical advisers and some of the Foreign Service officers. His name was Edward Hall. He had gotten his PhD at Columbia University, but apparently was not attracted to the resident Frankfurt men or to Trilling.[7] Hall was more a scholar than an intellectual.

THE SILENT LANGUAGE AS MASTER TEXT

Hall published his masterpiece, *The Silent Language,* in 1959. The tone of the book was clearly that of a popularizing scholar. He regularly made it clear that he had earned his scholarly credentials in the field, working with the Navajo, Hopi, Spanish American, and Trukese peoples; he had taught at several institutions, was a Fellow in the American Anthropological Association and the Society for Applied Anthropology, and a member of the Building Research Advisory Board of the National Academy of Sciences. He also regularly mentioned his government work throughout the book, and smirked a bit when talking about what life was like among public servants:

> College students are content to take subjects for their general interest. Point Four technicians and Foreign Service officers, on the other hand, are expected to go overseas and get results, and they have to be well prepared. In general I found that they are not too interested in the anthropologist's preoccupation with "what culture is" and tend to become impatient unless they have been abroad previously and have had some previous experience. Foreign Service officers in particular used to take great delight in saying that what the anthropologists told them about working with the Navajo didn't do them much good, for we didn't have an embassy on the Navajo reservation. . . . What was needed was something bold and new, not just more of the same old history, economics, and politics. (35–36)

That "something bold and new" that Hall wished to trumpet in *The Silent Language* was a linguistic model of culture, one he acknowledges developing with the linguist George Trager (13). More particularly, it was a linguistic model of "our silent language—the language of behavior" (10). That is, the central argument of the book was that culture-based behavior of peoples from different social backgrounds could be read semantically and syntactically as a language.[8] The overall framework for that argument was what we can call Hall's Identity: communication is culture and culture is communication (ch. 5). That is, communication processes are simultaneously culture-bound—and hence communication is culture—yet, they are the only means by which we can witness cultural standards for social behavior, and hence culture is communication.

Hall developed his theory of communication and culture around what he termed ten Primary Message Systems. He held himself to rigorous analytical rules when constructing the systems:

> In order to qualify as a cultural system, each system had to be:
>
> A. Rooted in a biological activity widely shared with other advanced living forms. It was essential that there be no breaks with the [biological] past.
>
> B. Capable of analysis in its own terms without reference to the other systems and so organized that it contained isolated components that could be built up into more complex units, and paradoxically—
>
> C. So constituted that it reflected all the rest of culture and was reflected in the rest of culture. (45)

Social activity, he believed, fell into ten categories: three were termed "core" systems (association, subsistence, and bisexuality) because they were essential to the maintenance of the human race; three were called "expression" systems (learning, play, and defense) because they were the mechanisms for passing on culture from one generation to another; two, exploitation and interaction, were uncategorized because they were means to all of the other ends; and two, temporality and territoriality, were called "orientation" systems because social positioning in time and space are people's primary means of knowing who and where they are symbolically and socially (see Figure 11.1). These ten dimensions of social activity were to Hall biobasic, that is, "rooted in biological activities. Infra-culture is the term which can be given to behavior that preceded culture but later became elaborated by man into culture as we know it today" (44).

To Hall, acculturation of individuals occurred in three ways: formally, that is, by admonition ("Do this"); informally, that is, by imitation ("Do what I do"); and technically, that is, by explanation ("Here's why we do this"). And thus in his map of culture ("human activity"), each of the ten Primary Message Systems manifested itself in three ways or, perhaps better, was taught to members of a culture in multiple dimensions. So, Hall believed, one could learn about a country's governmental system formally, through instruction, but about its caste system only through observation or imitation, and about the practical force of its class structure only by feeling it in direct statements aimed at oneself. One could learn language (grammar) formally; gestural systems, by watching people interact face-to-face; and the force of different tones of voice, only by being their object or having one's own tone-of-voice reacted to. In essence, therefore, Hall divided "culture" into 10 × 3, or thirty, cells or categories of human activity.

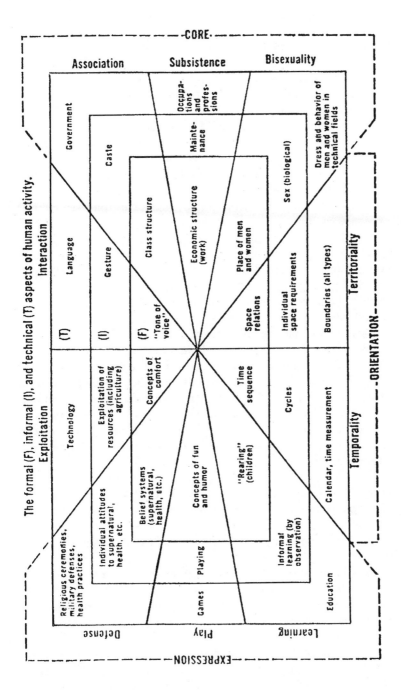

FIGURE 11.1. The Ten Primary Message Systems of culture. From Edward T. Hall, *The Silent Language*, 1959. Copyright 1959 by Fawcett World Library. Reprinted by permission.

It was particularly when wanting to explain culture technically that he urged his readers to employ the linguistic analogy. He said that "messages can be broken down into three components: sets (like words), isolates (like sounds), and patterns (like grammar or syntax)" (96). So, to Hall, isolates corresponded to phonemes, sets to spoken words, and patterns to correctly spoken sentences. As a trainer, Hall believed that he first should teach people the sets of other cultures, that is, the units of nonverbal behavior that had particular meanings. Then they could learn about isolates so as to distinguish relatively subtle differences in behavior, and, finally, they would learn about patterns—patterns of order, selection, and congruence. If one thinks of order in cultural behavior as something like word order, selection as something like choosing to call a police officer a "pig" or a "cop," and congruence as something like achieving a consistent tone or meeting generic expectations, one will have a general understanding of how Hall thought culturally significant behavior could and should be analyzed. Once an American was taught the sets, isolates, and patterns of, say, a Middle Eastern country and had learned them as a kind of language, then that person was ready for assignment as a technical adviser.

From this, the midpoint of his book, Hall moved into the most interesting and enduring aspects of his analysis—his studies of temporal and territorial or spatial orientations in different societies. While he could be embarrassingly reductionistic, writing about what all Americans or all Spaniards do or mean, Hall nonetheless opened the topic of temporal and spatial orientation as fundamental systems within which to comprehend the social dimensions of life experiences; distinguishing between and among, for example, formal, informal, and technical understandings of the sets, isolates, and patterns of time in a society gave him a comparatively powerful analytic tool (ch. 9) for probing American culture. Formally, time was analyzed in terms of:

ordering (first, second, the one millionth, etc.);
cyclicity (the sixty-cycle measure of seconds and minutes, the seasons, etc.);
synthesisity (adding-up time, as in forty-hour weeks, seventh-year sabbaticals);
valuation (the equation, e.g., of time with money or wisdom with age);
tangibility (time as a commodity to be bought, saved, sold, wasted);
duration (precise units of measurement of time's passing); and
depth (a sense of multiple pasts upon which the present rests).

Informally, time to Hall was marked with a much less precise—yet understandable—vocabulary, as when English speakers say "It'll take a while" or when we want something "now" or put something off "until later." Further, he ascribed social importance to quantifiable measures of time; getting "an hour with the president" as opposed to "ten minutes" is not only a matter of having six times as much time but of having been honored or taken much more seriously—immeasurably more seriously—by having been given that hour of attention. Learning to measure differences in so-called duration sets (an hour vs. ten minutes with the president) was viewed as a matter of coming to understand urgency in particular situations (the schedule of the president vis-à-vis an unemployed homebody), monochronism (e.g., having the president talk only to you rather than doing other things while chatting), variety (the freedom to "spend time" as opposed to a rigidly enforced schedule), and activity (what counts in a society as "an activity," which in turn determines the informal understanding of time use).

Additionally, Hall's technical discussion of interpersonal space, broken down into four distances between participants, has been reprinted countless times by scholars of personal relationships, and led into his next book, *The Hidden Dimension,* and to his hoary discussion of people's personal space bubbles. In *The Silent Language,* he talked about distances between communicators much more precisely: very close (3–6 inches), close (8–12 inches), near (12–20 inches), neutral-personal (20–36 inches), neutral-interpersonal (4.5–5 feet), public distance (5.5–8 feet), across the room (8–20 feet), and stretching the limits of distance (20–24 feet indoors, up to 100 feet outdoors). Such formal analyses of spatial relationships were again supplemented with discussion of more informal understandings of space: the social significance of spacing between people in different societies, who gets to stand next to whom on public occasions, the symbolism of spacing people of different rank or caste in various societies (see ch. 10).

Each of the ten Primary Message Systems could have been discussed in like manner, though he did not do them all in this little book. That was no problem, for what was important here is not whether Hall was right or even whether he was absolutely complete in his analysis of "cultures" generally. What was important is how he went about his study. In *The Silent Language,* Edward Hall advocated cultural studies based on *description, analysis, synthesis,* and *scientistic theorization.* Detailed description provided the raw material that required understanding and disassembly; analysis by means of category systems broke the behavior down into its constitutive isolates, sets, and patterns; synthesis reassembled the behavior so that it could be imitated in the case of training workshops or compared to like behavior in the case of cross-cultural study; and theorization—informally, modeling, and more formally, propositional theorems—completed the anthropologist's research into "the silent language" of culture-grounded social behavior.

The purpose of such studies was largely explanative: to bring culture (which is out-of-awareness) into awareness, to make vivid the semantics and syntactics of culture so that a person could competently, even properly, perform meaningfully in multiple societies. Cultural misunderstandings were, largely, ungrammatical acts that could be corrected by further instruction.[9]

In driving home this point, Hall made two of his only political comments in the entire book. He noted that Senator Joseph McCarthy was one of a number of "the more voracious, predatory, and opportunistic of their fellow men who take advantage of the fact that the public is not usually aware of those shared norms which give coherence to our society," and that "If the American public had great realization that formal norms are not individual but shared, they might save themselves from McCarthyism in any of its future manifestations" (166). And his last two sentences demonstrated his cognizance of the peace movement out of which so many post-World War II intellectuals had come:

> For the layman and scientist alike I would like to say that I feel very strongly that we must recognize and understand the cultural process. We don't need more missiles and H-bombs nearly so much as we need more specific knowledge of ourselves as participants in culture. (168)

The emphasis here was on cultural analysis as the tool for unmasking domestic devils and improving international relations, certainly not the political-cultural reformation so cherished by the Old Left. Salvation, to Hall, came from disinterested analysis and behavior-oriented instruction, not passionate transcendence of cultural forces. His mind worked as the teacher-scholar's, not the cultural critic's. Hall's true commitments were demonstrated immediately after that final paragraph of his book. From those sentiments he went right into Appendix I, his eight propositions concerning what he believed he had contributed to social science (169–170).[10] While the book became popularized as a handbook for effective and ineffective nonverbal communication inside and outside the United States, Hall certainly hoped that his work would be assessed on its scientific rigor.[11]

THE INFLUENCE OF EDWARD HALL

Hall's linguistic model of culture, his belief in the essential identity of culture and communication, his scientistic conception of cultural analysis (description/analysis/synthesis/theorization), his effort to make people aware of the unnoticed, and his voluminous examples from around the world gave *The Silent Language* peculiar status in the United States.[12] The explosion of pop culture (e.g., Marshall McLuhan), pop psychology (e.g., Eric Berne), and pop advice on interpersonal relations (e.g., t-group or sensitivity training) in the 1960s signaled an environment congenial to Hall's impulse to personal training based on applied research. From *The Silent Language* in 1959 to *The Hidden Dimension* in 1966, Hall's thinking about time and space—especially personal space—echoed through talk shows and supermarket checkout counter books.

But, his influence in the American scholarly world, I would suggest, was equally pervasive. His particular theories of the cultural conditioning of social interaction were afforded little credence, though his approach to cultural studies was often repeated. For example, Alfred Smith in 1966 put together an anthology called *Communication and Culture: Readings in the Codes of Human Interaction*. Now, the field was organized by Smith in the tradition of American semiotics as articulated by Charles Morris, with communication to be studied at three sites—semantics, syntactics, and pragmatics—and then conceptualized within three theories: the mathematical model, with its emphasis on clear transmission, the social psychological model, with its emphasis on "communal interaction" (4), and the linguistic anthropological model, with its emphasis on verbal and nonverbal coding apparatuses. Three foci of study times three models of analysis gave Smith a matrix of nine research sites.[13] He was pleased with the results of his sorting and organizing, for they could guide scholarly activity:

> The primary aim of this book is to build a theoretical framework for empirical research. Our organizational matrix gives the outlines of such a theory. This theoretical organization is important because the way a field is organized helps determine whether that field is accepted for research, and accepted for what kind of research. This is particularly important in the field of human communication because that is a teeming wilderness of facts and notions, instances and generalizations, proofs and surmises. (8)

And, in case his reader did not understand, he ended his introduction by saying that "This book is not directly concerned with the utility of these facts. It describes and explains how people interact, not how they should interact for greater effectiveness or enjoyment. This book is descriptive rather than prescriptive. But although it does not lead us on any specific line of flight, it does give us a chart from which we can take our bearings" (10). And so, the chapters dealing with social class, the powers of television, the status of immigrants, and the role of elites in opinion formation bypassed critical examination of race, class, and gender in favor of descriptive-analytical study. Hall's perspectives on and disinterested attitudes toward culture were reproduced in Smith's introduction. The matrix for charting categories of cultural behavior was becoming the mainstay of American social studies.

While Alfred Smith acknowledged Hall's influence and even included one of his essays, his successors did not mention Hall's thoughts; yet, they worked from an epistemological framework strongly reminiscent of his. So, in 1969 George Lewis assembled a delightful anthology of studies of popular culture called *Side-Saddle on the Golden Calf: Social Structure and Popular Culture in America.* A central tenet from Hall—that a culture is read by examining the behaviors and artifacts of those who live it—grounded the anthology. His views of popular culture paralleled Hall's views of nonverbal behavior, and Lewis quoted these remarks from Russel Nye in his introduction:

> Popular art confirms the experience of the majority, in contrast to elite art, which tends to explore the new. For this reason, popular art has been an unusually sensitive and accurate reflector of the attitudes and concerns of the society for which it is produced. Because it is of lesser quality, aesthetically, than elite art, historians and critics have tended to neglect it as a means of access to an era's—and a society's—values and ideas. The popular artist corroborates (occasionally with great skill and intensity) values and attitudes already familiar to his audience; his aim is less to provide a new experience than to validate an older one. (quoted in Lewis, xiii-xiv)[14]

Had these sentiments been expressed about the silent language of nonverbal communication rather than the artifacts of popular culture, they could have been Hall's. Both Nye and Hall were working from a primarily semantic understanding of popular cultural processes. Further, in Nye's words one even can hear a repudiation of the elitist critiques of the Frankfurt school and especially the literary coterie of the New York intellectuals. The elite perspective is shunted aside and the artist to Nye becomes, not an avant-garde bohemian laboring in the depths of anomie, but a socially sensitive representative of his or her culture. Aesthetically informed analysis of mind is displaced by socially framed goals for cultural study.

When Caleb Gattegno "discovered" television in 1966 and then wrote a book about television and education three years later, he was equally at home in the world of mass media approached descriptively and analytically. Though the title of his book, *Towards a Visual Culture: Educating through Television,* was promising, in fact he was an education school devotee who equated "culture" with "information" and acquisition of visual literacy with acquisition of frames of learning. The scientism and commitment to the description and analysis of micro-behavior were everywhere in evidence.

Even more promising was an anthology devoted to the historical-critical study of mass media, Francis and Ludmila Voelker's popular

Mass Media: Forces in Our Society, first released in 1972. In offering a full range of journalistic and scholarly statements on each of the major mass media, with Daniel Boorstein, Nicholas Johnson, George Gerbner, Ben Bagdikian, and Newton Minow having voices in the book, the Voelkers seemed on their way to developing a critical spirit in their readers. Yet, they carefully set off one essay, a segment of Theodore Peterson's 1963 book *Why the Mass Media Are That Way,* to serve as an introduction. That essay was a defense of the press and television against criticisms aimed at the political economy, the content of mass media, and the sorry state of media consumers. He reasserted the press's search for objectivity, representativeness, and a level of competitiveness that keeps one segment from going too far in any direction. The view that the mass media are electronically empowered social vehicles was framed in this paragraph:

> What one sees from the institutional perspective is that the mass media are but one aspect of human communication [symbolization] in general. Like the semaphore and tribal drum, they are technical extensions of this primary social process that I have been talking about. As purveyors of symbols, the mass media help society to function. They are carriers of the values, the beliefs, the distinctive tone of the society in which they operate. As Walter Lippmann observed some forty years ago, they interpose a sort of pseudo-environment between man and physical reality. But if they are a force for stability, they are also a force for change. And because they are technical extensions, they can transmit their message across vast sweeps of space and time. (quoted in Voelker and Voelker, 10)

Interestingly, Edmund Carpenter and Marshall McLuhan's writings about electronic media as new languages—and they both have reprinted essays on that idea in the anthology—are turned by Peterson into both analytic perspectives and shields with which to turn back critiques of television's economics and politics. Lippmann, one of the whipping boys of Macdonald ("just another 'creator of kitsch' " [quoted in Ricco, 9]), here is depicted as one of the true diviners of mass-mediated society. The linguistic model of mass communication is thus amalgamated with the linguistic model of culture in a defense of what Peterson proudly identifies as the libertarian theory of the press (Voelker and Voelker, 11).

Several other works could be examined, but one more is enough for our purposes. American cultural studies understood as the analysis of social behaviors and artifacts that provide us with access to the out-of-awareness aspects of culture reached its apex in 1977, with the publication of Michael Real's *Mass Mediated Culture.* Real's is undoubtedly the boldest and most penetrating work offered within a sociological orientation to media, cultural theory, and scientist analysis. Real's introductory chapter probably deserves a paper unto itself, for it is a virtuoso performance in taxonomy-building. It synthesizes the American work on the four types of culture—folk, elite, popular, and mass. It identifies six "evaluative positions" on the mass media—liberal apologists, empirical/descriptive/ historical objectivists, progressive elites, traditional elitists, cultural separatist radicals—and Marxist structural radicals, and then organizes those six categories into three (liberal, elitist, and radical) so as to formalize and cross-reference their positions on mass culture, history, art, judgment, attitudes, deficiencies, style, and goals (16–20). The chapter thereupon moves into questions of system and structure, in a model suggesting that institutional infrastructure (the "material organization" of media) and consciousness (the "symbolic organization" of media) are brought together into macro and micro communication processes. In other words, communication structures are the products of both personal subjectivity and institutional objectivity. This section then gives way to another, which models questions of symbolic form or what Real calls "cultural screens" (30) around the ways in which sensory data are sorted into what he calls "organized sensory information" categories, which is to say, into language, science, history, myth, religion, and art. Thus, the mass media as sensory stimuli are understood to be processed as symbolic languages that, in turn, are structured around systematic categories of knowledge. This represents, to Real, the "ecology of mass-mediated culture" (31).

Edward Hall is not mentioned by name in Real's book, though his influence is undeniable; his conceptual ghost haunts the work, putting a scientistic patina even on Real's critical essays. That Real would study mass communication languages—verbal, visual, material—so as to discover clues to states of consciousness and institutional infrastructures puts him squarely in the cultural lineage flowing from William Graham Sumner to the present. In the middle of that flow stood Edward Hall, who posited a relationship between communication and culture that is almost purely American.

Hall's *The Silent Language* can be thought of as a master text for American cultural studies not because it was so often quoted or even influential as a source of first-order theory, but because Hall's framing of cultural studies took hold. His textualization of social behavior and subsequent analysis of it as the manifestation of culture were widely imitated. His classic scientistic model of inquiry—description/analysis/synthesis/theorization—was likewise copied, especially, as we've seen, by scholars in the sociological and anthropological traditions of study. His exploration of everyday activity—vis-à-vis the elitists' study of the exceptional, the "best"—put him in step with the age. Marshall McLuhan may well have been the guru of the pop culture age, but Edward Hall was one of its serious researcher-scholars. He was one of a new breed who succeeded the free-floating intelligentsia of an earlier age, as Lionel Trilling's wife and literary partner Diana understood so clearly:

> The intellectual culture of this country as Lionel and I knew it in the earlier decades of the century no longer exists. It had begun to disappear even in Lionel's lifetime [he died in 1975]: it may be that when he complained that the younger men at the University no longer engaged him in easy intellectual exchange, what he was noting was not so much a response to his reputation as a change in the temper of the times. The New York intellectuals had their moment in history and it has passed. . . . Our best intelligences retreat into the universities and into their special fields of learning. They give up what earlier in this book I called the life of significant contention. Instead, they settle for the life of expertise. (D. Trilling, 420)

THE INTELLECTUAL AND THE SCHOLAR

To formalize Diana Trilling's sentiments: in thinking about why ideology as a totalizing thought pattern was at an historical end in the 1950s, Daniel Bell said the following about the intellectual and the scholar:

> The differences between the intellectual and the scholar, without being invidious, are important to understand. The scholar has a bounded field of knowledge, a tradition, and seeks to find his place in it, adding to the accumulated, tested knowledge of the pasts to a mosaic. The scholar, qua scholar, is less involved with his "self." The intellectual begins with *his* experience, *his* individual perceptions of the world, *his* privileges and deprivations, and judges the world by these sensibilities. Since his own status is of high value, his judgments of the society reflect the treatment afforded him. In a business civilization, the intellectual felt that the wrong values were being honored, and rejected the society. Thus there was a "built-in" compulsion for the free-floating intellectual to become political. (402)

Bell's thesis about the "end of ideology" in the 1950s may give us a clue to Edward Hall's peculiar relationships to the intellectual environment out of which he came and to that which grew up around his work. The sorts of cultural analysis that came out of the New York intellectual community following World War II were deeply politicized, the products of self-reflexive minds conditioned to think about art, expression, and criticism as vehicles for political praxis. Hook, Burnham, Macdonald, Trilling, Schlesinger, and the rest spent time teaching school, especially in the post-1940s era, but they were first and foremost public political analysts—intellectuals with what Bell identified as a " 'built-in' compulsion" to act politically. An essay, a novel, a speech—all were political acts to men who conceived of ideologies as what Bell terms "blueprints" for "a new utopia of social harmony" (402).

But, when such men no longer believed that there were blueprints capable of schematizing social change, or when they began to offer what Frankfurt School historian Helmut Dubiel identifies as "a purely theoretical critique incapable of being joined to political action" (86), then cultural analysis could change. If cultural studies no longer serve political ends, then they are free to become what they became to Edward Hall: scholarly vehicles capable of translating social observations into theorized structures and practical training rather than into partisan action. As well, they could be the grounds for a whole body of scholarship capable of operating like an Enlightenment science—the very practice, paradoxically, that Adorno and Horkheimer were out to disrupt in 1944.

From there, it was but a short step for Edward Hall's innovative approach to cultural studies to be institutionalized as a master text, as an articulation of a position arising out of particular historical and material circumstances but empowered to transcend those circumstances so as to frame the thought of subsequent investigators. A master text has epistemological and normative force. It controls answers to the questions of relevance: what factors and what investigator attitudes are relevant to some arena of thought? It silences the voices answering alternative questions, or, as we saw with Real, it packages those voices in such a way as to blunt their agitating force. Slowly but perceptibly, the master text becomes absorbed, turns into a background that no longer even needs to be articulated. Casual references to the linguistic character of culture, personal space bubbles, the temporal-spatial matrices of collective living, and high- and/or low-context systems of social activity, for example, can be made even without direct attribution.

Edward Hall's *The Silent Language*, especially, stands as a tribute to the scientistic turn in cultural studies that American scholars took in their reactions, perhaps, to the post-World War II culture wars, to McCarthyism, to the rise of the scientistic hegemony in American universities following the country's postwar romantic attachments to technology and consumer goods, and to the need for professional citizen training in etiquette as we assumed adaptive personae needed for waging peace and war internationally.

In the events that I have reviewed, scholars replaced intellectuals in the pursuit of cultural theory. Sumner triumphed over Arnold; the everyday rather than the artistically and politically exceptional was theorized and analyzed. Edward Hall's master text held sway especially among students of communication studies until science itself again was challenged as a useful approach to cultural phenomena and subjected to new criticism at the hands of the British and the French. The continental Cultural Studies of the late 1970s and 1980s could never have had its powerful impact upon the American humanities and social sciences had not political criticism of a normative kind been out of vogue. It was, I suspect, comparatively easy for Cultural Studies to seize the imagination of academic institutions where the human arts and sciences were dominated by scientists and descriptive-taxonomic literary critics. But that, the processes by which a master text is delegitimated, is the subject for another essay in cultural-rhetorical theory.

POSTSCRIPT: THE ACADEMICIAN'S ROMANCE WITH DICHOTOMIES

This essay has ridden the back of foundational epistemological and rhetorical dichotomies: the humanities-science dialectic (C. P. Snow's two cultures) and distinctions between acting (à la the Arnoldians) and knowing (à la the Sumnerites) as products of formal thinking and arguing. Dichotomies have grounded much of academic inquiry at least since Plato's disjunctive questioning and Aristotle's Square of Oppositions. Dichotomies are beloved in the academy because they are razors; they seemingly cut to the center of issues, exposing decision points, even while drawing enough blood to make the human contexts of inquiry exciting to observers. Intellectuals/scholars cannot help themselves. They drool in anticipation when faced with dichotomous disputes.

The rhetorical scholars of the United States are no exception. A range of issues similar to those showing up in this case study characterized the "One World or Two?" discussion of rhetorical and communication studies in the 1960s (Kenneth Williams), as well as the controversy surrounding "the ideological turn" in the 1980s (Wander). The one-world-or-two sermons ripped through convention papers, even settling into an explicit dichotomy where rhetoricians were asked to scavenge ideas for scientists to test (Bowers). The ideological turn has spawned a running battle between those who believe that analytically controlled rhetorical analysis generates human understanding (in the tradition of Black) and those who demand that critics must push past the disinterestedness of rational analysis and into the realm of ideological critique and political action (e.g., Nothstine, Blair, and Copeland). Similar battles rage between contemporary rhetorical theorists—between the likes of Farrell and Hariman writing in the civic tradition of rhetoric vis-à-vis the likes of McGee ("Text") and McKerrow, working out of poststructuralist thought.

The divides in contemporary rhetorical theory are relevant to this essay's subject matter. While I do not have the space to trace the reemergence of humane vis-à-vis scientistic theories of communication and culture, in fact they came knocking in the 1970s and 1980s, in multiple forms. The nascent thinking about everyday cultural practice that can be found as early as 1969 in Gregg, McCormack, and Pedersen's essay on the rhetoric of black power developed into Marxist cultural (ideological) analysis at the hands of Wander and into a rhetorical-constructionist analysis, then materialist analysis, at the hands of McGee ("In Search," "A Materialist's"). The analytical approach to matters of rhetoric, mass media, and ideological practice marking David Berg's 1972 essay on those topics was reframed in specifically critical-cultural terms in essays printed in Medhurst and Benson's anthology on rhetoric and the media. Hall was left behind in a series of attempts—and these are but illustrative—to continue negotiations between "rhetoric" and "culture," then "rhetorical studies" and "cultural studies," from the place Ernest Wrage had left them. Throughout such negotiations, the commitment to rational analysis of argument and argumentatively supported claims versus the commitment to political unmasking and empowerment—in discourses that often went well beyond the rational and formally valid argumentation of philosophically anchored theory—made the engagement of rhetorical studies and [C]ultural [S]tudies a noisy affair. It still is.

Let me be clear here: the humanities are not "better" than the sciences, nor is the reverse true. Both the civic and the critical-cultural impulses for theorizing about situated human communication tell us some important things about human agency (or the lack thereof). Rather, both sides of most epistemic and rhetorical dichotomies provide useful lenses through which to look at being-in-the-world. The New York intellectuals' call for examined and committed liberal-democratic social action was as useful in its way as was Hall's call for systematic, analytically secured generalizations about key points of human difference that ground misunderstanding and distrust. Hall's search for systemic differences between cultures served as a sort of corrective for the Old Left's belief in a more or less universal model of social democracy that could fit any society comfortably. Similarly, the intellectuals' exploration of the valuative worth of forms of cultural activity served as a sort of corrective to Hall's indifference to qualitative assessment within the primary message systems of a society.

Likewise, rhetoricians grounding their work in the scholarly revival of a classical tradition now enmeshed with Enlightenment thought about rhetorical propositions (a scientistically engineered *logos*) communicate visions of civic pieties and the reasoned bases of politics that are complemented by the others wishing to free the *demos* from the ideologically freighted discourses of the politically, economically, and socioinstitutionally elite rhetors owning the contemporary political economy. Rhetoric often in fact has been the tool of the political elite and, today, is the possession of the "scholar." Thus, it is little wonder that relationships between traditional rhetorical studies and the new champions of the discursive empowerment of the downtrodden—by champions who see themselves pridefully as "intellectuals" usually in a French tradition—are often tenuous and halting.

The halves of such dichotomies at least often, I would argue, can be compensatory to each other, and a choice between one horn or the other is less a matter of good and evil than a question of what one wants to examine with particular focus at a given time. I do not mean to suggest, however, that a choice between horns is arbitrary or capricious. I would hope that this study of the 1940s and 1950s makes it clear that intellectual inquiry is perforce knitted into the warp and weave of historically specific social valuations and tensions. The Old Left was much more comfortable and generally useful amid the tyrannies and oligarchies of the 1930s and 1940s than it was in the more democratically optimistic late 1950s. Edward Hall could not have prospered in an isolationist period characterized by spiritual crises—at least not to the extent that he did in the age of science and technology, material prosperity, and the cold war.

These are of course slippery, perhaps dangerous, generalizations. And they are born of what this entire essay is—the academician's romance with dichotomies. The stories that have been told herein about American cultural studies and, if briefly, about American rhetorical inquiry gain much of their vitality and conceptualizing force from dichotomous conflict. Insofar as one remembers that other stories about the same materials could be told, that narrativized interpretations can be as epistemically and characterologically suspect as propositional ones, and that the dialectic inherent in dichotomies is much more likely productive of understanding than of truth, then an essay such as this one becomes an engaging piece of cultural history and explanation.

NOTES

1. Macdonald himself, however, became reattached to political movements in the 1960s, and even has been termed by Irving Howe the progenitor of the 1960s radicals (Gewen, 14).
2. Aronowitz (62) discusses the idea of "cultural citizenship," wherein one's collective identity is tied to a subculture rather than to the nation state, even to such politically transcendent cultures as pan-Africanism or international women's solidarity. One senses in the early 1950s' writings of the New York intellectuals a sense of cultural citizenship.
3. The dating of the "culture industry" essay by Adorno and Horkheimer is difficult to pin down. Certainly it was published in Horkheimer and Adorno, 1944, but in German; and certainly that book was published in English translation in

1972. But, in between, its basic ideas had broad circulation, especially among the New York intellectuals. The parallels, for example, between their essay and Dwight Macdonald's "A Theory of Popular Culture" (originally published in 1944) have been noted by Wald (223). Their "combination of a trenchant critique of capitalism with the traditionally mandarin prejudices of high Germanic culture," in Ross's nicely turned phrase (50), allowed them to have appeal in both political and literary circles. Their association of capitalism and a degraded popular culture played well to the intelligentsia of mid-century (cf. Hardt, especially 136–138).

4. See Donnelly's intellectual obituary for a thoughtful consideration of Macdonald's views on middle culture.

5. The distinction between two types of politicians—"those who lived for politics and those who lived off politics"—was Max Weber's, a discussion of whom opened Wolpert's essay (240).

6. The elitists' sense of individualism as escape from or beyond culture should not be confused with the earlier brands worried over by Tocqueville (individualism as grounds for citizenship and voluntary associationism) or by Dewey (more or less the progressive commitment to the search for individual liberty). The individualism of many in the Old Left was an outering experience—transcending culture in the manner of an avant-garde so as to critique the collective and institutionalized aspects of one's society. For an examination of "the new individualism" preceding and absorbing the anti-Stalinist liberals, see Kutulas, 62–86.

7. Edward Hall, however, certainly knew of Trilling, alluding to his discussion of culture-as-prison late in his influential book (Hall, *Silent,* 166).

8. To read culture as a language certainly was an advance past the position of early communication theorist Colin Cherry, who believed that culture was encoded in verbal language (see Cherry, 17, 70, 72, 81, 106).

9. The parallel between Hall's focus on cross-cultural mistakes and I. A. Richards's definition in 1936 of rhetoric as the study of misunderstandings and their remedies is striking (3). Just as the General Semantics movement, among others, took up the cause of sanitizing human relationships through techniques that targeted misunderstanding in the 1940s and early 1950s, especially, with Richards as one of its heroes, so also the foreign relations community following a worldwide war and the establishment of the United Nations as a center for talk took up the task of trying to neutralize and correct cross-cultural interaction. Hall's mission as a proponent of applied research to train culturally sensitive communicators was in step with his times.

10. The eight propositions included the following: (1) communication is culture and culture is communication; (2) culture is biobasic and manifested in ten different bases; (3) culture is neither the sum of a society's institutions nor the aggregate of the psychological makeups of individuals, but instead comprises the modes of social interaction; (4) culture exists on formal, informal, and technical levels; (5) culture is better understood as particular messages than as message networks or control systems (i.e., than as Parsonian structures); (6) there is a Heisenberg-like indeterminacy to culture, for precise study often changes the character of that which is being studied; (7) culture is relative because each suc-

ceeding experience changes the nature of that which is experienced; and (8) cultural indeterminacy and cultural relativity suggest that social scientists should begin analysis at the microcultural level, and only in a step by step fashion move to larger patterns. These eight propositions—especially the last three—temper Hall's theory, though it seems obvious that in his enthusiastic generalizations about various societies he sometimes forgot about temperateness and caution in conclusion drawing.

11. To complete a picture of Edward Hall, I should add, one must go to his last book, *Beyond Culture* (1976). Here, his vision is broader and his mission, much more reformative—an attack on what he calls "cultural irrationality." One must escape culture to evolve. One must learn, too, to escape monochronic time ("M-time") and adapt to polychronic time systems ("P-time systems"); enable the individual to work and think in several spheres at once and thus move individuals away from the organizing principles of their culture. Were we exploring ideas of culture in the 1970s, working from this book, the story would be significantly different.

12. One might also note that as Hall textualized cultural analysis, he was one of the people responsible for making the American academy ready to receive the Saussurean/Barthesian semiotic model in later years.

13. Not all nine cells were occupied, however. To Smith, all three models focused on syntactics, though really only social psychology and linguistic anthropology featured semantics, and only social psychology had a strong interest in pragmatics. Hall's syntactic shadow falls across the models.

14. This reference to Russel Nye should remind readers that I am not dealing here with the so-called Bowling Green school of popular culture studies, founded in the 1960s by the likes of Nye and Ray Browne and institutionalized in the Popular Culture Association and its journal, the *Journal of Popular Culture*. This strain of work—for some (e.g., Aronowitz), inspired by McLuhan, for others (e.g., Browne), the more or less natural evolution of the literature-and-society school of criticism—was quintessentially American. Yet, two recent topical histories of popular culture studies, Strinati and Storey, do not mention this body of work. It deserves a good deal more attention from the popular culture studies community today than it is receiving, for it, like the scholarship following in the social or human sciences of the 1960s and 1970s, textualized culture, albeit in different ways.

TWELVE

ANTITHEORY
AND ITS ANTITHESES
Rhetoric and Ideology

Patrick Brantlinger

Various trends and "-isms" contributed to the heady mix that, in the late
1960s or early 1970s, came to be called just "theory," in the singular, and
to dominate the anxieties, if not always the practices, of scholars in humanities and sometimes social science disciplines.[1] Diverse though these trends
and -isms are, all have been commonly identified as one rough beast,
slouching (depending on one's politics, academic or otherwise) either
toward Bethlehem or toward Bedlam. Just how and when *theories* became
theory is uncertain, but a plausible answer is the 1966 conference at Johns
Hopkins University on The Languages of Criticism and the Sciences of
Man, which inaugurated on this side of the Atlantic both "the structuralist
controversy" and poststructuralism. Aspirations toward a "general *theory*
of signs and language systems" are expressed throughout the conference
proceedings (Macksey and Donato, xvi; emphasis added). Evident in all the
papers is the "linguistic turn" that had deeply affected European philosophy and that, for literary scholars, shifted attention from literature to language. According to the standard theory story, what preceded its hegemony
was New Criticism, often figured as the untheorized practice of close reading. But New Criticism was not theory-innocent; it was instead intensely,
combatively theoretical (see Wellek and Warren, *The Theory of Literature*)
even while it functioned as practical and as practice (see Brooks and Warren, *Understanding Poetry*). Espousing a practical theory or theoretical
practice of how to read and evaluate a poem or any other literary text,

New Criticism also had a theory (*the* theory, according to Wellek and Warren's title) of what constituted literature. After World War II, New Criticism offered literary scholars a united front, an intellectual hegemony with distinct disciplinary boundaries. Ironically, the more recent theory regime has involved the dissolution of those boundaries through conflicting claims and methodologies. Where there was once (apparent) unity, now there is disunity.[2]

One meaning of "theory" is just the intellectual arena, mostly academic, where conflicts over literature, culture, and interpretation now occur. In the midst of these conflicts, the main object of *literary* scholarship—literature—has been dethroned or at least somewhat marginalized. A corollary of the linguistic turn was a widening of focus from literature to textuality, including the writ-large texts of culture, society, and history. Literary theory transgresses the boundaries both of literature and of nonliterary disciplines because it is "a discourse about discourses" (Ralph Cohen, xv). In short, literary theory either ignores literature or treats it as the mere offshoot or effect of some larger category: textuality, communication, discourse, culture, or rhetoric. For theorists as different as Paul de Man and Terry Eagleton, theory's ultimate object proves to be "rhetoric," a category that overlaps with or is closely related to—perhaps indistinguishable from—"ideology" (de Man, 11; Eagleton, *Literary Theory*, 206–210).

For de Man, rhetoric takes precedence over ideology, which he defines as the tendency to overlook rhetoric—to treat it as transparent and nonmetaphoric. Ideology is rhetoric that persuades its audience that it is not rhetoric. The deconstruction of rhetoric, the revealing of its secret workings where it claims not to be working, is therefore ideological critique. In contrast, for Eagleton, ideology is the main category; rhetoric is just the set of linguistic conventions, tropes, and so forth that convey those aspects of ideology that get translated into discourse. From Eagleton's Marxist perspective, however, the distinction is minor, because whether one calls it "rhetoric" or "ideology," the discourse of a given social formation is the product of that social formation, and more specifically of its economic mode of production. Every social formation produces the discourse—the rhetoric or ideology—that rationalizes it. But for Eagleton it is not rhetoric that ideology occludes; rather, the rhetoric of ideology occludes social exploitation and injustice.

Over the past three decades, literary theory—or, better, just theory—has produced many variations on these two positions. The Marxist position, informing much of the work that identifies itself as cultural studies, privileges ideology over rhetoric. The poststructuralist position privileges discourse or rhetoric over ideology. In both cases, however, theory itself proves to be a sort of mirage. Theory becomes antitheory whenever it recognizes itself as the product of either ideology or rhetoric, or both. Perhaps the most notorious theoretical case against theory is Steven Knapp and Walter Benn Michaels's "Against Theory." For Knapp and Michaels, it does not make any difference whether the target of theory is rhetoric or ideology, because both of these terms are just alternative labels for theory's identity with practice—that is, for its identity with either rhetoric or ideology. But Knapp and Michaels's essay is only symptomatic of the general tendency whereby rhetoric and ideology become alternative names for theory's impossibility.

For Marx and Engels, ideology primarily meant the set of mystifications—false consciousness, a pre-Freudian version of the unconscious—that caused people to tolerate intolerable social conditions. Rhetoric was the main medium through which ideology was conveyed, but it was not for them a primary consideration. How rhetoric has come into focus as either a synonym for or a category that sometimes takes precedence over ideology concerns the much more recent, academic story of theory, and especially of antitheoretical literary and cultural theory.

THEORY AGAINST THEORY

When literary theory reaches the conclusion that its object is either rhetoric or ideology, it ceases to be literary and in a sense ceases to be theory. Much—perhaps most—literary and cultural theory, certainly since the poststructuralist turn of the late 1960s, has been relentlessly antitheoretical. Another way of stating this paradox is that theory uses the tools of philosophy to deconstruct philosophy; theory thereby aligns itself with the traditional antithesis of philosophy—namely, with rhetoric.[3]

The antiphilosophical tendency of theory is manifest in Derridean deconstructions of metaphysics and of all forms of essentialism; but it is also manifest in much modern so-called philosophy, from logical positivism to neopragmatism. Philosophy originally aspired to discover the general, absolute truths about existence. In contrast, theory, though it also asks fundamental questions, declares philosophy's main aspiration to be unattainable. Theory's simultaneously more modest and more radical aim is to understand how both knowledge and illusion are socially constructed, if only because necessarily expressed through language. This pared-down object of analysis—language or discourse rather than existence—in turn generates a series of subcategories, the most important of which have been rhetoric and ideology. Moreover, theory undermines philosophy by implying or declaring *itself* to be, in common with all forms of culture, socially constructed, and hence either rhetorical or ideological. The shift from literature to discourse, culture, or rhetoric has been paralleled by the also conflictual process of canon revision. But while it is often attributed to theory, canon revision has not depended upon theory. As even T. S. Eliot recognized, the literary canon is constructed in history rather than in heaven, and revising it is a main ongoing function of literary criticism, whether theorized or not. Like the New Critics, however, Eliot understood the literary canon to be based on a stable set of aesthetic criteria and also to be straightforwardly incremental. In contrast, just as its neoconservative opponents charge, recent canon revision has been based as much on a politics of democratic representation as on formalist literary criteria.[4]

Both canon revision and the shift from literature to rhetoric involve political as well as aesthetic questions. But why? As the opponents of theory often ask, doesn't the transformation of literary into cultural and social criticism involve a categorical error?[5] This question might be a theory-stopper if it weren't that literature is made out of language (and therefore rhetoric), that language is what binds people together in cultures and societies, and that—from even the most traditional perspective—literature plays or should play a significant educational and, hence, social role. Further, the category of the aesthetic is inherently political. In order to answer basic questions about literature, even the most traditional versions of literary criticism must operate as cultural and social theory some of the time. Just what kind of social theory the study of literature needs to be is a main source of controversy, to which the key terms rhetoric and ideology insistently point.[6] In common with philosophy, theory raises fundamental questions not just about the interpretation of works of literature, but about culture and society, language and identity, history and knowledge. Repeatedly, rhetoric and ideology, though not the answers to these questions, prove to be the media within which, it is hoped, the answers can be found.

The spate of new reference books focused on theory suggests that its hegemony is far from weakening. These include *A Dictionary of Critical Theory* (Orr, 1991), *Encyclopedia of Contemporary Literary Theory* (Makaryk, 1993), *A Glossary of Contemporary Literary Theory* (Hawthorn, 1994), and *The Johns Hopkins Guide to Literary Theory and Criticism* (Groden and Kreisworth, 1994). All of these books recognize the diversity of theory or, rather, theories—the very idea that there needs to be a dictionary or guide suggests as much—and their prefaces all emphasize this diversity.[7] But not only do all of these tomes use "theory" in the singular, perhaps equally symptomatic is that three out of the four do not even provide an entry for this singular term, suggesting, albeit by default, the taken-for-grantedness of "theory." It seems that theory is just all of the items for which entries are supplied.[8]

But the appearance of such reference works may also be symptomatic of theory's decline. Like the *Blue Guide* demythologized by Roland Barthes, guides to theory express a touristic nostalgia for history's monuments. Theory itself has been theorized as intellectual mourning for a lost or impossible coherence.[9] If these reference books are any guide, theory does not trail after practice, it has gone before—it has always already transpired—and it is the misfortune of those who come in its wake to be able only to catch a glimpse of its traces, its dawning spurs, its winged and shining heels, through the gaps and absences of monumental volumes like these. Theory, in other words, from the reference book standpoint, is a codifiable fait accompli, even though theory is forever in the vanguard: it is the future, or the promise of one. It's just that theory, like everything else, can never transpire in the present or be fully self-present. All that we have in theory's absence is rhetoric or ideology, or both. At least these guides signal that much of what has occurred under the theory rubric has been absorbed into academic routine.

In contrast to the other guides, Orr's *Dictionary* offers an entry labeled "theory, theoretical":

> . . . a coherent set of hypothetical, pragmatic, or conceptual principles forming the general frame of reference for a field of studies . . . ; abstract knowledge; a hypothetical entity . . . explaining . . . a set of facts; a working hypothesis giving probability by experimentation or by conceptual analysis. . . . Theory is generally the opposite of practice or application (but in Marxist terminology, "praxis" is practice informed by theory). (415)

Much could be said about this entry, starting with the observation that it is not directly relevant even to such standard critical practices as interpreting literary texts. Also, whatever else literary theory may be, its diversity suggests the opposite of "a coherent set of . . . principles forming the general frame of reference for a field of studies."

Moreover, a great deal of theory has been, like Knapp and Michaels's tour-de-polemic, "against theory." Insofar as much literary theory has been antitheory, Orr's definition does not match its object. In any event, the general spectacle has been one in which the philosophers—the theorists, that is—turn over the keys of the kingdom to the rhetoricians: theory tells us that rhetoric and/or ideology is all we can expect. This is not to say that the theorists, once they have reached their antitheoretical conclusion, stop theorizing. To conclude, as do Knapp and Michaels, on the basis of a lengthy theoretical argument, that theory as such is an impossibility, only generates more theory. Allegations of the death or decline of theory are often just the latest versions of theory taking its licks out on itself.[10]

Some of the participants in the 1966 Johns Hopkins University conference were more intent on deconstructing than on expressing the aspiration toward a "general theory" of semiosis. Such a deconstruction is implicit in the title of Jacques Lacan's contribution, "Of Structure as an Inmixing of an Otherness Prerequisite to Any Subject Whatsoever," while Derrida's "Structure, Sign, and Play in the Discourse of the Human Sciences," by decentering the necessarily centered concept of structure, subverts the goal of establishing a set of first principles or a central, unifying theory for any of "the human sciences."[11] Derridean deconstruction has been a potent antitheory theory, because the main object of its critique is the "logocentrism" of the Western metaphysical tradition, that highly influential canon of theories. "Deconstruction resists theory . . . because it demonstrates the impossibility of . . . the closure of an ensemble or totality on an organized network of theorems, laws, rules, methods" (Derrida, "Some Statements," 86). What we are left with is, for Derrida, just what all theories are made of: metaphors, language, rhetoric. But theory has higher aspirations than merely to recognize its entrapment within rhetoric or ideology, and therefore theory, according to Derrida, is productive of "monsters"; he suggests a theory of theory as "teratology," although "this teratology is our normality" ("Some Statements," 67).

The antitheoretical arguments of what is sometimes viewed as the most radical sort of theory (deconstruction) have not prevented its frequent identification as *the* vanguard theory among theories. Nor have these arguments prevented "theory" from being used in the singular, perhaps because the aspiration toward a grand, totalizing *Summa Theoretica* motivates deconstruction even while it emphasizes the inevitable frustration of that motivation, and even while other varieties of poststructuralism, neopragmatism, and postmodernism also emphasize (totalistically, theoretically) the nullity of all theoretically totalizing ambitions. So Jean-François Lyotard's claim that "postmodern" means "incredulity toward metanarratives" would seem to spell an end to aspirations toward grand or ultimate theories in any field (Lyotard, xxiv). But of course Lyotard's claim is both metanarrational and another instance of antitheory theory.

According to de Man's influential *The Resistance to Theory*, one result of literary theory's "self-resistance" (19) is the production of a "universal theory of the impossibility of theory" (18). de Man is less concerned with theory's external enemies than with its internal evasions of "its own project," which includes de Man's project, because:

> Nothing can overcome the resistance to theory since theory *is* itself this resistance. The loftier the aims and the better the methods of literary theory, the less possible it becomes. Yet literary theory is not in danger of going under; it cannot help but flourish, and the more it is resisted, the more it flourishes, since the language it speaks is the language of self-resistance. What remains impossible to decide is whether this flourishing is a triumph or a fall. (19–20; emphasis in original)

For de Man, what literary theory "resists" is specifically "the rhetorical or tropological dimension of language" (17), the constant temptation being to keep rhetoric under the sway of grammar and logic, and hence to reinforce "the claims of the *trivium* (and by extension, of language) to be an epistemologically stable construct" (17). By revealing the ways rhetoric always already overrides grammar and logic, theory becomes "a powerful and indispensable tool in the unmasking of ideological aberrations" (11), including its own aberrations. Accordingly, literary theory approximates Marxist ideological critique. "What we call ideology is precisely the confusion of linguistic with natural reality, of reference with phenomenalism" (de Man, 11). There are, of course, different, more obviously political definitions of ideology in Marx, Gramsci, Barthes, and Althusser (among others); nevertheless, de Man insists that "literary theory" comes under frequent attack because "it upsets rooted ideologies by revealing the mechanisms of their workings" (11).

MARXISM, NEOPRAGMATISM, AND RHETORIC

For de Man, "ideologies" work by occluding "rhetoric"; ideological critique, identical with deconstructive literary theory, entails the rigorous analysis of "the rhetorical and tropological dimension of language" against the claims of grammar and logic as well as of transparency, naturalness, and objectivity. Eagleton has no problem with de Man's perspective, so far as it goes; but it does not go far enough, because the rhetorical expression of ideology is only the tip of the iceberg.[12] In *Criticism and Ideology* and elsewhere, Eagleton models his conception of ideology on that of Althusser, for whom it is a structuring and causal principle that, if not exactly equivalent to the social totality, informs all aspects of that totality. "Ideology represents the imaginary relationship of individuals to their real conditions of existence," Althusser writes, but it is also more than just simple illusion or false consciousness; it is the very principle or power that creates individual identity in the first place: "ideology interpellates individuals as subjects" (Althusser, "Ideology," 162, 170). This proposition situates ideology beyond individual control while also granting it a positive force similar to an economic mode of production. Later elaborations of Althusser's theory—for instance, Slavoj Žižek's—come almost full circle to something like Foucault's theory of discourse: ideology does not produce illusions about social reality; it produces social reality.[13] In any event, from an Althusserian perspective, rhetoric and subjectivity (or individual identity) are both mere reflexes of ideology.

Poststructuralists, however, have developed powerful theories—or antitheories—that prioritize rhetoric and that are at least suspicious of the entire category of ideology. Foucault, for instance, gives three reasons why the "notion of ideology . . . cannot be used without circumspection": first, to identify ideology one must be able to identify its antithesis, "something else which is supposed to count as truth"; second, ideology "refers . . . to something of the order of a subject," that is, of a presumably reasoning or, at least, rationalizing mind that produces it in place of truth; and third, ideology "stands in a secondary position relative to something which functions as its infrastructure, as its material, economic determinant" (*Power/Knowledge*, 118). In contrast, for Foucault there is no outside to discourse that can be identified as truth, or as the integrated mind that produces it instead of the other way around, or as a nondiscursive mode of economic production. If one accepts the poststructuralist proposition that all that is available to analysis is discourse, then ideology cannot be understood as existing outside of rhetoric, much less as somehow shaping or determining rhetoric, as, say, the political unconscious to what appears within the conscious but illusionary frame of rhetoric. It then only makes sense to avoid using the term "ideology," as does Foucault, or else to restrict it to overtly politicized forms of discourse and propaganda.[14]

Both ideology and rhetoric ordinarily signify the untruths (mystifications), partial truths, or relative truths that are perhaps, theory in its various guises suggests, the only forms of enlightenment (or illusion?) attainable. Those theorists who privilege ideology also insist that all forms of consciousness are socially constructed, which may or may not mean socially determined.[15] Those who privilege rhetoric are less inclined to see everything in sociological, historical, or political terms, and more inclined to an at least quasi-Foucauldian pragmatism that treats the surfaces of discourse—rhetoric—as all that there is to analyze or all that can be analyzed.

Despite the different meanings that various theorists attach to rhetoric and ideology, both rhetorical and ideological critique have as their goal enlightenment or emancipation from the illusions generated by rhetoric and ideology. Eagleton ties his version of theory as ideological critique to an "emancipatory" politics (both Marxism and feminism) that is not part of de Man's agenda of theorized reading. Charges that de Man's version of theory is an evasion of history are surely correct to the extent that he insists on the literariness of what literary theory can and should deal with. Literary theory that becomes socially critical is necessarily, from de Man's perspective, itself an evasion of the main difficulty that properly literary theory struggles within and against. For de Man, any move away from literariness—that is, from the focus on rhetoric—expresses the very "resistance to theory" that he is trying to resist.

The critique of those illusions with which all individuals set forth in life has always been a principal aim of humanistic education. From this very general perspective, it perhaps hardly matters whether one calls these illusions rhetoric or ideology. In contrast, much current antitheory theory, speaking "the language of self-resistance" and repeatedly demonstrating its own impossibility, seems harmlessly self-deconstructive and also far too abstruse to have any effect on most individuals. The only way it can be held to threaten the subversion of Western civilization is if it is also held to have a central, influential place in Western civilization. This centrality the opponents of theory regularly deny, even while simultaneously accusing it of unhinging civilization. The belief that theory, in its persistent forms of ideological and rhetorical critique, is radical or subversive of the status quo also raises the question: just what is the ideology of theory? But if theory seeks to undo ideology by revealing its rhetorical construction, then how can theory be said to have an ideology or to be itself ideological and, hence, "radical"?

In "Against Theory," Knapp and Michaels contend that theory can have "no consequences"; it is just the illusory "attempt to escape practice" (30). On their account, all of the potential ways in which theory might oppose practice appear to be not just "resistance" to its own insights, but willful perversity: theory should know that it cannot "escape practice," and should therefore stop theorizing. But, like de Man, Knapp and Michaels depend on a definition of theory that narrows it to the question of literary interpretation, even while they attribute to it the impossible aspiration for some ultimate, grand theory that would settle all questions of interpretation. They blame theory both for its inability to stabilize the proliferation of meanings even within single literary texts *and* for its inability to be grandly totalizing. Furthermore, as Jonathan Crewe notes in his response to "Against Theory": "Practice [according to Knapp and Michaels] is always institutionally or otherwise given, always encompasses us, and belated attempts to seize control in the name of principle are consequently foredoomed. 'Doing' theory accordingly becomes a mode of impotent presumption equivalent to doing nothing" (53). But if this is so, then isn't the kind of antitheory theory that Knapp and Michaels practice also just "impotent presumption equivalent to doing nothing"? At least they have the good faith (or is it irony?) to acknowledge, echoing Stanley Fish, that their argument (like theory in general, according to them) can have no "practical consequences whatsoever" (26).

Despite—or because of—arguments like those in "Against Theory," the antitheoretical adventures of theory are bound to continue, in part because theory sophistication is now an aspect of the professionalization of most academics in literary and cultural fields. According to John Guillory, theory has emerged alongside literature as a distinct, in some ways rival, "theory-canon" (xii). Guillory speculates that the rise of the theory-canon has been a response to "the technobureaucratic restructuring of the university," itself a response to the rise of the new "professional-managerial class" for which "literature" is no longer a significant form of "cultural capital." As a discourse distinct from earlier forms of literary history and criticism, theory expresses the "technobureaucratic" values of the "professional-managerial class," though if this is the case it is difficult to understand why both academic and nonacademic members of that class so often find even antitheory theory threatening. But, from Guillory's perspective, "the emergence of theory is the symptom of a problem which theory itself could not solve" (xii).

Revising de Man's title, Mas'ud Zavarzadeh and Donald Morton, in *Theory as Resistance,* contend that "the dominant academy's antitheory theorists" are in effect all defenders of liberal pluralism and pragmatism, or the rationalizers "of (post)modern capitalism as an apparatus of crisis management" (3). What is being resisted is "new theoretical knowledge of the social totality"; but it turns out to be not exactly "new," because for Zavarzadeh and Morton the only sort of theory that counts is orthodox Marxism. Whether or not one agrees that theory as such, by definition, means socioeconomic critique of a sort that offers a "global understanding of capitalism" (3), the authors of *Theory as Resistance* are surely correct that much antitheory theory has been either apolitical or nonradical at least in its consequences. From their perspective, antitheory theory is mere academic collusion with "late capitalism": it is its intellectual superstructure and "alibi" (4).

Bruce Robbins also notes that "the history of literary criticism in its received versions [has been] a narrative of professionalization" (1) and hence of collaboration with capitalism, but he contends that "literature" in one direction and "theory" in another both function as "antiprofessional" discourses. If New Criticism saw itself as professionalizing literary studies by displacing the old-style belletrism of the "gentleman-amateur," theory today has claimed a similar professionalizing function against New Criticism. But much theory is not only antitheoretical, it is also antiprofessional, Robbins contends, in the sense of being both antidisciplinary and politically oppositional (as, for instance, both Marxists and feminists are oppositional), which also means opposed to the very institutions, including those of higher education, that employ and authorize professionals (that is, professors). For Robbins, being a professional and being an oppositional critic are not antithetical roles. Robbins suggests that one way to understand theory in humanities fields today is precisely as the discourse of socially critical or oppositional professionals.[16]

Robbins's argument will hardly reassure the neoconservative opponents of theory, for whom political radicalism in the academy is at least as threatening as the antitheory tendencies of theory. Those antitheory tendencies themselves add up to forms of relativism or antifoundationalism that, as Zavarzadeh and Morton believe, are disabling to Marxists, feminists, or African American theorists, and at the same time are more logically supportive of varieties of neopragmatism that, in turn, seem more consonant with liberal pluralism than with forms of political radicalism. But antifoundationalism in the case of Marxism reinforces the tendency to treat the interpretation of texts as ideological demystification. And antifoundationalism for feminists, queer theorists, and theorists of race and ethnicity alike reinforces the critique of biological determinism and essentialism in favor of, for example, Judith Butler's performance theory of gender.

Antifoundationalism is the main way that much current theory is antitheoretical. Theorists who argue that there is no ultimate grounding for understanding—that the knowledges generated by the "human sciences" are partial, relative, unscientific, and always socially constructed—must resist the temptation to believe that they themselves are approaching some ultimate truth or developing the Final Grand Theory. But such a position is very different from the claim that theory as such is impossible, or even that it is inconsequential. While the most compelling evidence of theory's failure comes from theorists, failure is not the same either as having no consequences or as decline or demise.

To return to Orr's definition, his familiar though strange claim that "theory is generally the opposite of practice" can be understood in at least three different ways. First, theory opposes practice because it critiques it, whether practice means just literary interpretation or culture, heterosexism, capitalism, history. Second, theory is a completely different enterprise from practice: it has no bearing on practice and, therefore, as Knapp and Michaels theorize, no practical consequences. A third meaning of "opposite," related to this second one, stems from the notion that theory always comes after practice (the owl of Minerva, Hegel declared, flies only at dusk). In this third sense, theory is not necessarily either irrelevant to practice (incapable of commenting on it at all) or critical of practice: it just comments on practice after the fact. Both the second and third meanings undermine the first meaning: theory as critically opposed to practice in ways capable of changing it.

A lot of antitheory theories, including Knapp and Michaels's neopragmatist manifesto, utilize disabling versions of the second and third meanings of "opposite" (irrelevant, belated). "The resistance to theory" from this perspective is also, as Zavarzadeh and Morton contend, a resistance to political radicalism (and not merely, following de Man, to the full recognition of "rhetoric"). In Knapp and Michaels's *reductio ad absurdum*, "theory . . . is taken preemptively to be an illegitimate imposition *on* practice, never a term dialectically paired with practice or the product of a theoretical moment that need not forever preclude the moment of practice" (Crewe, 55; emphasis in original). Orr's definition itself seems to restrict theory as critique to Marxism, because it concludes with the parenthetical remark that "in Marxist terminology, 'praxis' is practice informed by theory." So, one inference would seem to be that only Marxists worry about "praxis"; other forms of theory either cannot or do not try to "inform" or change practice.

Even though it identifies "praxis" with the Marxist tradition, Orr's definition does not explicitly preclude other critical relationships between theory and practice. If it is problematic, it is so mainly by being highly general and more oriented toward the sciences than toward literary or cultural fields. On its basis, it is possible to conclude that anyone who does any intellectual work whatsoever is theorizing: theory either is "abstract knowledge" or is a condition for the production of such knowledge. Similarly, in *The Significance of Theory* Eagleton says that "all social life is in some sense theoretical: even such apparently concrete, unimpeachable statements as 'pass the salt' . . . engage theoretical propositions of a kind, controvertible statements about the nature of the world" (24). This is no more helpful than Orr's definition, obviously in part because it fails to discriminate theory from any of its possible antitheses such as rhetoric or ideology. But, for Eagleton, "the significance of theory" resides in its ability to make such discriminations.

Perhaps the most widely read text on theory has been Eagleton's *Literary Theory: An Introduction* (1983). In his survey, Eagleton describes and critiques a number of the more prominent sorts of literary theory: phenomenology, hermeneutics, and reception theory; structuralism and semiotics; poststructuralism; and psychoanalysis. But his central purpose is to demonstrate that "literary theory . . . is really no more than a branch of social ideologies, utterly without any unity or identity which would adequately distinguish it from philosophy, linguistics, psychology, cultural and sociological thought" (204). Literary theory is "a chimera," because the object of its study is a chimera: "Literature, in the sense of a set of works of assured and unalterable value, distinguished by certain shared inherent properties, does not exist" (11). As a result, Eagleton declares that his book "is less an introduction than an obituary" for literary theory (204).

Eagleton's move from the literary text to rhetoric and the social text does not mean, however, that he is "against theory" in general. "Many valuable concepts" can be retrieved from literary theory "for a different kind of discursive practice altogether" (206). The recognition that literary theory is a form of ideology opens the way to social theory; merely literary criticism is or should become "political criticism" (194–217), which for Eagleton means rhetorical/ideological critique and both Marxist and feminist theory. How is this different from de Man's move from "literature" to "rhetoric" and "ideology"? de Man himself resists theory insofar as he accepts the idea that, once the theorist has identified "rhetoric" as the medium of all meanings and values, there is no definitive way to frame even relative truths as opposed to confronting the abyss of rhetoric (hence, there is no beyond to literary theory once it has deconstructed the distinction between literature and rhetoric). In contrast, Eagleton believes that the theoretical ability to identify rhetoric or ideology entails moving beyond their orbits, and therefore moving from literary into social theory. But of course arguments to the effect that theory as such is illusory or impossible do not stop with "literary theory"; they often also proclaim that social theory, at least in any grand or totalizing manner, is an impossibility. Eagleton himself contends, echoing Lyotard, that the ultimate object of theory-in-general is history, not literature, but since theory is also a product of history, constructing a "Grand Global" or "meta-theory" is "impossible" (*Significance*, 28).

Nevertheless, Eagleton thinks, theory is inevitable, because "all social life is . . . theoretical" (24). Since this argument merges theory with its usual antitheses (practice, rhetoric, ideology), Eagleton proceeds to speak of "emancipatory theory," by which he mainly means ideological critique in the Marxist tradition and which he sets over against other forms of theory that have been co-opted or "incorporated" by "late capitalism" and its well-paid professionals (including academics). "Theory can be seen as providing a flagging literary critical industry with a much-needed boost of spiritual plant and capital, largely imported" from Europe (31). But Marxism is also, for Americans and Britons alike, an import, and it also helps to give "a flagging literary critical industry . . . a . . . boost," as Eagleton's version of it has done. However, Eagleton rightly suggests that the theory hegemony can be understood *both* as an "incorporated" product of late capitalism *and* as resistance to its domination. As with Robbins, being professional and being oppositional are not necessarily antithetical. Further, theory begins precisely with the recognition of the socially situated and constructed nature of all discourse (including its own discourse). The sea of everyday life in which everyone swims consists of either rhetoric, or ideology, or both; if theory means anything (if it has any consequences), it means alertness to this condition, the human condition. But insofar as understanding anything is the necessary first step toward fixing it or letting it alone, theory also proffers the hope, at least, of opting for social change. Literary theory paradoxically becomes social theory via the linguistic turn, which means, as it does for both de Man and Eagleton, that it identifies, at least as a first stage, literature and all other discourse as rhetoric or ideology rather than either absolute truth or transcendent aesthetic value. But this opening onto rhetoric is necessarily also the opening onto the historical terrain of relative truths.

THEORIZING MODES OF DOMINATION

Perhaps the main antithesis of ideology is not theory, and certainly not science or truth of some absolute variety, but versions of critical utopianism, including works of literature and art that express the political, moral, and aesthetic claims to social justice and "the good life" mystified by ideology.[17] If theory is the space or moment in which literary criticism, on the hinge of linguistics, turns into social critique, it is also the case that an emancipatory politics is always already expressed and repressed in literature. This politics is both the ideology and the utopianism of the aesthetic, whose contradictory duality Eagleton has explored as fully as anyone since Adorno. "The construction of the modern notion of the aesthetic artefact is . . . inseparable from the construction of the dominant ideological forms of modern class-society"; nevertheless, "the aesthetic . . . provides an unusually powerful challenge and alternative to these dominant ideological forms" (Eagleton, *Ideology of the Aesthetic*, 3). The logic here is similar to that informing the idea of critic-theorists as oppositional professionals, except that now the critical "challenge and alternative" to the status quo is understood to reside within "the aesthetic artefact," or more specifically that *literature already implies, albeit in rhetorical or ideological forms, the social criticism that literary theory aspires to become.*

The various metamorphoses of literary theory into social critique by way of rhetoric and ideology are not arbitrary, but are instead responses to the "clash between the legitimation and the contestation of domination" that is "internal to expressive forms themselves" (Brenkman, 54). As "aesthetic artefact," literature may still be just as ideological as Eagleton declares it to be in *Literary Theory*; but it is simultaneously a "challenge and alternative" to the very social reality that produces it. Quite apart from those moments when works of literature explicitly voice social criticism, literature as such is a domain of the imagination antithetical to reality, and in this sense resistant also to the categories of rhetoric and ideology insofar as these work to reduce both theory and "the aesthetic dimension" to that reality.[18]

If Eagleton is right that the goals of a genuinely critical, emancipatory theory are, first, rhetorical and ideological demystification and, second, the undoing or subversion of capitalism, then everything else, from saying "pass the salt" to teaching deconstructive reading practices in graduate seminars, must be false theory or some form of ideology. But Marxism is not the only theory (or tradition of theory) that claims to be politically oppositional: so do Derridean deconstruction, feminism, queer theory, African American theory, postcolonialism, and some versions of postmodernism. In some measure, these forms of emancipatory theory draw much of their critical energy from the works of literature that each form valorizes or seeks to canonize. Emancipation from what? Logocentrism, racism, patriarchy, homophobia, and imperialism can today all be grouped under the rubric of late capitalism, which both reinforces and is reinforced by these other types of domination. But none of these types or, rather, modes of domination can be said to be the *product* of late capitalism in the same way that "the postmodern condition" is, according to Fredric Jameson, "the cultural logic of late capitalism" (*Postmodernism*). Each of these modes of domination has a history older than that of capitalism. Comparing "modes of domination" to Marx's "modes of production" makes theoretical sense, both because Marx's historical analyses of main economic configurations demonstrated that these have always also involved domination, and because, as Foucault contends, power-in-general is productive: the modes of domination are also ideological modes of production (symbolic or rhetorical capital) that are historically earlier but contributory to capitalism, the modern and modernizing economic mode of production through class domination.

Granted that social theory (literary theory may be a different, limited, or even illusory case, as Eagleton contends) should be emancipatory, which of the modes of domination should it challenge first? That there are multiple, interactive modes of domination should surprise no one except the most Panglossian believer in the status quo. That it is now possible to name, analyze, and seek to undo the common, historical modes of domination is one of the more hopeful signs of the times. Theory is one source of this hopefulness; like literature, theory speaks a language of possibility. Emancipatory theory is above all an expression of social, collective hope. It is the spark, the necessary intellectual beginning, if any of the many hopes for emancipation that both divide and unite people, societies, and cultures can be fulfilled.

Will the elimination of one mode of domination eliminate any or all of the others? Or will reaction set in and reinforce the others, as is now happening in the United States and Britain? Also, just how much (if any) domination is necessary for there to be any social formation whatever? How much emancipation is possible? No matter how pessimistically anyone answers these questions, and while anyone is free to believe that culture and literature are hopelessly ideological, culture is the site of struggle between dominant and resistant or emergent (hopefully progressive) forces, between power and (hopefully) emancipation.

Even to mention hope in this age of postmodern cynicisms, including cynical antitheory theories, is to risk being deemed hopelessly naive and untheoretical. Perhaps therefore what is needed is a theory of hope (which would also be a theory of mourning) in relation to the quite old-fashioned, yet utopian, ideals of liberty, equality, and social justice.[19] Despite cynicism, postmodernism itself can be understood in terms of utopianism (strongly laced with dystopianism). In the introduction to *Heterotopia*, Tobin Siebers writes: "It is no accident that the idea of utopia has emerged in the work of Donna Haraway, Fredric Jameson, and many others as the high concept of postmodernism" (3). So perhaps there is hope in and for the postmodern condition, after all. Further, perhaps heterotopias (plural) are new sorts of theoretical constructs to set over against the modes of domination: a multiplicity of places or prospects of freedom, based on equality-in-difference, or "a togetherness of diversity" beyond both "identity" and "contradiction" (Adorno, 150). Yet, given the collapse of the communist regimes in eastern Europe, reinforcing the global domination of a transnational capitalism to which there are currently no effective alternatives, going for rides on "the flying carpet of utopia" may seem merely fantastic, merely theoretical game playing and despair (Enzensberger, 20). Given the New World Disorder since 1989, such antiutopian, antitheoretical pessimism is understandable; nevertheless, it implies its opposite—the need for radical alternatives to the status quo.

Does each mode of domination necessitate a separate form of emancipatory theory (feminist for patriarchy, postcolonial for imperialism, etc.)? Is it really the case that, as Zavarzadeh and Morton believe, orthodox Marxism can adequately deal with the plurality of modes of domination? Even if Marxism still offers the most "global" emancipatory theory, the plurality itself—giving rise to a plurality of emancipatory theories—is not reducible to liberal pluralism. The mistake Zavarzadeh and Morton make is to conflate all versions of social critique (feminism, etc.) that are not self-evidently Marxist with capitulation to capitalism, so that only Marxism escapes being just more of the same: grist for the mill of the ruling class, under the twin complicit headings of "bourgeois literary and cultural studies" (167). Quite apart from whether the plurality of modes of domination require different emancipatory theories or forms of critique, that there can be effective but different degrees of critical enlightenment and opposition (even neopragmatism may be politically preferable to neoconservatism) Zavarzadeh and Morton do not appear to fathom.

Perhaps Derrida is right that a priority for any emancipatory theory should be the deconstruction of logocentrism. If there is a hierarchy of ideologies, then logocentrism may be at the apex, because it poses as pure theory, knowledge, truth disencumbered from common sense and practice, and from rhetoric and ideology. Thus, emancipatory theory must also be antitheory, because it deconstructs those logocentric illusions that pose as theory. Emancipatory theory does not aspire to be either an all-encompassing explanatory system or a methodology for cracking every rhetorical ploy or ideological code. It comes closer to being an intellectual stance toward other intellectual practices —one combining social critique with utopian aspiration. Certainly deconstruction can be an exemplary form of ideological critique, at least for those patient enough to follow its subtle maneuvers of discursive subversion. Every mode of domination, moreover, is obfuscated or rationalized by rhetoric and ideology, so emancipatory theory must involve rhetorical and ideological critique.[20] But to experience domination and to be aware of that experience is to begin to theorize in an emancipatory direction. Whether one calls it emancipation or enlightenment, moreover, the aim of all theory is in part the thoroughly classical one inscribed in both the Socratic and the Sophistic traditions. Even in its most apparently anti-Enlightenment forms, theory's utopianism—its desire for or goal of "noncoercive knowledge produced in the interests of human freedom" (Said, 29)—aligns it with the much-embattled Enlightenment ideals of democratic reason, liberty, equality, and fraternity (or community).

While it is possible to declare that all theory is mere rhetoric or mere ideology, or in other words that all theory is an inconsequential waste of time, such cynicism cannot begin to account for politics and history as common (communal but also everyday) struggles against modes of domination. While it is also possible to attribute such theorization to *ressentiment,* the obverse of a Nietzschean will-to-power, it makes equally good theoretical sense to attribute it to a will-to-emancipation. Moreover, the difficulty of distinguishing between theory and either rhetoric or ideology only increases the urgency to construct an adequately emancipatory theory (or theories). Given this urgency—indeed, given the current global domination of transnational capitalism—there does not seem to be any end to theory in sight. Where there is either rhetoric or ideology (which is everywhere), then there will be theory—that is, "theory as resistance" to rhetoric and ideology—for just the same reason that de Man understood theory as the resistant (in two senses) recognition of rhetoric.

Among many possible heterotopias, one can imagine an emancipatory university (or institution of critical theory), perhaps like the "free universities" of the sixties, in which each discipline or, better, antidiscipline, though in no sense rigidly separated from the others, would theorize and seek to dismantle a mode of domination through ideological and rhetorical critique. Women's and African American Studies programs are already doing so. Also, some departments of English have, tentatively, moved toward becoming departments of literary theory, poststructuralist, Marxist, feminist, gay and lesbian, postcolonial. When they haven't arisen simply as newfangled media studies with a critical edge, cultural studies programs have also encompassed several or all of these emancipatory trends. In any event, it is possible to construct, with the aid of one or more emancipatory theories, images of collective experience free of domination. It is the task of emancipatory theory to enable the construction of such images and to encourage the hope that they can be realized in practices both locally and globally, both among individuals and among all cultures and societies.

If nothing comes after theory except more rhetoric and ideology, that won't be because theory has no possible consequences, but because the central ideals of the Enlightenment remain unfulfilled—or in other words because, as Habermas has famously put it, "the project of modernity" remains "unfinished." In one direction, theory is the critique of Enlightenment; in another, it is its expression. "If we can and must be severe critics of the Enlightenment, it is Enlightenment which has empowered us to be so" (Eagleton, *Ideology of the Aesthetic*, 8). Or, as Adorno and Horkheimer declared, "the Enlightenment *must consider itself*" if humanity is "not to be wholly betrayed. The task to be accomplished is not the conservation of the past, but the redemption of the hopes of the past" (*Dialectic*; emphasis in original, xv). From this perspective, the answer to the question of what theory seeks, beyond mere rhetorical and ideological critique, becomes clear. When it isn't just cynical antitheory pointing to more of the same under the rubrics of rhetoric and ideology, theory seeks to understand and bring to practical realization the "concrete utopias" and emancipatory aspirations expressed in the aesthetic forms of all cultures and societies.

NOTES

1. The mix includes, in alphabetical but not exhaustive order, African American, ethnic, and postcolonial theories; cultural studies; deconstruction; feminism; hermeneutics; Marxism; neopragmatism; the new historicism; phenomenology; postmodernism; poststructuralism; psychoanalysis; queer theory; reader-response theory; semiotics; and structuralism.

2. But in *Professing Literature* Gerald Graff demonstrates that today's "conflicts" in the "theory wars" had their analogues, at least, throughout the history of the academic disciplining of English and American literary studies. Neoconservative and/or traditionalist narratives of decline-and-fall based on the prior "unity" provided by New Criticism ignore or downplay the contentiousness with which it was at first greeted.

3. On the antithesis between philosophy and rhetoric, see Neel, and also the introduction and several of the essays in Mailloux. For various studies focused upon the relationship between rhetoric and ideology, see Kneupper.

4. But in being based upon a politics, it is no different from older versions of canon formation, although this is something that the neoconservatives are loathe to acknowledge; to do so would entail the recognition that all literary canons, along with all other cultural hierarchies, are ideological.

5. Neoconservatives like Roger Kimball believe "theory" is how "tenured radicals" (Marxists, feminists, deconstructionists, and so on) continue their 1960s project of politicizing the academy. But this narrow view misses the fact that lit-

erary criticism has always tended to become cultural and social criticism. The neoconservatives often cite Matthew Arnold, but *Culture and Anarchy* is an obvious case of a presumably merely literary critic operating as a social critic.

6. Of course, not all versions of literary theory are overtly political, much less radical. And it is possible to be a quite traditional literary scholar, minus theory, while also being an ardent political radical and activist beyond and even within the academy.

7. As Groden and Kreisworth put it in their introduction, "The diverse, often apparently competing or incompatible approaches, perspectives, and modes of inquiry that flourish today under the generic label 'theory' have brought most scholars to a welcome awareness of the importance of attending at least to methodological concerns in critical practice" (ix).

8. Nor do they contain entries under "literary theory." Makaryk's *Encyclopedia* has an entry for "critical theory," meaning the work of the Frankfurt Institute philosophers (Adorno et al.).

9. "Reading in de Man's definition always expresses a rhetoric of mourning" (Siebers, "Mourning" 363). Heidegger's claim that spirit or *Geist* entails "nostalgia for its own essence" could be rewritten: theory is nostalgia or mourning for a theoretical finality that it knows it cannot attain (Heidegger quoted in Derrida, *Of Spirit*, 80).

10. Further, several recent publications whose titles announce the demise of theory also simultaneously imply its miraculous rebirth. *The Wake of Deconstruction* (Johnson) and *After Poststructuralism* (Easterlin and Riebling), for example, are titles whose double meanings involve the now familiar poststructuralist trope of the apocalyptic pun. Such-and-such is ending (history, for instance) but wait a minute . . . it is really just beginning, or anyway its aim or purpose or end has yet to be ascertained. "Rumors about the death of deconstruction," Johnson says, "have always already been exaggerated" (17).

11. Lacan insists that "there is no meta-language" (188), or in other words that there can be no theory about language (and therefore also about the unconscious, which "is structured like a language") that is not composed of words, those units of desire which, like Zeno's arrow, forever outrun themselves while never reaching their mark.

12. Eagleton sees de Man as offering "penetrating insights" into many subjects, but also as a key figure in the poststructuralist extension of Nietzsche's radical subversion of all forms of rationality and knowledge, through which "rhetoric took its terrible revenge" by "contaminating" everything. But this was a radicalism with depoliticizing effects. "In retreat from marketplace to study, politics to philology, social practice to semiotics, rhetoric was to end up as that vigorous demystifier of all ideology that itself provided the final ideological rationale for political inertia" (*Walter Benjamin*, 108).

13. According to Žižek: "Ideology is not a dreamlike illusion that we build to escape insupportable reality; in its basic dimension it is a fantasy-construction which serves as a support for our 'reality' itself. . . . The function of ideology is not to offer us a point of escape from our reality but to offer us the social reality itself as an escape from some traumatic, real kernel" (45).

14. In theorizing the relationship between ideology and rhetoric from a

poststructuralist perspective, moreover, one must also take account of Lacan's insistence that "the unconscious is structured like a language," and also that it is only through interminable speaking or writing that desire and subjectivity make themselves known. From this perspective, either ideology and rhetoric are just different words for the same category of our unknowing alienation through or within language, or else ideology is the creature of rhetoric, perhaps a specific and limited offshoot of the Symbolic Order or the language which speaks us more than the other way around.

15. Theories that assert the social-constructedness of all forms of knowledge, culture, subjectivity, gender identity, and so forth can either take a deterministic direction, as in Althusser's theory of ideology, or an apparently antithetical direction, toward claims of at least partial human and even individual agency, as in Judith Butler's performance theory of gender.

16. Robbins's main example is feminist critic-theorists.

17. One objection to such a view is that many familiar utopian fantasies (Plato's *Republic,* More's *Utopia,* and so forth) dissolve social contradictions and differences by way of a unifying ruthlessness that seems totalitarian. Such utopias, in other words, are versions of ideology all over again. But "concrete utopias," as Ernst Bloch contends, inform every emancipatory movement, and these are not necessarily marked by false ideological or rhetorical closure. "The mistake of traditional thinking is that identity is taken for the goal," Adorno writes; instead, "nonidentity is the secret *telos* of identification. It is the part that can be salvaged" (*Negative Dialectics,* 149). What Adorno has in mind involves a reconfiguration of utopian aspiration in terms of difference (or "nonidentity") rather than identity: "Utopia would be above identity and above contradiction; it would be a togetherness of diversity" (150). Compare Siebers on "heterotopias."

18. While, from a psychoanalytic perspective, literature may be reducible to collective daydreams or wish fulfillments (the rhetoric and/or ideology of the unconscious), these daydreams are, as Ernst Bloch argues, a repository of utopian images. But this is quite different from saying that every literary work is or should be an explicit utopian fantasy. Reducing literature and the other arts to the straightjackets of traditional utopian fantasies (many of which can easily be read as dystopias) is an error directly related to its apparent opposite: the reduction of "the aesthetic dimension" to an affirmative, idealistic transcendence of politics and the social.

19. Partly through Nietzsche, partly through psychoanalysis, and partly through feminism, *desire* has been central in recent theoretical discourse. A theory of hope would have to distinguish it as at least potentially collective and rational, making for the common good, as opposed to individual and irrational. Besides older starting points in political theory and ethics, some of the ingredients of a theory of hope are evident in, for instance, Derrida's stress on Walter Benjamin's "weak messianism" in *Specters of Marx* and Habermas's emphasis on "the ideal speech situation" in *Theory of Communicative Action.* See also Raymond Williams, *Resources of Hope;* Cornel West, *Prophetic Thought in Postmodern Times;* Ernst Bloch, *Das Prinzip Hoffnung;* and Tobin Siebers's anthology *Heterotopia.*

20. There are various names for each of the ideologies corresponding to each mode of domination, but playing double roles of signification are the names of the modes themselves: logocentrism, patriarchy, racism, homophobia, imperialism. Capitalism is an economic mode of domination/production whose most directly correspondent ideologies are: political conservatism and liberalism, economic free enterprise or free marketism, antiegalitarian rationalizations of social class hierarchies, and notions of value not based on labor.

THIRTEEN

Courting Community in Contemporary Culture

Thomas S. Frentz
Janice Hocker Rushing

But since, for better or worse, the mystery of hierarchy is forever
with us, let us, as students of rhetoric, scrutinize its range of
entrancements, both with dismay and in delight.
> —Kenneth Burke, *A Rhetoric of Motives*

Through our own habituated capacity as audience to reflect on,
engage in, or resist the call of discourse, we can help to decide
whether ours is a culture of wrath and destruction or a rhetorical
culture of *communitas*.
> —Thomas B. Farrell, *Norms of Rhetorical Culture*

And lo and behold! Apollo found it impossible to live without
Dionysos.
> —Friedrich Nietzsche, *The Birth of Tragedy*

With increasing regularity, communication conferences are scheduling panels featuring prominent spokespersons in rhetoric and cultural studies.
Typically, the promos for these affairs promise bracketed egos, suspended
ideologies, and invigorated dialogue. This never happens. Despite a common quest to understand the role of communication in culture, panelists
intellectually imitate the bellicose sporting events audience members must
often forego in order to attend instead of collaborating in a spirit of
give-and-take. While some of this can be bemusedly enjoyed as the cathar-
tic aggressive rituals of the academic elite, there seems to be something

more going on here, an animosity that belies the stylized posturing of each field's annointed "single-combat warriors."

Whereas we are not above relishing the leisure of the theory class, in our soberer moments we find these rites disappointing. We have strong ties to both fields, being raised on rhetoric—the language of democracy, but initiated by popular culture—the intercourse of the imagination. Because we believe that these two discourses are always related—indeed, in many instances are the same—we are distressed that the fields grown up to study them inhabit such different scholastic orbs. Separate living arrangements are also anathema to the origins of both fields. Rhetoric, conceived in classical times as the art of persuasion applicable to any subject matter, transgressed boundaries from its beginnings. And the original project of cultural studies, as Graham Murdock reminds us, "was precisely to disregard formal divisions between disciplines and fields and to work in the cracks, both theoretically and politically. It was a celebration of trespass and border violations in the interests of constructing a more complete analysis of culture" ("Across," 91). Neither rhetoric nor cultural studies by itself seems adequate to comprehend the intersections of institution and myth, to nourish the appetites for negotiation *and* narrative.

Like the children of divorce, we have sought fostering from a mix of surrogates—most importantly, for us, in depth psychology and cultural anthropology. With the optimism of the matchmaker and in the temper of this book, however, we think our ideal parents should make a date. As the following ethnographic interlude demonstrates, this may not be easy. Although some of what follows actually happened, most of it has been altered for rhetorical purposes.

>   *It's well after midnight, and we're holed up in the conference hotel bar. After our third grueling day of conventioneering, we are wearing down and* they *are wearing thin. Second-hand smoke coats our contacts and agitates our allergies. But we hang in there for our meeting with her—a friend and rising star in cultural studies—because, as she apologized to us earlier, this is the only time slot she has open.*
>
>   *But it's late. One of us, foolishly preempting some closing line of the other, ventures to her, "You know, as I was watching you this afternoon on that Rhetoric and Cultural Studies panel, well, I just got this feeling that you—how can I put this?—that you were really uncomfortable with those rhetoric types. Am I close here?"*
>
>   *"Let me tell you," she cuts us off, " 'uncomfortable' just doesn't get it. I mean where do those bozos get off? They just sit there with their prissy white male wannabe literary critic noses in the air as if they're slumming to be in the same room with me!"*

"They did seem a tad distant," we offer supportively.

"I mean they're totally innocent of how their own theories just reproduce the oppressive power structures they claim to explain. And that was true even when those theories were in vogue, and, lest we forget, 'in vogue' was 2,500 years ago."

"Huh," is about as good as we can do right now.

"And they still see a speech *as a 'hot' cultural practice, when the last one anybody can even remember was 'I Have a Dream.' They think if you add a dash of TV and a pinch of ideology to the Greek polis and stir, you'll get 'culture.' "*

"They haven't even theorized their own problematics," we offer, trying to talk the talk if not walk the walk.

"Exactly! And you know what else? They're old, stodgy, conservative, and don't know how to dress."

Thinking, *"but some of our best friends are rhetoricians,"* and trying not to check out our own attire, we slip away on the one-liner we should have used earlier, heading for the elevator. Almost out, we hear the familiar voice of one of these best friends, sitting alone at the end of the bar, preoccupied with the ice melting in his glass. We can't help but notice that he *does* look old and he *doesn't* know how to dress.

After a few *"and-how's-your-year-been?"* openers, he shifts uneasily on his barstool, as if he's not sure he wants to get into what he's already bringing up.

"You know, I probably shouldn't get started, but I couldn't help overhearing that little psychodrama just inflicted on you back there. I usually blow these things off as cases of arrested puberty, but seeing that I played an unnamed bit part on that panel this afternoon, I'm more than a little defensive."

"Oh, she was just tired," we suggest hopefully.

"Like hell she was!" he shouts, not sounding prissy or literary at all. *"I'll tell you something. I'm about as fed up with her type as she seems to be with mine."*

"So—just what is 'her type,' do you think?"

"It's that damn, self-righteous 'I speak for OTHER' garbage—that supercilious voice of the politically correct! You ever read their *stuff?"*

"Well, yes, actually—on occasion . . . "

"They have no respect for anything beautiful. They can reduce a van Gogh to neurotic desire—a Beethoven symphony to false consciousness. They're so busy 'fastening on to floating signifiers,' 'locating sites of resistance,' and 'decentering self-presence' (whatever that means) that they don't see the only 'cult'

in 'cultural studies' is groupies who think obscurity is cool. They produce this overtheorized, polysyllabic rubbish whose only meaning is that it doesn't mean anything."

"Yeah—well—their stuff can be sort of tedious," we inject, exchanging a glance acknowledging our hypocrisy.

"But they, of course, unlike any of us, do vitally important cultural work, like figuring out how some poor schluck is 'resisting hegemonic oppression' by decoding Monday Night Football oppositionally. Give me a break. And another thing, in my book, football is not a text *and you don't* read *it, you* watch *it! I'm sorry. It's late and I'm crabby. Time for my Geritol, as she would no doubt remind me."*

We make it to our room, leave a wake-up call because we can't set digital alarms, and hope that the rum will outweigh the Coke in the coming contest between slumber and insomnia. It doesn't, and we're left wondering how these two decent people, both reasonable and amiable in most ways, could live in such different worlds when it comes to culture.

Rhetorical and cultural studies scholars do share some common ground. Most from either realm would find little to dislike in Raymond Williams's notion that the analysis of culture is "the study of relationships between elements in a whole way of life," which includes art, learning, institutions, and ordinary behavior (*Long Revolution,* 57, 63). Both also profess a hope, if not always an optimism, that their respective fields will contribute to a better society. "Cultural studies," writes Lawrence Grossberg, "is driven by its attempt to respond to history, to what matters in the world of political struggle" (*We Gotta,* 18). And rhetoric, according to Thomas Farrell, "has always been a practiced imperfection, the worst fear of idealized reason and the best hope for whatever remains of civic life" (1). If both fields are politically committed to a better "whole way of life," why, then, the rancor? We think it stems from the different "elements" of Williams' "culture" in which each group invests its prospects for change.

Traditionally, rhetoricians have studied how people struggle for power and make collective decisions through persuasive discourse *within legitimate social institutions,* including government, mass media, the law, and education. Assuming the necessity of such structures, rhetoric values public speech, official rites, negotiation, consensus. Admittedly, our macroscopic perspective here underplays the focus of some on extrainstitutional rhetorics. Still, though he states the case more baldly than many (especially contemporary) rhetoricians would, Roderick Hart articulates the centrist rhetorical agenda when he argues:

(1) that deliberative, not cultural, discourse most powerfully affects the policy options available to the average citizen; (2) that discourse about the disbursement of public monies, and about the statutory regulation of private monies, ultimately constrains all other discourse in a modernist society; (3) that it takes a certain kind of expertise to track policy-impinging rhetoric. (74)

In radical opposition, cultural studies sees hierarchical structures as oppressive and repressive of individual freedoms, and wants to expose the constructedness of even those social relations, such as "everyday life," that seem the most "natural." Political empowerment of the oppressed occurs *outside legitimate social institutions,* and only in resistance to those structures. Arguing the historical contingency of such structures, cultural studies values popular culture, everyday behavior, resistance, conflict. Although its agenda is varied and conflicted, Graeme Turner aptly captures its impulse:

> Work in cultural studies has consistently addressed itself to the interrogation of society's structures of domination. It has focused most particularly on the experience of the working class and, more recently, on that of women as locations where the action of oppressive power relations can be examined. In its theoretical tradition, it is inextricably linked with a critical European Marxism that seeks to understand how capitalist societies work and how to change them. . . . Popular culture is a site where the construction of everyday life may be examined. (5)

At its most basic level, we would conclude, the conflict between rhetoric and cultural studies is over which aspect of culture contributes most directly to the good life.

Let us return for a moment to Williams's directions for the analysis of culture as "the study of relationships between elements in a whole way of life," this time with the accent on *relationships.* Changes in our way of life, he says, are fought out in the world of art and ideas, and "it is when we try to correlate change of this kind with the changes covered by the disciplines of politics, economics, and communications that we discover some of the most difficult but also some of the most human questions" ("Long Revolution," 12). What if we could forge a way of thinking that accepts the necessity of both hierarchy and equality, that not only theorizes, but *honors* the relationships between structures and resistance to them? Such a conception would meet people where they really live more completely than one that values one part of a whole. Furthermore, we think that such correlations are best assembled at the intersection of rhetoric and cultural studies. Thus, we offer here an integrated view of culture based on the necessary connections between structures and their antitheses, and on the way these connections have changed over time (see Figure 13.1). We then revisit the stereotypes enacted by our two barmates, attempting to mine their grudges to reveal how rhetoric and cultural studies both facilitate and inhibit the union we seek.

On the diagonals, *structure* is related to *communitas* by *degrees of connectedness,* while the vertical axis, bounded by *community* and *fragmentation,* defines a *continuum of cultural states* that changes over time. When structure and communitas are closely related to one another, we experience more communal forms of cultural life; that is, in terms of the figure, we move up the vertical axis. Conversely, when structure becomes disengaged from communitas, community atrophies and our cultural experience is more fragmented and individualistic—we move down the vertical axis.

Our framework synthesizes constructs from two eclectic thinkers, Kenneth Burke and Victor Turner. Curiously, Burke is lionized in rhetoric and ignored in cultural studies, while Turner is mostly overlooked by both. Richly steeped in Marx and Freud, two immensely influential figures in cultural studies, Burke keeps the right company. But because he uses Freudian and Marxist ideas more than he is used by them, he often says, at least to

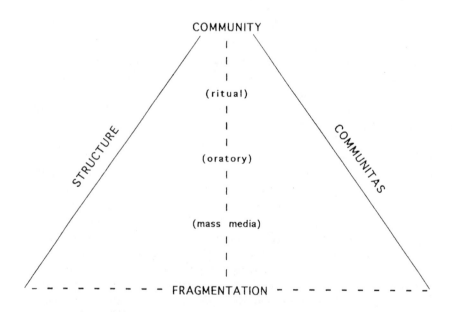

FIGURE 13.1. An integrated view of culture. This diagram schematizes how the major elements of culture change over time.

devotees, the wrong things about the right people. And it would seem that Turner, who has contributed much to the understanding of ritual in society, would appeal to the anthropological contingent within cultural studies, as well as to the recent "performance turn" within rhetoric (e.g., Ivie, "Rhetorical Knowledge," "Rhetorical Criticism"). Perhaps his concentration on so-called primitive societies is deemed irrelevant to contemporary rhetoric and culture, and his anthropological rather than semiotic view of myth and ritual marks him as unsuited to cultural studies theorizing.

Whatever their shortcomings among true believers, we want to bracket their misgivings for a while in order to explore how Burke and Turner think about culture in ways that preserve Williams's charge to study the relationships between elements in culture as a whole way of life. Specifically, we exploit their conceptualizations of a dialectical tension that is central to all cultures. For Burke, the dialectic is between *division* and *identification*, the "ambiguities of substance": "Identification is affirmed with earnestness precisely because there is division. Identification is compensatory to division. If men were not apart from one another, there would be no need for the rhetorician to proclaim their unity" (*Rhetoric*, 22). For Turner, it is between *structure* and *communitas*. There are two major models for human relatedness, he claims, "juxtaposed and alternating":

> The first is of society as a structured, differentiated, and often hierarchical system of politico-legal-economic positions with many types of evaluation, separating men in terms of 'more' or 'less.' The second . . . is of society as an unstructured or rudimentarily structured and undifferentiated *comitatus*, community, or even communion of equal individuals who submit together to the general authority of the ritual elders. (*Ritual Process*, 96)

"Spontaneous" or "existential" communitas, which exists in all societies, levels hierarchy and celebrates equality; it has something "magical" about it, generating a "feeling of endless power." But this feeling by itself is not sufficient for organizing the details of social existence, such as the need for mobilization of resources and social control. Thus, pure spontaneous communitas cannot substitute for lucid thought and sustained will (132–139). On the other hand, organized structure "swiftly becomes arid and mechanical if those involved in it are not periodically immersed in the regenerative abyss of communitas," which can, if only briefly, "burn out" or "wash away" the accumulated sins of structure (139, 180). These opposites, like figure and ground in Gestalt psychology, "constitute one another and are mutually indispensable" (97, 127), and "no society can function adequately without this dialectic" (129).

It could be objected, of course, that positing such an opposition merely retrofits the social world into yet another outdated, totalizing modernist dualism. We do not pretend to explain all of cultural life in terms of this single distinction. We do, however, claim that the tension is both ubiquitous and heuristic, as is evident in the fact that many of the theories central to both rhetoric and cultural studies have posited it in forms that are roughly analogous. Friedrich Nietzsche locates the apex of classical Greek art in tragedy, that ideal collaboration of the Apollonian worship of individuated forms and Dionysian force that forever dissolves and re-creates them. Marx invokes the tension between hierarchy and revolution to dramatize what he calls, significantly, "dialectical materialism." Thomas Kuhn casts the history of science into a normal science/revolutionary science opposition that foregrounds the rhetorical foundation of scientific progress. Sigmund Freud grounds his view of the psyche and the causes of neuroses, both individual and collective, in the relentless clash of consciousness with the unconscious. Jacques Lacan sees the opposition between the Symbolic and the Imaginary as pivotal to understanding how desire is worked out in language. In her feminist twist on Lacan, Julia Kristeva contrasts two levels of language, the symbolic and the chora, arguing that the latter always intrudes into and erupts through the former. Even Chaos Theory, the current scientific revolution disrupting normal science, posits an opposition between order and chaos, showing how simple physical systems exhibit complex underlying structures, and how complex, nonlinear systems have their own deeper stabilities. Our point here is not to claim innocence by association, but rather to suggest that the strains between structure and communitas, while perhaps no more "natural" than any other language opposition, offer a particularly rich inroad into varied aspects of cultural, aesthetic, psychological, and even physical life.

STRUCTURE AND COMMUNITAS

Although Turner focuses primarily on preliterate societies, all forms of cultural life, he maintains, pursue both hierarchical structure and egalitarian communitas. Similarly, Burke tells us, the principle of hierarchy "is inevitable to human thought" (*Rhetoric*, 141). As if already tuned to protests against essentialism, however, he qualifies:

> To say that hierarchy is inevitable is not to say that any particular hierarchy is inevitable; the crumbling of hierarchies is as true a fact about them as their formation. But to say that the hierarchic principle is indigenous to all well-rounded human thinking, is to state a very important fact

about the rhetorical appeal of dialectical symmetry. And it reminds us, on hearing talk of equality, to ask ourselves, without so much as questioning the possibility that things might be otherwise: "Just how does the hierarchic principle work in this particular scheme of things?" (141)

Although the criteria for hierarchical rankings may vary from physical strength to material possessions, the *principle* of hierarchy, Burke reminds us, is inevitable. But doesn't grounding culture in the inevitability of structure guarantee the continued oppression of the Other? Jean Baker Miller makes a pertinent distinction. She speaks of relationships based on "temporary inequality" like those between parents and children, teachers and students, doctors and patients, master craftsperson and novice. These are culturally defined disparities "*based in service* to the lesser party," the goal being the end of the inequality, as children become adults, students become citizens, patients become healed, and novices become craftspersons (4); thus, they are acceptable even when the ultimate goal is an egalitarian community. By contrast, "permanent inequalities" are those defined by ascription, such as race, sex, class, nationality, or religion (6). Miller paints in all too familiar strokes:

> Here, the terms of the relationship are very different from those of temporary inequality. There is . . . no notion that superiors are present primarily to help inferiors, to impart to them their advantages and "desireable" characteristics. There is no assumption that the goal of the unequal relationship is to end the inequality; in fact, quite the reverse. (6)

There are profound difficulties in terminating temporary asymmetries, which tend too often to freeze into permanent and debilitating dominator relationships, as cultural studies has so effectively documented. But hierarchical structures have always been central to the maintenance of cultural life. And since, as Burke implies, any specific hierarchy is rhetorically constructed, it can be deconstructed as well.

Burke claims that structure is grounded in division, and division produces mystery (*Rhetoric*, 114–117). We experience mystery, Burke says, as the estrangement among ranks in a hierarchy.

> Mystery arises at that point where different *kinds* of beings are in communication. In mystery there must be *strangeness*; but the estranged must also be thought of as in some way capable of communion . . . [T]he conditions for "mystery" are set by *any* pronounced social distinctions, as between nobility and commoners, courtiers and king, leader and people, rich and poor, judge and prisoner at the bar, "superior race" and underprivileged "races" or minorities. (115)

And, as Turner puts it, "There is a mystery of mutual distance, what the poet Rilke called 'the circumspection of human gesture,' which is just as humanly important as the mystery of intimacy" (*Ritual Process,* 138). We negotiate the mysteries of hierarchy, Burke continues, through rhetorical acts of "courtship" (*Rhetoric,* 115–116). Exploiting its psychoanalytic lineage as well as its aristocratic connotations, Burke implies in courtship a longing for relationship by moving up and down a hierarchy. Such relationship, however transient, is "identification," whereby estranged others become consubstantial, of one substance, by which Burke means an *acting-together,* as opposed to the more static alternative of possessing common essences (21).

The hierarchic principle, Burke explains, is "complete only when each rank accepts the *principle of gradation itself,* and in thus 'universalizing' the principle, makes a spiritual *reversal* of the ranks just as meaningful as their actual material arrangement" (138). What "courtship" seeks, in Turner's terms, is communitas, which produces this reversal of the ranks by "break[ing] in through the interstices of structure, in liminality; at the edges of structure, in marginality; and from beneath structure, in inferiority" (*Ritual Process,* 128). In communitas, individuals "are not segmentalized into roles and status but confront one another rather in the manner of Martin Buber's 'I and Thou' " (132). When humans relate in this way as "total beings," they tend to generate symbols and metaphors, and "art and religion are their products rather than legal and political structures" (128). Nietzsche's description of Dionysiac ritual, fundamental to the art and religion of ancient Greece, is a prime example:

> Now the slave emerges as a freeman; all the rigid, hostile walls which either necessity or despotism has erected between men are shattered. Now that the gospel of universal harmony is sounded, each individual becomes not only reconciled to his fellow but actually at one with him—as though the veil of Maya had been torn apart and there remained only shreds floating before the vision of mystical Oneness. (23)

The magic of the rite, however fleeting, reconstituted the bonds between person and person.

Attempts to stabilize communitas into permanent equality are doomed to " 'decline and fall' into structure and law," according to Turner, who examines several extended cases, such as the early Franciscans of medieval Europe, and the Sahajiyas of fifteenth- and sixteenth-century India (*Ritual Process,* 131–165). The more we try oxymoronically to structure communitas, the more it eludes our grasp. "Rhetoric," which Burke refers to as "the Scramble" and "the Human Barnyard," suffuses both the attempts to come and stay together, and the inevitability of "the state of

Babel after the Fall." It has its peaceful moments in which, Burke says, sounding much like Turner on communitas, "it can move from the factional to the universal."

> But its ideal culminations are more often beset by strife as the condition of their organized expression, or material embodiment. Their very universality becomes transformed into a partisan weapon. For one need not scrutinize the concept of "identification" very sharply to see, implied in it at every turn, its ironic counterpart: division. (*Rhetoric*, 23)

So, while communitas resists the excesses of structure, it can never substitute for it, for when it does, it transforms into that which it once stood against. Structure and communitas are necessarily symbiotic.

COMMUNITY AND FRAGMENTATION

The community-fragmentation axis depicts a continuum of cultural conditions varying from small, homogeneous, and close-knit on one end, to complex, heterogeneous, and fragmented on the other. Much has been made, of course, of "fragmentation" as a defining element of the postmodern condition; our particular take on its causes is that when the connections bonding structure to communitas weaken and begin to break down, cultural life becomes increasingly splintered. This has happened over time with changes in the forms of communication that contest structure in an attempt to reestablish communitas.[1] In a macroscopic sense, these communicative forms have changed from ritualistic in tribal or preliterate times to oratorical in classical times to technologically mediated in modern and postmodern times. While it might be objected that the structure-communitas dialectic is irrelevant to contemporary, mass-mediated societies in which structure is more something to be resisted than mediated, we believe that such a claim assumes too clean a break between historical eras. "We have abandoned," James Carey says, "the struggle to find the irreducible difference between the 'primitive' and the modern mind":

> Once the intellectual membrane separating the primitive from the modern mind was pierced, influence ran in both directions. The mind of the savage [sic] slowly yielded its logical structure, and patterns of primitive, though not therefore erroneous, forms of intellection among modern man, stood out in bolder relief. ("Mass Communication Research," 423)

The impulse to juxtapose structure and communitas persists in the postindustrial era, we think, even though the relationship between them is more one of struggle than of rhythmical alternation. In what follows, we complete the integrated view of culture we are developing by discussing in very general terms the changes from ritual to oratorical to mass-mediated communication as the primary ways to intercede with structure. This should further enable us to highlight reasons for the enmity between rhetoric and cultural studies, as well as ways in which they may be able to come together.

Ritual

In tribal and agrarian cultures, according to Turner, communitas takes the form of performed rituals that reflect or comment upon structure from a frame that is temporarily or permanently removed from it. Following Arnold Van Gennep's treatment of *rites de passage,* Turner discusses "liminal rituals" as marked by three phases: separation, margin or *limen* ("threshold"), and aggregation. Individuals are first separated from a fixed status or set of cultural conditions and placed in a liminal realm of the now that has few attributes of the past or future. As a transition rather than a state, liminality is frequently likened to death, being in the womb, invisibility, darkness, bisexuality, wilderness, or the eclipse of the sun or moon (*Ritual Process,* 95). For example, the installation rites of a tribal chief and his wife may induce a liminal condition in which they are ritually chided and ridiculed, made to go naked, stripped of their wealth, and otherwise humiliated (97–102). The whole tribe participates in a reversal of status that can be compared to comedy, for both involve mockery and inversion, but not destruction, of structural rules and overzealous adherence to them (201). Though the chief couple is eventually reintegrated into the tribe, the humility of the liminal condition ideally carries over into their position, tempering their pride. "Liminality," says Turner, "implies that the high could not be high unless the low existed, and [s/]he who is high must experience what it is like to be low" (97).

Communitas may also manifest itself in characters who are inferior or marginal to structured society. Many cultures believe in "the powers of the weak" that attach to someone poor, deformed, or mentally defective (109). Symbolic figures such as "simpletons," "third sons," "holy beggars," and "little tailors" frequently populate folk literature; their role is to "strip off the pretensions of holders of high rank and office and reduce them to the level of common humanity and mortality" (110). The long tradition of the court jester or fool, often a person of low class, a dwarf, or another such oddity, is an example of a marginal and "inferior" character who is given license to gibe at the king and courtiers, or lord of the manor, allowed to express comically feelings of outraged morality, whereas others could not (109). The fool and the king are thought to be divinely inspired, and it is the fool's function to remind the king of his mortality, to help him guard against *hubris*. His presence in the inner court "serve[s] the ruling powers as a constant reminder that the urge to anarchy exists in human nature and that it must be taken into account" (Sallie Nichols, 29–30). Prophets and artists also tend to be marginal and liminal people, according to Turner, "edgemen" who strive to get beyond the cliches of status.

In sum, liminality, marginality, and structural inferiority are conditions that reclassify humanity's relationship to nature and to society, and that, according to Turner, incite people to action as well as to thought (*Ritual Process,* 128–129). Acts of communitas mock hierarchy in a symbolic reminder that any structure built to serve the many can be deconstructed when it comes to privilege the few. In preindustrial cultures, then, structure is closely connected, by implicit social contract, to its own negation in communitas. At regular intervals and in physical proximity with one another, the high and the low participate together in rituals designed to remind them that they are identified, even within the divisions of rank. In "being there," these rituals liquefy the solids of hierarchy, if only for a time.

Oratory

Classical Greece obviously does not adequately represent all cultures at a midpoint between preliterate and postmodern. Neither is it the only tradition of rhetoric, which certainly exists in unsystematized forms in preindustrial cultures such as those studied by Turner. But it is the flowering of oratory in fifth-century B.C. Athens, particularly as documented by Aristotle in the *Rhetoric,* that carries the discipline of rhetoric into the twentieth century, and thus is relevant to our present concerns. As the twin of democracy, the golden idea of rhetoric is that disputes among equals over contingent issues can be mediated by *reasoned argument* among citizens of the *polis* in an arena designed for public speaking. "Formally speaking," writes Farrell in his defense of Aristotelian rhetoric for contemporary life, "rhetoric is the collaborative art of addressing and guiding decision and judgment—usually public judgment about matters that cannot be decided by force or expertise" (1). The rationality and immediacy of classical oratory—that is, speaker and audience share the same unmediated space in reasoned debate—is no doubt one source of contemporary rhetorical scholars' nostalgia for this "better way."

Although by almost any measure a noble and necessary invention, already divisions between structure and communitas that would amplify in modernity had sprouted in the ancients' rhetorical culture. As coperformed rituals gave way to structured *address,* contemporary divisions between encoder and decoder were prefigured in speaker and audience. When rea-

soned argument replaced performance rituals as a way to check the aspirations of power, the dualities that create "other" intensified, for, as we are
now acutely aware, difference is inscribed in language; it is "always already
there" as the carrier of meaning. Indeed, rhetoric always worked more
within structure than against it, having been conceived as the art of negotiating differences within the legitimate institutions of the state. Furthermore,
Athenian society was divided into three tiers, a ruling *polis* (the primary
participants in rhetoric); ordinary citizens; and women, slaves, and barbari-
ans. Not only could individuals of the latter two categories rarely enter the
rhetorical arena, but if they did their argumentative premises had to be
based in opinions shared by members of the *polis*. Liminal regions where
hierarchy could be critiqued or dissolved were sustained in other art forms,
most particularly drama, but they were not entered into incarnate by those
making the decisions of government. Setting a pattern that persists in the
academic frictions that open this essay, rhetoric thus became more allied
with structure than its opposition, as the homogeneous communities of
premodernity were replaced by the relatively heterogeneous *polis* and complex social orders of the Renaissance and the Enlightenment eras.

Mass-Mediated Communication

The move from ritual and oratory to electronic mass media profoundly
reconfigures the relationship between structure and communitas. The old
connections, based upon face-to-face contact and shared linguistic premises, are irreparably severed. Some theorists of technological media see
new kinds of connections being forged, but most agree that communities
becomes increasingly fragmented as media insert themselves between governing hierarchies and their egalitarian critiques. We attempt here briefly to
capture some of the controversy about the effects of electronic media in
terms of what happens to the relationship between structure and
communitas.

As one of the earliest visionaries of media's massive effects on human
relationships, Marshall McLuhan is the most prominent exception to the
theoretical tilt toward fragmentation. Viewing what Turner calls "structure" as divisions among people caused by the unconscious effects of linear
media, especially print, McLuhan sees the pure informational qualities of
electricity as "retribalizing" the world into a sort of hard-wired "global village" in which each person participates intimately in the lives of others,
reestablishes oral over visual modes of communication, and lives according
to myth rather than logic (3–21). In this decentralized planetary community, the hierarchies dominating the industrial age are flattened, seemingly
replaced with one giant form of perpetual worldwide communitas.

Certainly, McLuhan is one of the first to recognize the radically reconfiguring potential of electronic media. But Turner, no doubt, would temper McLuhan's grand utopianism, for he does not share the view that tribal cultures themselves, supposedly reinstantiated by electricity, are nonstructured. McLuhan would seem to make the same error as Turner attributes to Rousseau and to Marx—the confusion between communitas, a dimension of all societies, and primitive or archaic societies (*Ritual Process*, 130). Structure is not eliminated by mass communication, in Turner's view, but it is mediated in a fundamentally different way—by what he calls the "liminoid" (meaning "like," "resembling" liminal) productions of postindustrial societies (*Ritual to Theatre*, 20–60). Technology has proliferated the forms of communitas, for the dismemberment of ritual provides the opportunity for the many desacralized performative genres that now reflect on culture. Liminoid forms of communitas are no longer tied to the sacred, and can be found at various levels of class structure. Whereas Turner sees the liminoid productions of mass mediated cultures as freer than the liminal acts of tribal ones, they achieve this posture through the progressive *separation* of communitas from structure, and thus their consequences for structure are not nearly as profound.

Adopting Carey's ritual view of mass communication as " 'not directed toward the extension of messages in space but the maintenance of society in time; not the act of imparting information but the representation of shared beliefs' " (504), Horace Newcomb and Paul Hirsch also see mass communication as more fragmenting than liminal rituals, but still able to negotiate, rather than merely to reflect, dominant structures. They invoke Turner's discussion of the liminal (they really mean liminoid, as they imply in a footnote) to study television, which they think performs what John Fiske and John Hartley call the "bardic function" of contemporary societies (85). That is, television "does not present firm ideological conclusions . . . so much as it *comments on* ideological problems. . . . " "Our most traditional views, those that are repressive and reactionary, as well as those that are subversive and emancipatory, are upheld, examined, maintained, and transformed" (Newcomb and Hirsch, 508, 506). Concentrating on "viewing strips" that transgress the boundaries of individual programs and genres, they suggest that television reconstitutes a "cultural forum" within which issues are raised for viewer consideration. As they point out, theirs is a decidedly rhetorical approach, similar to the classical sense in which participants actively deliberate about political issues, and it opposes the view that sees media as always upholding the values of structure. Still, television is a pluralistic forum within the very real limits of American monopoly-capitalism (508). As in Turner's view, then, the cultural forum cannot have the same immediate effects as do liminal rituals within a society in which structure and communitas are parts of an integrated whole.

Unlike McLuhan's mythic retribalization and the less celebratory ritual views of communication based on Turner, the last three theorists we consider—Donna Haraway, Jean Baudrillard, and Vivian Sobchack—cast their bets boldly with the fragmenting rather than with the communalizing effects of mass communication technology. Haraway shares McLuhan's optimistic vision concerning technology in general, but for radically different reasons. In this technological age, she declares, we are all cyborgs—penetrating and penetrated by the machine. When technology fuses with people, the old linguistic dichotomies such as male-female are replaced with the unstable trichotomy male/female/cyborg. It is the very *shattering* of these patriarchal structures that liberates the "other." But, whereas McLuhan celebrates the intimacy of a reconnected, imploded world, Haraway cheers the loss of the mythic "garden," for it is just that kind of "innocence" that gives rise to dualities.

> That is why cyborg politics insist on noise and advocate pollution, rejoicing in the illegitimate fusions of animal and machine. These are couplings which make Man and Woman so problematic, subverting the structure of desire, the force imagined to generate language and gender, and so subverting the structure and modes of reproduction of "Western" identity, of nature and culture, of mirror and eye, slave and master, body, and mind. (176)

Lauding cyborg imagery as "a powerful infidel heteroglossia," it is as if she discovers a sort of communitas within the breakdown of structure—definitely not as an alternating and alternative collective participatory act, but as a kind of fortuitous accident. Culture *is* fragmenting, says Haraway, and it's about time.

Finally, both Sobchack and Baudrillard agree that postmodern culture is progressively fragmenting, but their views constitute a lament. Technology fosters the illusion that nothing has changed, when, in fact, everything has changed. Like McLuhan, they see the change in terms of the decentralization of structure, but this has certainly not retribalized us. As Sobchack puts it, "[o]ur new electronic technology has . . . spatially dispersed capital while consolidating and expanding its power to an 'everywhere' that seems like 'nowhere' " (233). For Baudrillard, technology does not *mediate* between structure and its critiques, but *is* structure, an obscene, all-pervasive, and ever penetrating force that, in a sort of inertia with no original source, produces copies of itself without cessation (*Ecstacy*; *Simulations*). Thus for Sobchack and Baudrillard, electricity in concert with late capitalism so empowers structure that it meets no resistance from communitas and becomes the totality of cultural life.

Although the precise state of contemporary culture is (and must be) disputed, what seems clear from our brief review is that structure and communitas are no longer seen as halves of an integrated whole, directly impacting each other in an intimate and effective way. For most, the result is increasingly fragmented communities, although for some this is reason for jubilation and for others, regret.

REVISITING THE STEREOTYPES

At the outset of this essay, we wished for a way of thinking that would honor the connections *between* hierarchical structures and egalitarian oppositions, and that would fulfill Williams's idea that the analysis of culture is "the study of relationships between elements in a whole way of life." While we recognize, with Turner, that the breakup of the close tribal circle liberates the individual, and we can even share Haraway's exultation over the breakdown of oppressive dualisms in a cyborg society, we do not think most people want to live without community. As David Zarefsky puts it: "Our society . . . is highly diverse, and diversity is a source of strength. But, lest it fracture, our society also needs the anchors of community, at the national level as well as the local. Reconciling diversity and community is among our most significant problems . . . " ("State," 1). We agree with Turner that no society can function adequately without some kind of dialectic between structure and communitas. If this relationship has deteriorated in contemporary mass-mediated culture, then it needs to be fixed.

We also suggested that such correlations are best assembled, theoretically, at the intersection of rhetoric and cultural studies. Ironically, in their current antagonistic states, the two fields too often only echo the divisions between structure and communitas that erode community in the society at large. With its roots in what we have called the middle phase of communication history—when oratory attempted to mediate between structure and communitas—rhetoric has strong ties to structure, and in its central tendencies is less attuned to the technologies of contemporary society. On the other hand, by affirming the everyday behaviors of working-class cultures and the electronic technologies that construct their meanings, cultural studies is suspicious of hierarchies and celebratory of resistance. But, as Turner points out, academic work itself is "liminoid," for "it takes place in 'neutral spaces' or privileged areas—laboratories and studies—set aside from the mainstream of productive or political events," and it partakes of the subjunctive, of possibility, of the "what if." It can "generate and store a plurality of alternative models for living, from utopias to programs, which are capable of influencing the behavior of those in mainstream social and political roles . . . in the direction of radical change, just as much as they can serve as instruments of political control . . . " (*Ritual to Theatre,* 33). If rhetoric and cultural studies were to join their liminoid theorizing against a new enemy—not that of *structure,* but that of the *disconnection between structure and communitas* that erodes community, perhaps they could together realize the hope for change that animates them both. As Burke has made so clear, division gives way to identification when former rivals unite against a common enemy.

So let us return to the stereotypes enacted by our two nocturnal companions and reconfigure their respective portraits in light of what we have done so far. In this liminoid process of give-and-take, we hope to offer some ideas for how the two fields might work together.

Rhetoric

Rhetorical theories stand accused of reproducing the power structures they purport to explain—and of obsolescence. The former reproach seems to some extent warranted, for they have often limited their explanatory power by uncritically invoking assumptions favorable to a particular social class. As feminist and intercultural scholarship increasingly makes clear, for example, rhetorical theory has largely reflected the Euro-American patriarchies in which it has been produced.[2] Similarly, when rhetorical theories are based solely on speech and language use, or when they treat electronic media as if they were linguistic signs, they are surely out of touch with the formal peculiarities of the dominant communication media in the current era.

But few among even the most persistent critics of hegemony would really wish to live without institutions, we suspect, if only the ones that enable them to do their liminoid work. Unchecked by effective communitas, structures certainly oppress, but, as Turner reminds us, "[c]ommunitas cannot stand alone if the material and organizational needs of human beings are to be adequately met" (*Ritual Process,* 129). It is the practice of rhetoric that has traditionally armed societies to meet these needs, through persuasion, conflict, and consensus—through what Aristotle called *phronesis,* or practical reason—and it is the study of rhetoric that helps us understand how this happens and teaches us to do it better. Recovering the multiple voices and forms of rational deliberation implied by *phronesis,* Farrell writes, "[r]eason can never be sufficient for all that judgment implies and involves; yet the idea of judgment as something divorced from reason would make both terms virtually nonsensical" (8). Although rhetorical theories have sometimes been unconscious of their complicity with oppression, a rhetoric revised to meet the needs of contemporary times still seems necessary if we are to rehabilitate institutions through moments of communitas, not just resist them.

But even if rhetoric can reanimate communitas, would any collectivity capable of action still be around to effect change? Many think not, and charge rhetorical theory with inadequately responding to the ways modern technologies have changed the classical *polis*. The market-driven, mass-mediated consumer economy of late capitalism fractures, not only structure from communitas, but *all* collectivities into individualistic enclaves of experience (Gaonkar, "Very Idea," 336). Even the Marxist counterpoint that rhetoricians temporarily bring publics into existence by giving shape to dormant myths (McGee, "In Search of") is unconvincing for some simply because contemporary suasory practices seem to lack sufficient grounds for a collective identity, no matter how short-lived that identity might be. Thus, rhetorical theories must reconceptualize audiences in more complex and ephemeral terms than they have done in the past. In this light, cultural studies' multidimensional understandings of how viewer-listeners respond to mediated messages could enrich rhetoric's notions of how audiences are formed.

Finally, we often hear the complaint, mostly at panels such as the ones alluded to here, that rhetoric is "undertheorized." Certainly, rhetorical theory is plural and conflicting, and it has not yet dealt adequately with the contingencies of technologically mediated culture nor with its own unconscious Euro-American, masculinist assumptions. Nevertheless, its history is theoretically rich, for comprehending not only structures, but also how they are mediated and resisted. It would seem that Burke, to mention only the most obvious case, offers untapped potential for students of contemporary culture. For example, Burke's convictions that rhetoric as identification exists within poetic discourses and nondiscursive forms and often operates outside of the conscious awareness of agents to overcome division (as hierarchy) are widely accepted in rhetoric, and also seem fundamental to, if unacknowledged by, cultural studies theorizing (*Rhetoric*, 3–46). His diverse and subtle treatments of the ways this happens, captured in suggestive metaphors such as "courtship," might offer something to a field so influenced by theories of desire. Or again, his notion of how acting out of a "comic" as opposed to a "tragic frame" can reconfigure hierarchy without either reproducing or destroying it would appear to illuminate Turner's suggestions that structure is critiqued in liminoid genres (*Attitudes*, 1959).

We have relied here on Burke's treatment of the relationship between identification and division. Tempered by Turner's cultural dialectic, Burke's views could be expanded to help explain the contradictory status of community, particularly in contemporary times. Given his Marxist orientation,

Burke treats division as both the cultural mirror of language structure and as a materialization of property distribution in a class-structured economy, as the primary motivating impulse behind rhetorical identification. "Put identification and division ambiguously together, so that you cannot know for certain just where one ends and the other begins, and you have the characteristic invitation to rhetoric" (*Rhetoric*, 25). Although division is always *entailed* in acts of identification, as when people unite against a common enemy (22), Burke does not seem to think division is *motivated* by, or compensatory to, identification. Indeed, both identification and division take on a semi*natural* and all-pervasive status, as when he speaks of humans as always attempting to overcome the separation occurring at birth (137–142), as "goaded by hierarchy," and as the "symbol-using animal" (*Language as Symbolic Action*, 8–9). In "pure persuasion," he finds an example of the unadulterated delight of phatic communication. He writes: "Pure persuasion involves the saying of something, not for an extraverbal advantage to be got by the saying, but because of a satisfaction intrinsic in the saying. It summons because it likes the feel of a summons. It would be nonplused if the summons were answered" (*Rhetoric*, 269).

But in Turner's view, communitas, as "pure" a state of identification as occurs in society, eventually gives way to structure because of humans' motives for organization (and, less charitably, for domination). If this is so, then division is *rhetorically* constructed out of identification as much as identification is produced from division. Thus, cultural studies' insistence on the preservation of heterogeneity over homogeneity, even at the expense of community, may be seen from this framework as a rhetorical compensation for the excesses of identification—that is, of a false unity that disguises difference at the expense of the different.

Cultural Studies

Some rhetoricians have been taking popular culture seriously for quite some time, but others are condescending about the trivialities of such "trash," preferring to concentrate on canonical speeches as their field's contribution to the *real* work of culture. But, as cultural studies has amply demonstrated, popular communication functions in complex ways to maintain and critique the hierarchies that govern us. The focus in cultural studies upon how the politically disempowered construct their own life worlds in the face of proliferating structures is a vital agenda, not only because it values the texts of marginalized others, but also because, in its best moments, it shows how they can fuse people into collectivites for specific political purposes (Grossberg, *We Gotta*, 79–87). For example, Ernesto Laclau and Chantal Mouffe theorize how diverse forms of subordinated people might resist the increasingly overdetermined strictures of power without having to embrace some foundational identity like "class." "Plurality is *radical*," they write, "only to the extent that each term of this plurality of identities finds within itself the principle of its own validity, without this having to be sought in a transcendent or underlying positive ground for the hierarchy of meaning of them all and the source and guarantee of their legitimacy" (167). Extending this politics of difference to gender representation in cinema, Judith Butler not only underscores Laclau's and Mouffe's call for nonfoundational cultural identities, but radicalizes the resistance still further by arguing that even constructed identities are unstable and performed:

> The deconstruction of identity is not the deconstruction of politics; rather, it establishes as political the very terms through which identity is articulated. . . . The task here is not to celebrate each and every new possibility *qua* possibility, but to redescribe those possibilities that *already* exist, but which exist within cultural domains designated as culturally unintelligible and impossible. If identities were no longer fixed as premises of a political syllogism, and politics no longer understood as a set of practices derived from the alleged interests that belong to a set of ready-made subjects, a new configuration of politics would surely emerge from the ruins of the old. (148–149)

For us, these attempts to derive innovative forms of political resistance from the textual fabric of mediated "popular" communication constitute one of cultural studies' significant contributions to political action.

Cultural studies, especially in some of its more poststructuralist forms, is also sometimes chided by rhetoricians for generating endless overtheorized textual analyses that seem light years removed from the political agenda upon which the field was originally founded. Even from within cultural studies itself, we detect grumblings over what can appear as a fetishistic attachment to the text. "I am frustrated," Ben Agger complains, "by the mounting tendency to turn cultural studies into a vacuous methodology for reading cultural texts that has no real political grounding. This is very much the fate of the poststructuralism methodologized into deconstruction in American literary departments" (1–2). This tendency to displace political struggles into texts seems to correlate, Terry Eagleton notes, with Charles de Gaulle's crushing defeat of the 1968 student uprisings in France. "Unable to break the structures of state power, post-structuralism found it possible instead to subvert the structures of language" (*Literary Theory*, 142). In this displacement, various forms of logocentrism came to stand in for empowered structures, while the endlessly playful varieties of linguistic figuration come to represent the resistance of other. It was, and still is for many cultural studies writers, an empty sort of struggle with little payoff for winning. "Such deconstruction," Eagleton wickedly notes, "is a power game, a mirror-image of orthodox academic competition. It is just that now, in a religious twist on an old ideology, victory is achieved by *kenosis* or self-emptying; the winner is the one who has managed to get rid of all his [or her] cards and sit with empty hands" (147). If Eagleton is even partially correct here, rhetoric's charge that cultural studies' political agenda can be hypocritical when compared to its practice will have to stand.

Even with certain misgivings about the poststructuralist turn in cultural studies, we still defend their overall commitment to resistance to cultural oppression as a welcome antidote to the overly conventional tendencies of the academy. We want to question, though, just *what* is being resisted. Still enthralled with the Marxian dialectic, cultural studies sees resistance primarily as an opposition to power as/in structure, whether that be language or the state. Living "the good life" is invariably reduced to opposing "the bad life." But if, as we've argued above, the current fragmented state of culture stems in part from a rift between structure and communitas, then resistance, as cultural studies continues to think about it, presupposes a relationship that is tenuous at best. It seems far more important these days to confront *fragmentation* than structure—that is, to craft lines of connection between institutions and their critiques rather than just to critique.

It is not as if cultural studies is unaware of fragmentation; the word is a ubiquitous complaint in the postmodern age, often invoked by cultural studies writers themselves. However, some of the more influential scholars continue to see fragmentation as an effect of structure rather than as the disjunction of structure from communitas. Thus, while many in cultural studies congratulate Stuart Hall for discovering resistance in television viewers through his distinctions among preferred, negotiated, and oppositional viewing strategies ("Encoding/Decoding," 136–138), others detect an ironic political impotence in the individualism of such acts. For example, feminist rhetorician Bonnie Dow, while still reaffirming the Marxist assumption that resistance must confront hegemonic structures, provocatively asks of the viewer response literature, "If we celebrate the active audience to prove that viewers are not dominated by cultural hegemony, then what have we proven when their resistance does not go beyond negotiating with the messages of television?" (*Prime-Time Feminism,* 14). In other words, television decoding, no matter how complex, multifaceted, and active it may be, rarely cycles back to alter in significant ways the hegemonic codes of production that generate television texts. Although Dow is not operating within the same dialectic we posit here between structure and communitas, her skepticism about the political import of viewer response work in cultural studies (reflected in the rhetorician's remarks in our opening ethnography) seems consistent with our argument that the focus of political resistance today ought to be the fragmentation that proliferates when institutional power loses contact with potential sources of critique.

Cultural studies' concern with resisting *structure* also contributes to its tendency to interpret many forms of resisting *fragmentation* as conservative attempts to maintain structure. This helps explain the field's hostility toward myth (a hostility that does not necessarily extend, strangely enough, toward ritual, often defined as the enactment of myth; ritual is generally seen as the performance of everyday life, whereas myth is oppressive ideology). Strongly influenced by Roland Barthes's equation of myth with the second level of signification—conventionalized meaning or ideology—cultural studies tends to limit the functions of myth to the reaffirmation of power.[3] Patrick Brantlinger's critique of the American Studies movement, especially the myth and symbol school, as a response to the disciplinary fragmentation of twentieth-century higher education aptly exemplifies the stance and is worth quoting at length:

> The old, usually conservative idea of society as organism reinforces the "life" of the nation as the main subject of American Studies. . . . As [Cecil F.] Tate points out, by "myth" the early practitioners of American Studies—Roy Harvey Pearce, Henry Nash Smith, R. W. B. Lewis, and others—meant any widely diffused idea or theme expressive of the "life" or "mind" of the nation—again, close to some anthropological definitions of myth and culture. Of course "myth" often refers to irrational forms of social delusion (its most common meaning in a secular age), and in this way it tends to merge with the concept of ideology. But whereas "myth" has frequently retained a religious connotation, "ideology" commonly refers to secular political beliefs. The stress on myth thus involves a political ambiguity not shared by ideology. That is, "myth" can be used in demystifying critiques of social illusions, virtually as a synonym for "ideology"—this is how, for example, Roland Barthes uses it in *Mythologies*. Or in an older, less critical and more conservative inflection, "myth" can be used neutrally—even reverently or patriotically—to refer to essential, characteristic cultural forms (though ones which, no doubt, the wise scholar can see through or beyond). Tate cites Ernst Cassirer's definition of myth as " 'the primary cognitive form under which all reality is viewed' " by any society. By such a definition, "myth" is thus both universalized and deprived of its critical edge as illusion or false consciousness—it is instead *the* fundamental form of all knowing, all consciousness. (29)

Brantlinger, like most in cultural studies, clearly prefers that the term "ideology" replace the term "myth." But one can read the above passage itself ideologically by listing its set of stated and implied oppositions, the terms on the left (reflecting critical use of the term ideology) now forming the new standard, with those on the right (reflecting the uncritical use of the term myth) constituting the old view that should be discarded:

Ideology	*Myth*
critical	conservative
oppositional	organic
cultural studies	anthropology
rational	irrational
secular	religious
clear	ambiguous
sane	delusional
demystifying	mystifying
skeptical	reverential
unpatriotic	patriotic
constructed	essential
wise	unwise
cultural	universal

Brantlinger's point—that the myth and symbol school often analyzed major American myths uncritically, thus unconsciously valorizing dominant values and marginalizing the Other—is well-taken. But there is more than a little valorization going on in this passage. Myth can certainly be all those things in the righthand column; that is, it can mystify structure, naturalizing the interests of power by offering a symbolic solution to a historical problem or encouraging passivity by repressing dissent.[4] But cultural studies violates its own dictum against "totalizing" when it sees myth as *only* those things. In fact, by thus bridling myth to a conservative horse, cultural studies misses how myth's transformative potential can serve its own interests—to critique power and uproot its petrified structures—as well as to resist the sort of fragmentation that is our concern here.

Both Turner and Nietzsche tend to regard myth as more within the realm of communitas or opposition to rigidified forms than of structure. For example, as Turner explains, tribal initiations abolish the minutiae of structural differentiation in the domains of kinship, economics, and political structure, and thus "liberate the human structural propensity and give it free reign in the cultural realm of myth, ritual, and symbol" (*Ritual Process*, 133). Nietzsche's insistence on the forcefulness of Dionysiac rapture, what he calls "the shattering of the *principium individuationis*," often accompanied by physical intoxication and sexual promiscuity (22, 25–26), pinpoints the capacity of myth to rupture what we have seen here as the basis of hierarchy, i.e., the division among persons: "It is as though in these Greek festivals a sentimental trait of nature were coming to the fore, as though nature were bemoaning the fact of her fragmentation, her decomposition into separate individuals" (27). Indeed, one purpose of myth has always been to dissolve the ossifications of structures by obliterating their boundaries. Although he is articulating a grammar not just of myth but of discourse in general, Burke reminds us with regard to his "dramatistic pentad" that transformations take place only at points of ambiguity:

> Distinctions among the pentadic terms . . . arise out of a great central moltenness, where all is merged. They have been thrown from a liquid center to the surface, where they have congealed. Let one of these crusted distinctions return to its source, and in this alchemic center it may be remade, again becoming molten liquid, and may enter into new combinations, whereat it may be again thrown forth as a new crust, a different distinction. (*Grammar*, xix)[5]

Burke hints here of the necessity for the borders of structure to melt away in order for anything new to be born. This is the way that myth often opposes and reforms a structure, for example, by images of death, darkness, or *descent* that shadow the immortality, lightness, and upperworld dominance of a culture's conscious outlook.[6]

Furthermore, as Brantlinger's passage illustrates, there is an equation within cultural studies of "religious" and "mythic" with "conservative." Again, such associations may be legitimate when they refer to religious *institutions,* but are totalizing when reduced to equivalencies. Those who assume that religious myth always supports the dominant ideology forget that religious movements generally begin as attempts to rupture structure. Like tribal initiation, the genesis of religious movements, claims Turner, is liminal in that it arises "in times of radical social transition, when society itself seems to be moving from one fixed state to another . . . " (*Ritual Process*, 133).

We must distinguish, Turner says, between "ideal and praxis, existential communitas and normative communitas" (140), or, in Nietzsche's terms, between myth, the prerequisite of all religion, and theology, "the baneful virus of our society . . . " (110). Existential communitas, illustrated by St. Francis's vows of poverty and vagabondage (similar to the behavior of the hippies in the Haight-Ashbury community in St. Francis's American namesake), was in radical opposition to the opulence of the Catholic Church and the worldly commercial system of buying and selling. Francis's habit of thinking, as in most existential communitas, was in the primary, visual images of dream, myth, and parable; he seemed incapable of, or unwilling to indulge in, abstract thought and normative principles. "It was no doubt the very concreteness of his thinking and . . . the multivocality of his symbolism that made Francis a poor legislator" (*Ritual Process*, 142).

Never having intended to found an order, Francis relinquished its governance several years before his death. But, as the Franciscan order endured afterwards, it developed in time into a structural system with legalistic definitions, divisions into factions, and, inevitably, the erosion of the poverty ideal. It is an illustration of how quickly existential communitas gives way to normative communitas that his first successor, Elias, with a talent for organization lacking in Francis, was the driving force behind the building of the large basilica at Assisi to entomb Francis's body. Elias thus contributed more to the development of the city's tourism than to the Franciscan ideal, and completed the transformation from existential into normative communitas and then into structure (146–149). Nietzsche remarks:

> It is the sure sign of the death of a religion when its mythic presuppositions become systematized, under the severe, rational eyes of an orthodox dogmatism, into a ready sum of historical events, and when people begin timidly defending the veracity of myth but at the same time resist its natural continuance—when the feeling for myth withers and its place is taken by a religion claiming historical foundations. (68)

When myth is expressive of liminality, then, it is more opposed to than supportive of dominant ideology—indeed, more "critical" than it is "conservative." It is only when it calcifies into the religious institution that it loses its capacity to disrupt.

But what of our own times, which, as we have argued, are plagued more by fragmentation than by structure—does myth sport anything to counteract this, and thereby justify our claim that scholars often attack the very thing that resists this condition of postmodernity? Elsewhere, we have recounted at length the evolution of a Frankenstein myth within American film that arises imagistically as the terrible, dark underside to the more dominant myth of technological progress (*Projecting the Shadow*). As the "shadow" of the light-motif of progress, this tale narrativizes Nietzsche's warning that "science, spurred on by its energetic notions, approaches irresistibly those outer limits where the optimism implicit in logic must collapse," and his prophecy that the scientific inquirer, "having pushed to the circumference, realizes how logic in that place curls about itself and bites its own tail . . . " (95). If it is true, as we have argued above, that technological media tend to fragment community by separating structure from communitas, then this shadow myth resists this very state of fragmentation not only by critiquing its isolating and dangerous effects but also by metaphorically suggesting cures. Although this myth is primarily dystopian, it contains within itself the healing seeds of reversal. Since the hero of the more utopian myth is rational, scientific, de-spiritualized *man* dominating all that is Other, the shadow story implies, his conversion occurs only in contact with dreams, visions, spiritual mentors, women, and the experience of enslavement. Such metamorphosis is more by force than by consent, and it does not always occur. But the frequent hints in these directions, even within a myth of the apocalypse, are signs that point toward a coming together of progress and its critique—of institutional structures and their antitheses. It would seem a loss not to inquire into similar signs in other myths because of an antipathy toward a whole genus rather than certain species.

The portraits that begin this essay include the opposition "old/young"; each spokesperson seems to resent the age of the other, as well as the stereotypical characteristics that go with it. Now, surely, the line of latitude between rhetoric and cultural studies is not so simple as post– and pre–Baby Boom, but there are reasons beyond the longevity of the two fields and their practitioners for the ageist stereotypes in both directions—structure being typically aligned with the responsibilities of maturity and communitas with the liberties of youth. Writing of the values of communitas in the literature and behavior of such "cool" members of adolescent and young-adult categories as the beat and hippie generations, Turner notes that, without benefit of national *rites de passage*, these people opt out of the status-bound social order and take on the characteristics of the lowly. "They stress personal relationships rather than social obligations, and regard sexuality as a polymorphic instrument of immediate communitas rather than as the basis for an enduring structured social tie" (*Ritual Process*, 112–113).

From this perspective, it is predictable that cultural studies would eventually discover "pleasure," not just as determined by ideology, but as "a category separate from ideology"—a revolt against meaning, which is always socially constructed (G. Turner, 218). Following Mikhail Bakhtin's theory of the "carnivalesque" (which shares much with Turner's discussions of communitas) and Barthes's description of "*jouissance,*" the body, as Graeme Turner puts it, "has been separated off and made the location for the last stand, as it were, against cultural determination" (220). Although the degrees to which pleasure can be liberated from ideology, as well as the ways it can mold collective in addition to merely individualistic utopias, are still very much contested (222), it is clear that cultural studies sees pleasure as a potential form of resistance to structures of domination.

In this sense, as well as in its often close association with Freudian and Lacanian concepts, cultural studies contributes an important corollary to rhetoric's long acknowledgment of how "emotional appeals" endow a speech with persuasiveness. The pleasures of the body can be activated to disrupt, in addition to bring an audience into compliance with, the social order, as the work of Barbara Biesecker in rhetoric demonstrates. Those in cultural studies who laud the pleasures of the body as a political agenda can be seen as part of a long line of enactors of, or at least apologists for, communitas as a form of resistance to structure, although Turner is careful not to *reduce* communitas to "instinctual energies," but to include "rationality, volition, and memory . . . " (*Ritual Process,* 128). They qualify as "a case of arrested puberty," as our rhetorical spokesman puts it, only when they remain stuck in a sort of stasis of pleasure—which is a distortion of the ebb and flow or balancing of structure and communitas, an assumption that it is best to remain in a permanent marginalized state of resistance, to turn the phallic into the phatic. We do think this is a proclivity of some in cultural studies (and of the deconstructionist turn in criticism) who, for the understandable reason of wishing to avoid victimizing the marginalized or capitulating to power, refuse to enter into any hierarchy at all. Such a wish is the classic idealism of youth, usually expressed as opposition to those of age who run the institutions. One purpose of the *rites de passage* of which Turner and many anthropologists speak, the passage from adolescence into maturity, is to initiate the young person into the social order. This involves a sacrifice of the hubristic innocence of youth, the illusion that one can maintain a life without "sin." Whereas this is in some sense tragic—that is, one cannot live a perfect life that hurts no one—the acceptance of hierarchy is a necessary stage in growing up, and this would seem as true in academic theorizing as in tribal initiation.

Finally, although there have been some notable attempts, now mostly notorious, strictly to differentiate rhetoric from art (e.g., Wichelns), rhetoric, sometimes termed the art of "eloquence," has historically maintained a shifting but close relationship with aesthetics, from Aristotle's frequent cross-referencing in the *Rhetoric* to his *Poetics,* to Longinus's treatise *On the Sublime,* to the post-Renaissance rhetorics of *belles-lettres,* to the early-twentieth-century elocutionary movement, to Burke's focus upon rhetoric within literature. Thus, the complaint that cultural studies has abandoned aesthetics or, as our rhetorician put it, that "they have no respect for anything beautiful," is to be expected. There are good reasons, of course, for cultural studies' dissociation from aesthetics—namely, the desire to avoid the elitism of dividing culture into the "high" and the "low," of disguising ideology under the banner of "taste." The fear of aesthetics seems to stem from the same antipathy cultural studies has toward myth—that it requires a theory of the universal over the particular, and that it elevates dominant values over the marginalized.

From Turner's point of view, though, art lies within the realm of the liminal/liminoid as an alternative to institutional life. Free from the restraints of structure and able to "play" with its precepts, it can reorganize them into novel configurations. McLuhan accords artists the special function of prophecy:

In the history of human culture there is no example of a conscious adjustment of the various factors of personal and social life to new extensions except in the puny and peripheral efforts of artists. The artist picks up the message of cultural and technological challenge decades before its transforming impact occurs. [S]he, then, builds models or Noah's arks for facing the change that is at hand. (64–65)

In this, he echoes Mircea Eliade, who writes, "Through their creation the artists anticipate what is to come—sometimes one or two generations later—in other sectors of social and cultural life" (73). Art is important, it would seem, not just in terms of power or its critique, but for its peculiar oracular properties. Or, as Nietzsche would have it, the greatest art, which he finds embodied in Greek tragedy, is able to balance the Apollonian and the Dionysian impulses, to give each its due. A society gets its bearings from its visionaries, and any study of culture that makes no room for these would seem to be a radical breach of history.

CONCLUSION

We began this work with Raymond Williams's sage observation that any study of culture must necessarily include the relationships among all of its forms of life. Whether those cultural elements cohere into the tribal communities enacted through performance rituals, the prototypes of democracy crafted by classical oratory, or even the fragmented lifeworld (de)constructed by the technological media of our own times, the many diverse practices of culture cluster into two recurrent forms we have called, following Turner, structure and communitas, a dialectic of alternating realities marked by hierarchical institutions and their egalitarian levelings. For a culture even to exist as we commonly understand the meaning of that term—that is, as some form of communal life and not merely as an aggregate of disconnected individuals—some linkage between structure and communitas must be preserved.

It is that linkage that both rhetoric and cultural studies continue to presuppose, and that we, with a little help from our friends, have called into question here. If we are correct that increasing fragmentation—understood now as the dissociation of structure from communitas and no longer as the singular machinations of structure itself—is a profound threat to community, then a political agenda seems to emerge for rhetoric and cultural studies. The first task, somewhat ironically, is for these two fields to move beyond their own split to an interdisciplinary community as a collective base of operations, for the after-hours barroom antipathies with which we began can now be seen as a microcosm of cultural fragmentation in general. As we have maintained throughout, there is nothing wrong or ill advised in scholarship that concentrates on only structure or communitas; it is just that those orientations, when divorced from one another, inhibit the one collective goal of both fields—namely, to build a better way of living.

We conclude with some general projects that rhetoric and cultural studies might undertake in a joint effort to improve community. If the diminishing relationship between institutions and their critique depotentiates political agendas by undercutting the forms of collective action necessary for empowerment, then clearly we need to probe those communicative practices that promote these disjunctions, publicize current attempts to reconnect them, and suggest further ways that this can be done. Taking a cue from Burke, we could strategically construct "perspectives by incongruity" with the scholarship of our two fields, thus providing a space for the insights arising from the collision of contrary terms. How does official persuasion get dramatically embodied and massaged into forms of entertainment, and how are those depictions in turn recycled into official public address? What are the links and disjunctions between consensus building inside and outside the institution? How might disparate forms of mass media decoding reform our understanding of audiences for political address? How can we distinguish between cultural narratives and art forms that maintain the system, that flatten it, and that rejoin it with its human components? Such questions, wrought from theoretical and practical antitheses, seem both affluent and fertile. Perhaps this book, itself the collective effort of rhetorical and cultural studies scholars, is such a beginning.

NOTES

1. Obviously, the changes in cultural conditions that we ascribe here to changes in communication modes are not isolated from multiple causes, but involve historical shifts of enormous significance in society, technology, economics, government, religion, aesthetics, etc. We concentrate here on communication because it is the subject of this essay.
2. This scholarship is richly exemplified in the work of Barbara Biesecker, Sonja K. Foss and Cindy L. Griffin, Mary Garrett, and Jane Sutton.
3. Like cultural studies, rhetoric holds a limited view of myth. Some treat it as a hegemonic legitimation for structure, while others see it as an aesthetic fiction, a sort of fourth "artistic proof," i.e., *ethos, pathos, logos,* and *mythos,* while still others envision it as a narrative form of disposition.
4. These functions of myth are well documented in cultural studies; we have addressed these ideological functions of mythic rhetoric in Rushing, "Mythic

Evolution," and in Rushing and Frentz, "Integrating Ideology," and *Projecting the Shadow.*

5. Cultural studies typically does not share this Nietzschean/Burkean understanding or endorsement of communitas/identification; as pointed out above, their preference is for coalitions over consensus, and for the retaining of individual boundaries within such coalitions. The melting away of distinctions into "nature" suggests a sort of essentialism that would irk most cultural studies scholars. The relationship between this preference for individual partitions and the general suspicion of individualism as the bane of collectivism would make an interesting future inquiry.

6. See, for example, Sylvia Perera's analysis of the descent myth of Inanna, and Janice Hocker Rushing's examination of the descent motif in *Alien* and *Aliens.*

BIBLIOGRAPHY

Abrahams, Roger D. "Introductory Remarks to a Rhetorical Theory of Folklore."
Journal of American Folklore 81 (1968): 143–58.

Abramson, Daniel. "Maya Lin and the 1960s: Monuments, Time Lines, and
Minimalism." *Critical Inquiry* 22 (1996): 679–709.

Adams, Judith A. *The American Amusement Park Industry: A History of Technology and Thrills.* Boston: Twayne, 1991.

Aden, Roger C. "Back to the Garden: Therapeutic Place Metaphor in *Field of
Dreams.*" *Southern Communication Journal* 59 (1994): 307–317.

Adler, Jerry. "Putting Names in the Sky: 'Space Mirror' honors America's dead
astronauts." *Newsweek,* 31 May 1991: 69.

Adorno, Theodor. *Negative Dialectics.* Trans. E. B. Ashton. New York: Continuum,
1973.

Adorno, Theodor, and Max Horkheimer. "The Culture Industry: Enlightenment as
Mass Deception." 1944. Trans. John Cumming. Reprinted in *The Cultural
Studies Reader.* Ed. Simon During. New York: Routledge, 1993. 29–43.

_____. *Dialectic of Enlightenment.* Trans. John Cumming. New York: Seabury,
1972.

Agger, Ben. *Cultural Studies as Critical Theory.* London: Falmer, 1992.

The Air Up There. Dir. Paul Michael Glaser. Buena Vista Pictures, 1984.

Allor, Martin. "Between Discourse and Rhetoric: Textuality and Epistemes." *Communication* 12 (1990): 65–71.

Althusser, Louis. "Ideology and Ideological State Apparatuses." In Althusser.
127–185.

_____. *Lenin and Philosophy and Other Essays.* Trans. Ben Brewster. New York:
Monthly Review Press, 1971.

Altman, R. (1986). "Television/sound." *Studies in Entertainment.* Ed. Tanya
Modleski. Bloomington: Indiana University Press,. 39–54.

Armstrong, Robert Plant. *The Powers of Presence: Consciousness, Myth, and
Affecting Presence.* Philadelphia: University of Pennsylvania Press, 1981.

Arnold, Matthew. *Culture and Anarchy: An Essay in Political and Social Criticism.*
1869. New York: Macmillan, 1916.

Aronowitz, Stanley. *Roll Over Beethoven: The Return of Cultural Strife.* Hanover,
NH: Wesleyan University Press, 1993.

Aronowitz, Stanley, and William DiFazio. *The Jobless Future: Sci-Tech and the Dogma of Work.* Minneapolis: Minnesota University Press, 1994.

Asante, Molefi Kete. *The Afrocentric Idea.* Philadelphia: Temple University Press, 1987.

Ashdown, Dwight. Letter to Gary Koepke. Holt Hinshaw files. San Francisco. 23 February 1989.

Astronauts Memorial Foundation. "Facts About the Astronauts Memorial, Kennedy Space Center, Florida." Press Release, n.d.

———. "National Design Competition for a Memorial and Site Design." Competition Program, 1987.

Aune, James Arnt. "Burke's Late Blooming: Trope, Defense, and Rhetoric." *Quarterly Journal of Speech* 69 (1983): 328–340.

———. "Marxism and Rhetorical Theory." *Communication* 11 (1990): 265–276.

———. *Rhetoric and Marxism.* Boulder, CO: Westview Press, 1994.

Ball, Moya Ann. "A Case Study of the Kennedy Administration's Decision-Making Concerning the Diem Coup Press, of Nov. 1963." *Western Journal of Speech Communication* 54 (1990): 557–574.

Baltrušaitis, Jurgis. *Anamorphic Art.* Trans. W. J. Strachan. Cambridge, UK: Chadwyck-Healey, 1977.

Barker, David. " 'It's Been Real': Forms of Television Representation." *Critical Studies in Mass Communication* 5 (1988): 42–56.

———. "Television Production Techniques as Communication." *Critical Studies in Mass Communication* 2 (1985): 234–246.

Barthes, Roland. *Camera Lucida.* London: Vintage, 1993.

———. "From Work to Text." *Image-Music-Text.* Trans. Stephen Heath. New York: Hill & Wang, 1977. 155–164.

———. *Mythologies.* New York: Hill & Wang, 1957.

———. *S/Z.* Trans. Richard Miller. New York: Hill & Wang, 1974.

Baskerville, Barnet. "Must We All Be 'Rhetorical Critics'?" *Quarterly Journal of Speech* 63 (1977): 107–116.

Bateson, Gregory. *Mind and Nature: A Necessary Unity.* New York: Dutton, 1979.

———. *Steps to an Ecology of Mind.* New York: Ballantine, 1972.

Baudrillard, Jean. "Simulacra and Simulations." *Jean Baudrillard: Selected Readings.* Ed. Mark Poster. Stanford: Stanford University Press, 1988. 166–184.

———. *The Ecstacy of Communication.* Trans. Bernard Schutze and Caroline Schutze. New York: Semiotext(e), 1988.

———. *Fatal Strategies.* Trans. Philip Beitchman and W. G. J. Niesluchowski. 1983. New York: Semiotext(e), 1990.

———. *Simulations.* Trans. Paul Foss, Paul Patton, and Philip Beitchman. New York: Semiotext(e), 1983.

Baudry, Jean-Louis. "Ideological Effects of the Basic Cinematographic Apparatus." In *Narrative, Apparatus, Ideology: A Film Theory Reader.* Ed. Philip Rosen. New York: Columbia University Press, 1986.

Becker, Samuel L. "Rhetorical Studies for the Contemporary World." *The Prospect of Rhetoric: Report of the National Developmental Project.* Eds. Lloyd F. Bitzer and Edwin Black. Englewood Cliffs, NJ: Prentice-Hall, 1971. 21–43.

Bederman, Gail. *Manliness and Civilization: A Cultural History of Gender and*

Race in the United States, 1880–1917. Chicago: University of Chicago Press, 1995.

Bell, Daniel. *The End of Ideology: On the Exhaustion of Political Ideas in the Fifties*. 1960. New York: Free Press, 1962.

Ben-Amos, Dan. "Toward a Definition of Folklore in Context." *Toward New Perspectives in Folklore*. Eds. Americo Paredes and Richard Bauman. Austin: University of Texas Press, 1972. 3–15.

Benjamin, Walter. *Charles Baudelaire: A Lyric Poet in the Era of High Capitalism*. Trans. Harold Zohn. London: New Left Books, 1973.

Bennett, Tony. "Putting Policy into Cultural Studies." In Grossberg, Nelson, and Treichler. 23–34.

Bennett, Tony, and Janet Woollacott. *Bond and Beyond: The Political Career of a Popular Hero*. New York: Methuen, 1988.

Benson, Thomas. "Rhetorical Structure and *Primate*: Commentary." In Nothstine, Blair, and Copeland. 184–188.

_____. "The Rhetorical Structure of Frederick Wiseman's 'Primate.' " *Quarterly Journal of Speech* 71 (1985): 204–217.

_____, ed. *Speech Communication in the 20th Century*. Carbondale: Southern Illinois University Press, 1985.

Berg, David M. "Rhetoric, Reality, and Mass Media." *Quarterly Journal of Speech*, 58 (1972): 255–263.

Berger, John. *About Looking*. London: Writers and Readers Publishing Cooperative, Ltd., 1980.

_____. *Ways of Seeing*. London: Penguin Books, 1977.

Berger, Peter L. *A Rumor of Angels: Modern Society and the Rediscovery of the Supernatural*. Garden City, NY: Anchor/Doubleday, 1969.

Berger, Peter L., and Thomas Luckmann. *The Social Construction of Reality: A Treatise in the Sociology of Knowledge*. Garden City, NY: Anchor/Doubleday, 1966.

Berlin, James A. *Rhetorics, Poetics, and Cultures: Refiguring College English Studies*. Urbana, IL: National Council of Teachers of English, 1996.

Bernard-Donals, Michael F. *Mikhail Bakhtin: Between Phenomenology and Marxism*. Cambridge, UK: Cambridge University Press, 1994.

Berub,, Michael. "Public Image Limited: Political Correctness and the Media's Big Lie." *The Village Voice* 18 June 1991. Reprinted in *Debating P.C.: The Controversy over Political Correctness on Campuses*. Ed. Paul Berman. New York: Dell, 1992. 124–149.

Biesecker, Barbara. "Towards a Transactional View of Rhetorical and Feminist Theory: Rereading Helene Cixous's 'The Laugh of the Medusa.' " *The Southern Communication Journal* 57 (1992): 86–96.

Billig, Michael. "From Codes to Utterances." In Ferguson and Golding. 205–226.

Birnbaum, Stephen, ed. *Birnbaum's Walt Disney World, 1996*. New York: Hyperion and Hearst, 1995.

Bitzer, Lloyd. "The Rhetorical Situation." *Philosophy and Rhetoric* 1 (1968): 1–14.

Bizell, Patricia, and Bruce Herzberg, eds. *The Rhetorical Tradition: Readings from Classical Times to the Present*. Boston: St. Martin's Press, 1990.

Black, Edwin. *Rhetorical Criticism: A Study in Method*. New York: Macmillan, 1965.

_____. "The Sentimental Style as Escapism, or The Devil with Dan'l Webster." *Form and Genre: Shaping Rhetorical Action.* Eds. Karlyn K. Campbell and Kathleen H. Jamieson. Falls Church, VA: Speech Communication Association, 1978. 75–86.

Blair, Carole. "Contested Histories of Rhetoric: The Politics of Preservation, Progress, and Change." *Quarterly Journal of Speech* 78 (1992): 403–428.

_____. " 'We are all just prisoners here of our own device': Rhetoric in Speech Communication after Wingspread." *Making and Unmaking the Prospects for Rhetoric.* Eds. Theresa Enos, Richard McNabb, Carolyn Miller, and Roxanne Mountford. New York: Lawrence Erlbaum, 1997. 29–36.

Blair, Carole, Marsha S. Jeppeson, and Enrico Pucci, Jr. "Public Memorializing in Postmodernity: The Vietnam Veterans Memorial as Prototype." *Quarterly Journal of Speech* 77 (1991): 263–288.

Blair, Carole, and Neil Michel. "Constructing Memories . . . of What? Reading the Landscape of the Astronauts Memorial." *Places of Commemoration: The Search for Identity and Landscape Architecture.* Ed. Joachim Wolschke-Bulmahn. Washington, DC: Dumbarton Oaks, in press.

Blankenhorn, David. *Fatherless America: Confronting Our Most Urgent Social Problem.* New York: Basic Books, 1995.

Bloch, Ernst. *Das Prinzip Hoffnung.* 1959. Frankfurt: Suhrkamp, 1969.

Bloom, Allan. *The Republic of Plato.* 2nd ed. New York: Basic Books, 1991.

Bly, Robert. *Iron John: A Book about Men.* Reading, MA: Addison-Wesley, 1990.

Borisoff, Deborah and Dan F. Hann. "Thinking with the Body: Sexual Metaphors." *Communication Quarterly* 41 (1993): 253–260.

Bowers, John Waite. "The Pre-Scientific Functions of Rhetorical Criticism." *Essays in Rhetorical Criticism.* Ed. Thomas R. Nilsen. New York: Random House, 1968. 126–145.

Brande, David. "The Business of Cyberpunk: Symbolic Economy and Ideology in William Gibson." *Virtual Realities and Their Discontents.* Ed. Robert Markley. Baltimore: Johns Hopkins University Press, 1996. 79–106.

Brantlinger, Patrick. *Crusoe's Footprints: Cultural Studies in Britain and America.* New York: Routledge, 1990.

Braveheart. Dir. Mel Gibson. Perf. Mel Gibson, Sophie Marceau, Patrick MacGoohan, Catherine McCormack. Paramount, 1995.

Brenkman, John. *Culture and Domination.* Ithaca: Cornell University Press, 1987.

Brennen, Bonnie. "Newsworkers During the Interwar Era: A Critique Of Traditional Media History." *Communication Quarterly* 43 (1995): 210–224.

Brimelow, Peter. *Alien Nation: Common Sense about America's Immigration Disaster.* New York: HarperCollins, 1995.

Brinson, Susan L. "The Myth of White Supremacy in *Mississippi Burning.*" *Southern Communication Journal* 60 (1995): 211–221.

Brock, Bernard L., and Robert L. Scott, eds. *Methods of Rhetorical Criticism: A Twentieth-Century Perspective.* 1st ed., New York: Harper, 1972; 2nd ed., Detroit: Wayne State University Press, 1980.

Brookeman, Christopher. *American Culture and Society Since the 1930s.* London: Macmillan, 1984.

Brooks, Cleanth, and Robert P. Warren. *Understanding Poetry.* 4th ed. Fort Worth, TX: Harcourt, 1976.

Brooks, Van Wyck. *America's Coming-of-Age.* New York: Huebesch, 1915.

Brown, William R. "Mass Media and Society: The Development of Critical Perspectives." In Benson. 196–220.

Browne, Ray. *Against Academia: The History of the Popular Culture Association/American Culture Association and the Popular Culture Movement, 1967–1988.* Bowling Green, OH: Bowling Green State University Popular Press, 1989.

Browne, Stephen H. "Edmund Burke's 'Discontents' and the Interpretation of Political Culture." *Quarterly Journal of Speech* 77 (1991): 53–66.

_____. " 'Like Gory Spectres': Representing Evil in Theodore Weld's *American Slavery as It Is,*" *Quarterly Journal of Speech* 80 (1994): 277–292.

Brummett, Barry. "How to Propose a Discourse—A Reply to Rowland." *Communication Studies* 41 (1990): 128–135.

_____. *Rhetoric in Popular Culture.* New York: St. Martin's Press, 1994.

_____. *Rhetorical Dimensions of Popular Culture.* Tuscaloosa: University of Alabama Press, 1991.

_____. "Some Implications of 'Process' or 'Intersubjectivity': Postmodern Rhetoric." *Philosophy and Rhetoric* 9 (1976): 21–51.

Brummett, Barry, and Margaret Carlisle Duncan. "Theorizing without Totalizing: Specularity and Televised Sports." *Quarterly Journal of Speech* 76 (1990): 227–246.

Bryman, Alan. *Disney and His Worlds.* London: Routledge, 1995.

Budd, Mike, Robert M. Entman, and Clay Steinman. "The Affirmative Character of U.S. Cultural Studies." *Critical Studies in Mass Communication* 7 (1988): 169–184.

Burgchardt, Carl, ed. *Readings in Rhetorical Criticism.* State College, PA: Strata Publishing, 1995.

Burgess, Parke G. "The Rhetoric of Black Power: A Moral Demand?" *Quarterly Journal of Speech* 44 (1968): 122–133.

Burke, Kenneth. *Attitudes Toward History.* 2nd ed., rev. Boston: Beacon, 1959.

_____. *A Grammar of Motives.* Berkeley: University of California Press, 1969.

_____. *Language as Symbolic Action: Essays on Life, Literature, and Method.* Berkeley: University of California Press, 1968.

_____. *A Rhetoric of Motives.* Berkeley: University of California Press, 1969.

Burroughs, William S. *Naked Lunch.* New York: Grove Press. 1959.

Bush, Harold K., Jr., "A Brief History of PC, with Annotated Bibliography." *American Studies International* 33 (April 1995): 42–64.

Butler, Judith. *Gender Trouble: Feminism and the Subversion of Identity.* New York: Routledge, 1990.

Buxton, Rodney A. "The Late-Night Talk Show: Humor in Fringe Television." *Southern Speech Communication Journal* 52 (1987): 377–389.

Cain, William E., ed. *Reconceptualizing American Literary/Cultural Studies: Rhetoric, History, and Politics in the Humanities.* New York: Garland, 1996.

Campbell, John Angus. "Scientific Revolution and the Grammar of Culture: The Case of Darwin's *Origin.*" *Quarterly Journal of Speech* 72 (1986): 351–376.

Campbell, Karlyn Kohrs. "Conventional Wisdom-Traditional Form: A Rejoinder." *Quarterly Journal of Speech* 58 (1972): 451–460.

_____. "The Forum: 'Conventional Wisdom-Traditional Form': A Rejoinder." *Quarterly Journal of Speech* 58 (1972): 451–460.

_____. "Response to Forbes Hill." *Central State Speech Journal* 34 (1983): 126–127.

_____. "In Silence We Offend." *Toward the Twenty-First Century: The Future of Speech Communication*. Eds. Julia T. Wood and Richard B. Gregg. Cresskill, NJ: Hampton, 1995. 137–150.

_____. *Man Cannot Speak for Her: A Critical Study of Early Feminist Rhetoric*, vol. 1. New York: Praeger, 1989.

Campbell, Karlyn Kohrs, and Kathleen H. Jamieson. "Form and Genre in Rhetorical Criticism: An Introduction." In *Form and Genre: Shaping Rhetorical Action*. Eds. Karlyn Kohrs Campbell and Kathleen H. Jamieson. Falls Church, VA: Speech Communication Association, 1978. 9–32.

Campbell, Richard. "Securing the Middle Ground: Reporter Formulas in *60 Minutes*." *Critical Studies in Mass Communication* 4 (1987): 325–350.

Carbaugh, Donal. "Communication and Cultural Interpretation." *Quarterly Journal of Speech* 77 (1991): 336–342.

_____. " 'Soul' and 'Self': American and Soviet Cultures in Conversation." *Quarterly Journal of Speech* 79 (1993): 182–200.

_____. "Cultural Terms and Tensions in the Speech at a Television Station." *Western Journal of Speech Communication* 52 (1988): 216–237.

Carey, James W. *Communication as Culture: Essays on Media and Society*. Boston, MA: Unwin Hyman, 1989.

_____. "Mass Communication Research and Cultural Studies: An American View." *Mass Communication and Society*. Eds. James Curran, Michael Gurevith, and Janet Woollacott. London: Open University Press, Edward Arnold, 1977. 409–425.

_____. "Reflections on the Project of (American) Cultural Studies." In Ferguson and Golding. 1–24.

Carlson, A. Cheree. "Defining Womanhood: Lucretia Coffin Mott and the Transformation of Femininity." *Western Journal of Communication* 58 (1994): 85–97.

Carr, Stephen, Mark Francis, Leanne G. Rivlin, and Andrew M. Stone. *Public Space*. New York: Cambridge University Press, 1992.

Carroll, David, ed. *The States of "Theory": History, Art, and Critical Discourse*. New York: Columbia University Press, 1990.

Chaitin, Gilbert. *Rhetoric and Culture in Lacan*. Cambridge, UK: Cambridge University Press, 1996.

Chakrabarty, Dipesh. "Provincializing Europe: Postcoloniality and the Critique of History." *Cultural Studies* 6 (1992): 337–357.

Charland, Maurice. "Constitutive Rhetoric: The Case of the Peuple Quebecois." *Quarterly Journal of Speech* 73 (1987): 133–150.

_____. "Rehabilitating Rhetoric: Confronting Blindspots in Discourse and Social Theory." *Communication* 11 (1990): 253–264.

Cherry, Colin. *On Human Communication*. 1957. Science Editions. New York: John Wiley & Sons, 1961.

Cleary, Sandra Vonvelsen. "Of No Party: The Independent Newspaper and the Rhetoric of Revolution, 1765–1775." *Communication Studies* 44 (1993): 157–167.

Clifford, James. "Traveling Cultures." In Grossberg, Nelson, and Treichler. 96–112.

Cloud, Dana L. "The Limits of Interpretation: Ambivalence and the Stereotype in *Spenser: For Hire.*" *Critical Studies in Mass Communication* 9 (1992): 311–324.

———. "The Materiality of Discourse as Oxymoron: A Challenge to Critical Rhetoric." *Western Journal of Communication* 58 (1994): 141–163.

Cochran, Thomas C. *The Inner Revolution: Essays on the Social Sciences in History.* New York: Harper & Row, 1964.

Cohen, Herman. *History of Speech Communication: The Emergence of a Discipline.* Annandale, VA: Speech Communication Association, 1994.

Cohen, Jodi R. "Interesting and Competing Discourses in Harvey Fierstein's *Tidy Endings.*" *Quarterly Journal of Speech* 77 (1991): 196–207.

Cohen, Ralph, ed. *The Future of Literary Theory.* New York and London: Routledge, 1989.

Collins, Steven E. " 'For the Greater Good': Trilateralism and Hegemony in *Star Trek: The Next Generation.*" *Enterprise Zones: Critical Positions on Star Trek.* Eds. Taylor Harrison, Sarah Projansky, Kent A. Ono, and Elyce Rae Helford. Boulder, CO: Westview Press, 1996. 137–156.

Condit, Celeste M. "Contributions of the Rhetorical Perspective to the Placement of Medical Genetics." *Communication Studies* 46 (1995): 118–129.

———. *Decoding Abortion Rhetoric: Communicating Social Change.* University of Illinois Press, 1990.

———. "Interpellating Rhetoric, Politics, and Culture: 'Hail' or 'Greetings'?" *Communication* 11 (1990): 241–252.

———. "Kenneth Burke and Linguistic Reflexivity: Reflections on the Scene of the Philosophy of Communication in the Twentieth Century." *Kenneth Burke and Contemporary European Thought.* Ed. Bernard Brock. Tuscaloosa, AL: University of Alabama Press, 1995. 207–262.

———. "The Need for a Materialist Rhetoric: Reflections on the Genetic Code." Invited presentation, Pennsylvania State Conference on Rhetoric, June 1997.

———. "The Rhetorical Limits of Polysemy." *Critical Studies in Mass Communication* 6 (1989): 103–122.

Condit, Celeste M., and John L. Lucaites. *Crafting Equality: America's Anglo-African Word.* University of Chicago Press, 1993.

Condit, Celeste M., and Melanie Williams. "Audience Responses to the Discourse of Medical Genetics: Evidence Against the Critique of Medicalization." *Health Communication* 9 (1997): 219–235.

Conquergood, Dwight. "Rethinking Ethnography: Towards a Critical Cultural Politics." *Communication Monographs* 58 (1991): 179–194.

Corcoran, Farrell. "KAL 007 and the Evil Empire: Mediated Disaster and Forms of Rationalization." *Critical Studies in Mass Communication* 3 (1986): 297–316.

———. "Pedagogy in Prison: Teaching in Maximum Security Institutions." *Communication Education* 34 (1985): 49–58.

Crewe, Jonathan. "Toward Uncritical Practice." *Against Theory.* Ed. W. J. T. Mitchell. 53–64.

Cuklanz, Lisa. *Rape on Trial: How the Mass Media Construct Legal Reform and Social Change.* Philadelphia: University of Pennsylvania Press, 1996.

Dates, Jannette L., and William Barlow, eds. *Split Image: African Americans in the Mass Media.* Washington, DC: Howard University Press, 1990.

Davies, Ioan. *Cultural Studies and Beyond: Fragments of Empire.* London: Routledge, 1995.

deCerteau, Michel. *The Practice of Everyday Life.* Trans. Steven Rendall. Berkeley: University of California Press, 1984.

Delany, Samuel R. *Flight from Neveryon.* New York: Bantam Books, 1985.

de Man, Paul. *The Resistance to Theory.* Minneapolis: University of Minnesota Press, 1986.

Deleuze, Gilles, and Félix Guattari. *A Thousand Plateaus: Capitalism and Schizophrenia.* Trans. B. Massumi. Minneapolis: University of Minnesota Press, 1987.

Derrida, Jacques. "Afterword: Toward an Ethic of Discussion." Trans. Samuel Weber. *Limited Inc.* Evanston: Northwestern University Press, 1988. 111–60.

_____. *Of Spirit: Heidegger and the Question.* Trans. Geoffrey Bennington and Rachel Bowlby. Chicago: University of Chicago Press, 1991.

_____. "Some Statements and Truisms about Neo-Logisms, Newisms, Postisms, Parasitisms, and Other Small Seismisms." In Carroll. 63–94.

_____. *Specters of Marx: The State of Debt, the Work of Mourning, and the New International.* New York: Routledge, 1994.

_____. "Structure, Sign, and Play in the Discourse of the Human Sciences." In Macksey and Donato. 247–265.

Dewey, John, et al. *Creative Intelligence: Essays in the Pragmatic Attitude.* New York: Holt, 1917.

Diggins, John Patrick. *The Promise of American Pragmatism: Modernism and the Crisis of Knowledge and Authority.* Chicago: University of Chicago Press, 1994.

Dionisopoulos, George N., and Steven R. Goldzwig. " 'The Meaning of Vietnam': Political Rhetoric as Revisionist Cultural History." *Quarterly Journal of Speech* 78 (1992): 61–79.

Dirks, Nicholas B., Geoff Eley, and Sherry B. Ortner, eds. *Culture/Power/History: A Reader in Contemporary Social Theory.* Princeton, NJ: Princeton University Press, 1994.

Disraeli, Benjamin. *Sybil, or The Two Nations.* Harmondsworth: Penguin, 1980.

Donnelly, Jerome. "Dwight Macdonald: Critic of Mass Culture." *America,* 1 Oct., 1983: 173–174.

Dow, Bonnie J. *Prime-Time Feminism: Television, Media Culture, and the Women's Movement Since 1970.* Philadelphia: University of Pennsylvania Press, 1996.

_____. "Feminism, Cultural Studies, and Rhetorical Studies." *Quarterly Journal of Speech* 83 (1997): 90–106

Dubiel, Helmut. *Theory and Politics: Studies in the Development of Critical Theory.* 1978. Trans. Benjamin Gregg. Cambridge, MA: MIT Press, 1985.

Duncan, James, and David Ley, eds. *Place/Culture/Representation.* London: Routledge, 1993.

Dundes, Alan. "Texture, Text, and Context." *Southern Folklore Quarterly* 28 (1964): 251–265.

Dunn, Jerry Camarillo, Jr. "Hollywood in Florida: Disney-MGM Studios Theme-park." *National Geographic Traveler,* November/December 1991: 36–49.

Eagleton, Terry. *Criticism and Ideology: A Study in Marxist Literary Theory.* London: Verso, 1986.

_____. *Ideology: An Introduction.* London: Verso, 1991.

_____. *The Ideology of the Aesthetic.* Oxford: Basil Blackwell, 1990.

_____. *Literary Theory: An Introduction.* Minneapolis: University of Minnesota Press, 1983.

_____. *The Significance of Theory.* Oxford: Basil Blackwell, 1990.

_____. *Walter Benjamin: or Towards a Revolutionary Criticism* London: Verso Books, 1981.

Easterlin, Nancy, and Barbara Riebling, eds. *After Poststructuralism: Interdisciplinarity and Literary Theory.* Evanston: Northwestern University Press, 1993.

Eco, Umberto. *A Theory of Semiotics.* Bloomington: Indiana University Press, 1976.

Ehninger, Douglas. "On Systems of Rhetoric." *Philosophy and Rhetoric* 1 (1968): 131–144.

Ehrenreich, Barbara. *Fear of Falling: The Inner Life of the Middle Class.* New York: Pantheon, 1989.

Eley, Geoff, and Ronald Grigor Suny, eds. *Becoming National: A Reader.* New York: Oxford University Press, 1996.

Eliade, Mircea. *Myth and Reality.* Trans. Willard R. Trask. New York: Harper Colophon, 1975.

Ellis, Carolyn. *Final Negotiations: A Story of Love, Loss, and Chronic Illness.* Philadelphia: Temple University Press, 1995.

Engen, David. "The Making of a People's Champion: An Analysis of Media Representations of George Foreman." *Southern Communication Journal* 60 (1995): 141–151.

Engnell, Richard. "The Spiritual Potential of Otherness in Film: The Interplay of Scene and Narrative." *Critical Studies in Mass Communication* 12 (1995): 241–262.

Enzensberger, Hans Magnus. "Ways of Walking: A Postscript to Utopia." *After the Fall: The Failure of Communism and the Future of Socialism.* Ed. Robin Blackburn. London: Verso Books, 1991. 18–24.

Ethnic Notions. Dir. and Prod. Marlin Riggs. California Newsreel, 1989.

Fallon, Richard H., Jr., "What Is Republicanism and Is It Worth Reviving?" *Harvard Law Review* 102 (1989): 1695–1735.

Faludi, Susan. *Backlash: The Undeclared War Against American Women.* New York: Crown, 1991.

Farrell, Thomas B. *Norms of Rhetorical Culture.* New Haven: Yale University Press, 1993.

Farrell, Thomas B., and Thomas G. Goodnight, "Accidental Rhetoric: the Root Metaphors of Three Mile Island." *Communication Monographs* 48 (1981): 271–300.

Ferguson, Marjorie, and Peter Golding, eds. *Cultural Studies in Question.* Thousand Oaks, CA: Sage, 1997.

Findlay, John M. *Magic Lands: Western Cityscapes and American Culture After 1940.* Berkeley: University of California Press, 1992.

Fish, Stanley. "Rhetoric." *Critical Terms for Literary Study.* 2nd ed. Eds. Frank Lentricchia and Thomas McLaughlin. Chicago: University of Chicago Press, 1995. 203–222.

Fisher, Andrew. *William Wallace.* Edinburgh: John Donald Publishers, 1986.

Fisher, Thomas. "Case Study: Holt Hinshaw Pfau Jones, Introduction." *Progressive Architecture,* July 1991: 72–78.

Fisher, Walter R. *Human Communication as Narrative: Toward a Philosophy of Reason, Value, and Action.* Columbia: University of South Carolina Press, 1987.

Fiske, John. "For Cultural Interpretation: A Study of the Culture of Homelessness." *Critical Studies in Mass Communication* 8 (1991): 455–474.

_____. "Critical Response: Meaningful Moments." *Critical Studies in Mass Communication* 5 (1988): 246–251.

_____. "Cultural Studies and the Culture of Everyday Life." In Grossberg, Nelson, and Treichler. 154–165.

_____. *Media Matters: Race and Gender in U.S. Politics.* Rev. ed. Minneapolis: University of Minnesota Press, 1996.

_____. "Television and Popular Culture: Reflections on British and Australian Critical Practice." *Critical Studies in Mass Communication* 3 (1986): 200–216.

_____. *Television Culture.* London: Routledge, 1994.

_____. "Television: Polysemy and Popularity." *Critical Studies in Mass Communication* 4 (1986): 391–408.

_____. *Understanding the Popular.* Boston: Unwin Hyman, 1989.

_____. "Writing Ethnographies: Contribution to a Dialogue." *Quarterly Journal of Speech* 77 (1991): 330–335.

Fiske, John, and John Hartley. *Reading Television.* London: Routledge, 1989.

Fitch, Kristine L. "Rev. of *Cultural Studies,* ed. Lawrence Grossberg, Cary Nelson and Paula Treichler." *Quarterly Journal of Speech* 80 (1994): 240–242.

Fjellman, Stephen M. *Vinyl Leaves: Walt Disney World and America.* Boulder, CO: Westview, 1992.

Fjelstad, Per. "Legal Judgment and Cultural Motivation: Enthymematic Form in *Marbury V. Madison.*" *Southern Communication Journal* 60 (1994): 22–32.

Foss, Karen A., and Belle A. Edson. "What's in a Name? Accounts of Married Women's Name Choices." *Western Journal of Speech Communication* 53 (1989): 356–373.

Foss, Sonja K. "Equal Rights Amendment Controversy: Two Worlds in Conflict." *Quarterly Journal of Speech* 65 (1979): 275–288.

_____. "Feminism Confronts Catholicism: A Study of the Use of Perspective by Incongruity." *Women's Studies in Communication* 3 (1979): 7–15.

Foss, Sonja K., and Cindy L. Griffin. "Beyond Persuasion: A Proposal for an Invitational Rhetoric." *Communication Monographs* 62 (1995): 2–18.

Foster, Hal. *The Return of the Real.* Cambridge, MA: MIT Press, 1996.

Foucault, Michel. "Archaeology and the History of Ideas." *The Archaeology of*

Knowledge. Trans. A. M. Sheridan Smith. New York: Pantheon Books, 1972. 135–140.

_____. "Afterword: The Subject and Power." *Michel Foucault: Beyond Structuralism and Hermeneutics.* Eds., Trans. H. L. Dreyfuss and P. Rabinow. Chicago: University of Chicago Press, 1983. 208–226.

_____. *Madness and Civilization: A History of Insanity in the Age of Reason.* 1965. Trans. Richard Howard. New York: Vintage Books, 1988.

_____. *Power/Knowledge: Selected Interviews and Other Writings, 1972–1977.* New York: Pantheon Books, 1980.

Franklin, Sarah, Celia Lury, and Jackie Stacey. *Off-Centre: Feminism and Cultural Studies.* London: Harper-Collins Academic, 1991.

Frentz, Thomas S., and Janice Hocker Rushing. "Integrating Ideology and Archetype in Rhetorical Criticism, Part II: A Case Study of *Jaws.*" *Quarterly Journal of Speech* 79 (1993): 61–81.

Gamman, Lorraine, and Margaret Marshment. *The Female Gaze: Women as Viewers of Popular Culture.* London: The Women's Press, 1988.

Gaonkar, Dilip Parameshwar. "The Idea of Rhetoric in the Rhetoric of Science." In Gross and Keith. 25–85.

_____. "Object and Method in Rhetorical Criticism: From Wichelns to Leff and McGee." *Western Journal of Speech Communication* 54 (1990): 290–316.

_____. "The Oratorical Text: The Enigma of Arrival." In Leff and Kauffeld. 255–75.

_____. "The Very Idea of a Rhetorical Culture." *Quarterly Journal of Speech* 80 (1994): 333–338.

Garchik, Leah. "Their Viewing Pleasure." *San Francisco Chronicle,* 2 Feb. 1996: D16.

Garrett, Laurie. "The Future of Death/A Report on an Aging World's Diseases Sets Up a Debate on How to Allocate Health Resources." *Newsday,* 8 Oct. 1996: B21.

Garrett, Mary. "Pathos Reconsidered from the Perspective of Classical Chinese Rhetorical Theories." *Quarterly Journal of Speech* 79 (1993): 19–39.

Gates, Henry Louis, Jr. *The Signifying Monkey.* New York: Oxford University Press, 1988.

Gattegno, Caleb. *Towards a Visual Culture: Educating Through Television.* 1969. New York: Avon Books, 1971.

Geertz, Clifford. *The Interpretation of Cultures.* New York: Basic Books, 1973.

Gewen, Barry. "Writers & Writing: Dwight Macdonald's Legacy." *The New Leader,* 11–15 Feb. 1985: 13–14.

Gibson, William. *Neuromancer.* New York: Ace Books, 1984.

Gibson, William, and Bruce Sterling. *The Difference Engine.* New York: Bantam Books, 1991.

Gilbert, James. "Scolding American Liberalism." *Reviews in American History* 25 (1997): 107–112.

Gilder, George. *Life After Television: The Coming Transformation of Media and American Life.* Rev. ed. New York: Norton, 1994.

Gingrich, Newton L. "Speech given to the Washington Research Group: 11 November 1994." Online. Internet. 15 April 1997. Available at http://dolphin.gulf.net./Gingrich.html.

Giroux, Henry A. *Fugitive Cultures: Race, Violence, and Youth.* New York: Routledge, 1996.

Gitlin, Todd. "The Anti-Political Populism of Cultural Studies." In Ferguson and Golding. 25–38.

Glynn, Kevin. "Reading Supermarket Tabloids as Menippean Satire." *Communication Studies* 44 (1993): 19–37.

Goffman, Erving. *Frame Analysis: An Essay on the Organization of Experience.* New York: Harper-Colophon, 1974.

Gold, Ellen Reid. "Ronald Reagan and the Oral Tradition." *Central States Speech Journal* 39 (1988): 159–176.

Goodnight, G. Thomas. "*The Firm, The Park,* and the University: Fear and Trembling on the Postmodern Trail." *Quarterly Journal of Speech* 81 (1995): 267–290.

Gorman, Paul R. *Left Intellectuals and Popular Culture in Twentieth-Century America.* Chapel Hill: University of North Carolina Press, 1996.

Gouldner, Alvin W. *Against Fragmentation: The Origins of Marxism and the Sociology of Intellectuals.* New York: Oxford University Press, 1985.

Graff, Gerald. *Beyond the Culture Wars: How Teaching the Conflicts Can Revitalize American Education.* New York and London: Norton, 1992.

_____. *Professing Literature: An Institutional History.* Chicago: University of Chicago Press, 1989.

Greenblatt, Stephen. *Shakespearean Negotiations.* Berkeley: University of California Press, 1988.

Greene, Ronald W. "Policy: Mapping the Terrain of Power at the Intersection of Rhetoric and Cultural Studies." Speech Communication Association Convention. San Antonio, TX, 21 Nov. 1995.

Greenough, Beverly Sills. "Breaking the Genetic Code." *Newsweek,* 5 April 1993: 10.

Gregg, Richard B., A. Jackson McCormack, and Douglas J. Pedersen. "The Rhetoric of Black Power: A Street-Level Interpretation." *Quarterly Journal of Speech* 55 (1969): 151–160.

Griswold, Charles L. "The Vietnam Veterans Memorial and the Washington Mall: Philosophical Thoughts on Political Iconography." *Critical Inquiry* 12 (1986): 688–719.

Groden, Michael, and Martin Kreisworth, eds. *The Johns Hopkins Guide to Literary Theory and Criticism.* Baltimore: Johns Hopkins University Press, 1994.

Gronbeck, Bruce E. "Rhetorical Timing in Public Communication." *Central States Speech Journal* 25 (1974): 84–94.

Gross, Alan G., and William M. Keith, eds. *Rhetorical Hermeneutics: Invention and Interpretation in the Age of Science.* Albany: State University of New York Press, 1997.

Grossberg, Lawrence. "Can Cultural Studies Find True Happiness in Communication?" *Journal of Communication* 43.4 (1993): 89–97.

_____. "The Circulation of Cultural Studies." *Critical Studies in Mass Communication* 6 (1989): 413–420.

_____. "Cultural Studies and/in New Worlds." *Critical Studies in Mass Communication* 10 (1993): 1–22.

_____. "Toward a Genealogy of the State of Cultural Studies: The Discipline of

Communication and the Reception of Cultural Studies in the United States." In Nelson and Gaonkar. 131–148.

_____. *We Gotta Get Out of This Place: Popular Conservatism and Postmodern Culture.* London: Routledge, 1992.

Grossberg, Lawrence, Cary Nelson, and Paula A. Treichler, eds. *Cultural Studies.* New York: Routledge, 1992.

Grossberg, Lawrence, and Janice Radway. "Editorial Statement." *Cultural Studies* 8 (1994), ii–iii.

Grossberg, Lawrence, and Jennifer Daryl Slack. "An Introduction to Stuart Hall's Essay." *Critical Studies in Mass Communication* 2 (1985): 87–90.

Guillory, John. *Cultural Capital: The Problem of Literary Canon Formation.* Chicago: University of Chicago Press, 1993.

Gunn, Giles. *Thinking Across the American Grain: Ideology, Intellect, and the New Pragmatism.* Chicago: University of Chicago Press, 1992.

Hacker, Andrew. *Two Nations: Black and White, Separate, Hostile, Unequal.* New York: Charles Scribner's Sons, 1992.

Habermas, Jürgen. *The Theory of Communicative Action.* 2 vols. Boston: Beacon Press, 1984, 1989.

Haden-Guest, Anthony. "The Pixie-Dust Papers." *The Paradise Program: Travels through Muzak, Hilton, Coca-Cola, Texaco, Walt Disney and Other World Empires.* New York: William Morrow, 1973. 220–310.

Halberstam, David. *The Fifties.* New York: Villard Books, 1993.

Hall, Edward. *Beyond Culture.* Garden City, NY: Anchor Press/Doubleday, 1976.

_____. *The Hidden Dimension.* 1966. Garden City, NY: Anchor Books, 1969.

_____. *The Silent Language.* 1959. New York: Fawcett World Library, 1961.

Hall, Stuart. "Cultural Studies and Its Theoretical Legacies." In Grossberg, Nelson, and Treichler. 277–286.

_____. "Cultural Studies: Two Paradigms." *Media, Culture and Society* 2 (1980): 57–72.

_____. "Encoding/Decoding." *Culture, Media, Language.* Eds. Stuart Hall, Dorothy Hobson, and Paul Willis. London: Hutchinson, 1980. 128–138.

_____. *The Hard Road to Renewal: Thatcherism and the Crisis of the Left.* London: Verso, 1988.

_____. "Notes on Deconstructing the Popular." *People's History and Socialist Theory.* Ed. Raphael Samuel. New York: Routledge, 1981. 227–239.

_____. "Signification, Representation, Ideology: Althusser and the Post-Structuralist Debates." *Critical Studies in Mass Communication* 2 (1985): 91–114.

_____. ed. *Representation: Cultural Representations and Signifying Practices.* Thousand Oaks, CA: Sage, 1997.

Hall, Stuart, and Martin Jacques. *The Politics of Thatcherism.* London: Lawrence Wishart, 1983.

Hall, Stuart, Chas Critcher, Tony Jefferson, John Clarke, and Brian Roberts. *Policing the Crisis: Mugging, the State, and Law and Order.* London: Macmillan, 1978.

Handelman, Don. "Play and Ritual: Complementary Frames of Meta-Communication."

It's a Funny Thing, Humour. Eds. Anthony J. Chapman and Hugh C. Foot. Oxford: Pergamon Press, 1977. 185–192.

Haraway, Donna J. "A Cyborg Manifesto: Science, Technology, and Socialist-Feminism in the Late Twentieth Century." *Simians, Cyborgs, and Women: The Reinvention of Nature.* New York: Routledge, 1991. 149–181.

Hardt, Hanno. *Critical Communication Studies: Communication, History and Theory in America.* New York: Routledge, 1992.

Hariman, Robert. *Political Style: The Artistry of Power.* Chicago: University of Chicago Press, 1995.

———. "Time and the Reconstitution of Gradualism in King's Address: A Response to Cox." In Leff and Kauffeld. 205–218.

Hart, Roderick. "Wandering with Rhetorical Criticism." In Nothstine, Blair, and Copeland. 71–81.

Hartley, John. "Critical Response: The Real World of Audiences." *Critical Studies in Mass Communication* 5 (1988): 234–238.

———. "Culture." In O'Sullivan et al. 68–70.

———. "Rhetoric." In O'Sullivan et al. 266–267.

Hasian, Marouf A. *The Rhetoric of Eugenics in Anglo-American Thought.* Athens: University of Georgia Press, 1996.

Hawthorn, Jeremy. *A Glossary of Contemporary Literary Theory.* 2nd ed. London: Edward Arnold, 1994.

Heath, Stephen. "Film and System: Terms of Analysis," Part 1: *Screen* 16, 1 (1975); Part 2: *Screen* 16, 2 (1975): 7–77.

Hebdige, Dick. "What Is 'Soul'?" *Video Icons and Values.* Eds. Alan M. Olson, Christopher Parr, and Debra Parr. Albany: State University of New York Press, 1991. 121–134.

Heller, Scott. "New Curriculum at Syracuse U. Attacked by 2 Marxist Professors." *Chronicle of Higher Education,* 3 August 1988: A17.

———. "Some English Departments Are Giving Undergraduates Grounding in New Literary and Critical Theory." *Chronicle of Higher Education,* 3 August 1988: A15–A17.

Hicks, Granville. "The Future of Socialism: II. On Attitudes and Ideas." *Partisan Review.* Mar.–Apr. 1947: 117–129.

Hill, Forbes. "Conventional Wisdom—Traditional Form: The President's Message of November 3, 1969." *Quarterly Journal of Speech* 58 (1972): 373–386.

———. "Reply to Professor Campbell." *Quarterly Journal of Speech* 58 (1972): 451–460.

———. "A Turn Against Ideology: Reply to Professor Wander." *Central States Speech Journal* 34 (1983): 121–126.

Hinshaw, Marc. Interview with Carole Blair. 10 June 1994.

Hogben, Gavin. "Life in the Machine." *Progressive Architecture,* July 1991: 79, 142.

Hoggart, Richard. *The Uses of Literacy.* 1958. New York: Oxford University Press, 1970.

Holland, Norman. *The Dynamics of Literary Response.* New York: Oxford University Press, 1968.

Holt, Paul. Letter to Design Review Committee, Astronauts Memorial Foundation. Holt Hinshaw files. San Francisco. 6 December 1989. 1–4.

Hook, Sidney. "The Future of Socialism." *Partisan Review,* Jan.–Feb. 1947: 23–36.

hooks, bell. *Art on My Mind.* New York: The New Press, 1995.

_____. *Black Looks: Race and Representation.* Boston: South End Press, 1992.

_____. *Killing Rage: Ending Racism.* New York: Henry Holt and Co, 1995.

_____. *Outlaw Culture.* New York: Routledge, 1994.

_____. "Postmodern Blackness." *Postmodern Culture* 1 (1990): 1–15.

_____. *Yearning: Race, Gender, and Cultural Politics.* Boston: South End Press, 1990.

Horne, Janet. "Rhetoric After Rorty." *Western Journal of Speech Communication* 53 (1989): 247–259.

Hubbard, Ruth, and Elijah Wald. *Exploding the Gene Myth: How Genetic Information Is Produced and Manipulated by Scientists, Physicians, Employers, Insurance Companies, Educators, and Law Enforcers.* Boston: Beacon Press, 1993.

Husband, Charles. *White Media and Black Britain.* London: Arrow Books, 1975.

Information Summaries: Spinoffs. Washington, DC: n.p., 1988.

Ivie, Robert L. "The Performance of Rhetorical Knowledge." *Quarterly Journal of Speech* 80 (1994): 128.

_____. "Scrutinizing Performances of Rhetorical Criticism." *Quarterly Journal of Speech* 80 (1994): 248.

Jablonski, Carol J. "Rhetoric, Paradox, and the Movement for Women's Ordination in the Roman Catholic Church." *Quarterly Journal of Speech* 74 (1988): 164–183.

Jacobs, Norman, ed. *Culture for the Millions?* Princeton, NJ: Van Nostrand, 1961.

James, William. *Pragmatism and The Meaning of Truth.* 1907. Cambridge, MA: Harvard University Press, 1978.

_____. "The Moral Philosopher and the Moral Life." *William James: The Essential Writings.* Ed. Bruce W. Wilshire. 1891. Albany: State University of New York Press, 1984.

Jameson, Fredric. *Fables of Aggression: Wyndham Lewis, the Modernist as Fascist.* Berkeley: University of California Press, 1979.

_____. "Marx's Purloined Letter." *New Left Review* 209 (January/February 1995): 75–109.

_____. *The Political Unconscious: Narrative as a Socially Symbolic Act.* Ithaca, NY: Cornell University Press, 1981.

_____. *Postmodernism, or, The Cultural Logic of Late Capitalism.* Durham, NC: Duke University Press, 1991.

_____. *Signatures of the Visible.* New York: Routledge, 1992.

Jamieson, Kathleen M. "Antecedent Genre as Rhetorical Constraint." *Quarterly Journal of Speech* 61 (1975): 406–415.

_____. "Generic Constraints and the Rhetorical Situation." *Philosophy and Rhetoric* 6 (1973): 162–170.

Jasinski, James. "Instrumentalism, Contextualism, and Interpretation in Rhetorical Criticism." In Gross and Keith. 195–224.

Jeffords, Susan. *Hard Bodies: Hollywood Masculinity in the Reagan Era.* New Brunswick, NJ: Rutgers University Press, 1994.

Jenkins, Henry. *Textual Poachers: Television Fans and Participatory Culture.* New York: Routledge, 1992.

Jewett, Robert, and John Shelton Lawrence. *The American Monomyth.* Garden City, NY: Anchor/Doubleday, 1977.

Johannesen, Richard J. "The Ethics of Plagiarism Reconsidered: The Oratory Of Martin Luther King, Jr." *Southern Communication Journal* 60 (1995): 185–194.

Johnson, Barbara. *The Wake of Deconstruction.* Cambridge, MA: Blackwell, 1994.

Johnson, Richard. "What Is Cultural Studies Anyway?" *Social Text* 16 (1986): 38–80.

Jones, Paul. "The Myth of 'Raymond Hoggart': On 'Founding Fathers' and Cultural Policy." *Cultural Studies* 8 (1994): 394–416.

Kaplan, E. Ann, and Michael Sprinker, eds. *The Althusserian Legacy.* London and New York: Verso, 1993.

Katriel, Tamar. "Rhetoric in Flames: Fire Inscriptions in Israeli Youth Movement Ceremonials." *Quarterly Journal of Speech* 73 (1987): 444–459.

———. "Sites of Memory: Discourses of the Past in Israeli Pioneering Settlement Museums." *Quarterly Journal of Speech* 80 (1994): 1–20.

Kellner, Douglas. "Overcoming the Divide: Cultural Studies and Political Economy." In Ferguson and Golding. 102–120.

Kennedy Space Center Visitor Center. N.p.: n.d. [acquired September 1996].

Kielwasser, Alfred P., and Michelle A. Wolf. "Mainstream Television, Adolescent Homosexuality, and Significant Silence." *Critical Studies in Mass Communication* 9 (1992): 350–373.

Kipnis, Jeffrey. "The Mechanism of Power." *Progressive Architecture,* July 1991: 79, 142.

Knapp, Steven, and Walter Benn Michaels. "Against Theory." In Mitchell. 11–30.

Kneupper, Charles, ed. *Rhetoric and Ideology: Compositions and Criticisms of Power.* Arlington, TX: Rhetoric Society of America, 1989.

Koestler, Arthur. *The Act of Creation.* New York: Dell, 1964.

Kolata, Gina. "Parents Take Charge, Putting Gene Hunt Onto Fast Track." *The New York Times,* 16 June 1996: sec. C, p. 1.

Kovel, Joel. *White Racism: A Psychohistory.* New York: Columbia University Press, 1984.

Kuhn, Annette. *The Power of the Image.* London: Routledge & Kegan Paul, 1985.

———. *Women's Pictures.* London: Routledge & Kegan Paul, 1982.

Kurtti, Jeff. *Since the World Began: Walt Disney World, the First 25 Years.* New York: Hyperion, 1996.

Kutulas, Judy. *The Long War: The Intellectual People's Front and Anti-Stalinism, 1930–1940.* Durham, NC: Duke University Press, 1995.

Lacan, Jacques. *Écrits: A Selection.* Trans. Alan Sheridan. New York: Tavistock, 1979.

———. *The Four Fundamental Concepts of Psychoanalysis.* Ed. Jacques-Alain Miller. Trans. Alan Sheridan. New York: Norton, 1981.

———. "Of Structure as an Inmixing of an Otherness Prerequisite to Any Subject Whatever." In Macksey and Donato. 186–195.

LaCapra, Dominick. *Rethinking Intellectual History: Texts, Contexts, Language.* Ithaca, NY: Cornell University Press, 1983.

Laclau, Ernesto, and Chantal Mouffe. *Hegemony & Socialist Strategy: Towards a Radical Democratic Politics*. London: Verso, 1985.

Laing, Stuart. *Representations of Working-Class Life, 1959–64*. London: Macmillan, 1986.

Laird, Donald A. "Intelligence and Heredity." *Today's Health* 30 (August 1952): 23–24.

Lake, Randall A. "Enacting Red Power: The Consummatory Function in Native American Protest Rhetoric." *Quarterly Journal of Speech* 69 (1983): 127–142.

_____. "Order and Disorder in Anti-Abortion Rhetoric: A Logological View." *Quarterly Journal of Speech* 70 (1984): 425–443.

Lakoff, George. *Moral Politics: What Conservatives Know That Liberals Don't*. Chicago: University of Chicago Press, 1996.

Lange, Jonathan. "Refusal to Compromise: The Case of Earth First!" *Western Journal of Speech Communication* 54 (1990): 473–494.

Langiulli, Nino. "On the Location of Socrates' Feet: or the Immanence of Transcendence." *Telos* 96 (1993): 143–147.

_____. *Possibility, Necessity, and Existence: Abbagnano and His Predecessors*. Philadelphia: Temple University Press, 1992.

_____. "Syracuse University and the Kool-Aid Acid Curriculum." *Measure* 88 (September 1990): 5–8.

Laplanche, J., and J.-B. Pontalis. *The Language of Psychoanalysis*. Trans. Donald Nicholson Smith. New York: Norton, 1974.

Lappe, Marc. *Broken Code: The Exploitation of DNA*. San Francisco: Sierra Club Books, 1984.

Lasch, Christopher. *The Revolt of the Elites and the Betrayal of Democracy*. New York: Norton, 1995.

The Last of the Mohicans. Dir. Michael Mann. Perf. Daniel Day-Lewis, Madeleine Stowe, and Jodhi May. Twentieth Century Fox, 1992.

Leff, Michael C. "Interpretation and the Art of the Rhetorical Critic." *Western Journal of Speech Communication* 44 (1980): 337–349.

_____. "Rhetorical Timing in Lincoln's 'House Divided' Speech." Evanston, IL: Northwestern University School of Speech, 1984.

_____. "Textual Criticism: The Legacy of G. P. Mohrmann." *Quarterly Journal of Speech* 72 (1986): 377–389.

_____. "Things Made by Words." *Quarterly Journal of Speech* 78 (1992): 223–231.

Leff, Michael C., and Fred Kauffeld, eds. *Texts in Context: Critical Dialogues on Significant Episodes in American Political Rhetoric*. Davis, CA: Hermagoras, 1989.

Leff, Michael C., and Margaret Organ Procario. "Rhetorical Theory in Speech Communication." *Speech Communication in the 20th Century*. Ed. Thomas Benson. Carbondale, IL: Southern Illinois University Press, 1985. 3–27.

Leff, Michael C., and Andrew Sachs. "Words the Most Like Things: Iconicity and the Rhetorical Text." *Western Journal of Speech Communication* 54 (1990): 252–273.

Leong, Wai-Teng. "Culture and the State: Manufacturing Traditions for Tourism." *Critical Studies in Mass Communication* 6 (1989): 355–375.

Lévi-Strauss, Claude. "The Structural Study of Myth." *Journal of American Folklore* 68 (1955): 428–444.

Levy, Renee Gearhart. "PC'ed Out." *Syracuse University Magazine* 7 (December 1991): 29–35.

Levy, Steven. *Hackers.* Garden City, NY: Anchor Press/Doubleday, 1984.

Lewis, George H., ed. *Side-Saddle on the Golden Calf: Social Structure and Popular Culture in America.* Pacific Palisades, CA: Goodyear, 1969.

Lewis, Peter H. "New concerns raised over a computer smut study." *The New York Times,* 16 July 1995: A22.

Lind, Michael. *The Next American Nation: The New Nationalism and the Fourth American Revolution.* New York: Free Press, 1996.

Lindenberger, Herbert. "The Western Culture Debate at Stanford University." *Comparative Criticism* 11 (1989): 225–234.

Lippmann, Abby. "Prenatal Genetic Testing and Geneticization: Mother Matters for All." *Fetal Diagnosis and Therapy* 8 (suppl. 1) (1993): 175–188.

Lloyd, David, and Paul Thar. "Culture and Society or 'Culture and the State.' " *Cultural Materialism: On Raymond Williams.* Ed. Christopher Prendergast. Minneapolis: University of Minnesota Press, 1995. 268–279.

Logue, Cal M., and Thurmon Garner. "Shifts in Rhetorical Status of Blacks After Freedom." *Southern Communication Journal* 54 (1988): 1–39.

Lucaites, John, Celeste M. Condit, and Sally Caudill. *Contemporary Rhetorical Theory: A Reader.* New York: Guilford, 1998.

Lucas, Stephen E. "The Renaissance of American Public Address: Text and Context in Rhetorical Criticism." *Quarterly Journal of Speech* 74 (1988): 241–260.

Lyne, John. "Culture of Inquiry." *Quarterly Journal of Speech* 76 (1990): 192–208.

Lyotard, Jean-Francois. *The Differend: Phrases in Dispute.* Trans. Georges Van Den Abbeele. Minneapolis: University of Minnesota Press.

Macdonald, Dwight. *Against the American Grain.* London: Victor Gollancz, 1963.

_____. *The Responsibility of Peoples and Other Essays in Political Criticism.* Westport, CT: Greenwood Press.

Mackay, James. *William Wallace: Brave Heart.* Edinburgh: Mainstream Publishing, 1995.

Macksey, Richard, and Eugenio Donato, eds. *The Structuralist Controversy: The Languages of Criticism and the Sciences of Man.* Baltimore: Johns Hopkins University Press, 1972.

Mailloux, Steven. "Rhetoric Returns to Syracuse: Curricular Reform in English Studies." *English Studies/Culture Studies: Institutionalizing Dissent.* Eds. Isaiah Smithson and Nancy Ruff. Urbana and Chicago: University of Illinois Press, 1994.

_____. "Rhetorically Covering Conflict: Gerald Graff As Curricular Rhetorician." *Teaching the Conflicts: Gerald Graff, Curricular Reform, and the Culture Wars.* Ed. William E. Cain. New York and London: Garland, 1994. 79–91.

_____, ed. *Rhetoric, Sophistry, Pragmatism.* Cambridge, UK: Cambridge University Press, 1995.

Mairston, Alan. "The Everglades: Dying for Help." *National Geographic* 185 (April 1994): 2–35.

Makaryk, Irena R., ed. *Encyclopedia of Contemporary Literary Theory.* Toronto: University of Toronto Press, 1993.

Makay, John J., and Alberto Gonzalez. "Dylan's Biographical Rhetoric and the Myth of the Outlaw-Hero." *Southern Speech Communication Journal* 52 (1987): 165–180.

Makus, Ann. "Stuart Hall's Theory Of Ideology: A Frame for Rhetorical Criticism." *Western Journal of Speech Communication* 54 (1990): 495–514.

Mayer, Michael E. "Explaining Choice Shift: An Effects Coded Model." *Communication Monographs* 52 (1985): 92–101.

McCoy, Michael. "Attitudes Toward Technology: Between Nature and Culture." *Progressive Architecture,* April 1991: 106–107.

McGee, Michael Calvin. "The 'Ideograph': A Link Between Rhetoric and Ideology." *Quarterly Journal of Speech* 66 (1980): 1–16.

_____. "In Search of 'The People': A Rhetorical Alternative." *Quarterly Journal of Speech* 61 (1975): 235–249.

_____. "A Materialist's Conception of Rhetoric." *Explorations in Rhetoric: Studies in Honor of Douglas Ehninger.* Ed. Raymie McKerrow. Glenview, IL: Scott, Foresman, 1982. 23–48.

_____. "Social Movement As Meaning." *Central States Speech Journal* 34 (1983): 74–77.

_____. "Text, Context, and the Fragmentation of Contemporary Culture." *Western Journal of Speech Communication* 54 (1990): 274–289.

McKeever, James. "SU Takes a New Look at the Classics." Syracuse *Post-Standard,* 30 August 1990: C1–C2.

McKerrow, Raymie E. "Critical Rhetoric: Theory and Praxis." *Communication Monographs* 56 (1989): 91–111.

McLuhan, Marshall. *Understanding Media: Extensions of Man.* New York: McGraw-Hill, 1965.

Mechling, Elizabeth Walker. "From Paradox to Parody: A Socio-Rhetorical Theory of Counter-Institutional Movement Organizations, Applied to the Free Clinic Movement." Diss. Temple University, 1979.

Mechling, Elizabeth Walker, and Jay Mechling. "The Campaign for Civil Defense and the Struggle to Naturalize the Bomb." *Western Journal of Speech Communication* 55 (1991): 105–133.

_____. "Hot Pacifism and Cold War: The American Friends Service Committee's Witness for Peace in 1950s America." *Quarterly Journal of Speech* 78 (1992): 173–196.

_____. "The Jung and the Restless: The Mythopoetic Men's Movement." *Southern Communication Journal* 59 (1994): 97–111.

_____. "The Sale of Two Cities: A Semiotic Comparison of Disneyland with Marriott's Great America." *Journal of Popular Culture* 15 (1981): 166-170. Reprinted in Medhurst and Benson. 400–413.

_____. "Sweet Talk: The Moral Rhetoric against Sugar." *Central States Speech Journal* 34 (1983): 19–32.

_____. "Youthful Citizenship in the Cold War United States." Unpublished essay, 1996.

Mechling, Jay. "Introduction: William James and the Philosophical Foundations for the Study of Everyday Life." *Western Folklore* 44 (1985): 303–310.

_____. "The Jamesian Berger." *Making Sense of Modern Times: Peter L. Berger and the Vision of Interpretive Sociology.* Eds. James Davison Hunter and Stephen C. Ainley. London: Routledge & Kegan Paul, 1986. 197–220.

Medhurst, Martin J. "Reconceptualizing Rhetorical History: Eisenhower's Farewell Address." *Quarterly Journal of Speech* 80 (1994): 195–218.

_____. "Public Address and Significant Scholarship: Four Challenges to the Rhetorical Renaissance." In Leff and Kauffeld. 29–42.

Medhurst, Martin, and Thomas Benson, eds. *Rhetorical Dimensions of the Media: A Critical Casebook.* Dubuque, IA: Kendall/Hunt, 1984.

Meehan, Eileen R. "Conceptualizing Culture As Commodity: The Problem of Television." *Critical Studies in Mass Communication* 3 (1986): 448–457.

Meguiar, George. Interview with Carole Blair and Neil Michel. 6 April 1994.

Meyers, Marian. "Reporters and Beats: The Making of Oppositional News." *Critical Studies in Mass Communication* 9 (1992): 75–90.

Miller, J. Hillis. *The Ethics of Reading.* New York: Columbia University Press, 1987.

Miller, Jacques-Alain. (1988) "Extimité." *Prose Studies* 11.3 (December 1988): 121–131.

Miller, Jean B. *Toward a New Psychology of Women.* Boston: Beacon Press, 1976.

Mills, C. Wright. *The Sociological Imagination.* New York: Oxford University Press, 1959.

Mitchell, W. J. T. "Introduction." *Landscape and Power.* Ed. W. J. T. Mitchell. Chicago: University of Chicago Press, 1994. 1–4.

_____, ed. *Against Theory: Literary Studies and the New Pragmatism.* Chicago: University of Chicago Press, 1985.

Mohrmann, G. P., and Michael C. Leff. "Lincoln at Cooper Union: A Rationale for Neo-Classical Criticism." *Quarterly Journal of Speech* 60 (1974): 459–467.

Moon, Dreama. "Concepts of 'Culture': Implications For Intercultural Communication Discourse." *Communication Quarterly* 44 (1996): 70–84.

Moore, Robert, and Douglas Gillette. *King, Warrior, Magician, Lover: Rediscovering the Archetypes of the Mature Masculine.* San Francisco: HarperCollins, 1990.

Morley, David. "Postmodernism: The Rough Guide." *Cultural Studies and Communication.* Eds. James Curran, David Morley, and Valerie Walkerdine. London: Arnold, 1996. 50–65.

_____. *Television, Audiences, and Cultural Studies.* New York: Routledge, 1992.

Morris, Richard. "Modernity's Prometheus." *Western Journal of Communication* 57 (1993): 139–146.

Morse, Margaret. "An Ontology of Everyday Distraction: The Freeway, the Mall, and Television." *Logics of Television: Essays in Cultural Criticism.* Ed. Patricia Mellencamp. Bloomington: Indiana University Press, 1990. 193–221.

Morton, Donald, and Mas'ud Zavarzadeh. "The Nostalgia for Law and Order and the Policing of Knowledge: The Politics of Contemporary Literary Theory."

Syracuse Scholar: An Interdisciplinary Journal of Ideas Published by Syracuse University, Supplementary Issue (Spring 1987). 25–71.

Mumby, Dennis K., ed. *Narrative and Social Control: Critical Perspectives.* Newbury Park, CA: Sage, 1993.

Mumby, Dennis, and Carole Spitzack. "Ideology and Television News: A Metaphoric Analysis of Political Stories." *Central States Speech Journal* 34 (1983): 162–171.

Munns, Jessica, and Gita Rajan, eds. *A Cultural Studies Reader: History, Theory, Practice.* London: Longman, 1995.

Murdock, Graham. "Across the Great Divide: Cultural Analysis and the Condition of Democracy." *Critical Studies in Mass Communication* 12 (1995): 89–94.

_____. "Cultural Studies: Missing Links." *Critical Studies in Mass Communication* 6 (1989): 436–440.

Nakagawa, Gordon. "Deformed Subjects, Docile Bodies: Disciplinary Practices and Subject-Constitution in Stories of Japanese-American Internment." *Narrative and Social Control: Critical Perspectives.* Ed. Dennis K. Mumby. Newbury Park, CA: Sage, 1993. 143–163.

_____. " 'What Are We Doing Here with All These Japanese?': Subject-Constitution and Strategies of Discourse Closure Represented in Stories of Japanese American Internment." *Communication Quarterly* 38 (1990): 388–402.

NASA Public Affairs, Kennedy Space Center. *The Kennedy Space Center Story.* Orlando, FL: Graphic House, 1991.

Neel, Jasper. *Plato, Derrida, and Writing.* Carbondale: Southern Illinois University Press, 1988.

Negroponte, Nicholas. *Being Digital.* New York: Knopf, 1995.

Nelkin, Dorothy, and Susan M. Lindee. *The DNA Mystique: The Gene As a Cultural Icon.* New York: W. H. Freeman and Company, 1995.

Nelson, Cary. *Manifesto of a Tenured Radical.* New York: New York University Press, 1997.

Nelson, Cary, and Dilip P. Gaonkar. "Cultural Studies and the Politics of Disciplinarity: An Introduction." In Nelson and Gaonkar. 1–19.

—, eds. *Disciplinarity and Dissent in Cultural Studies.* New York: Routledge, 1996.

Nelson, Cary, Paula A. Treichler, and Lawrence Grossberg. "Cultural Studies: An Introduction." In Grossberg, Nelson, and Treichler. 1–16.

Nelson, Jeffrey. "Homosexuality in Hollywood Films: A Contemporary Paradox." *Criticla Studies in Mass Communication* 2 (1985): 54–64.

Nelson, John S., Allan Megill, and Donald N. McClosky, eds. *The Rhetoric of the Human Sciences: Language and Argument in Scholarship and Public Affairs.* Madison: University of Wisconsin Press, 1987.

Nelson, Steve. "Walt Disney's EPCOT and the World's Fair Performance Tradition." *The Drama Review* 30 (1986): 106–146.

Newcomb, Horace, and Paul Hirsch. "Television As a Cultural Forum." *Television: The Critical View.* 5th ed. Ed. Horace Newcomb. New York: Oxford University Press, 1994. 503–515.

Newfield, Christopher, and Ronald Strickland, eds. *After Political Correctness: The Humanities and Society in the 1990s*. Boulder: Westview Press, 1995.

Nichols, Bill. *Ideology and the Image*. Bloomington: Indiana University Press, 1981.

Nichols, Sallie. *Jung and Tarot: An Archetypal Journey*. Maine: Samuel Weiser, 1980.

Nietzche, Friedrich. *The Birth of Tragedy*. 1909. Trans. Francis Golffing. New York: Doubleday, 1956.

Nothstine, William L., Carole Blair, and Gary A. Copeland, eds. *Critical Questions: Invention, Creativity, and the Criticism of Discourse and Media*. New York: St. Martin's Press, 1994.

Oberg, James. "Black astronaut's sacrifices ignored." *USA Today*, 26 November 1996: 13A.

O'Connor, Alan. "The Problem of American Cultural Studies." *Critical Studies in Mass Communication* 6 (1989): 405–412.

Olson, Gary A. "Fish Tales: A Conversation with 'The Contemporary Sophist.' " *Journal of Advanced Composition* 12 (1992): 253–277.

_____. "Jacques Derrida on Rhetoric and Composition: A Conversation." *Journal of Advanced Composition* 10 (1990): 1–21.

Olson, Kathryn M., and G. Thomas Goodnight. "Entanglements of Consumption, Cruelty, Privacy, and Fashion: The Social Controversy over Fur." *Quarterly Journal of Speech* 80 (1994): 249–276.

Ong, Walter. *The Presence of the Word*. New York: Clarion, 1967.

Orr, Leonard. *A Dictionary of Critical Theory*. New York: Greenwood Press, 1991.

Orwell, George. "The Future of Socialism: IV. Toward European Unity." *Partisan Review*, July–Aug. 1947: 346–351.

Osborn, Michael. "Archetypal Metaphor in Rhetoric: The Light-Dark Family." *Quarterly Journal of Speech* 53 (1967): 115–126.

_____. "The Evolution of the Archetypal Sea in Rhetoric and Poetic." *Quarterly Journal of Speech* 63 (1977): 347–363.

_____. *Orientations to Rhetorical Style*. Chicago: Science Research Associates, 1976.

_____. "Rhetorical Depiction." *Form, Genre, and the Study of Political Discourse*. Eds. Herbert W. Simons and Ara A. Aghazarian. Columbia: University of South Carolina Press, 1986. 79–107.

O'Sullivan, Tim, John Hartley, Danny Saunders, Martin Montgomery, and John Fiske, eds. *Key Concepts in Communication and Cultural Studies*. 2nd ed. New York: Routledge, 1994.

Owen, A. Susan. "Oppositional Voices in *China Beach*: Narrative Configurations of Gender and War." In Mumby. 207–231.

Parlin, Carol A. Syracuse *Record*, 16 July 1990: 1ff.

Perera, Sylvia Brinton. *Descent to the Goddess: A Way of Initiation for Women*. Toronto: Inner City Books, 1981.

Peterson, Eric E. "The Stories of Pregnancy: On Interpretation of Small Group Cultures." *Communication Quarterly* 35 (1987): 39–47.

Pierce, Fred. "SU Curriculum Challenges 'Classics.' " Syracuse *Post-Standard*, 19 July 1990: A1ff.

Pocock, J. G. A. *The Machiavellian Moment*. Princeton: Princeton University Press, 1975.

Poulakos, John. *Sophistical Rhetoric in Classical Greece*. Columbia: University of South Carolina Press, 1995.

Pratt, Mary Louise. "Humanities for the Future: Reflections on the Western Culture Debate at Stanford." *South Atlantic Quarterly* 89 (Winter 1990): 7–25.

Proctor, David E. "The Dynamic Spectacle: Transforming Experience into Social Forms of Community." *Quarterly Journal of Speech* 76 (1990): 117–133.

The Project on Disney. *Inside the Mouse: Work and Play at Disney World*. Durham, NC: Duke University Press, 1995.

Propp, Vladimir. *Morphology of the Folktale*. Ed. Svatava Pirkova-Jakobson. Trans. Laurence Scott. Bloomington: Indiana University Press, 1958.

Radway, Janice A. *Reading the Romance: Women, Patriarchy, and Popular Literature*. Chapel Hill: University of North Carolina Press, 1984.

Railsback, Celeste Condit. "The Contemporary American Abortion Controversy: Stages in the Argument." *Quarterly Journal of Speech* 70 (1984): 410–424.

Real, Michael. *Mass-Mediated Culture*. Englewood Cliffs, NJ: Prentice-Hall, 1977.

Reed, T. V. *Fifteen Jugglers, Five Believers: Literary Politics and the Poetics of American Social Movements*. Berkeley: University of California Press, 1992.

Ricco, Barry D. "Popular Culture and High Culture: Dwight Macdonald, His Critics and the Ideal of Cultural Hierarchy in Modern America." *Journal of American Culture* 16:4 (Winter 1993): 7–18.

Richards, I. A. *The Philosophy of Rhetoric*. 1936. New York: Oxford University Press, 1965.

Roach, Jannette, and Petal Felix, P. "Black Looks." *The Female Gaze: Women As Viewers of Popular Culture*. Eds. Lorraine Gamman and Margaret Marshment. London: The Women's Press, 1988. 130–142.

Rob Roy. Dir. Michael Caton-Jones. Perf. Liam Neeson, Jessica Lange, John Hurt, Tim Roth, Eric Stoltz, and Brian Cox. United Artists, 1995.

Robbins, Bruce. "Oppositional Professionals: Theory and the Narratives of Professionalization." *Consequences of Theory*. Eds. Jonathan Arac and Barbara Johnson. Baltimore: Johns Hopkins University Press, 1991. 1–21.

Robin Hood: Prince of Thieves. Dir. Kevin Reynolds. Perf. Kevin Costner, Morgan Freeman, Mary Elizabeth Mastrontonio, Christian Slater, and Alan Rickman. 1991.

Rochberg-Halton, Eugene. *Meaning and Modernity: Social Theory in the Pragmatic Attitude*. Chicago: University of Chicago Press, 1986.

Rodman, Gilbert. *Elvis After Elvis: The Posthumous Career of a Living Legend*. New York: Routledge, 1996.

Rogers, Everett M. *A History of Communication Study*. New York: Free Press, 1994

Rorty, Richard. *Consequences of Pragmatism*. Minneapolis: University of Minnesota Press, 1982.

_____. *Contingency, Irony, and Solidarity*. Cambridge, UK: Cambridge University Press, 1989.

Rose, Jaqueline. *Sexuality in the Field of Vision*. London: Verso, 1986.

Rosenberg, Bernard, and David Manning White, eds. *Mass Culture: The Popular Arts in America.* Glencoe, IL: Free Press, 1957.

Ross, Andrew. *No Respect: Intellectuals & Popular Culture.* New York: Routledge, 1989.

Rosteck, Thomas. "Cultural Studies and Rhetorical Studies." *Quarterly Journal of Speech* 81 (1995): 386–403.

———. "Rhetorical Criticism and the Context of Culture: Rereading Ernest Wrage." Southern States Communication Association Annual Convention. Peabody Hotel, Memphis, 30 Mar. 1996.

———. See It Now *Confronts McCarthyism: Television Documentary and the Politics of Representation.* Tuscaloosa: University of Alabama Press, 1994.

Rosteck, Thomas, and Michael Leff. "Piety, Propriety, and Perspective: An Interpretation and Application of Key Terms in Kenneth Burke's *Permanence and Change.*" *Western Journal of Speech Communication* 53 (1989): 327–341.

Rushing, Janice Hocker. "Evolution of 'the New Frontier' in *Alien* and *Aliens*: Patriarchal Co-optation of the Feminine Archetypal." *Quarterly Journal of Speech* 75 (1989): 1–24.

———. "Mythic Evolution of 'The New Frontier' in Mass Mediated Rhetoric," *Critical Studies in Mass Communication* 3 (1986): 265–296.

———. "Power, Other, and Spirit in Cultural Texts." *Western Journal of Communication* 57 (1993): 159–168.

———. "Ronald Reagan's 'Star Wars' Address: Mythic Containment of Technical Reasoning." *Quarterly Journal of Speech* 72 (1986): 415–433.

Rushing, Janice Hocker, and Thomas S. Frentz. "The Frankenstein Myth in Contemporary Cinema." *Critical Studies in Mass Communication* 6 (1989): 61–80.

———. "Integrating Ideology and Archetype in Rhetorical Criticism." *Quarterly Journal of Speech* 77 (1991): 385–406.

———. *Projecting the Shadow: The Cyborg Hero in American Film.* Chicago: University of Chicago Press, 1995.

———. "The Rhetoric of 'Rocky': A Social Value Model of Criticism." *Western Journal of Speech Communication* 42 (1978): 63–72.

Rybaak, Spider. "The Corruption of SU English." Syracuse *New Times,* 20–27 November 1991: 9–10.

Said, Edward W. "Traveling Theory." In Said. 226–247.

———. *The World, the Text, and the Critic.* Cambridge, UK: Harvard University Press, 1983.

Salvador, Michael. "The Rhetorical Subversion of Cultural Boundaries: The National Consumers' League." *Southern Communication Journal* 59 (1994): 318–332.

Scheibel, Dean. "Graffiti and 'Film School Culture': Displaying Alienation." *Communication Monographs* 61 (1994): 1–18.

———. " 'Making Waves' with Burke: Surf Nazi Culture and the Rhetoric of Localism." *Western Journal of Communication* 59 (1995): 253–269.

Scheinfeld, Amram. "You, Your Child and Heredity." *Parents Magazine* (1953): 40–41, 78–79.

Schiappa, Edward. "The Rhetoric of Nukespeak." *Communication Monographs* 56 (1989): 253–272.

Schlesinger, Arthur M., Jr., "The Future of Socialism: III. The Perspective Now." *Partisan Review,* May–Jun. 1947: 229–242.

Schramm, Wilbur. *The Beginnings of Communication Study in America.* Thousand Oaks, CA: Sage, 1997.

Schudson, Michael. "The New Validation of Popular Culture: Sense and Sentimentality in Academia." *Critical Studies in Mass Communication* 4 (1987): 51–68.

Schutz, Alfred. *Collected Papers I: The Problem of Social Reality.* Ed. Maurice Natanson. The Hague: Martinus Nijhoff, 1973.

Schwarz, Bill. "Where Is Cultural Studies?" *Cultural Studies* 8 (1994): 377–393.

Scott, Robert L. "Diego Rivera at Rockefeller Center: Fresco Painting and Rhetoric." *Western Speech Communication* 41 (Spring 1977): 71–82.

Sehlinger, Bob. *The Unofficial Guide to Walt Disney World & EPCOT.* New York: Macmillan, 1996.

Seigfried, Charlene Haddock. *Pragmatism and Feminism: Reweaving the Social Fabric.* Chicago: University of Chicago Press, 1996.

Serge, Victor. "The Future of Socialism: V. The Socialist Imperative." Trans. George Schloss. *Partisan Review,* Sep.–Oct. 1947: 511–517.

Shannon, Christopher. *Conspicuous Criticism: Tradition, the Individual and Culture in American Social Thought, from Veblen to Mills.* Baltimore: Johns Hopkins University Press, 1996.

Shaw, Gareth, and Allan M. Williams. *Critical Issues in Tourism: A Geographical Perspective.* Oxford: Blackwell, 1994.

Shaw, Kenneth A. "The Chancellor's Report: Restructuring Syracuse University." 17 February 1992. Special Insert Section in *Syracuse University Magazine,* 8 (March 1992).

Shaw, Punch. "General Refinement on the Fringe: The Game Show." *Southern Speech Communication Journal* 52 (1987): 403–410.

Shome, Raka. "The Rhetoric of NEO/imperialism: The Discourse of National Identity in the Jewel in the Crown." Diss. University of Georgia, 1996.

Siebers, Tobin. "Mourning Becomes Paul de Man." *Responses: On Paul de Man's Wartime Journalism.* Ed. Werner Hamacher, Neil Hertz, and Thomas Keenan. Lincoln: University of Nebraska Press, 1989. 363–367.

_____, ed. *Heterotopia: Postmodern Utopia and the Body Politic.* Ann Arbor: University of Michigan Press, 1994.

Sillars, Malcolm. "Rhetoric as Act." *Quarterly Journal of Speech* 50 (1964): 277–284.

Silverman, Kaja. *Male Subjectivity at the Margins.* New York: Routledge, 1992.

_____. *The Threshold of the Visible World.* New York: Rouledge, 1996.

Silverstone, Roger. "Television and Everyday Life: Towards an Anthropology of the Television Audience." *Public Communication: The New Imperatives.* Ed. Marjorie Ferguson. Newbury Park, CA: Sage, 1990. 173–189.

Simons, Elizabeth Radin. "The NASA Joke Cycle: The Astronauts and the Teacher." *Western Folklore* 45 (1986): 261–273.

Simpson, David. "Raymond Williams: Feeling for Structures, Voicing 'History.' "

Cultural Materialism: On Raymond Williams. Ed. Christopher Prendergast. Minneapolis: University of Minnesota Press, 1995. 29–50.

Simpson, Gailyn. Interview with Carole Blair. 20 May 1992.

Sloop, John M. "The Parent I Never Had: The Contemporary Construction of Alternatives to Incarceration." *Communication Studies* 43 (1992): 1–13.

Slotkin, Richard. *Gunfighter Nation: The Myth of the Frontier in Twentieth Century America.* New York: Atheneum, 1992.

_____. *Regeneration Through Violence.* Middlebury, CT: Wesleyan University Press, 1973.

Smith, Alfred G., ed. *Communication and Culture: Readings in the Codes of Human Interaction.* New York: Holt, Rinehart and Winston, 1966.

Smith, Henry Nash. "Can 'American Studies' Develop a Method?" *American Quarterly* 9 (1957): 197–208.

Smith, Jonathan. "The Lie That Blinds: Destabilizing the Text of Landscape." In Duncan and Ley. 78–92.

Smith, Michael L. "Making Time: Representations of Technology at the 1964 World's Fair." *The Power of Culture: Critical Essays in American History.* Eds. Richard Wightman Fox and T. J. Jackson Lears. Chicago: University of Chicago Press, 1993. 223–244.

Sobchack, Vivian. *Screening Space: The American Science Fiction Film.* New York: Ungar, 1987.

Solomon, Martha. "The Positive Woman's Journey: A Mythic Analysis of the Rhetoric of STOP ERA." *Quarterly Journal of Speech* 65 (1979): 262–274.

_____. "The Rhetoric of Dehumanization: An Analysis of Medical Reports of the Tuskegee Syphilis Project." *Western Journal of Speech Communication* 49 (1985): 233–247.

_____. "The Things We Study: Texts and Their Interactions." *Communication Monographs* 60 (1993): 62–68.

Sontag, Susan. *On Photography.* New York: Farrar, Straus and Giroux, 1977.

Sorkin, Michael. "See You in Disneyland." *Variations on a Theme Park: The New American City and the End of Public Space.* Ed. Michael Sorkin. New York: Noonday, 1992. 205–232.

Spaceport USA. n.p.: Kennedy Space Center, 1992.

Spartacus. Dir. Stanley Kubrick. Perf. Kirk Douglas, Laurence Olivier, Jean Simmons, and Tony Curtis. 1960.

Springer, John L. "Small Wonder Called the Gene." *The New York Times Magazine,* 23 November 1958: 15, 24–27.

Sproul, J. Michael. "The New Managerial Rhetoric and the Old Criticism." *Quarterly Journal of Speech* 74 (1988): 474–481.

Staples, Clifford L. "White Male Ways of Knowing." *Postmodern Culture* 2 (1992): 1–33.

Stearney, Lynn M. "Feminism, Ecofeminism, and the Maternal Archetype: Motherhood As a Feminine Universal." *Communication Quarterly* 42 (1994): 142–159.

Steedman, Carolyn. "Culture, Cultural Studies, and the Historian." In Grossberg, Nelson, and Treichler. 613–621.

Steiner, Linda. "Oppositional Decoding As an Act of Resistance." *Critical Studies in Mass Communication* 5 (1988): 1–15.

Stephenson, Neal. *The Diamond Age, or, A Young Lady's Illustrated ÿ20Primer.* New York: Bantam, 1995.

_____. *Snow Crash.* New York: Bantam Books, 1992.

Sterk, Helen M. "In Praise Of Beautiful Women." *Western Journal of Speech Communication* 50 (1986): 215–226.

_____. "The Metamorphosis of Marilyn Monroe." *Central States Speech Journal* 36 (1985): 294–304.

Stevens, Wallace. *Harmonium.* New York: Knopf, 1923.

Stewart, Charles J. "Rhetorical Criticism in Twentieth-Century America." *Explorations in Rhetorical Criticism.* Eds. G. P. Mohrmann, Charles J. Stewart, and Donovan Ochs. University Park, PA: Pennsylvania State University Press, 1973. 1–31.

Stewart, Susan. *On Longing: Narratives of the Miniature, the Gigantic, the Souvenir, the Collection.* Durham: Duke University Press, 1993.

Stock, Brian. "Reading, Community, and a Sense of Place." In Duncan and Ley. 314–328.

Stone, A. R. (1993). "What Vampires Know: Transsubjection and Transgender in Cyberspace." Online. Internet. 15 April 1997. Available from http://www. actlab.utexas.edu/~sandy

Stone, Allucquère Roseanne. *The War of Desire and Technology at the Close of the Mechanical Age.* Cambridge, MA: MIT Press, 1995.

Storey, John. *Cultural Studies and the Study of Popular Culture: Theories and Methods.* Athens: University of Georgia Press, 1996.

Strinati, Dominic. *An Introduction to Theories of Popular Culture.* New York: Routledge, 1995.

Sturken, Marita. "The Wall, the Screen, and the Image: The Vietnam Veterans Memorial." *Representations* 35 (1991): 118–142.

Sumner, William Graham. *Folkways: A Study of the Sociological Importance of Usages, Manners, Customs, Mores, and Morals.* 1906. Boston: Ginn & Co., 1911.

Sussman, Herbert. "Cyberpunk Meets Charles Babbage: *The Difference Engine* As Alternative Victorian History." *Victorian Studies* 38 (1994): 1–23.

Sutton, Jane. "The Taming of Polos/Polis: Rhetoric As an Achievement Without Woman." *The Southern Communication Journal* 57 (1992): 97–119.

Taylor, Bryan C. "Register of the Repressed: Women's Voice And Body in the Nuclear Weapon's Organization." *Quarterly Journal of Speech* 79 (1993): 267–285.

Thomas, Laurence. "Group Autonomy and Narrative Identity: Blacks and Jews." *Blacks and Jews: Alliances and Arguments.* Ed. Paul Berman. NY: Delacorte Press, 1994. 143–156.

Thompson, E. P. *The Making of the English Working Class.* 1963. New York: Vintage, 1966.

Toffler, Alvin. *The Culture Consumers: Art and Affluence in America.* Baltimore, MD: Penguin, 1965.

Toffler, Alvin, and Heidi Toffler. *Creating a New Civilization: The Politics of the Third Wave*. Atlanta: Turner Publishing, 1995.

Tomasso, Melissa. Telephone interview with Carole Blair. 21 October 1996.

Trevor-Roper, Hugh. "The Invention of Tradition: The Highland Tradition of Scotland." *The Invention of Tradition*. Eds. Eric Hobsbawm and Terence Ranger. Cambridge, UK: Cambridge University Press, 1983. 15–41.

Trilling, Diana. *The Beginning of the Journey: The Marriage of Diana and Lionel Trilling*. New York: Harcourt Brace & Co., 1993.

Trilling, Lionel. *Beyond Culture: Essays on Literature and Learning*. 1955. New York: The Viking Press, 1965.

_____. *A Gathering of Fugitives*. Boston: Beacon Press, 1956.

Turner, Graeme. *British Cultural Studies: An Introduction*. London: Routledge, 1992.

Turner, Victor. *From Ritual to Theatre: The Human Seriousness of Play*. New York: Performing Arts Journal Publications, 1982.

_____. *The Ritual Process*. Chicago: Aldine, 1969.

Tuttleton, James W. "Back to the Sixties with Spindoctor Graff." *The New Century* 11 (March 1993): 33–34.

_____. *Vital Signs: Essays on American Literature and Criticism*. Chicago: Ivan R. Dee, 1996.

United States. Central Intelligence Agency. Origins of the Congress for Cultural Freedom, 1949–50. Online. Available at www.odci.gov/csi/studies/95unclas/war.html.

United States. Congress. H.J. Res. 214. *Congressional Record* 30 April 1991: H2578-79; *Congressional Record* 6 May 1991: S5359-60.

_____. Congress. S.J. Res. 372. Senate Committee on Energy and Natural Resources. *Hearings*. 99th Cong., 2d sess. Washington: GPO, 1986. 36–37.

van Dijk, Teun. *Racism and the Press*. London: Routledge, 1991.

Van Maanen, John. *Tales of the Field: On Writing Ethnography*. Chicago: University of Chicago Press, 1988.

Vanderford, Marsha L. "Vilification and Social Movements: A Case Study of Pro-Life and Pro-Choice Rhetoric." *Quarterly Journal of Speech* 75 (1989): 166–182.

Vaughn, Thomas. "Voices of Sexual Distortion: Rape, Birth, and Self-Annihilation Metaphors in the Alien Trilogy." *Quarterly Journal of Speech* 81 (1995): 423–435.

Voelker, Francis H., and Ludmila A. Voelker, eds. *Mass Media: Forces in Our Society*. 1972. 4th ed. New York: Harcourt Brace Jovanovich, 1978.

Wald, Alan M. *The New York Intellectuals: The Rise and Decline of the Anti-Stalinist Left from the 1930s to the 1980s*. Chapel Hill: University of North Carolina Press, 1987.

Wallace, Mike. *Mickey Mouse History, and Other Essays on American History*. Philadelphia: Temple University Press, 1996.

The Walt Disney Company. *1996 Annual Report*. 1996.

_____. *Disney-MGM Studios Guide Map*. Orlando: Walt Disney World. September 8–14, 1996.

_____. *Disney-MGM Studios Theme Park*. Orlando: Walt Disney World, n.d. (acquired June 1994).

_____. *Disney-MGM Studios Theme Park.* Orlando: Walt Disney World, n.d. (acquired September 1996).

_____. *Epcot Guide Map.* Orlando: Walt Disney World, 15–21 Sept. 1996.

_____. *Magic Kingdom Guide Map.* Orlando: Walt Disney World. 8–14 Sept., 1996.

_____. *Walt Disney World Vacation Planning.* Videocassette. Orlando: The Walt Disney Company, 1997.

Wander, Philip C. "At the Ideological Front." *Communication Studies* 42 (1991): 199–218.

_____. "The Ideological Turn in Modern Criticism." *Central States Speech Journal* 34 (Spring 1983): 1–18.

_____. "The Third Persona: An Ideological Turn in Rhetorical Theory." *Central States Speech Journal* 35 (Winter 1984): 197–216.

Warnick, Barbara. "Leff in Context: What Is the Critic's Role?" *Quarterly Journal of Speech* 78 (1992): 219–237.

_____. "A Ricoeurian Approach to Rhetorical Criticism." *Western Journal of Speech Communication* 51 (1987): 227–244.

Warren, Stacy. " 'This Heaven Gives Me Migraines': The Problems and Promises of Landscapes of Leisure." In Duncan and Ley. 173–186.

Watzlawick, Paul, Janet Helmick Beavin, and Don D. Jackson, eds. *Pragmatics of Human Communication: A Study of Interactional Patterns, Pathologies, and Paradoxes.* New York: Norton, 1967.

Weissman, Judith. "Masters of the Universe: Deconstruction and the Yuppies." *Syracuse Scholar: An Interdisciplinary Journal of Ideas Published by Syracuse University.* Supplementary Issue (Spring 1987): 11–23.

Wellek, Ren,, and Austin Warren. *The Theory of Literature.* New York: Harcourt, Brace, 1949.

Wess, Robert. "Notes Toward a Marxist Rhetoric."ÿ20 *Bucknell Review* 28.2 (1983): 126–148.

West, Cornel. *The American Evasion of Philosophy: A Genealogy of Pragmatism.* Madison: University of Wisconsin Press, 1989.

_____. "Marxist Theory and the Specificity of Afro-American Oppression." *Marxism and the Interpretation of Culture.* Eds. Lawrence Grossberg and Cary Nelson. Urbana: University of Illinois Press, 1988. 17–29.

_____. *Prophetic Thought in Post-Modern Times.* Monroe, ME: Common Courage Press, 1993.

West, James T. "Ethnography and Ideology: The Politics Of Cultural Representation." *Western Journal of Communication* 57 (1993): 209–220.

White, Hayden. *The Content of the Form: Narrative Discourse and Historical Representation.* Baltimore: Johns Hopkins University Press, 1987.

_____. *Tropics of Discourse: Essays in Cultural Criticism.* Baltimore: Johns Hopkins University Press, 1978.

Wichelns, Herbert A. "The Literary Criticism of Oratory." *Studies in Rhetoric and Public Speaking in Honor of James A. Winans.* New York: Century, 1925. 181–216.

Williams, Jeffrey, ed. *PC Wars: Politics and Theory in the Academy.* New York and London: Routledge, 1995.

Williams, Kenneth R. "Speech Communication Research: One World or Two?" *Central States Speech Journal* 21 (1970): 175–180.

Williams, Raymond. *The Country and the City.* New York: Oxford University Press, 1973.

———. *Keywords: A Vocabulary of Culture and Society.* Rev. ed. New York: Oxford University Press, 1985.

———. *Resources of Hope: Culture, Democracy, Socialism.* London: Verso, 1989.

———. *The Long Revolution.* New York: Columbia University Press, 1961.

———. *Marxism and Literature.* 1977. Oxford: Oxford University Press, 1985.

Williamson, Judith. *Decoding Advertisements: Ideology and Meaning in Advertising.* 1979. London: Boyars, 1984.

Wilson, Alexander. *The Culture of Nature: North American Landscape from Disney to the Exxon Valdez.* Cambridge, MA: Blackwell, 1992.

Wilson, John K. *The Myth of Political Correctness: The Conservative Attack on Higher Education.* Durham and London: Duke University Press, 1995.

Wise, Gene. "Some Elementary Axioms for an American Culture Studies." *Prospects: An Annual Review of American Cultural Studies.* Ed. Jack Salzman. New York: Burt Franklin, 1979. 517–547.

Wolpert, J. F. "Notes on the American Intelligentsia." 1947. Reprinted in *The Scene Before You: A New Approach to American Culture.* Ed. Chandler Brossard. New York: Rinehart and Co., 1955. 239–254.

Wrage, Ernest J. "The Little World of Barry Goldwater." *Western Journal of Communication,* 27 (Fall 1963): 207–215.

———. "Public Address: A Study in Social and Intellectual History." *Quarterly Journal of Speech* 33 (1947): 451–457.

Wright, Will. *Six Guns and Society: A Structural Study of the Western.* Berkeley: University of California Press, 1975.

Zagacki, Kenneth S., and Andrew King. "Reagan, Romance, And Technology: A Critique Of 'Star Wars.' " *Communication Studies* 40 (1989): 1–12.

Zarefsky, David. "The Roots of American Community." The Carroll C. Arnold Distinguished Lecture. San Antonio, Texas, 1995.

———. "State of the Art in Public Address Scholarship." In Leff and Kauffeld. 13–28.

Zavarzadeh, Mas'ud. " 'The Stupidity That Consumption Is Just As Productive As Production' (Marx, *Theories of Surplus-Value*): In the Shopping Mall of the Post-al Left." *The Alternative Orange* 4 (Fall/Winter 1994): 8–12.

Zavarzadeh, Mas'ud, and Donald Morton. *Theory as Resistance: Politics and Culture after (Post)structuralism.* New York: Guilford Press, 1994.

———. *Theory, (Post)Modernity, Opposition: An "Other" Introduction to Literary and Cultural Theory.* Washington, DC: Maisonneuve Press, 1991.

———. "War of the Words: The Battle of (and for) English." *In These Times* 11 (October 28–November 3, 1987): 18–19.

Žižek, Slavoj. *The Sublime Object of Ideology.* London: Verso Books, 1989.

INDEX

CONTRIBUTORS

James Arnt Aune (PhD, Northwestern University, 1980) is Associate Professor of Speech Communication at Texas A&M University. He is the author of *Rhetoric and Marxism* (1994), as well as several articles on rhetorical theory and the relationship between rhetoric and political theory. He is currently at work on *Beyond Economic Correctness: Studies in Free Market Rhetoric*.

Carole Blair, Professor of American Studies at the University of California, Davis, is coeditor of *Critical Questions: Invention, Creativity, and the Criticism of Discourse and Media* (1994) as well as author of numerous monographs and anthology articles. She has been a fellow of the UC Davis Humanities Institute and of the University of California Washington Center, and she has won national awards for several of her monographs, including "Disciplining the Feminine" (1994). She is working now, with Neil Michel, on a critical-historical-photographic study of U.S. commemorative art and its construction of collective memory and national identity.

Detine L. Bowers's interests are in nineteenth-century and contemporary African American speaking, Afrocentric rhetoric, and public speaking. She has published several articles and presented several convention papers. She received her PhD from Purdue University.

Patrick Brantlinger is Professor of Literature at Indiana University, Bloomington. He has written many essays exploring the relationship between discourse and culture. Most recent are *Fictions of State: Culture and Credit in Britain* (1996), *Crusoe's Footprints: Cultural Studies in Britain and America* (1990), and a coedited collection, *Modernity and Mass Culture* (1991).

Barry Brummett's interests are in rhetorical theory and criticism, and in the rhetorical analysis of popular culture. He is the author of *Rhetorical Dimensions of Popular Culture* (1991), *Rhetoric in Popular Culture*

(1994), *Recent Apocalytic Rhetoric* (1991), and many other essays on communication and culture. He received his PhD from the University of Minnesota.

Celeste Michelle Condit (PhD, University of Iowa, 1982) is Professor of Speech Communication at the University of Georgia. Her research explores the way in which public discourse participates in processes of social change. Her books include *Decoding Abortion Rhetoric: Communicating Social Change* (1990), *Crafting Equality: America's Anglo-African Word* (with John Louis Lucaites, 1993), and *Evaluating Women's Health Messages: A Resource Book* (with Roxanne Parrott, 1996). She has also published a variety of essays in the *Quarterly Journal of Speech*, *Communication Monographs*, and other journals and edited collections.

Thomas S. Frentz (PhD, University of Wisconsin, Madison, 1970) is Professor of Communication at the University of Arkansas. He is interested in how psychological processes affect rhetorical and cultural practices in the media. He has recently coauthored a book with Janice Hocker Rushing, *Projecting the Shadow: The Cyborg Hero in American Film* (1995).

Bruce E. Gronbeck, A. Craig Baird Distinguished Professor of Public Address at the University of Iowa, has long been interested in the relationships among rhetoric, media, and culture. His publications include *Presidential Campaigns and American Self-Images* (1994), and *Media, Consciousness, and Culture: Explanations of Walter Ong's Theories* (1991).

Henry Krips is Professor of Communication and of History and Philosophy of Science at the University of Pittsburgh, where he teaches in the areas of rhetoric of science and cultural studies. His publications include *The Metaphysics of Quantum Theory* (1990); as coeditor, *Science, Reason, and Rhetoric* (1995); and *Fetish: An Erotics of Culture* (forthcoming). He is currently writing a book on science, discourse, and new technologies.

Steven Mailloux, Professor of English at the University of California, Irvine, is the author of *Interpretive Conventions: The Reader in the Study of American Fiction* (1982) and *Rhetorical Power* (1989). He coedited (with Sanford Levinson) *Interpreting Law and Literature: A Hermeneutic Reader* (1988) and recently edited another collection, *Rhetoric, Sophistry, Pragmatism* (1995). His latest book is *Reception Histories: Rhetoric, Pragmatism, and American Cultural Politics* (1998).

Elizabeth Walker Mechling is Professor of Speech Communication at the California State University, Fullerton, and **Jay Mechling** is Professor of

American Studies at the University of California, Davis. Together they write about a range of topics, from social movements (nuclear, animal rights, peace) to discourses in popular culture. Presently they are writing about the ten-year anniversaries of the Hiroshima bombing and working on a large project on the social and rhetorical construction of young "citizenship" in cold war America.

Neil Michel is a partner in Axiom Photo and Design, Davis, California. His photographic work has been published in *The New York Times, The Chronicle of Higher Education, Science*, the *San Jose Mercury News*, and *San Francisco Focus Magazine*. His client list includes Visa International, the National Park Service, the University of California, and Bravo Cable Network.

Cary Nelson is Jubilee Professor of Liberal Arts and Sciences, Professor of English, and founding director of the Unit for Criticism and Interpretive Theory at the University of Illinois at Urbana-Champaign. He is the author of a number of volumes including *Repression and Recovery: Modern American Poetry and the Politics of Cultural Memory* (1992) and *Manifesto of a Tenured Radical* (1997). He is the editor of *Theory in the Classroom* (1986) and the coeditor of several books including *Marxism and the Interpretation of Culture* (1988), *Cultural Studies* (1992), and *Disciplinarity and Dissent in Cultural Studies* (coedited with Dilip Gaonkar, 1996). His most recent book is *Academic Keywords: A Devil's Dictionary for Higher Education* (1998).

Mark Olson is in the graduate program at the University of North Carolina at Chapel Hill.

Thomas Rosteck is Associate Professor of Communication at the University of Arkansas, Fayetteville. His interests are in in the connections between media, culture, and rhetorical discourse. He frequently writes about the role of documentary film and television in public argument, and is the author of *See It Now Confronts McCarthyism: Television Documentary and the Politics of Representation* (1994).

Janice Hocker Rushing (PhD, University of Southern California, 1976) is Professor of Communication at the University of Arkansas. She is interested in the rhetorical criticism of the media, particularly in the expression of American values through myth in contemporary film. She has published articles in this area, and has coauthored a book with Thomas S. Frentz, *Projecting the Shadow: The Cyborg Hero in American Film* (1995).

John M. Sloop (PhD, University of Iowa, 1992) is Assistant Professor of Communication Studies at Vanderbilt University. He is the author of *The Cultural Prison: Discourse, Prisoners, and Punishment* (1996), an editor of *Mapping the Beat* (1997), as well as the author of a number of theoretical and critical essays dealing with public arguments, popular music, and the intersection between poststructuralism and rhetorical theory.